Western sociologists on Indian society

International Library of Sociology

Founded by Karl Mannheim

Editor: John Rex, University of Warwick

Arbor Scientiae
Arbor Vitae

A catalogue of the books available in the **International Library of Sociology** and other series of Social Science books published by Routledge & Kegan Paul will be found at the end of this volume.

Western sociologists on Indian society

Marx, Spencer, Weber, Durkheim, Pareto

G. R. Madan
Department of Sociology and Social Work
Lucknow University

Routledge & Kegan Paul
London, Boston and Henley

First published in 1979
by Routledge & Kegan Paul Ltd
39 Store Street,
London WC1E 7DD,
Broadway House,
Newtown Road,
Henley-on-Thames,
Oxon RG9 1EN and
9 Park Street,
Boston, Mass. 02108, USA
Set in Times 327
and printed in Great Britain by
Thomson Litho Ltd, East Kilbride, Scotland

British Library Cataloguing in Publication Data

Madan, G R

Western sociologists on Indian society.
—(International library of sociology).
1. Indian—Social conditions—1947—
2. Sociology—History—20th century
1. Title   II. Series
309. 1'54   HN683.5   79–40447 ✓

ISBN 0 7100 8782 9

Dedicated to my teacher and guide,
Professor S. L. Andreski, a renowned British sociologist
who has been a constant source of inspiration in
completing this work

Contents

Preface

This work was undertaken in the year 1970 at the kind suggestion of my learned guide, Professor S. L. Andreski, head of the Department of Sociology, University of Reading, when I went there for a year to do some advanced work in sociology under the Commonwealth University Interchange Scheme of the British Council, London. The first two chapters were submitted in the form of a thesis as part of the requirement for the M.A. degree in sociology in the said university. However, the scope of the work proved to be extensive and could not be finished within that limited period. On returning from England the work was continued for another three years or so to bring it to its present form.

These sociologists were selected from among the important Western sociologists who have done some work on Indian society and whose writings were available in English. Of the five sociologists whose views on Indian society have been presented here, two viz. Marx and Weber, have made a special study of some aspects of Indian society while the rest studied them only as a part of their larger studies and from a comparative point of view, in order to draw some general sociological conclusions.

While in England, I visited the British Museum Newspaper Library, Hendon, to consult certain articles by Karl Marx. The staff of Reading University Library secured some books for me on inter-library loan from London. On returning to India I found that certain important books on Weber and Pareto were not available in our university library and I would only obtain them on loan or by visiting other libraries personally. It was with the kind co-operation and the helpful attitude of the staff of the libraries at Lucknow, Agra and Delhi that this work was completed. My thanks are due to all these people.

I owe a debt of gratitude to my learned guide, Professor S. L.

Andreski, who suggested this stimulating topic to me and then guided me throughout the venture. His encouragement has been a constant source of inspiration to me. Without his help it would have been difficult to complete the work. I am thankful to my colleagues in Lucknow University, particularly to those in the Departments of Sanskrit and Ancient and Modern History, and to those in the Oriental Department with whom I had some consultations. I visited the Sarnath Temple at Varanasi to discuss some points on Buddhism with the head monk of the sanctuary. Some points on Jainism were discussed with Sri K. C. Jain, Research Officer in the Uttar Pradesh Civil Secretariat. My thanks are due to both of these. My wife was a constant source of help to me—I often discussed my difficulties with her, in England as well as in India—and I am indebted to her for constant advice and help and for making the home environment conducive to study. I am thankful to the British Council, London, for awarding me a travel grant under the Commonwealth University Interchange Scheme as well as an overseas student fee award in England for my advanced work in sociology. My thanks are due to Miss L. M. Bloomfield and Sri R. D. Saxena who typed the manuscript. My publishers Messrs Routledge & Kegan Paul, London, should be thanked for their assistance with publication.

G. R. MADAN

1 Karl Marx (1818–83)

Karl Mark was, first and foremost, the sociologist and economist of the capitalist regime.[1] He was interested in historical materialism, and not only of one country but of many countries. It is generally believed that Marx and Engels's observations on pre-capitalist epochs rest on far less thorough study than Marx's description and analysis of capitalism. However, as Mr Hobsbawm points out, it is true that the literature available to them on pre-capitalist societies at that time was far scantier than it is at present. But this does not mean that their knowledge was insufficient for the elaboration of their theories of pre-capitalist societies.[2]

There are two periods in the life of Marx when his mind was intensely occupied with the history of pre-industrial or non-European societies. These periods were the 1850s, i.e. the period which preceded the drafting of the *Critique of Political Economy* in 1859, and the 1870s after the publication of *Capital I* and substantial drafting of *Capital II* and *III*. Marx's exile in England, the political developments of the 1850s, and Marx's interest in economic studies soon transformed his knowledge about the Orient. He read and re-read the works of classical economists in the early 1850s. Among these the most important were J. S. Mill's *Principles,* Adam Smith and Richard Jones's introductory lecture in 1851.[3] He began to write articles on China and India for the *New York Daily Tribune* in 1853. In this year both he and Engels were deeply preoccupied with the historical problems of the Orient, and there is a lot of reference to these studies in the correspondence between the two friends during this year. Their correspondence and writings in this period refer to certain relevant books, for example, Rev. C. Foster's *A Historical Geography of Arabia,* Bernier's *Voyages,* Sir William Jones's *The Orientalist,* G. Campbell's *Modern India* (1852), J. Child's *Treatise on the East India Trade* (1681), J. von

1

Hammer's *Geschichte des Osmanischen Reiches* (1835), James Mill's *History of India* (1826), Thomas Mun's *A Discourse on Trade, from England into the East Indies* (1621), J. Pollexfen's *England and East India* (1697), Soltykov's *Lettres sur l'Inde* (1848) and parliamentary papers on India.

In the 1870s, apart from the agrarian orientation of his work in *Capital III,* there were perhaps two other reasons for the concentration of Marx's interests on primitive communal societies. First, the development of a Russian revolutionary movement increasingly led Marx and Engels to place their hopes for a European revolution in Russia. Since the position of the village community was a matter of fundamental theoretical disagreement among Russian revolutionaries, who consulted Marx on this point, it was natural for him to investigate the subject at greater length.

Second was his growing hatred of and contempt for capitalist society in his old age. It is said that Marx, who had earlier welcomed the impact of Western capitalism as an inhuman but historically progressive force on the stagnant pre-capitalist economies, found himself increasingly appalled by this inhumanity. He had always admired the positive social values embodied, in however backward a form, in the primitive community. And so in *Capital III* (pp. 365–6) and in the subsequent Russian discussions with Narodnik, he increasingly stressed the viability of the primitive commune, its powers of resistance to historical disintegration and even its capacity to develop into a higher form of economy without prior destruction.[4]

Our appreciation of Marx's observations on various aspects of Indian society during that period is mostly based on his various articles on India in the *New York Daily Tribune* in 1853, correspondence between Marx and Engels (*Pre-capitalist Economic Foundations* by Hobsbawm), *Notes on Indian History (664–1858)* and *Capital III.*[5] It may not be out of place to mention here that Karl Marx made most important observations on Indian society during the period June to August 1853, when the debate on the India Bill was going on in the British Parliament. The charter of the East India Company was to expire in 1854 and it was for the Parliament to decide whether the charter should be renewed for another twenty years as it had been in the past or if the charge should be taken over directly by the British government. Karl Marx pointed out that the responsibility for the governance of India not being fixed on any one authority was not conducive to the welfare of the people of that country. He stressed that this responsibility should be directly assumed by the Parliament itself and that more positive steps should be taken for the development of India. The princely states should also come under direct British rule and the princes be deposed, as they were an unnecessary burden on the poor people. His views on various aspects of Indian society may conveniently be discussed under the following heads:

1 India's woes more under British rule than in the past
2 Principle of *laissez faire* and neglect of irrigation
3 No responsible authority to look after people's welfare
4 Undue burden of Indian princes
5 Destruction of hand industries
6 Village communities and their role in historic development
7 Property rights in arable land
8 Indian land tenure
9 Indian revenue and taxation
10 Dual role of England–destructive and regenerative
11 Indian social structure and human progress

India's woes more under British rule than in the past

Marx observes that Hindustan is an Italy of Asiatic dimensions, the Himalayas for the Alps, the Plains of Bengal for the Plains of Lombardy, the Deccan for the Apennines and the Isle of Ceylon for the Island of Sicily. There is the same rich variety in the products of the soil and the same dismemberment in the political configuration. Just as Italy has from time to time been compressed by the conqueror's sword into different national masses, so do we find Hindustan, when not under the pressure of the Mohammedan or the Mogul or the British, dissolved into as many independent and conflicting states as it numbered towns or even villages. Yet, from a social point of view, Hindustan is not the Italy, but the Ireland of the East. And this strange combination of Italy and Ireland, of a world of voluptuousness and a world of woes, is anticipated in the ancient traditions of the religion of Hindustan. This religion is at once a religion of sensualist exuberance and a religion of self-torturing asceticism; a religion of the lingam (cult of the deity Shiva widespread in southern India) and of Juggernaut (cult of the deity Vishnu); the religion of the monks and of the bayaderes.

He does not share the opinion of those who believe in a golden age of Hindustan. Take for example the times of Aurangzebe, or the epoch when the Mogul appeared in the north, and the Portuguese in the south; or the age of Mohammedan invasion and of the Heptarchy in southern India; or if you will, go still further back to antiquity, take the mythological chronology of the Brahmin himself, who places the commencement of Indian misery in an epoch even more remote than the Christian creation of the world.

There cannot, however, remain any doubt but that the misery inflicted by the British on Hindustan is of an essentially different

3

and infinitely more intensive kind than anything Hindustan has had to suffer before. Marx does not allude to European despotism, planted upon Asiatic despotism by the British East India Company, forming a more monstrous combination than any of the divine monsters which startle us in the temple of Salsette.

He does say that British colonial rule has been actuated solely by the spirit of gain and, viewing their subjects with less regard or consideration than a West Indies planter formerly viewed a gang upon his estate, not having paid the purchase money of human property which the latter had, the British have employed all the existing machinery of despotism to squeeze from the people their last mite of contribution, the last dregs of their labour, and thus aggravated the evils of a capricious and semi-barbarous government by working it with all the practised ingenuity of politicians and all the monopolizing selfishness of traders. All the civil wars, invasions, revolutions, conquests and famines, strangely complex, rapid and destructive as the successive action in Hindustan may appear, did not go deeper than its surface. England has broken down the entire framework of Indian society, without any symptoms of reconstitution having yet appeared.[6] This loss of his old world, with no gain of a new one, imparts a particular kind of melancholy to the present misery of the Hindu and separates Hindustan, ruled by Britain, from all its ancient traditions and from the whole of its past history.

In what ways the Britishers, solely actuated by their own desire for gain, destroyed the old traditions and social structure of India, he explains in the subsequent pages.

Principle of *laissez-faire* and neglect of irrigation

According to Marx there have been in Asia generally, from time immemorial, but three departments of government; that of finance, or the plunder of the interior; that of war, or the plunder of the exterior; and, finally, the department of public works. Climate and territorial conditions, especially the vast tracts of desert extending from the Sahara, through Arabia, Persia, India and Tartary, to the most elevated Asiatic Highlands, made artificial irrigation by canals and waterworks the basis of oriental agriculture. As in Egypt and India, inundations are used for fertilizing the soil in Mesopotamia, Persia, etc.; advantage is taken of a high level for feeding irrigative canals. This prime necessity of an economical and common use of water, which in the Occident drove private enterprise to voluntary association, as in Flanders and Italy, necessitated, in the Orient where civilization was too low and the territorial extent too vast to call into life voluntary association, the interference of the centralizing power of government. Hence an economic function devolved upon all Asiatic governments the function of providing public works. This artificial fertilization of the soil, dependent on a central government and immediately decaying with the neglect of irrigation and drainage, explains the otherwise strange fact that we now find whole territories barren and desert that were once brilliantly cultivated, as Palmyra, Petra, the ruins in Yemen, and large provinces of Egypt, Persia and Hindustan; it also explains how a single war of devastation has been able to depopulate a country for centuries and to strip it of all civilization.

Now, the British in East India accepted from their predecessors the departments of finance and of war, but have neglected entirely that of public works. Hence the deterioration of an agriculture which is not capable of being conducted on the British principle of free competition, of *laissez faire* and *laissez aller*. But in Asiatic empires we are quite accustomed to see agriculture deteriorating under one government and reviving again under some other government, as they change in Europe with good or bad seasons. Thus the oppression and neglect of agriculture, bad as it is, could not be looked upon as the final blow dealt to Indian society by the British intruder, had it not been attended by a circumstance of quite different importance, a novelty in the annals of the whole Asiatic world.

However, it may be mentioned that owing to a series of famines in different parts of the country from the 1860s onward, which sometimes led to riots, and because of the Britishers' own self-interest, to have raw material (particularly cotton) for their own mills, some attempts were made to improve irrigation facilities through the repair of old tanks or the opening of new canals. Reference to this fact is also made by Marx at another place. But it needs to be pointed out, that the repair and maintenance of tanks in the south was the responsibility of the village local self-governments and their higher organs. These received grants from the government from time to time for this purpose. Unfortunately the British government did not recognize these organizations and took up this work through newly set up district boards, which were not so effective. Thus the initiative of people in the maintenance of such works was killed.

No responsible authority to look after people's welfare

When the question of renewal of the charter of the East India Company came before Parliament in June 1853, Karl Marx advocated that the British government should take direct responsibility for looking after the affairs of the Indian people rather than leaving it in the Company's hands. After dealing with the history of the East India Company in detail since 1702, and how it grew from a commercial into a military and territorial power, Marx points out that the question of India's governance by a proper authority has been postponed for many years. But it must now be tackled earnestly as the boundaries of the British Empire have grown extensively involving a large mass of people. He observes,

> It is only since 1849, that the one great Anglo-Indian Empire has existed. The British Government has been fighting under the company's name for two centuries, till at last the natural limits of India were reached. So the position of the Indian question is altered in the present year compared with all former periods of charter renewal.[7]

Different interests, i.e. the manufacturers, the commercial class and oligarchy, have been exploiting Indian people in different ways, while since 1784 the Indian finances have got more and more deeply into difficulty. The whole question is who shall be the governing power? The question is a perplexing one and this riddle has not been solved so far. He remarks,

> That there is in India a permanent financial deficit, a regular over supply of wars, and no supply at all of public works, an abominable system of taxation, and a no less abominable state of justice and law, that these five items constitute, as it were, the five points of the East Indian charter, was settled beyond all doubt in the debates of 1853, as it had been in the debates of 1833, and in the debates of 1813, as in all former debates on India. The only thing never found out, was the party responsible for all this.[8]

There exists, unquestionably, a Governor General of India, holding the supreme power, but that Governor is governed in his turn by a home government. Who is that home government? Is it the Indian Minister, disguised under the modest title of President of the Board of Control, or is it the twenty-four Directors of the East India Company? On the threshold of the Indian religion we find a divine trinity, and thus we find a profane trinity on the threshold of the Indian government. However, leaving the Governor General altogether on one side, we find the double government. Pitt's Act of 1784, by entering into a compromise with the company, by subjecting it to the superintendence of the Board of Control and by making the Board of Control an appendage of the Ministry, accepted, regulated and settled that double government arose from circumstances in name as well as in fact. The Act of 1833 strengthened the Board of Control and since then the East India

Company has no longer existed except in name and on sufferance. While there seems to be no difficulty in getting rid of the Company altogether, it is considered indifferent whether the English nation (i.e. Ministerial Board of Control) rules over India in the personal name of Queen Victoria, or through the traditional form of an anonymous society. The whole question, therefore, appears to turn about a technicality of very questionable importance. Still, the thing is not quite so plain.

Marx goes on to add that, along with the Board of Control, the Court of Directors also had certain powers. They appointed, with the sanction of the crown, the Supreme Government of India, the Governor General and his councillors, and could recall the highest servants and even the Governor General. Along with that there are two thousand shareholders who have no other interest in India except to be paid their dividends out of Indian revenue and to elect twenty-four directors for the Company's court.

No wonder, then, that there exists no government by which so much is written and so little is done, as the government of India. Even in India House no real work is done. The clerical establishments of Leadenhall Street and Cannon Row cost the Indian people the trifle of £160,000 annually. The oligarchy involves India in wars, in order to find employment for its younger sons; the 'moneyocracy' consigns it to the highest bidder; and a subordinate bureaucracy paralyses its administration and perpetuates its abuses as the vital condition of its own perpetuation.

The above observations made by Marx are quite apt. The ultimate authority for the governance of India was quite confusing and different authorities exploited the situation in their own way. Soon afterwards, in 1857 when the Sepoy Mutiny arose, Parliament had to assume the direct responsibility for the governance of the country.

Undue burden of Indian princes

Karl Marx observes that during the debate on the India Bill (in 1853) in Parliament the East Indian Reform Association have published certain pamphlets. However, their only merit until now has been to draw public attention to Indian affairs in general, and they cannot go further in their present form of eclectic opposition. For instance, while they attack the doings of the English aristocracy in India, they protest against the destruction of the Indian aristocracy of native princes.

After the British intruders had once set foot in India and made up their mind to hold on to it, there remained no alternative but to break the power of the native princes by force or by intrigue. After having won over their allies, in the way of ancient Rome,

7

the East India Company executed them, in the modern manner of Change Alley. In order to discharge the engagements they had entered into with the Company, the native princes were forced to borrow enormous sums from Englishmen at usurious interest. When their embarrassment had reached the highest pitch, the creditor became inexorable, 'the screw was turned' and the princes were compelled to concede their territories amicably to the Company, or to begin war, to become pensioners on their usurpers in one case, or to be deposed as traitors in the other. At this moment the native states, however, are no longer the allies, only the dependants, of the British government, subject to multifarious conditions, and to the various forms of subsidiary and protective systems. All of them have to pay a tribute, either in hard cash or in a contingent of armed forces commanded by British officers.

The final absorption or annexation of these native states is at present eagerly disputed between the reformers who denounce it as a crime and the men of business who excuse it as a necessity.

In Marx's opinion the question itself is altogether improperly put. As to the native states, they virtually ceased to exist from the moment they became subsidiary to or protected by the Company. If you divide the revenue of a country between two governments, you are sure to cripple the resources of the one and the administration of both. Under the present system the native states succumb to the double incubus of their native administration and the tributes and inordinate military establishments imposed upon them by the Company. The conditions under which they are allowed to retain their apparent independence are at the same time the conditions of a permanent decay and of an utter inability of improvement. Organic weakness is the constitutional law of their existence as of all existences under sufferance. It is, therefore, not the native states, but the native princes and courts on whose maintenance the question revolves. Now, is it not a strange thing that the same men who denounce

> the barbarous Splendors of the Crown and Aristocracy of
> England are shedding tears at the downfall of Indian Nabobs,
> Rajahs and Jagheerdars, the great majority of whom possess not
> even the prestige of antiquity, being generally usurpers of very
> recent date, set up by English intrigue. There exists in the whole
> world no despotism more ridiculous, absurd and childish than
> that of those *Schazenans* and Schariars of Arabian Nights.[9]

Many members of the House want the *status quo,* because the native troops under English rule need to be employed in the petty warfare with their own countrymen, in order to prevent them from turning their strength against their own European masters, because the existence of independent states gives occasional employment to the English troops.

Leaving aside all the arguments, which state in so many words that the native princes are the strongholds of the present abominable English system and are the greatest obstacle to Indian progress, he comes to Sir Thomas Munro and Lord Elphinstone, who were at least men of superior genius and of real sympathy for the Indian people. They think that without a native aristocracy there can be no energy in any other class of the community, and that the subversion of that aristocracy will not raise but will debase a whole people. They may be right, as long as the natives under direct English rule are systematically excluded from all superior offices, military and civil. Where no men can achieve greatness by their own exertions, there must be great men by birth, to leave to a conquered people some greatness of their own. That exclusion, however, of the native people from the English territory has been effected only by the maintenance of the hereditary princes in the so-called independent territories. And one of these two concessions had to be made to the native army, on whose strength all British rule in India depends. Perhaps Mr Campbell is right when he says that the native Indian aristocracy are the least enabled to fill higher offices; that for all fresh requirements it is necessary to create a fresh class; and that from the acuteness and aptness to learn of the inferior classes, this can be done in India as it can be done in no other country.

The native princes themselves are fast disappearing through the extinction of their houses, but the British Government has observed the policy of allowing them to make heirs by adoption, or of filling up their vacant seats with puppets of English creation. As for the pensioned princes, the £2,468,969 assigned to them by the British government from the Indian revenue is a most heavy charge upon a people living on rice and deprived of the first necessaries of life.

The above observations of Marx are mostly correct. With few exceptions, whereas some princes had a broader outlook and took an active part in the development of their states (e.g. Baroda and Mysore), the other princes lived in aristocratic style and spent the state revenues lavishly on pomp and show. Moreover they had little power to take action independently without consulting the British Resident. This dual authority led to the crippling of administration and unnecessary expenses. In some cases the old nabobs and princes received pensions, which made them parasites on society. However, it also needs to be pointed out that when attempts were made by the East India Company to annex these princely states and merge them into British territory there was great resentment among the local people. It was one of the reasons for the outbreak of the Mutiny in 1857 and then the British government had to assure them that in future such states will not be merged into British territory. It was only after independence that these states were amalgamated with other provinces, while the pensions of princes only stopped in 1971.

Destruction of hand industries

Karl Marx observes that the British Parliament, following this prejudicial policy because of pressure from the industrial class, discouraged Indian manufacturers in order to encourage the rising manufacturers of England. The policy was to make Indian industries subservient to those of Great Britain, and to make the Indian people grow raw produce only, in order to supply material for the looms and factories of Great Britain. He remarks, however, that a change in the political aspect of India's past must come about, its social condition having remained unaltered from remotest antiquity right up to the first decade of the nineteenth century. The handloom and the spinning wheel, with their regular myriads of spinners and weavers, were the pivots of the structure of that society. From time immemorial, Europe has received the admirable textiles produced by Indian labour, sending in return for them her precious metals, thereby furnishing that indispensable member of the Indian society, the goldsmith, with his raw material. It was the British intruder who broke up the Indian handloom and destroyed the spinning wheel.

Parliamentary intervention was claimed, not by the commercial, but by the industrial class at the latter end of the seventeenth century, and during the greater part of the eighteenth century, when the importation of East Indian cotton and silk stuffs was declared to ruin the poor British manufacturers. It was enacted under William III that wrought silks and printed or dyed calicos from India, Persia and China should be prohibited and a penalty of £200 imposed on all persons having or selling the same. Similar laws were enacted under George I, George II and George III so that during the greater part of the eighteenth century Indian manufactures were generally imported into England in order to be sold on the continent, and were excluded from the English market itself.

Till 1813 India had been chiefly an exporting country, while it has now become an importing one and the rate of exchange has sunk from 2s 6d per rupee to 2s per rupee. After its own products had been excluded from England, or only admitted on the most cruel terms, British manufactures were poured into India at a small and merely nominal duty, to the ruin of the native fabrics once so celebrated. England began by driving the Indian cotton from the European markets; she then introduced twist into Hindustan and, in the end, inundated the very mother country of cotton with cottons. From 1818 to 1836 the export of twist from Great Britain to India rose in the proportion of 1 to 5200. At the same time the population of Dacca decreased from 150,000 to 20,000. This decline of Indian towns celebrated for their fabrics was by no means the worst consequence. British steam and science sundered, over the whole surface of Hindustan, the union between agricultural and manufacturing industry.[10]

The ruin of hand industries in urban centres was really a great blow to the Indian economy. In the words of Dr Mukerjee,

> India between 1600 and 1800 experienced vicissitudes that have fallen to the lot of few countries in the world's history. The seventeenth century saw India as the agricultural mother of Asia and the industrial workshop of the world. The end of the eighteenth century witnessed the rapid decline of Indian industries, the complete ruin of Indian trade and shipping, and the loss of her political power.[11]

Not only was the export industry affected, but local consumption went down owing to changes in the tastes of the ruling classes, who preferred artistic goods of European origin, in contrast to those of the previous rulers who encouraged local workers. Regarding the union of agriculture and manufacturing industry in the villages more shall be said later.

Village communities and their role in historic development

Here Marx critically examines the role of village communities in the historic progress of Indian society. He observes that these are small, isolated, independent republics, superstitious and narrow in outlook, dependent upon central government for irrigation, unconcerned with national affairs and offering no resistance to new invaders. Under British rule these self-sustained communities have disintegrated because of the destruction of home industries. But this disintegration may bring a social revolution as with new means of communication some of the rural people may migrate to towns to take up employment in modern factories and this may broaden their outlook.

Karl Marx gives two main reasons for the stationary, independent and self-centred village communities in India. These are (1) that the Hindu, like all oriental peoples, leaves to the central government the care of the great public works, the prime condition of his agriculture and commerce, and (2) that they are dispersed over the surface of the country, and agglomerated in small centres by the domestic union of agricultural and manufacturing pursuits. These two factors had

11

brought about, since the remotest times, a social system with
particular features—the so-called village system, which gave to each
of these small unions their independent organization and distinct
life. The peculiar character of this system may be judged from the
description contained in an old official report of the British House
of Commons on Indian affairs.

A village, geographically considered, is a tract of country
comprising some hundred or thousand acres of arable and waste
land; politically viewed it resembles a corporation or township.
Its proper establishment of officers and servants consists of the
following description: The *Potail,* or head inhabitant, who has
generally the superintendence of the affairs of the village, settles
the disputes of the inhabitants, attends to the police, and performs
the duty of collecting the revenue within his village, a duty which
his personal influence and minute acquaintance with the situation
and concerns of the people render him the best qualified for this
charge. The *Kurnum* keeps the accounts of cultivation, and
registers everything connected with it. The *Tallier* and the *Totie,*
the duty of the former of which consists in gaining information
of crimes and offences, and in escorting and protecting persons
travelling from one village to another; the province of the latter
appearing to be more immediately confined to the village,
consisting among other duties, in guarding the crops and assisting
in measuring them. The *boundary man,* who preserves the limits of
the village or gives evidence respecting them in case of dispute. The
superintendent of tanks and water courses distributes the water for
the purposes of agriculture. The Brahmin, who performs the
village worship. The schoolmaster, who is seen teaching the
children in the village to read and write in the sand. The calendar-
Brahmin, or astrologer, etc.[12] These officers and servants generally
constitute the establishment of a village; but in some parts of the
country it is of less extent; some of the duties and functions above
described being united in the same person; in others it exceeds the
above-named number of individuals. Under this simple form of
municipal government, the inhabitants of the country have lived
from time immemorial. The boundaries of the villages have been
but seldom altered; and though the villages themselves have been
sometimes injured and even desolated by war, famine and disease,
the same name, the same limits, the same interests and even the
same families, have continued for ages. The inhabitants gave
themselves no trouble about the breaking up and divisions of
kingdoms; while the village remains entire, they care not to what
power it is transferred, or to what sovereign it devolves; its internal
economy remains unchanged. The *Potail* is still the head habitant,

and still acts as the petty judge or magistrate, and collector or rentor of the village.[13] In some of these communities the lands of the village are cultivated in common, in most cases each occupant tills his own field. The waste lands are for common pasture. Domestic weaving and spinning is done by wives and daughters.[14]

He further observes that these small stereotyped forms of social organism have been to the greater part dissolved, and are disappearing owing to the effect of English steam power and English free trade. Those family communities were based on domestic industry, in that peculiar combination of hand-weaving, hand-spinning and hand-tilling agriculture which gave them self-supporting power. English interference, having placed the spinner in Lancashire and the weaver in Bengal, or having swept away both Hindu spinner and weaver, dissolved these small semi-barbarian, semi-civilized communities, by blowing up their economic balance, and thus produced the greatest and, in truth, the only social revolution ever heard of in Asia.

Now, sickening as it must be to human feeling to witness those myriads of industrious, patriarchal and inoffensive social organizations disorganized and dissolved into their units, thrown into a sea of woes, and their individual members losing at the same time their ancient form of civilization and their hereditary means of subsistence, we must not forget that these idyllic village communities, inoffensive though they may appear, had always been the solid foundation of oriental despotism, and that they restrain the human mind within the smallest possible compass, making it the unresisting tool of superstition, enslaving it beneath traditional rules, depriving it of all grandeur and historical energies. We must not forget the barbarian egotism which, concentrating on some miserable patch of land, had quietly witnessed the ruin of empires, the perpetration of unspeakable cruelties, the massacre of the population of large towns, with no other consideration bestowed upon them than on natural events, itself the helpless prey of any aggressor who deigned to notice it at all. This undignified, stagnatory and vegetative life, and this passive sort of existence evoked on the other part, in contradistinction, wild, aimless, unbounded forces of destruction and rendered murder itself a religious rite in Hindustan. These little communities were so contaminated by distinctions of caste and by slavery, that they subjugated man to external circumstances instead of elevating him to be the sovereign of circumstances, that they transformed a self-developing social state into never-changing natural destiny, and thus brought about a brutalizing worship of nature, exhibiting its degradation in the fact

13

that man, the sovereign of nature, fell down on his knees in adoration of *Kanuman,* the monkey, and *Sabbala,* the cow.

England, it is true, in causing a social revolution in Hindustan, was actuated only by the vilest interests and was stupid in her manner of enforcing them. But that is not the question. The question is, can mankind fulfil its destiny without a fundamental revolution in the social state of Asia? If not, whatever may have been the crimes of England, she was the unconscious tool of history in bringing about that revolution.

Here Marx makes many observations about the village communities in India; of these, some are correct, some partly correct, while others are incorrect.

(1) His observation that villagers wholly depended upon central government for irrigation purposes leading to despotism is not wholly correct. I have already mentioned that some of the works were maintained by the village panchayats or their higher organs, which sometimes obtained assistance from government for repair work. The British government did not recognize these bodies and this led to inefficiency in their working. If some great works were left to government, which were beyond their control, how it led to despotism is not clear. Government ought to perform such functions and the provision of irrigation facilities is now recognized to be one of the important functions of a modern democratic state.

(2) His observation that village communities were small, scattered and self-dependent, combining agricultural and manufacturing pursuits, and that this led to a peculiar social system known as the village system is only to be expected when there was lack of means of communication before the industrial revolution. To some extent the same type of system prevailed in Europe. This system started disintegrating as soon as communication became easy and there was the opportunity of education, employment etc., in the cities.

(3) His observation that these small stereotyped social organisms had been dissolved to a great extent and were disappearing because the effects of English steam power and English free trade is not wholly correct. The cheap, British, machine-made goods mostly affected the urban centres, where, owing to easy communications by railways and roads, the competition was keen and many spinners and weavers became unemployed. In the villages the number of such spinners and weavers was small. And this spinning and weaving was mostly done in the home as part-time work, as Marx himself mentions at one place, and continued to be so for a considerable time. On the other hand the urban industrial workers migrated to the villages bringing more pressure on land.

(4) His observation that they restrained the human mind within the smallest possible compass, that people were superstitious and traditional in outlook, that there were distinctions of caste and slavery, animal worship and sacrifices etc., is all true to some extent. And the village is always the place of such phenomena, where there is lack of education.

(5) His assertion that villagers were unconcerned with the town or country as a whole, never raising any protest against the despotic ruler or against the new invader, is only partly true. None of the invaders who came to India before the British could ever subjugate the whole territory. There was always some resistance and this was particularly tough in the south. The villagers co-operated with the king when given such a call. The major causes of defeat of the Indian kingdoms were: (1) that the smaller kingdoms did not make a united front, either because of caste or personal rivalries or lack of a good communications system which created difficulties in making such a front. Marx himself mentions this fact elsewhere.

> How came it that English supremacy was established in India? The paramount power of the Great Mogul was broken by the Mogul Viceroys. The power of the Viceroys was broken by Mahrattas.... A country not only divided between Mohammedan and Hindoo, but between tribe and tribe, between caste and caste; a society whose framework was based on a sort of equilibrium, resulting from a general repulsion and constitutional exclusiveness, between all its members. Such a country and such a society, were they not the predestined prey of conquest? If we knew nothing of the past history of Hindustan, would there not be one great and incontestable fact, that even at this moment India is held in English thraldom by an Indian army maintained at the cost of India?[15]

(2) that sometimes the arms of the invaders and their ways of fighting were superior to that of the local rulers, which led to the latter's defeat; (3) that often villages were not given military training to be useful during a war.

Property rights in arable land

Marx was not clear about the property rights in arable land, as it was really a complex question. First in his letter to Engels on 2 June, 1853 he says, 'Bernier rightly considered the basis of all phenomena in the East—he refers to Turkey, Persia, Hindustan—to be the absence of private property in Land. This is the real key, even to the Oriental Heaven'.[16] However, as stated earlier, he mentions in

15

another letter that although in some communities the lands of the village are cultivated in common, in most cases each occupant tills his own field. The waste lands are for common pasture.[17] In the same letter he concludes

> As to the *question of property,* this is a very *controversial* one among the English writers on India. In the broken hill-country south of Krishna, property in land does seem to have existed. In Java on the other hand Sir Stamford Raffles, former English Governor of Java in his History of Java observes that the sovereign was absolute landlord of the whole surface of the land, where rent to any considerable amount was attainable. In any case it seems to have been the Mohammedans who first established the principle of 'no property in land' throughout the whole of Asia.[18]

It is evident that the British had no clear idea about the property rights in land. Actually the land belonged to the tiller of the soil during the Hindu period; whether it was held separately by each cultivator or jointly is a different question. The king had no right to disturb the ownership of the cultivator unless he was in default of payment of the rent due from him. In areas where land was held jointly by the village it was distributed periodically among families on the basis of their share in the total land so as to give good quality land on an equitable basis. Views differ as to whether the arable land was held on an individual basis or jointly by the villagers. Among supporters of the former view we may include such authorities as Messrs A. S. Altekar, Baden-Powell, and M. Elphinstone, while the latter view is supported by Sir Henry Maine, Dr R. K. Mukerjee and many others. Mr Altekar is of the view that, as the Vedas, Jataka stories and Hindu Smritis reveal, the system of peasant proprietorship has been prevalent in India since very early times. The separate record of each owner of land in the village kept by the village accountant during the Maurya period as mentioned in the Arthasastra is proof of the same. The joint holdings villages in the north, where a group of persons in the village community hold the village land, not in joint tenancy but in tenancy in common, came into appearance in the medieval period when the Punjab and the United Provinces were subjected to invasions both in Hindu and Muslim periods. A daring chief conquered and occupied a tract of land, which he assigned to his followers by way of reward. Each assignee became the owner of the village land. In the course of time his family multiplied and, in a century or so, instead of one owner there was a co-sharing body of village proprietors, descended from a common ancestor. Each had a clear idea of his ownership in the joint land though they became jointly responsible for the government revenue. The joint cultivation was done to keep better community life, while joint responsibility for payment of land revenue was undertaken to avoid rulers' oppression.[19]

On the other hand Sir Henry Maine contends that in the earliest times the whole village land belonged to the community without any individual rights in the property, as was the case with the ancient European communities, and that the ryotwari system (peasant proprietorship) is a decayed form of the joint holdings system. He also holds the view that in these villages, later on, though the individual rights in property were recognized, the land was re-distributed among the villagers equalizing the fertility of the soils.[20] Whatever the case, there were two systems prevalent in India before the British came, the ryotwari system (or the system of peasant proprietorship) and the mahalwari system (or the system of joint ownership). However, the British, following their own tradition that the king was the sole proprietor of land, imposed the same system, first in Bengal and later on in other parts of northern India. But this system had soon to be given up because of resistance from the local people. However, even the ryotwari system and mahalwari system introduced later on were not satisfactory as the land revenue charged was very high and fluctuated from one time to another. Karl Marx strongly protested against all these systems as we shall see below.

Indian land tenure

Karl Marx observes that as the various kinds of Indian land tenure have recently been described in so many places, and in popular style, too, he proposed to limit his observations on the subject to a few general remarks on the zemindari and ryotwari systems.[21]

The zemindari and the ryotwari were both of them agrarian revolutions, effected by British ukases, and opposed to each other; the one aristocratic, the other democratic; the one a caricature of English landlordism, the other of French peasant proprietorship; but they were pernicious: both combined the most contradictory character; both were made not for the people, who cultivate the soil, nor for the holder, who owns it, but for the government that taxes it.

By the zemindari system, the people of the presidency of Bengal were dispossessed at once of their hereditary claims to the soil in favour of the native tax-gatherers, called zemindars.

> Lord Cornwallis suddenly without warning passed a motion in the Council which at once assumed the force of law, that the *Zemindars* were to be henceforth considered as possessing all (the territory) they claimed ... as hereditary owners of all the soil

17

of the district, paying annually, not their quota of public taxes which they collected for the government, but a sort of tribute into the treasury. The measure was as illegal as it was sudden and unexpected, for the English were supposed to be legislating for the Hindus as a race and, as far as possible, administering to them their own laws, and that was wholesale destruction of Indian tradition. Simultaneously the English Government passed several laws giving the ryot remedies in the civil courts against the zemindars and protecting them from increase of rent. These were nugatory, dead-letter (laws), considering the state of the country; for the ryots were so absolutely at the mercy of their landlords that they seldom dared to raise a finger in self-defence. . . .
Thus Cornwallis and Pitt artificially expropriated the rural population of Bengal. . . . First product of this plunder of 'communal and private property' of the ryots; whole series of local risings of the ryots against the landlord.[22]

By the ryotwari system introduced into the presidencies of Madras and Bombay, the native nobility, with their territorial claims, merassees, jagheers, etc., were reduced with the common people to the holding of minute fields, cultivated by themselves, in favour of the Collector of the East India Company. But a curious sort of English landlord was the zemindar, receiving only one-tenth of the rent, while he had to make over nine-tenths of it to the government. A curious sort of French peasant was the ryot, without any permanent title in the soil, and with the taxation changing every year in proportion to his harvest. The original class of zemindars, notwithstanding their unmitigated and uncontrolled rapacity against the dispossessed mass of the ex-hereditary landholders, soon melted away under the pressure of the Company, in order to be replaced by mercantile speculators who now hold all the land of Bengal, with the exception of estates returned under the direct management of the government. These speculators have introduced a variety of the Zemindari tenure called 'patree'. Not content to be placed with regard to the British government in the situation of middlemen, they have created in their turn a class of 'hereditary' middlemen called 'patnetas' who created again their sub-patnetas, etc., so that a perfect scale of hierarchy of middlemen has sprung up, which presses with its entire weight on the unfortunate cultivator. As to the ryots in Madras and Bombay, the system soon degenerated into one of forced cultivation, and the land lost all its value. 'The land,' says Mr Campbell, 'would be sold for balances by the Collector, as in Bengal, but generally is not, for a very good reason viz; that nobody will buy it'.[23]
Thus, in Bengal, we have a combination of English landlordism,

the Irish middlemen system, the Austrian system, transforming the landlord into the tax-gatherer, and of the Asiatic system making the state the real landlord. In Madras and Bombay we have a French peasant proprietor who is at the same time a serf, and a *metayer* of the state. The drawbacks of all these various systems accumulate upon him without his enjoying any of their redeeming features. The ryot is subject, like the French peasant, to the extortion of the private usurer; but he has no hereditary, or permanent title in his land, like the French peasant. Like the serf he is forced to cultivate, but he is not secured against want like the serf. Like the *metayer* he has to divide his produce with the state, but the state is not obliged, with regard to him, to advance the funds and the stock, as it is obliged to do with regard to the *metayer*. In Bengal, as in Madras and Bombay, under the *zemindari* as under the ryotwari, the ryots—and they form eleven-twelfths of the whole Indian population—have been wretchedly pauperized; and if they are, morally speaking, not sunk as low as the Irish cottiers, they owe it to their climate, the men of the South having fewer wants and more imagination than the men of the North.

Later on Marx observed,

> The Zemindars and Ryotwar themselves, abominable as they are, involve two distinct forms of private property in land—the great *desideratum* of Asiatic Society.... They are the defenders of property, but did any revolutionary party ever originate agrarian revolutions like those in Bengal, in Madras and in Bombay? Did they not, in India, to borrow an expression of the great robber, Lord Clive himself, resort to atrocious extortion, when simple corruption could not keep pace with their rapacity?[24]

In *Capital III* he says,

> If any nation's history, then the history of the English in India is a string of futile and really absurd (in practice infamous) economic experiments. In Bengal they created a caricature of large-scale English landed estates, in south-eastern India, a caricature of small parcelled property; in the north-west they did all they could to transform the Indian economic community with common ownership of the soil into a caricature of itself.[25]

As pointed out by Marx all three systems, i.e. zemindari, ryotwari and mahalwari were unsatisfactory. But the first two were more full of abuses than the third, i.e. the mahalwari. The zemindari system was really very inappropriate and against Hindu traditions. The ryots were exploited by the zemindars who charged exorbitant rents and also got illegal exactions in the form of forced labour from them. The ryotwari system was also oppressive as tax was

19

heavy and often beyond the capacity of the ryot. Even in the mahalwari system the revenue was not permanently fixed. About the position at that time Mr Dutt observes, 'Agriculture is now virtually the only remaining source of national wealth in India, and four-fifths of the Indian people depend upon agriculture. But the Land Tax levied by the British Government is not only excessive, but what is worse, it is fluctuating and uncertain, in many provinces'.[26] Although later on attempts were made to fix the land tax for a longer period, say twenty to forty years, the demand was still excessive, compared to that made during the Hindu period. Because of excessive tax the cultivator was forced to borrow from the moneylender at an exorbitant rate of interest, and got into heavy debt. Many times the land passed from the hands of cultivators to those of moneylenders. Although legislative measures were taken to restrict such transfers, they were not very effective.

After a series of famines from 1860 to 1900, the government took steps to improve irrigation facilities, to advance cheap loans through co-operative societies or to disseminate scientific information on agriculture; yet all these steps were not commensurate with the needs. It was only after Independence that various land reform measures were taken to abolish the intermediaries, to fix the rent on an equitable basis and to advance finance to cultivators at reasonable rate of interest. However, the problem of tiny holdings still remains to be solved.

Indian revenue and taxation

Karl Marx observes that the utilization of public revenues and the taxation system are both defective. While the bulk of the public revenue goes out of the country in the form of home charges, very little is spent on developmental activities. The taxation is lopsided and falls on the poor man. He observes,

> The Home Establishment absorbs 3 per cent of the net revenue, and the annual interest for Home Debt and Dividends 14 per cent, together 17 per cent. If we deduct these annual remittances from India to England, the military charges amount to about two-thirds of the whole expenditure available for India, or to 66 per cent, while the charges for public works do not amount to more than $2\frac{3}{4}$ per cent of the general revenue, or for Bengal 1 per cent, Agra $7\frac{3}{4}$, Punjab $\frac{1}{8}$, Madras $\frac{1}{2}$ and Bombay 1 per cent of the respective revenues. These figures are the official ones of the Company itself.
>
> On the other hand nearly three-fifths of the whole net revenue are derived from the land, about one-seventh from opium, and

upward of one-ninth from salt. These resources together yield 85 per cent of the whole receipts.

As to minor items of expenditure and charges, it may suffice to state that the Moturpha revenue maintained in the Presidency of Madras, and levied on shops, looms, sheep, cattle, sundry professions, etc., yields somewhat about £50,000 while the yearly dinners of the East India House cost about the same.[27]

He further adds that land tax is not only excessive but fluctuates from time to time. Conjointly with the land tax we have to consider the salt tax. Notoriously the Company retains the monopoly of that article which they sell at three times its mercantile value—and this in a country where it is furnished by the sea, by the lakes, by the mountains and the earth itself. The practical working of this monopoly was described by the Earl of Albemarle in the following words:

A great proportion of the salt for inland consumption throughout the country is purchased from the Company by large wholesale merchants at less than 4 rupees per maund; these mix a proportion of sand, chiefly got a few miles to the south-west of Dacca, and send the mixture to a second, or, counting the Government as the first, to a third monopolist at about 5 or 6 rupees. This dealer adds more earth or ashes, and thus passing through more hands, from the large towns to villages, the price is still raised from 8 to 10 rupees and the proportion of adulteration from 25 to 40 per cent. It appears then that the people pay from £21 17s. 2d. to £27 6s. 2d. for their salt, or in other words, from 30 to 36 times as much as the wealthy people of Great Britain.

As an instance of English bourgeois morals, he alleges that Mr Campbell defends the opium monopoly because it prevents the Chinese from consuming too much of the drug, and that he defends the brandy monopoly (licences for spirit-selling in India) because it has wonderfully increased the consumption of brandy in India.

The zemindar tenure, the ryotwari and the salt tax, combined with the Indian climate, were the hotbeds of cholera—India's scourge of the Western world—a striking and severe example of the universality of human woes and wrongs.

The above observations made by Marx with regard to Indian revenue and taxes are quite correct. Mr R. C. Dutt, who studied the Indian finances of that period, almost concurred with Marx's findings and to remove these defects suggested moderate and regulated land tax, reduction in the rate of interest on public debt, the bearing of civil and military charges incurred in England by the British government, reduction of civil charges in India by

21

employment of more Indians, reduction in military charges and more investment in public works.[28] Mahatma Gandhi later on agitated against the salt monopoly in 1930 from the Congress platform.

Dual role of England—destructive and regenerative

In his article entitled 'The Future Results of British Rule in India' Marx observes that England had to fulfil a double mission in India: one destructive, the other regenerating—the annihilation of the old Asiatic society, and the laying of the material foundations of Western society in Asia.

Arabs, Turks, Tartars, Moguls, who had successively overrun India, soon became Hinduized, the barbarian conquerors being, by an eternal law of history conquered themselves by the superior civilization of their subjects. The British were the first conquerors superior, and therefore inaccessible, to Hindu civilization. They destroyed it by breaking up the native community, by uprooting the native industry, and by levelling all that was great and elevated in the native society. The historic pages of their rule in India report hardly anything beyond that destruction. The work of regeneration hardly transpires through a heap of ruins. Nevertheless it has begun.

The political unity of India, more consolidated and extending further than it ever did under the Great Moguls, was the first condition of its regeneration. That unity, imposed by the British sword, will now be strengthened and perpetuated by the electric telegraph. The native army, organized and trained by the British drill-sergeant, was the *sine qua non* of Indian self-emancipation, and of India ceasing to be the prey of the first foreign intruder. The free press, introduced for the first time into Asiatic society, and managed principally by the common offspring of Hindu and European, is a new powerful agent of reconstruction. From the Indian natives, reluctantly and sparingly educated at Calcutta, under English superintendence, a fresh class is springing up, endowed with the requirements for government and imbued with European science.

Steam has brought India into regular and rapid communication with Europe, has connected its chief ports with those of the whole south-eastern ocean, and has revindicated it from the isolated position which was the prime law of its stagnation. The day is not far distant when, by a combination of railways and steam vessels the distance between England and India, measured by time, will be shortened to eight days, and when that once fabulous country will thus be actually annexed to the Western world.

The ruling classes of Great Britain have had, till now, but an accidental, transitory and exceptional interest in the progress of India. The aristocracy wanted to conquer it, the moneyocracy to plunder it, and the millocracy to undersell it. But now the tables are turned. The millocracy have discovered that the transformation of India into a reproductive country has become of vital importance to them, and that, to that end, it is necessary, above all, to gift her with means of irrigation and of internal communication. They intend now drawing a net of railways over India. And they will do it. The results must be inappreciable.

The introduction of railways may be easily made to subserve agricultural purposes by the formation of tanks, where ground is required for embankment, and by the conveyance of water along the different lines. Thus irrigation, the *sine qua non* of farming in the East, might be greatly extended, and the frequently recurring local famines, arising from want of water, would be averted.

The railways will afford the means of diminishing the amount and the cost of the military establishments. Stores would not be required to the same extent at the various depots and the number of troops might be diminished in direct proportion to their effectiveness.

He further adds,

I know that the English millocracy intend to endow India with railways with the exclusive view of extracting at diminished expenses the cotton and other raw materials for their manufactures. But when you have once introduced machinery into the locomotion of a country, which possesses iron and coals, you are unable to withhold it from its fabrication. You cannot maintain a net of railways over an immense country without introducing all those industrial processes necessary to meet the immediate and current wants of railway locomotion, and out of which there must grow the application of machinery to those branches of industry not immediately connected with railways. The railway-system will therefore become, in India, truly the forerunner of modern Industry.

He also believed that the great mass of the Indian people possesses a great industrial energy, is well fitted to accumulate capital, and remarkable for a mathematical clearness of head, and talent for figures and exact sciences as was evinced by some English writers. Modern industry, resulting from the railway-system, will dissolve the hereditary division, upon which rests the Indian castes, those decisive impediments to Indian progress and Indian power.

All that the English bourgeoisie may be forced to do will neither emancipate nor materially mend the social conditions of the mass of

23

the people, depending as they do not only on the development of the productive power but also on its appropriation by the people. But what they will not fail to do is to lay down the material premises for both. Has the bourgeoisie ever done more? Has it ever effected progress without dragging individuals and peoples through blood and dirt, through misery and degradation?

The Indians will not reap the fruits of the new elements of society scattered among them by the British bourgeoisie, till in Great Britain itself the now ruling classes shall have been supplanted by the industrial proletariat, or till the Hindus themselves shall have grown strong enough to throw off the English yoke altogether. At all events, we may safely expect to see, at a more or less remote period, the regeneration of that great and interesting country, whose gentle natives are, to use the expression of Prince Soltykov, even in the most inferior classes *'plus fins et plus adroits que les Italiens'*,[29] whose submission even is counterbalanced by a certain calm nobility, who notwithstanding their natural langour, have astonished the British officers by their bravery, whose country has been the source of our languages, our religions, and who represent the type of the ancient German in the *Jat* and the type of the ancient Greek in the brahman.[30]

Most of the observations made by Marx in connection with the future results of the British rule in India turned out to be true. (i) India was for the first time united into one country after a very long time. The railways, post and telegraph, the press and the other means of communication further strengthened it. (ii) The native army, organized and trained by the British drill-sergeant once tried to revolt against the foreign yoke in 1857, but the revolt was unsuccessful. However, it was for the first time in the history of India that both Hindus and Muslims fought together against the British rule. A similar type of attempt was again made by the Indian National Army in 1943 during the Second World War under the leadership of Subhas Chandra Bose, when he tried to organize Indian War prisoners in the Eastern front. They were forced to leave India as the ratings of Royal Indian Navy rose in mutiny against them in 1946. His prophecy that with the new, organized and trained army India would cease to be a prey of the first foreign intruder also turned out to be true when, in 1965, the attack of Pakistan was made unsuccessful although the latter had enough arms.[31] (iii) The free press, introduced and managed by the common offsprings of Hindus and Europeans was a powerful agent of reconstruction. It helped in bringing together the leaders from different parts of the country on a common platform, to agitate against the foreign rule and helped in forging the unity in the country. The grievances of the public were voiced by the leaders through the press. (iv) Many Indians trained and educated by modern methods of education were recruited in government service while the rest joined other professions as scientists, doctors, teachers and lawyers having a new outlook. The modern educated young man proved a boon in setting up a good bureaucracy in government and other business organizations and industries. (v) He correctly read the the motives of the English bourgeoisie in spreading the railway in India and the irrigation system. By expansion of irrigation, of course, they wanted to minimize famines, but were at the same time interested in procuring raw material for their mills in Britain. During the American Civil War there was short supply of cotton from America and British mills were affected by that. Similarly in the expansion of railways they wanted a cheap supply of raw materials for their industries and to sell finished goods to the Indian masses at a cheaper rate. After the construction of railways discriminatory rates were used for exporting raw materials to Great Britain and importing finished goods into India. Of course, another motive in the expansion of means of communications was better military control. (vi) However, the opening of railways brought many indirect advantages to India. The workshops opened to repair engines and prepare many other accessories did help the native population in getting training in new industrial techniques and also provided them with employment. After independence the network of railways proved beneficial in the industrial development of the country, goods and machinery being easily transported from one place to another.

Another advantage of railways and modern industries, as pointed out by Marx, has been the dissolution of hereditary division of labour and caste distances. Many people have joined the industries, leaving their hereditary occupations and working together at one place. However, it needs pointing out that many of the upper castes still prefer non-manual jobs and are not interested in taking up industrial enterprises. Travelling together in the railways and eating in hotels has broken the barriers of untouchability and eating with other castes. (vii) His observation that all the English bourgeoisie may be forced to do will neither emancipate nor materially mend the social conditions of the mass of the people till in Great Britain itself the ruling class is replaced by industrial proletariat or the Hindus themselves shall have grown strong enough to throw off the English yoke altogether, has also proved true. India got independence in 1947 only when the Labour government with Mr Attlee as Prime Minister came to power, although promises were made earlier from time to time by various other parties in power to give independence to India.

In respect of material progress also there was not much improvement in the country during the British rule, because of the *laissez faire* policy followed in the interest of the millocracy in England. The real industrial advancement began only after the country gained independence.

Indian social structure and human progress

Karl Marx studied all the aspects of Indian society, including political, economic, social, religious, rural–urban, familistic, cultural etc., with the exception of population. Many of his observations were incisive, but in certain respects he was not very clear. For example, when he said that the village community was disintegrating because of English steam and free trade, he was rather incorrect. Actually it was the urban artisans who were hit hard and became unemployed. Similarly he said that the village people were unconcerned with the country as a whole; but the facts were otherwise. By his remarks on the 'closed' nature of the communal units he meant that cities hardly belonged to the economy at all arising

> only where the location is particularly favourable to external trade or where the ruler and his satraps exchange their revenue (surplus product) for labour, which they expend as labour fund. This Asiatic system is therefore not yet a class society or if it is a class society, then in its most primitive form.[32]

But there were certain good cities in India, where many home industries flourished. Under the conditions existing at that time, when communication was very slow, big cities like London and Paris were not possible in India. And as soon as conditions were favourable such cities rapidly emerged. As Marx anticipated, India is now on the road of material progress. The difficulties hindering her development are a rapidly growing population, the caste system, lack of education and technical know-how and certain other bottlenecks.

In his earlier writings Marx did not mention the evolution of Asiatic societies. In the Manifesto of the Communist Party (1847) he mentions the three historical epochs of Western society, i.e. ancient, medieval and modern. He states,

> In the earlier epochs of history, we find almost everywhere a complicated arrangement of society into various orders, a manifold gradation of social rank. In ancient Rome we have patricians, knights, plebians, slaves; in the Middle Ages, feudal lords, vassals, guild-masters, journey-men, apprentices, serfs; in almost all of these classes, again, subordinate gradations....

Our epoch, the epoch of the bourgeoisie, possesses, however, this distinctive feature: it has simplified the class antagonisms. Society as a whole is more and more splitting up into two great hostile camps, into two great classes directly facing each other: Bourgeoisie and Proletariat.[33]

But after his migration to England, he and Engels both were absorbed in the Eastern Question and whether those countries would also pass through the same stages. In his 'Preface to A Contribution to the Critique of Political Economy', he does mention the Asiatic mode of production as a historical epoch, when he states, 'In broad outlines Asiatic, ancient, feudal, and modern bourgeois modes of production can be designated as progressive epochs in the economic formation of society'.[34] However, Marx did not consider that the Indian society would have to pass through these stages ultimately to become a Communist society. But he firmly believed that all people, of whatever race or historical background, are equally capable of all the achievements of modern civilization once they are free to pursue them.

2   Herbert Spencer (1820–1903)

After Comte, Herbert Spencer was undoubtedly the scholar chiefly responsible for the foundation of sociology during the nineteenth century.[1] His theoretical master-key was the concept of evolution.[2] He was the first sociologist who formulated a comprehensive theory of society based on concrete empirical data. As such he left Comte far behind and set an example which, consciously or otherwise, every sociologist has followed ever since. An organism in Spencer's view is the more perfect according as it is more complex and its parts are differentiated. This involves greater division of functions between the different organs, which means that the parts would have to be more closely integrated. Social evolution and progress consists essentially in an increase of social differentiation and integration, in an increase of the division of labour, and in a transition from the state of undifferentiated homogeneity to a state of heterogeneity.[3] After de Tocqueville Spencer was an outstanding sociologist who recognized clearly the importance of the comparative method in analysing social facts.

Spencer made no special study of Indian society as a whole, as Marx did, or of any of its particular parts, as Weber did. In reply to a letter from an Indian lady in July 1890 who had sought his advice on legislation about early marriages in India, he admits that he had not studied Indian affairs to any great extent and therefore would not be able to say much in the matter.[4] However, he did study certain aspects of Indian society such as religious beliefs and political, ecclesiastical and other institutions so as to fit his comparative analysis in the *Principles of Sociology*. Among oriental societies his study of China and Japan was deeper than that of India, as is indicated by the use of data in the works referred to above.

As he tried to apply the concept of evolution to every aspect of social phenomena, whether religious beliefs, forms of family, or institutions political, ecclesiastical or industrial, he takes his data from many primitive societies as a basis of induction. He compiled this data in the eight volumes of *Descriptive Sociology*. One of these volumes, no. V, deals with Asiatic races including some hill tribes of India. As these tribes are a part of Indian society, reflecting some traces of Indian civilization, it might be appropriate to discuss some of their salient features as pointed out by Spencer, before dealing with Indian society as such. According to Spencer most of these hill tribes had lived in plains in the past and had fled from the invading people. They found localities here and there in which they were able to carry on their peaceful occupations unmolested; in most cases it was their ability to live in a malarious atmosphere, fatal to the Aryan races, which kept them free from molestation. Besides these hill tribes Spencer also makes reference to some tribes living on the plains in his work *Principles of Sociology*. These include the Bhat, Bawras, Domras, Bunjaras, Kanjars, etc.

Tribes of India

The tribal population of India is accepted to be the oldest population of the land. These communities have lived for centuries in the forest and hilly regions. Besides these, there were certain other tribes, including criminal ones, living on the plains. They were made up of a few pastoral communities which could not adjust themselves to the economy of settled life and found it profitable to take advantage of concentrated properties in settled colonies rather than to earn their livelihood by productive labour. Many of them developed peculiar concepts of property and practised anti-social activities, i.e. thieving, begging, etc. Out of a total population of 361 millions in 1951, the tribal population made 19 millions and criminal tribes 4 millions. The tribes whose details are given in *Descriptive Sociology* include Todas, Khonds, Gonds, Bhils, Santals, Karens, Kukis, Nagas, Bodo, Dhimals, Mishmis, Puttooahs and Lepchas. Some of these tribes such as Todas, Khonds, Santals, Bodo and Dhimals possess certain good characteristics which are not found in many of the tribal populations in other countries. Therefore, Spencer praises these tribes for such characteristics, that is, their high moral character, voluntary co-operation in industrial and other activities and better treatment of women and children, and makes reference to these features again and again in various volumes of his works. However, he also mentions some of their weak features which are often anti-social or lead to their ruin. Let us discuss these in brief.

High morals

Spencer refutes the presumption that civilized large nations must be morally advanced. He says that characters are to be found among rude people which compare well with those of the best among cultivated people. With little knowledge and but rudimentary arts there in some cases go virtues which might shame even those whose education and polish are the highest. Surviving remnants of some primitive races in India have natures in which truthfulness seems to be organic. Not only to the surrounding Hindus, intellectually and relatively advanced in culture, are they in this respect superior; but they are superior to Europeans. Of certain of these hill peoples it is remarked that their assertions may always be accepted with perfect confidence, which is more than can be said of manufacturers who use false trademarks and of diplomatists who intentionally delude. As having these traits may be named the Santals, of whom Hunter says, 'they were the most truthful set of men I ever met'.[5] Notwithstanding their sexual relations being of a primitive and low type, even the Todas are described as considering falsehood one of the worst of vices.[6] Similarly in respect of honesty some of these people classed as inferior read lessons to those classed as superior. Among these he mentions Todas, Gonds, Khonds, Bodo and Dhimals. Among the Khonds the denial of a debt is a breach of this principle which is held to be highly sinful. 'They say, let a man give up all he has to his creditors'.[7] Among some of these tribes crime is rare and theft is almost unknown.

Voluntary co-operation in industrial activities

Spencer observes that few examples exist among uncivilized societies, which show with tolerable clarity the outlines of the industrial type of society in its rudimentary form—the form which it assumes where culture has made but little progress. Among these, Bodo and Dhimals are wholly unmilitary, as lacking political organization, as being without slaves or social grades, and as aiding one another in their heavier undertakings. Todas lead tranquil lives 'without any of those bonds of union which man in general is induced to form from a sense of danger'.[8] And they settle their disputes by arbitration or by a council of five. Santals again are quite unoffensive. These people are industrious cultivators and enjoy their existence unfettered by caste. While there is a patriarch who is honoured, but who rarely interferes, 'every village has its council place . . . where the committee assemble and discuss the affairs of the village and its inhabitants. All petty disputes, both of a civil and criminal nature, are settled there'.[9]

Better treatment of women and children

Spencer also mentions the high status of women in these tribes and higher work assigned to them as in modern industrial societies but not in militant societies. He remarks that people unallied in race and living in regions remote from one another show that where exceptional conditions have made possible a perfectly peaceful life, and where men are no longer occupied in war and the chase, the division of labour between the sexes becomes humane in its character: the men do the heavy, outdoor work and the women the light indoor work. For example, in the Bodo and Dhimals tribes, while the men clear the fields, till the ground and make the houses, 'the women aided by the girls, are fully employed within doors in spinning, weaving and dyeing the clothing of the family, in brewing, and in cooking'.[10] Bodo and Dhimals also use their wives and daughters well; treating them with confidence and kindness. Among them infanticide is utterly unknown and it is deemed shameful to leave old parents entirely alone.

Marriage system

Spencer observes that while Bodo and Dhimals are monogamous, among Todas there is polyandry joined with polygyny. Dr Shortt tells us,

> if there be four or five brothers, and one of them, being old enough, gets married, his wife claims all the other brothers as her husbands, and as they successively attain manhood, she consorts with them; or if the wife has one or more younger sisters, they in turn, on attaining a marriageable age, become the wives of their sister's husband, or husbands, and thus in a family of several brothers, there may be, according to circumstances only one wife for them all, or many; but one or more, they all live under one roof, and cohabit promiscuously.[11]

Beliefs and religious practices

Spencer points out that among many uncivilized people there is a belief in an after-life. Having this conception they place with the deceased not only his inanimate possessions like weapons and implements, clothing, ornaments and other movables but also sacrifice his domestic animals and servants, so that he may enjoy them in his after-life. Thus among the Dyaks burial-rites frequently reduce survivors to poverty. And if on the death of a Toda 'his entire herd of oxen was sacrificed',[12] the implication is that his widow and children had to suffer great want and such want is indeed alleged.

31

Spencer mentions that robbery as well as murder has had, and still has in some places a religious sanctification. Of the robber-tribe among the Chibchas, Piedrahita writes, 'they regard as the most acceptable sacrifice that which they offer up out of the robbery to certain idols of gold, clay and wood, whom they worship'. And at the present time in the north-western provinces of India, we have freebooters like the Domras, among whom 'a successful theft is always celebrated by a sacrifice to their chief god Gandak'.[13] This practice is characteristic of all the lowest and barbarous Indian societies. The Doms or Domras live on the edge of the forests under the Himalayas and are one of the most utterly degraded and irreclaimable tribes in all these parts.

Regarding the Kanjars another tribe living in plains, Nesfield observes,

> The man-god whom the Kanjar worship is Mana. The worshippers collect near a tree, under which they sacrifice a pig or goat, or sheep, or fowl and make an offering of roasted flesh and spirituous liquor. Formerly (it is said) they used to sacrifice a child, having first made it insensible with fermented palm juice and toddy. They dance round the tree in honour of Mana and sing the customary songs in commemoration of his wisdom and deeds of valour. At the close of the ceremony there is a general feast, in which most of the banqueters get drunk.[14]

Most of the observations made by Spencer about these Indian tribes are quite correct. It is true that high morals are not always connected with higher civilization or higher religion, but it cannot be denied that religion does play a part in raising the morals of peoples, as asserted by Weber and certain other philosophers. Social habits once formed take root in a society and it takes time to efface them. We find that some of these tribes, when they come in contact with civilized people for a considerable time, also change their morals and become unscrupulous. Similar is the position with regard to criminal tribes. Some of these communities have already settled down and only a small section follow their old predatory habits. During the British rule certain restrictions were put on their movements and they were forced to confine themselves to certain areas. However, after Independence, under the new Indian constitution no such restriction could be put on anyone, unless he was proved to be guilty in a court of law. So the existing Criminal Tribal Acts had to be repealed.

Under the five-year plans special schemes have been drawn up to settle them on new agricultural lands or in cottage industries. A well-thought-out scheme of education for their children has been chalked out so that they are gradually weaned away from their present practices. For the tribal people living in forests and hilly areas, special welfare programmes have been drawn up under the five-year plans to improve their living conditions. To avoid their exploitation by contractors, merchants and moneylenders, state governments have tried to organize co-operatives among them. Other programmes include improvements in communications, the education of their children, the development of tribal economy and the provision of water supply and health services. For those tribes who practise shifting cultivation, efforts have been made to settle them at one place by providing them with suitable land for cultivation and also by improving their agricultural practices. However, so far as their religious and social life is concerned, no changes are brought about unless the initiative comes from the tribal people themselves.

Having discussed some salient aspects of the tribal communities in India let us move on to the civilized population of the country. Here Spencer discusses the beliefs and institutions of Hindus who formed the largest part of the population in the country.

Indian civilization

Indian civilization is one of the oldest in the world. Some of the other civilizations to which he makes reference in his works are the Egyptian, Greek, Roman, etc. Indian civilization is generally dealt with in three periods, i.e. ancient, medieval and modern, and he makes reference to all the three. The special aspects to which he refers may be dealt with under the following main heads:

1 Religious beliefs
2 Priestly organization
3 Marriage and family structure
4 The caste system and industrial progress
5 Village communities and communal regulations
6 Ancient Hindu law and its effects
7 Slavery in ancient India
8 The development of sciences and philosophy in ancient India
9 The military system in medieval India
10 Political organization and colonial rule
11 Indian society and social progress

Religious beliefs

In part I of his book *Principles of Sociology* Spencer points out at the outset that social phenomena are complex, comprised of many components which interact with one another. Among these he includes external environments—both organic and inorganic—population growth, social interaction between the individual and society and how they stimulate each other, social environments or relations with neighbouring societies, and advancement of material and non-material culture. Then, after discussing some of these in brief, he devotes the major portion of this part to the beliefs people form about themselves or of other beings and the surrounding world, as such beliefs affect their conduct in many ways. Here he discusses the beliefs of Hindus along with those of many other societies, primitive and civilized.

He stresses that Indian religion is a complex one where, besides ancestor-worship, people believe in various kinds of gods and goddesses. However, there are some who do not believe in such things. Let us discuss some of these beliefs as he describes them.

(a) Temple and tope combined   Spencer points out that while in some societies in the beginning people erected temples for worship, in others they started worshipping the tombs, while in still others both were combined. In India there was combined the altar and the temple as in some other countries like Egypt. He observes that when, from tracing the origin of the sacred chamber, be it a cave, or deserted houses, or special mortuary-house, or temple, we proceed to trace the origin of the sacred structure within it—the altar—we come first to something intermediate. In India there are highly developed sacred structures uniting the attributes of the two. Instead of a sacred edifice evolved from the sepulchral chamber, we have in India the tope, a sacred edifice evolved from the grave-heap itself. 'The Tope is the lineal and direct descendant of the funereal Tumulus',[15] says Ferguson; as defined by Cunningham in his elaborate work, it is 'a regularly-built cairn'[16] as its name implies. Of these Indian topes, some contain relics of Sakya Muni, and certain other relics of his principal disciples, priests and saints. The tope is a tomb; and the prayers offered at topes, the processions made round them, and the adorations paid to them (as shown in the sculptures on their own surfaces), prove that they are simply solid temples instead of hollow ones. Further evidence of this remains: the name given to certain of them, chaitya, means, in Sanskrit 'an altar, a temple, as well as any monument raised on the site of a funeral pile'.

(b) Ancestor-worship along with worship of other gods   Spencer observes that Aryans, while worshipping their greater deities, also worshipped their ancestors who, according to their remoteness, were regarded as divine, semi-divine and human. To support his contention he quotes A. C. Lyall who observes,

So far as I have been able to trace back the origin of the best known minor provincial deities, they are usually men of past generations who have earned special promotion and brevet rank among disembodied ghosts by some peculiar acts or accidents of their lives or deaths. ... Of the numerous local gods known to have been living men, by far the greater proportion derive from the ordinary canonization of holy personages. ... The number of shrines thus raised in Berar alone to these authorities and persons deceased in the odour of sanctity is large, and it is constantly increasingly. Some of them have already attained the ranks of temples.[17]

This fact, that generally the holy personages are worshipped, has also been stressed by other writers, as has been seen above.

Regarding ancestor-worship, he continues, there are specific passages in the laws of Manu. There we have the statement that the manes eat of the funeral meal; we have the direction to the head of the family to make a daily offering to obtain the goodwill of the manes, and also a monthly offering. However, Manu also points out that in making offerings to the manes the master of the house must commence with an oblation to the gods, so that the gods may not appropriate what is intended for the manes. In other words he gives higher rank to gods than to ancestors. He says,

Let an offering to the gods be made at the beginning and end of the Sraddha: it must not begin and end with an offering to ancestors; for he who begins and ends it with an oblation to the pitris; quickly perishes with his progeny.[18]

(c) New genesis of cults We have mentioned above that holy or great men were deified among the Hindus. But it is not always the case that the same deities or gods are worshipped for ever; with the passage of time some old deities are dropped and new ones are taken up. To substantiate this fact Spencer quotes some reports which he received from certain persons in India. A magistrate of Gorakhpur writes,

It may perhaps be interesting to know that a weekly pilgrimage has been instituted within the last year to the tomb of a Fakir in the compound next my own. The Fakir died two centuries ago, it is said. A 'Jhundi' was struck over his grave—somebody got cured there last year, and a concourse of people now visit it every Thursday, with drums beating, etc. I counted once seven graves within a mile or so of my house, at which offerings are presented by the Hindu public, on fixed days. The tombs are generally those of Mahomedans, but this is immaterial. As my

Honorary Magistrate Babu Durga Pershad explained one day, when pointing out a tree frequented by a 'Jin', a 'bhut' is generally a Hindu, rather harmless and indistinct, but a 'Jin' is always a wicked old Mahomedan, and there is no appeasing him. The number of 'Devis' is also innumerable, new ones are always springing up, and the most fashionable shrines are generally very recent. The principal Mahadeo on this side of the town was discovered by two herd boys, some years ago, in the Ramgarh Tal. One boy struck it, it began to bleed and the boy fell dead. There is a famous Kali at the corner of my compound, another Devi lives in the judges' compound and her image is carried home every evening by the mali who officiates.[19]

This statement harmonizes entirely with that given by Sir Alfred Lyall in his Asiatic studies. To the instances he cites, he adds the remark, 'The saint or hero is admitted into the upper circles of divinity, much as a successful soldier or millionaire is recognized by fashionable society, takes a new title and is welcomed by a judiciously liberal aristocracy'.[20]

(d) Fetish worship Spencer observes that besides the worship of ancestors, holy men and other gods possessing superhuman qualities, some other objects supposed to possess some extraordinary power are also worshipped in many primitive societies. And this was also done by Hindus. It is the unusualness which makes an object a fetish and it is supposed to imply an indwelling ghost—an agent without which deviation from the ordinary would be inexplicable. There is no tendency gratuitously to ascribe duality of nature; but only when there is an unfamiliar appearance, or motion, or sound, or change in a thing does there arise this idea of a possessing spirit. First a stone is the abode of some spirit; its curious shape or situation betraying possession. Next, this strange form or aspect argues some design, or handiwork, of supernatural beings.

And, Spencer adds, 'If we ask where fetishism has culminated, we are referred to a people whose civilization, older in date than our own, has created vast cities, elaborate industries, a highly-structured language, great poems, subtle philosophies'.[21] In India a woman adores the basket which serves to bring or to hold her necessaries; and she offers sacrifices to it, as well as to the rice-mill and other implements that assist her in her household labours. A carpenter pays like homage to his hatchet, his adze and his other tools; and likewise he offers sacrifices to them. A Brahmin does so to the style with which he is going to write; a soldier to the arms he is to use in the field; a mason to his trowel.[22] And this statement of Dubois, quoted by Sir John Lubbock, coincides with that of A. C. Lyall who says, 'Not only does the husbandman pray to his plough, the fisher to his net, the weaver to his loom; but the scribe adores his pen, and the banker his account-books'.[23]

The Hindus worship not only their tools and the implements which are a source of their bread-winning, but they also worship animals, plants and stones and other inanimate objects, as is done in some other primitive tribes. Spencer mentions that serpent-gods are common in India; and the serpent habitually sculptured as a god, is the cobra.[24] Among plants a typical case is the worship of the soma which is an intoxicating plant. There are many references to it in the Rig-Veda as quoted by Dr J. Muir. According to him, 'The rishis had come to regard Soma as a god, and apparently to be passionately devoted to his worship'.[25] Similarly they also worship natural objects like the moon, the sun, etc.

(e) Demon worship   According to Spencer ghost-theory gives rise to a belief in ghosts that may be either friendly or malicious; the last, usually not ancestral, are feared more than the first, and often in a greater degree propitiated. He then quotes Mr M. J. Walhouse who gives good illustration of this fact in an essay on the beliefs in bhutas among the people in western India. Mr Walhouse observes,

> But the last three classes, of whom more particularly it is now intended to speak, are of exclusively human origin, being malignant, discontented beings, wandering in an intermediate state between Heaven and Hell, intent upon mischief and annoyance to mortals; chiefly by means of possession and wicked inspiration, every aspect of which ancient ideas, as well as of the old doctrine of transmigration, they exemplify and illustrate. They are known by the names of *Bhutas, Preta,* and *Pisacha,* the first name being ordinarily applied to all the three, and even vulgarly to the seven superior classes. These beings, always evil, originate from the souls of those who have died untimely or violent deaths, or been deformed, idiotic, or insane; afflicted with fits and unusual ailments; or drunken, dissolute, or wicked during life.... The death of any well-known bad character is a source of terror to all the neighbourhood, as he is sure to become a *Bhuta* or demon, as powerful or malignant as he was in life. Some of the *Bhutas* now most dreaded were personages of old days.... In their haunts and modes of appearance Bhutas repeat the beliefs of many countries. They wander borne upon the air, especially in uninhabited, dry, and desert places; and tall trees are a favourite abode.... As the

ancient Jews would speak to none whom they met after midnight, for fear they might be addressing a devil, so Hindu villagers will speak to no one they may meet at that time, lest he should be a *Bhut*, nor, indeed, willingly then stir out of their houses. The before-mentioned classes are believed more particularly to afflict human beings by entering into and possessing them. Gaping or drawing deep breaths are supposed to give them opportunities for this, and no Brahman ever gapes without snapping his fingers before his mouth, as a charm to prevent an evil spirit entering. . . . Should a member of the family be stricken with any unusual attack, such as apoplexy, paralysis, cholera, etc., or should disease break out amongst the cattle, it is at once ascribed to the anger of the Bhut, and a propitiatory sacrifice is offered.[26]

From the above account which Spencer gives of beliefs about supernatural beings, whether among Hindus or other people, he concludes two things. First that anything which transcends the ordinary is considered by man as supernatural or divine; the remarkable man among the rest. And thus using the phrase ancestor-worship in its broadest sense as comprehending all worship of the dead, be they of the same blood or not, he comes to the conclusion that ancestor-worship is the root of every religion.

Secondly he concludes that a system of superstitions arises by continuous growth, each stage of which leads to the next, and here the general formula of evolution is conformed to by the changes gone through. In ghosts there soon arise the concept of a contrast of goodness between the ghosts of relatives and the ghosts of other persons, which are often malicious. Eventually there is formed a hierarchy of partially-deified ancestors, demigods, great gods and, among the great gods, one who is supreme; there is simultaneously formed a hierarchy of diabolical powers. Then come those further differentiations which specialize the functions and habitats of these supernatural beings, until each mythology has its major and minor presiding agents from Apollo down to dryad, from Thor down to a water-sprite, from a saint down to a fairy.[27]

Ultimately, there results under favouring conditions a gravitation towards monotheism. It is true that for a long time there may continue in the minds of a polytheistic people, a fluctuating conflict among the beliefs respecting the relative powers of their gods. Here he supports his argument by quoting Max Muller. Of the ancient Aryans, he says,

It would be easy to find, in the numerous hymns of the Veda, passages in which almost every single god is represented as supreme and absolute. . . . Agni is called the ruler of the universe... Indira is celebrated as the strongest god... and the burden of one of the songs... is... Indra is greater than all. Of Soma it is said that... he conquers every one.[28]

Thus eventually the position of 'father of gods and men' becomes settled in the minds of the believers.

However, from monotheism people move further, led by critical and speculative philosophy, to agnostic and heterodox opinions. And this happened in India too. The reference to philosophical schools is made later under 'The development of sciences and philosophy'.

Most of the observations made by Spencer regarding the religious beliefs of Hindus are correct. There is no doubt that the Hindu religion is a polytheistic one where, besides ancestor-worship, people believe in various types of gods and goddesses. Not only is there a hierarchy of certain gods, but there are special gods that are worshipped on particular occasions. The types of gods worshipped varies from place to place and sometimes from caste to caste. It is also true that some new gods are added and old ones are dropped. There is a fetish worship and people worship stones, plants and animals because of their usefulness or unusualness or some extraordinary power in them. The belief in demons i.e. *bhutas, preta* and *pisacha* are found among rural folk, who try to propitiate them by various means. However, it may be mentioned that Spencer makes no reference to worship of the guru, who is the living deity for many persons. In whatever god or goddess a man may believe, the key to heaven lies with the living guru and this point is rightly stressed by Weber.[29] Nor does he make any reference to certain rational beliefs among the modern educated classes who did not believe in all these things, though he does mention such beliefs in the past.

His idea that ancestor-worship is the root of all religions does not seem to be tenable as it is equally possible that people might have just begun to believe in certain other supernatural things like the sun, the moon, clouds, etc. which had some extraordinary power, and then would have arrived at the conclusion that there was some super-power controlling all these things, as asserted by Max Muller.

Priestly organization

Spencer divides priests into two groups, i.e. semi-priest and the priesthood proper. In the first category he includes the family heads who propitiate their ancestors. He observes that although in the early stages sacrifices to the ghost of the dead man are made by descendants in general, gradually the propitiatory function is performed by the father of the family. Among Hindus the daily offering to ancestors is made by the head of the family, who must be a male member. Sir Henry Maine observes that not only must the ancestor worshipped be a male ancestor, but the worshipper must be the male child or other male descendant.[30] And according to Duncker the law of the brahmans enjoins that every man ought to marry, so that he may have a son who may one day pour for him the libations for the dead.[31]

Regarding the priesthood proper, Spencer points out that in the beginning the king or chief was the main priest. But gradually this function was transferred to some relation of his, as the territory of the king increased and along with that his activities. In tribal communities, where the dead ruler or other remarkable person had become the traditional god, so well established that propitiation of him became imperative, migrating portions of the tribe, carrying their cult with them, must have someone to perform the rites on their behalf. And always the probability is that a man related to the chief of the parent tribe may perform this function, generally being the eldest male member, and hence priestly caste becomes intelligible. Similarly, along with the worship of an apotheosized founder of the tribe, there may be worship of their respective ancestors or local people, who for one reason or another strike the popular imagination thus giving rise to a number of gods and their respective priests.

The spread of a particular religion from above, or the integration of local units may give rise to the hierarchy in priesthood. Thus there may be bishops, priests, deacons, sub-deacons, exorcists, etc., and an unrecognized hierarchy depending upon the god whom they serve.

Regarding the functions of the priest, besides their usual function of propitiating and serving the gods, they also performed some military and civil functions. Sometimes priests went with the army to pray for their people and curse the enemy. They were appointed as judges and advisers to the king. For example, in ancient Egypt, next to the king, the priests held the first rank and from them were chosen his confidential and responsible advisers. Among some Hindu kings, 'all is regulated by the opinion of the Brahmins, so that not even the king shall presume to take any step without their advice'.[32]

Concerning the influence of priesthood, he points out that the original duty of the priest was the carrying on of worship; the derived duty is the insistence on rules of conduct. Worship in the beginning is often characterized by atrocious observances. For example, in some societies priests urged the kings to wage war in order to procure captives to be sacrificed before the idols who were starving with hunger. In some Indian tribes (Domras) a successful theft is always celebrated by a sacrifice to their chief god Gandak. Similarly prostitution in temples was a religious observance among Hindus. The extreme attention to other religious rites also characterized many societies, so that the living were the slaves of the dead. Regarding the Aryans Mr Mitra observes,

> The Vedas represent the ancient Indo-Aryans to have been eminently religious in all their actions. According to them, every act of life had to be accompanied by one or more mantras, and no one could rise from his bed, or wash his face, or brush his teeth, or drink a glass of water, without going through a regular system of purifications, salutations and prayers.[33]

Speaking of the existing Hindu the Reverend Sherring says, 'He is a religious being of wonderful earnestness and persistency. His love of worship is a passion, is a frenzy, is a consuming fire. It absorbs his thoughts; it influences and sways his mind on every subject'.[34] In all societies we find the kindred connections.

However, he also observes that 'the evidence furnished by many peoples and times shows that the propitiatory element, which is the primary element, diminishes with the advance of civilization, and becomes qualified by the growing ethical element'.[35] The conduct of life, parts of which are already the subject-matter of sermons, may hereafter probably be taken in its entirety as the subject of sermons. Ideas of right and wrong, now regarded as applying only to actions of certain kinds, will be regarded as having applications co-extensive with actions of every kind.

Some of the observations made by Spencer regarding the priestly organization do not seem to concur with the facts available in Hindu literature. Spencer mentions that in the beginning the king was the main priest and this function was later on transferred to some of his kin. However, we find no such evidence in Hindu literature. On the other hand it is often stated that the priestly function was performed by a separate group from the very beginning. But his assertion that the hierarchy among the priests arose with the worship of different gods appears to be correct, as different castes were formed among brahmans on this basis. His observation that besides their usual function the priests also performed certain military and civil functions is probably correct. In India the Hindu kings were often guided by an advisory council of brahmans, and they also served as judges. His contention that the original duty of the priest was the carrying on of worship and insistence on rules of conduct was a derived one is also debatable. Along with the worship of the deity there was also some preaching about the observance of certain rules

41

of conduct. How far those rules were observed by the laity depended upon the social environment of the time. If the upper classes themselves did not follow those rules, not much could be expected from the lower classes.

Marriage and family structure

Spencer observes that although monogamy has been the rule in most of the societies, yet polygamy also exists in some societies both primitive and civilized. Among Nairs, a Hindu caste,

> it is the custom for one woman to have attached to her two males, or four, or perhaps more, and they cohabit according to rules.
> With this account that of Hamilton agrees, excepting that he states that a Nair woman could have no more than twelve husbands, and had to select these under certain restrictions as to rank and caste.[36]

In an ancient Hindu epic, the Mahabharata, a princess is described as married to five brothers.

Along with polyandry there goes polygyny in many societies. This is more common, because some rich people think it a matter of prestige to marry more women, or because of death of men in war, men are allowed to marry more than one woman. Among Hindus the chief reason for allowing polygamy was that a son must necessarily be born to the father to offer libations for the dead. If the legitimate wife was barren, or brought forth daughters only, the defect must be remedied by a second wife. How strongly the necessity for a son was felt in ancient times is shown by an indication of the Rig-Veda, where the childless widow summons her brother-in-law to her bed, and by the narrative in the Epos of the widows of the king who died without a son, for whom children are brought up by a relation, and these children pass for the issue of the dead king. Even the law shows that such a custom did exist and is not a poetic invention. It permits a son to be begotten by the brother of the husband, or the nearest kin after him; in any case by a man of the same race (gotra), even in the lifetime of the husband with his consent.[37]

Regarding the family structure, Spencer refutes the arguments advanced by Sir Henry Maine that the patriarchal system was the only one prevalent in all societies, where the authority in family affairs rested in the male head in respect of property and of authority over wife, children, slaves and all those included in the primitive social group. However, he agrees with him to the extent that in the highest societies, on passing from the wandering pastoral life to the settled agricultural life, the patriarchal type of family, with its established traits, persisted and gave its stamp to the social structures which gradually rose.[38]

According to Sir Henry Maine, 'In the joint undivided family of the Hindus, the stripes, or stocks, which are only known to European law as branches of inheritors, are actual divisions of the family and live together in distinct parts of the same dwelling'.[39] Mr J. C. Ghosh observes,

A Hindu joint family signifies (1) that the members all mess together; and (2) live in the same house; (3) that the male members and unmarried girls are descended from a common ancestor; and (4) that the male members put their income together.... The integral character of the family is destroyed when the joint mess and common purse cease to exist. However, the branches thus disunited continue to observe certain close relations as *gnatis* up to some seven or fourteen generations from the common ancestor. Beyond that limit they are said to be merely of the same Gotra.[40]

Further multiplication of families produces the village community, in which households and, in part, landed properties have become distinct. Along with the persistence of the patriarchal structure under new conditions goes the persistence of patriarchal principles. There is supremacy of the eldest male, sometimes continuing, as in Roman Law, to the extent of life and death power over wife and children.

With few exceptions men, having by gift of nature the mastery, universally use that mastery in every way, dictating to all members of the family group in respect of their occupations as in other respects. Along with the father's despotic regulation of them in all else, there goes despotic regulation of their labours. So, too, unlimited paternal power is insisted upon by the sacred books of the Hindus.

In the code of Manu it is written, 'Three persons—a wife, a son and a slave are declared by law to have in general no wealth exclusively their own; the wealth which they may earn is regularly acquired for the man to whom they belong'.[41] And according to Nelson this relationship still continues.

It is undoubted fact that among the so-called Hindus of the Madras province the Father is looked upon by all at the present day as the Rajah or absolute sovereign of the family.... He is entitled to reverence during life, as he is to worship after death. His word is law, to be obeyed without question or demur.[42]

This authority of the head passes at his death to his eldest male descendant (or, if he is not alive, then to his eldest son) making him the governor of the group. The authority of the head above and beyond filial obedience is fostered by two additional factors, viz. ancestor-worship and control over property. There is a belief in the ghost of the dead father who is propitiated by sacrifices and who is supposed to inflict evils if he is angered. The father has full control over property and the sons may not inherit that property if he is displeased. The parallel is also drawn between the domestic regime of the patriarchal family and the political regime. As Mommsen describes him, the early Roman ruler, once in office, stood towards the citizens in the same relation that the father of the family did to wife, children and slaves.[43]

Preference for the male child Regarding the difference in the status of children of the two sexes, Spencer points out that the urgent need to augment the number of warriors leads to a preference for male children, and everywhere we find either the destruction of daughters or their low estimation and ill-usage. The sacred duty of blood revenge, earliest of recognized obligations among men, survives so long as societies remain predominantly warlike; and it generates an anxiety to have a male representative who shall retaliate against those from whom injuries have been received. The development of ancestor-worship, requiring each man to make sacrifices to immediate and more remote male progenitors, initiates yet another motive for cherishing male children rather than females. And this practice was common among ancient Aryans whether Hindu, Greek or Roman, as daughters were incapable of performing such rites.

However, he also notes that the status of children, in common with that of women rises in proportion as the compulsory co-operation characterizing militant activities becomes qualified with the voluntary co-operation characterizing industrial activities.

He agrees with Sir Henry Maine that disintegration of the joint family proceeds with the development of industrial society. Though need for mutual protection causes cohesion of relations in clusters, there was at work from the beginning a cause of dissolution ready to show its effects as soon as surrounding conditions allowed. Always the diligent and skilful felt annoyance at being unable to profit by their superiority. They were vexed on seeing the idle taking an equal share of the benefits with themselves. As Sir Henry Maine on the South Slavonian house-communities says, 'The adventurous and energetic member of the brotherhood is always rebelling against its natural communism. He goes abroad and makes his fortune, and strenuously resists the demands of relatives to bring it into the common account'.[44] The reasons for the dissolution in other communities are similar, i.e. dissatisfaction with the leader, excursions of members in search of work and their eventual separation, and the desire to retain what they have earned. The same essential causes operate in the Hindu joint families. As Mr J. C. Ghosh points out, jealousies within the family and facilities offered by the British courts to secure separate enjoyment of communal property led to their disintegration. He says, 'Hence it has been that under the Dayabhaga law the communal relations generally break off in the third or second generation, counting from the founder of the family'.[45]

Spencer concludes by saying that though different types of domestic relations may prevail in different societies, in civilized nations the monogamic form of the sexual relation is manifestly the ultimate form, and any changes to be anticipated must be in the direction of its completion and extension. While an average increase of juvenile freedom may be anticipated we may suspect that in some cases (the USA, for example) the increase has already gone too far. They get too early the excitements proper to maturity which tend to exhaust the interests of life before it is half spent. The care of parents by offspring at present is not as great as might be desired. A basis for a stronger affection to be displayed by the child for the parent in later life could be established by a closer intimacy between parents and children in early life. This means that children should not be sent away from home for a long time as was done in ancient China and in other societies.

Most of the observations made by Spencer in connection with marriage and family structure among Hindus of that time are correct. However, a few remarks need to be added. As regards polyandry among Hindus, the instances quoted are correct, but they were the exception rather than the rule. It is true that polyandry was practised among a few castes like Nairs in South India, but monogamy was the general rule among the Hindus. The case given of a princess in Mahabharata who was married to five brothers was also an exception and was disapproved of by society in general.[46] Polygyny was also prevalent in some higher castes because of hypergamous marriages. However, with the passing of the Hindu Marriage Act 1955 both polyandry and polygyny have gone out of practice. Under the Act no spouse can enter another marriage during the lifetime of his or her spouse, except under certain circumstances, or before the dissolution of the first marriage.

Although the joint family system is still the rule in the villages among agricultural families, yet with the easy division of property under the new law and better employment opportunities outside the village the system is now disintegrating. The status of females has also changed as, under the Hindu Women's Right to Property Act 1937 and the Hindu Succession Act of 1956, wives and daughters have been given equal property rights with males.

The caste system and industrial progress

Spencer observes that during social evolution among the civilized the fact that there were, in the beginning, specializations of function caused by natural aptitudes needs no showing. Concerning the Hindus in ancient periods Mr Dutt observes, 'The Aryan Vaisyas followed different trades and professions in ancient India without forming separate castes; they were scribes and physicians, goldsmiths and blacksmiths, etc.',[47] all these occupations of the relatively skilled kind having fallen into the hands of the most intelligent. During the intermediate stages in which men's occupations were regulated by castes and guilds, individuals were restrained from following their natural bents. This was the practice in India too among the Hindus, and it was perhaps more rigorously followed, as indicated below.

Spencer defines a caste as a group of families produced by intermarriages under restrictions of the exogamy of the *gotras* and endogamy of the caste with the inheritance of occupation. The inheritance of occupation is very rigorously applied and it is universally recognized that every caste is bound to follow one particular occupation and no other.[48] The members come together to hold sacrificial and other feasts. The caste councils control the private conduct of members and excommunicate those who transgress its rules.

Although fixity of occupation through inheritance is good for the stability of society, says Spencer, it stands in the way of change and further advancement later on. The maintenance of class divisions which arise as political organization advances implies the inheritance of a rank and a place in each class. The same thing happens with those sub-divisions of classes which, in some societies, constitute castes and, in other societies, are exemplified by incorporated trades. Where custom or law compels the son of each worker to follow his father's occupation, there result in the industrial structure obstacles to change analogous to those which result in the regulative structures from impassable divisions of ranks. India shows this to an extreme degree; and to a lesser degree it was shown by the craft guilds of early days in England, which facilitated adoption of a craft by the children of those engaged in it, and hindered adoption of it by others. Thus, whereas succession by descent favours the maintenance of that which exists, succession by fitness favours transformation and makes possible something better. In other words social change is facile in proportion as men's places and functions are determinable by personal qualities.

Craft guilds Here it may be appropriate to refer to the craft guilds which were formed in towns among persons following the same occupation and were analogous to caste organization. Spencer points out that the guild in its primitive form arose out of a cluster of relatives following the same occupation. Perhaps the strongest bond which held its members together was the religious bond implied by periodical meetings for joint worship. Among Christian nations this points back to pre-Christian times when there doubtless existed among the peoples of northern Europe, as among those of southern Europe, and as still among the Hindus, occasions on which the eldest male of the family group made sacrifices to the spirits of ancestors.

Just like village communes mentioned below, they had their own regulations—a kind of local governing agency. As Mr J. C. Ghosh points out, in India 'a natural development of the Indian village communities' was the caste 'distinguished not only by the autonomy of each guild, but by the mutual relations between these autonomous guilds' and being so internally organized 'that caste government does not recognize the finding or verdict of any court other than what forms part of itself'.[49]

Most of the observations made by Spencer regarding the caste system and how it stifled further progress are quite correct. However, it should be mentioned that, with the expansion of education, there has been some change in the outlook of the people and they are taking up new occupations to suit the industrial needs.

Village communities and communal regulations

Spencer first traces the evolution of village communities and then discusses some of their characteristics. He observes that in early days social groups were held together by blood-ties. In those days relations were ready-made friends, as they are now; but non-relations were either actual or potential foes. Hence the result that the communal group was primarily an aggregate of kindred, and its cohesion all along was maintained for joint protection against those who did not belong to the kindred. Cohesion was great in proportion as external dangers were great, and diminished along with the diminution of external dangers. As simple family groups grow into compound family groups, so these, becoming too large for a single household, grow into clusters of households; house communities develop into village communities. There is evidence that in the fourth century B.C., such rillage communities existed in India. Nearchus, one of the Alexander's generals, is reported by Strabo as observing that,

Among other tribes the ground is cultivated by families and in common; when the produce is collected, each takes a load

sufficient for his subsistence during the year; the remainder is
burnt, in order to have a reason for renewing their labour,
and not remaining inactive.[50]

During two thousand and odd years, distorting changes have
produced various forms, but the essential nature of these social
groups remains traceable. Mr J. C. Ghosh tells us that in certain
parts of India, villages are 'extensive habitations, which are far too
big and too irregular, to be called single dwelling-house, and of
which the external appearance may not be very remote from that of
a walled village' to keep away the barbarians. The defensive
purpose of these united dwellings, as well as of the disunited
clusters derived from them which are found elsewhere, is implied
in a passage quoted by him from a 'Report on the Meerut
Settlement'.

> During the misrule and disorganisation of the former Govern-
> ments, it was necessary for the brotherhood to combine for the
> purpose of resisting the unlawful encroachments of their
> neighbours, and the attacks of predatory hordes; it was not the
> interest of a party to have his separate share divided off, which
> would be of no use to him so long as he could not protect
> it from violence.[51]

The introduction of outsiders has gradually complicated these
communities, but their family origin is sufficiently shown by Mr
Elphinstone. He observes, 'The popular notion is that the village
landholders are all descended from one or more individuals who
first settled the village. . . . The supposition is confirmed by the fact
that to this day there are only often single families of landholders
in small villages'.[52] Speaking of the existing structure Sir Henry
Maine observes,

> There are first, a certain number of families, who are traditionally
> said to be descended from the founder of the village. . . . Below
> these families, descended from the originators of the colony,
> there are others distributed into well ascertained groups. The
> brotherhood, in fact, forms a sort of hierarchy, the degrees of
> which are determined by the order in which the various sets of
> families are amalgamated with the community.[53]

At another place in the same book he observes that in certain
villages of central and southern India, there is an hereditary class
of 'outsiders' who are looked upon as 'essentially impure', and who,
though

> not included in the village . . . are an appendage solidly connected
> with it; they have definite village duties, one of which is the

settlement of boundaries.... They evidently represent a population of alien blood, whose lands have been occupied by the colonists or invaders forming the community.[54]

The village communities have a local self-government. As Mr Ghosh observed. 'The village life of our small communities comprises an agricultural and a governmental element' and that 'the village community have to decide all manners of questions; judicial, criminal, social, fiscal or any other which may arise'.[55] Regarding industrial regulation Sir Henry Maine observes,

> The Indian cultivating group includes a nearly complete establishment of occupations and trades for enabling them to continue their collective life without assistance from any person or body external to them.... They include several families of hereditary trades; the blacksmith, the harness maker, the shoemaker.... There is invariably a village accountant.... But the person practising any one of these hereditary employments is really a servant of the community as well as one of its component members. He is sometimes paid by an allowance in grain, more generally by the allotment to his family of a piece of cultivated land in hereditary possession.[56]

Spencer observes that these facts lead us to the conclusion that these developed family unions, maintained for mutual protection, show at once the original identity of political and industrial rule, the differentiation of occupations within the group, and the partial development of an individual ownership beyond that of personal belongings, which, in some of the Hindu tribes, readily passes into complete ownership by separation of shares.[57]

The observations made by Spencer in connection with the working of village communities are mostly correct. However, he does not go deeply into the existing property rights of villagers in arable land in different parts of the country. He makes no reference to new land tenure systems, i.e. zemindari, ryotwari or mahalwari, introduced by the East India Company to which Karl Marx refers in detail. Again, he mentions certain functions performed by local self-government in villages, such as taking decisions in judicial, criminal, social and fiscal matters. But he does not state how the working of these village governments (popularly known as village *panchayats*) had been affected by the British rule in India. Besides the functions mentioned above, another important function entrusted to these panchayats was the collection of land revenue from the cultivators. A part of this revenue was returned to them by the central government to perform certain civic functions.[58] The British government entrusted the function of revenue collection to the collector or zemindar, while judicial work was given to the new

49

civil and criminal court set up by the government. No part of the revenue collected was returned to the panchayats to perform the civic functions. All these steps resulted in the disintegration of village panchayats. It also needs to be stated that after Independence these village panchayats have again been revived and old functions entrusted to them.

Ancient Hindu law and its effects

Spencer observes that in rude societies men are guided by customs and these customs and usages are generally those left by their ancestors. However, the rule of the dead also means the rule of the deity. The seeking of information and advice from ghosts, takes here a supplicatory and there a coercive form. As among the Todas an appeal for supernatural guidance was sought in judicial matters. 'When any dispute arises respecting their wives or their buffaloes, it has to be decided by the priest, who affects to become possessed by the Bell-god and ... pronounces the deity's decision upon the point in dispute'.[59] Among the Hebrews, laws for general guidances were supposed to be divinely communicated. Similarly, in common with other Indian codes, the code of Manu 'according to Hindu mythology, is an emanation from the supreme God'.[60] Thus, in the beginning, little distinction is made between sacred and secular law, and the code of Manu was a kindred mixture of sacred and secular regulations of moral dictates and rules for carrying on ordinary affairs. Originating in this manner, law acquires stability. Possessing a supposed supernatural sanction, its rules have a rigidity enabling them to restrain men's actions in greater degree than could any rules having an origin recognized as natural.

While the unchangeableness of law, due to its supposed sacred origin, greatly conduces to social order during those early stages, there, of course, results an unadaptiveness which impedes progress when there arise new conditions to be met.

In societies which become large and complex, there arise forms of activities and intercourse not provided for in the sacred code, and in respect of these the ruler is free to make regulations. As such regulations accumulate, there comes into existence a body of laws of known human origin; and though this acquires an authority arising from reverence for the man who made it, yet it has not the sacredness of the god-descended body of laws.

The law of adoption and inheritance Besides laws in general, Spencer also mentions the adoption law and the law of inheritance among the Hindus. In his view the primitive and long-surviving belief in an after-life, repeating the first in its needs, prompted the practice of adoption which supplies the childless with heirs. As Professor Hunter points out, there was a great desire on the part of the ancients to have vacant inheritances filled up, in order that there might be someone to perform the sacred rites, which were specially called for at the time of death. It was thus with the eastern Aryans. Sir Henry Maine, speaking of the elaborate liturgy and ritual for ancestor-worship among the Hindus says, 'In the eyes of the ancient Hindu sacerdotal lawyer, the whole law of Inheritance is dependent on its accurate observance'.[61] Or as Professor Hunter remarks of these people, 'The earliest notions of succession to deceased persons are connected with duties rather than with rights, with sacrifices rather than with property'.[62]

The observation made by Spencer with regard to ancient Hindu law are correct, where sacred and secular law were combined. It was only during the British rule that rational law was gradually introduced in India which was equally applicable to all strata of society, except in certain spheres where personal law was applicable to Hindus and Muslims, such as the law of inheritance, marriage, adoption, etc.

Slavery in ancient India

Spencer observes that during recent times habit has generated the idea that slavery is an exceptional institution; whereas observation of all societies in all times shows that slavery is the rule and freedom the exception. However, owing to different treatment being meted out to slaves in different societies their status varied from society to society. The most extreme power of the master naturally existed where political restraints did not exist. The much higher status of the Greek slave was shown by the fact that he had a legal remedy for personal outrage.

Where a man's possession of himself is absent or greatly restricted, his possession of other things is likely to be either absent or greatly restricted. It was thus according to some authorities among the Hebrews; probably the custom varied. So it was in early India, where the slave's inability to hold property was definitely instituted. In other cases, the capacity for possession, beginning by usage, eventually became legal. Along with the gradually established ability to possess, there soon came the ability to purchase freedom. When slave-labour and free labour came into competition, slave-labour, other things being equal, decreased as being less economical. However, in certain cases slaves were set free by legislation or voluntarily as liberation was considered to be an act of pious sacrifice.

It seems to be true as asserted by Spencer that the lower castes, known as untouchables, were generally not allowed to hold landed property during the Hindu period; but they were not slaves in the sense that they could be sold or that they could not hold even movable property.

The development of sciences and philosophy in ancient India

Spencer deals in part VII of volume III with professional institutions. In professional organizations he traces the origin of various professions like that of physicians and surgeons, dancers, musicians, orators, poets, actors, historians, scientists, judges, lawyers, teachers, architects, etc. He makes reference to various Indian professions and how they evolved. He points out that once the sustenance protection and regulation of life have been achieved, men turned to its augmentation, which function is subserved by the professions. The medical man removes pains and cures diseases, wards off premature deaths and increases the amount of life. Similarly, other professions like music, dance, poetry and drama yield pleasurable feelings and so increase life.

(a) *The science of medicine and surgery* In the beginning diseases were supposed to be caused either by angry gods or indwelling demons who have either to be driven out by making the body an intolerable residence, or have to be expelled by superior spirits who are invoked. But there is often a simultaneous use of natural and supernatural means, and thus the doctors are said to have arisen as one division of the priestly class.

Concerning the origin of the medical man among the Hindus, whose history has been so complicated by successively superposed governments and religions, the evidence is confused. Accounts agree, however, in the assertion that medicine was of divine origin: evidently implying its descent through the priesthood. In the introduction to Charaka's work, medical knowledge is said to have indirectly descended from Brahma to Indra, while, 'Bharadvaja learnt it from Indra, and imparted it to six Rishis of whom Agnivasa was one'.[63]

Gradually the medical agency separates from the ecclesiastical agency and then separations occur within the medical agency itself. While both physician and surgeon had to cure bodily evils, the one was concerned with evils supposed to be supernaturally inflicted, and the other with evils that were naturally inflicted—the one with diseases ascribed to possessing demons, the other with injuries caused by human beings, by beasts and by inanimate bodies. Hence we find in the records of early civilization more or less decided distinctions between the two. As Mr Wise observes,

The Brahmin was the physician; but the important manual department of the profession could not be properly exercised by the pure Brahmin; and to meet this difficulty, at an early period, another caste was formed, from the off-spring of a brahmin with a daughter of a Vaishya.[64]

Along with this leading differentiation, there have gone on, within each division, minor differentiations. In ancient India, as Professor Hunter observes, 'A special branch of surgery was devoted to rhinoplasty, or operations for improving deformed ears and noses, and forming new ones'.[65] That the specialization thus illustrated was otherwise marked, is implied by the statement that 'no less than 127 surgical instruments were described in the works of the ancient surgeons';[66] and by the statement that in the Sanskrit period, 'The number of medical works and authors is extraordinarily large. The former are either systems embracing the whole domain of the science, or highly special investigations of single topics'.[67]

(b) *Science and philosophy* Spencer points out that among savages there is little knowledge to be named as rudimentary science except some knowledge of medicinal herbs, with perhaps a little information about minerals, often joined with such observations of weather-signs as enabled them to foresee coming changes. Only when there has arisen that settled life which yields facilities for investigation and for transmitting the knowledge gained, can we expect priests to display a character approaching the scientific. Hence we pass at once to early civilizations.

Evidence from the books of ancient India indicates that science was originally a part of religion. Both astronomy and medicine, says Weber, 'received their first impulse from the exigencies of religious worship'.[68] More specific is the statement of Dr Thibaut,

> The want of some norm by which to fix the right time for the sacrifices, gave the first impulse to astronomical observations; urged by this want, the priests remained watching night after night the advance of the moon ... and days after days the alternate progress of the sun towards the north and the south. ... The laws of phonetics were investigated, because the wrath of the gods followed the wrong pronunciation of a single letter of the sacrificial formulas; grammar and etymology had the task of securing the right understanding of the holy text.[69]

Further, according to Mr Dutt, geometry was developed in India from the rules for the construction of altars.[70] According to him there also arose a differentiation of the learned class from the ceremonial class as he observes, 'Astronomy had now come to be regarded as a distinct science, and astronomers by profession were called Nakshatra Darsa and Ganaka... sacrificial rites were regulated by the position of the moon in reference to these lunar asterisms'.[71]

So, too, we have proof that philosophy, originally forming a part of the indefinite body of knowledge possessed by the priesthood, eventually developed independently. As Hunter writes, 'The Brahmans, therefore, treated philosophy as a branch of religion.... Brahman philosophy exhausted the possible solutions... of most of the other great problems which have since perplexed the Greek and Roman ages, the medical schoolmen, and the modern man of science'.[72]

And in this, as in other cases, the speculative and critical activity soon led to rationalism. There came 'a time when philosophers and laymen were alike drifting towards agnostic and heterodox opinions'.[73]

(c) *Educational system*   Teaching implied knowledge of things to be taught; and, for various reasons, the priest came to be distinguished by his possession of knowledge. As ghosts and gods are believed to be everywhere and always influencing men's lives for good or evil, of chief importance is information concerning the ways in which conduct may be so regulated as to obtain their favours and avoid their vengeance. This knowledge is communicated by the elder to the younger priests. However, Spencer also mentions that sons of rulers were given education in many societies.

Concerning ancient India, Mr Dutt states that education consisted of learning the Vedas and that in the later, as in the earlier, periods it was under the control of the priests. He also observes, 'There were Parishads or Brahmanic settlements for the cultivation of learning... and young men went to these Parishads to acquire learning'.[74] To this there may be added the significant fact that in the Epic Period (*ca.* 1400 to 1000 B.C.),

> Besides these Parishads, individual teachers established what would be called private schools in Europe, and often collected round themselves students from various parts of the country.... Learned Brahmans who had retired to forests in their old age often collected such students round them, and much of the boldest speculation in the Epic Period has proceeded from these sylvan and retired seats of sanctity and learning.[75]

This shows that teaching, which in the beginning was exclusively concerned with religious doctrines and rites, eventually gave rise to teaching which in some measure was detached from the religious institutions and at the same entered upon other subjects than the religion.

(d) *Architecture, sculpture and painting* The earliest architecture bequeathed by ancient nations was the outcome of ancestor-worship. Its first phases were exhibited in either tombs or temples. As both were facilities for worship, now simple and now elaborate, both came under the control of the priesthood; and the inference to be drawn is that the first architects were priests. In ancient India, according to Mr Manning, architecture was treated as a sacred science by learned Hindus.[76] Hunter adds, 'Indian architecture, although also ranked as an *upa-veda* or supplementary part of inspired learning, derived its development from Buddhist rather than from the Brahmanical impulses'.[77]

The association between architecture, sculpture and painting is so close that the description of their origins, considered as distinct from one another, is not easy. Spencer does not mention sculpture and painting in India, though they both developed during the Brahmanic and Buddhist period and the paintings and sculptures of Anjanta and Ellora are very famous. However, he does mention these subjects among the Buddhists of Ceylon.

> The labours of the sculptor and painter were combined in producing these images of Buddha, which are always coloured in imitation of life, each tint of his complexion and hair being in religious conformity with divine authority, and the ceremony of painting of the eyes is always observed by the devout Buddhists as a solemn festival.[78]

Most of the account given by Spencer of the development of sciences and philosophy in ancient India is correct as he quotes quite reliable sources about these facts. However, it needs to be mentioned that he does not make reference to many other of the professions and arts of India such as poetry, drama and music, which also developed well during the ancient period, i.e. before A.D. 1000. Just as there were in Europe the dark ages, when the further development in various fields was checked, so were there the dark ages in India. As Mr Dutt rightly points out,

> Indeed, in many respects the tenth and eleventh centuries in India resembled the Middle Ages in Europe. A noble religion had become the monopoly of priests, and had been all but smothered with childish legends and image worship.... The people were kept in ignorance, fed with unwholesome superstition, beguiled with gorgeous and never-ending festivals. Everything bore the appearance of disintegration and decay; and national life seems extinct.[79]

The military system in medieval India

While tracing the origin of the military system, Spencer points out that in rude societies all adults are warriors and their primary military gathering is also the primary political gathering. Thus the assemblies which are summoned for the purposes of defence and offence, are the assemblies in which public questions at large are decided. In the normal course of social evolution, the military head grows into the political head. Later on, where political subordination is established, the army usually coincides with the body of freemen who are also the body of landowners. Captives are made slaves to do the manual work in the fields. This happened in Egypt, Greece, Rome and Germany. How natural this incidence of military obligation is. We find in ancient Japan and medieval India systems of military tenure like those of the middle ages in Europe.

A dissociation of military duty from landownership begins when land ceases to be the only source of wealth. The growth of a class of free workers, accumulating property by trade, is followed by the obligation to fight or to provide fighters being imposed on them. The widening civil functions of the political head, leads to the delegation of military functions to a separate head. The discharge of both offices becomes increasingly difficult as the nation enlarges so the political headship separates from the military headship. The above observations made by Spencer regarding the military system in medieval India apply only to a certain part of the country. Generally the peasants were the owners of land and the regular military men were paid out of the taxes collected by the kings.

Political organization and colonial rule

Spencer points out that political organization is essential for every nation to maintain law and order within its territory and to save it from foreign aggression. But it must not be oppressive, and should have a representative government of the local people and not of foreigners who have a different culture. The political control of any nation by foreigners is unnatural and unjustified. He stresses this aspect in *Principles of Sociology* as well as in *Social Statics* and points out that colonial rule by European nations of various colonies including India is oppressive and these latter should be allowed to have their own governments.

He first points out that political organization, as it extends itself throughout masses of increasing size, directly furthers welfare by removing that impediment to co-operation which the antagonisms of individuals and of tribes cause. It indirectly furthers it in another way. With the increase in population within the territory there is more specialization and complex division of labour leading to economical methods of production and also creating a greater demand for the commodities within the territory. However, this political organization is not without disadvantages if it becomes oppressive. In medieval France, while internal peace and its blessings were achieved when feudal nobles became subordinated to the king, yet, with extension of political organization, there grew up evils as great or greater—multiplication of taxes, forced loans, groundless confiscations and a universal corruption of justice consequent upon the sale of offices; the results were that many people died by famine, some committed suicide, while others, deserting their homes, led a wandering life.[80] The position in India in the nineteenth century was similar. He adds that

> notwithstanding the boasted beneficence of our rule in India, the extra burdens and restraints it involves, have the effect that the people find adjacent countries preferable: the ryots in some parts have been leaving their homes and settling in the territory of the Nizam and in Gwaliar where the local rulers reigned.[81]

He also stresses that for political integration certain conditions are essential. These include the homogeneity of nature among the population within a territory, which is ensured by greater or less kinship in blood, community of religion, i.e. a likeness of ideas and sentiments embodied in the worship of a common deity, community of tradition, ideas and sentiments, as well as a community of speech. In the absence of considerable likeness, the political aggregates formed are unstable and can be maintained only by a coercion which, some time or other, is sure to fail. So from this point of view the governing of India and other territories by the British was unjustified. He remarks, 'Our own Indian Empire too, held together by force in a state of artificial equilibrium, threatens some day to illustrate by its fall the incohesion arising from lack of congruity in components'.[82]

He earlier pointed out in his book *Social Statics* that not only was colonial rule unnatural but it was also unjustified on many grounds.

(a) *The burden on mother countries* A government cannot undertake to administer the affairs of the colony, and to support for it a judicial staff, a constabulary, a garrison, and so forth, without trespassing on the parent society. Any expenditure for these purposes, be it, like our own, some three and a half millions sterling a year, or but a few thousands, involves a breach of state duty. The taking away from men of property beyond what is needful for the better securing of their rights is an infringement of their rights. Colonial expenditure cannot be met without property being so taken. Colonial expenditure is therefore unjustifiable.[83]

(b) *No advantage in trade*   Though trade is a simple enough thing that will grow up wherever there is room for it, yet according to statesmen, it must be created by a gigantic and costly machinery. Only that trade is advantageous to a country which brings in return what is directly and indirectly given, a greater worth of commodities than could otherwise be obtained. But statesmen recognize no such limit to its benefits. Here is some scrubby little island, or wild territory—unhealthy or barren—which by right of discovery, conquest, or diplomatic manoeuvring, may be laid hands on. Possession is forthwith taken; a high-salaried governor is appointed; officials collect round him, then follow forts, garrisons, guardian-ships; from these by-and-by come quarrels with neighbouring peoples, incursions, war; and these again call for more defensive works, more force, more money. And to all protests against this reckless expenditure, the reply is, 'Consider how it extends our commerce'.

(c) *No proper safeguards of their welfare*   Not only is there no advantage in foreign trade, but the interests of the native people cannot be properly looked after by a foreign government. He observes that dotted on the earth here and there, there are forty-six communities, consisting of different races, placed in different circumstances. And the affairs of these numerous, far-removed communities—their commercial, social, political and religious interests—cannot be properly looked after by six functionaries and their twenty-three clerks sitting at desks in Downing Street. These transplanted societies could probably manage their affairs better than the British officials sitting in London can.

(d) *Evil effects of colonial rule*   On the other hand great evils have been afflicted upon the aborigines of the conquered countries. Whether we think of the extinct West Indian tribes, who were worked to death in mines; or of those nine thousand Chinese whom the Dutch massacred one morning in Batavia; or of the Arabs lately suffocated in the caves of Dahra by the French, we do but call to mind solitary samples of the treatment commonly received by subjugated races from so-called Christian nations. Even the English are not guiltless of such barbarities. Imagine how black must have been their deeds, when even the directors of the East India Company admitted that, 'The vast fortunes acquired in the inland trade have been obtained by a scene of the most tyrannical and oppressive conduct that was ever known in any age or country'. Conceive the atrocious state of society described by Vansittart, who tells us that the English compelled the natives to buy and sell at just what rates they pleased, on pain of flogging or confinement. Judge to what a pass things must have come when, in describing a journey, Warren Hastings says, 'Most of the petty towns and serais were deserted at our approach'. A cold-blooded treachery was the established policy of the authorities. Princes were betrayed into war with each other; and one of them having been helped to overcome his antagonist, was then himself dethroned for some alleged misdemeanour. Always some muddied stream was at hand as a pretext for official wolves.

There is the grievous salt monopoly, and the pitiless taxation that wrings from the poor ryots nearly half the produce of the soil. Undue exhortions by wealthy scamps in league with police authorities and other cruelties and treacheries to which reference has been made above are mainly due to the carrying on of colonization under state management, and with the help of state funds and state force.

No one can doubt that had the East India Company been denied military aid and state-conferred privileges, both its own affairs, and the affairs of Hindustan would have been in a far better condition than they are now. The energy that has been expended in aggressive wars would have been employed in developing the resources of the country. Unenervated by monopolies, trade would have been much more successful.

The natural rulers influenced by a superior race on friendly terms with them, would have facilitated improvements; and we should not have seen, as now, rivers unnavigated, roads not bridged or metalled, and the proved capabilities of the soil neglected. Private enterprise would long ago have opened up these sources of wealth, as in fact it is at length doing; in spite of the discouragements thrown in its way by conquest-loving authorities. And had the settlers thus turned their attention wholly to the development of commerce, and conducted themselves peacefully, as their defenceless state would have compelled them to do, England would have been better supplied with raw materials, the markets for her goods would have been enlarged, and something appreciable toward the civilization of the East would have been accomplished.

And Spencer points out that even later on the policy of repression and iniquities continued when India was directly governed by the Crown. He observes that people talk of communism at home. But how can there be established communism, unless there is basic change in human nature. He says, it is true that a state of universal brotherhood is very tempting while the existing one of competitive strife appears to be full of miseries. But such a system seems to be impracticable under the existing conditions. A community which can fulfil this ideal must be composed of men having sympathies so strong that those who, by their greater powers, achieve greater benefits, willingly surrender the excess to others.[84] But the real human nature exhibited around us shows the inability of the socialistic hopes. Observe what is done by these men who are expected to be so regardful of one another's interest. If, in our days, the name 'birds of prey and of passage', which Burke gave to the English in India at the time of Warren Hastings' trial when auditors wept at the accounts of the cruelties committed, is not applicable as it was then; yet the policy of unscrupulous aggrandizement continues. As was remarked by an Indian officer, Deputy Surgeon-General Paske, all our conquests and annexations are made from base and selfish motives alone. Major Raverty of the Bombay Army condemns 'the rage shown of late years for seizing what does not, and never did, belong to us, because the people happen to be weak and very poorly armed while we are strong and provided with the most excellent weapons'.

> So-called savages who according to numerous travellers behave
> well until they are ill-treated, are taught good conduct by the
> so-called civilized, who presently subjugate them—who inculcate
> rectitude and then illustrate it by taking their lands. The policy
> is simple and uniform—bible first, bomb-shells after. Such being
> the doings abroad, what are the feelings at home? Honours,
> titles, emoluments, are showered on the aggressors. 'British
> power', 'British pluck', 'British interests' are words on every
> tongue; but of justice there is no speech, no thought. Out of men
> who do these things and men who applaud them, is to be formed a
> society pervaded by the sentiment of brotherhood.[85]

Herbert Spencer was a great liberal who advocated freedom and the protection of civic rights, not only for the citizens of his own country, but also for the citizens of other countries. In his view a colonial rule did not bestow any advantage on the governing country in foreign trade. However, this was not wholly correct as colonies provided a good market for machine-made goods as well as for the supply of raw material.

But Spencer was quite correct in pointing out that the interests of the colonies could not be well looked after by a few officials of the governing country sitting in London. The account of the treacheries and cruelties committed by the East India Company narrated by Spencer is mostly correct. But it is difficult to say that had the East India Company been denied military aid the affairs of Hindustan would have been in a better state. The country had already disintegrated, the law and order situation was unsatisfactory, and how much progress a country could make under such conditions is difficult to guess. However, it cannot be denied that had the British administered the country in a better way, the position would have been much better. As mentioned by Spencer the high taxation extracted from the ryot did not allow him much with which to make further investment. Government did not pay much attention to the development of resources such as the provision of more irrigation facilities, the extension of communication, the improvement in agricultural methods, etc. as was done by independent Western states. Spencer's belief that natives were capable of developing the country's resources as private enterprise had done in Europe was also correct. Thus he did not believe in the racial superiority of European nations.

Indian society and social progress

Taking into consideration Spencer's views as a whole we may say that he was of the opinion that Indians (or Hindus) were capable of making progress as they had done in the past, provided they were made politically independent. He was a great critic of the British government for the selfish and repressive policy they followed in India. They maintained the salt monopoly, charged excessive land revenue from the poor cultivators, allowed extortions by scamps, put hindrances in the way of the development of local industries and made no efforts to develop resources. They annexed the territories of the princes without much reason. He observed that Indian people believed in various kinds of gods and goddesses, as was the case in some other societies, yet he did not see that such beliefs in any way stood in the way of social progress. On the other hand he correctly saw that the caste system with its rigidity of occupations was a great obstacle in the way of industrial development. He anticipated that, with the growth of industries and better employment opportunities in the cities, people would migrate to urban areas and there would be disintegration of the joint family system as had occurred in the West. He also observed that with the advancement of civilization monogamous marriage would be the rule and women and children would enjoy more freedom. To cope with new situations the sacred law would be replaced by rational law. Almost all his assertions have proved to be true, and India is now marching towards progress.

Views of Karl Marx and Herbert Spencer—a comparative analysis

Both Karl Marx and Herbert Spencer were great sociologists of the nineteenth century, who made a systematic study of modern society.

However, their views about this society were similar in certain respects but dissimilar in other respects.[86]

As regards Indian society both saw the Hindu religion as being full of superstition and the caste system as being a great hindrance to industrial progress. Both thought that Indians were capable of developing their society once they were given the opportunity to do so. Both were optimistic that India would achieve independence, though the circumstances which would lead to such a situation were given as different. While Spencer believed that the advanced nations should set free their colonies on moral grounds, Marx was of the view that the British would not leave India unless either a proletarian government was formed in England or the Indian people themselves had grown strong enough to throw off the English yoke. Here perhaps Marx was more correct than Spencer. Regarding the role of village communities in historic progress, Marx disdained the present communities which were self-contained and narrow in their outlook. He therefore wanted them to disintegrate before regeneration started. Spencer believed that such self-sufficient communities were natural in the beginning. With the progress of industries in cities and of easy communication people would automatically migrate to towns with better employment opportunities. Here Spencer was more correct than Marx. As regards property rights of villagers in arable land, Spencer was of the view that there would be joint ownership of property so long as the individual could not protect his land from external groups. But with the formation of political organizations, which could maintain law and order within the territory and protect it from foreign invasions, individual ownership in land would arise. However, Spencer did not go deeply into the question of how there came to exist joint ownership in arable land in some parts of the country along with individual rights in other parts, as did Marx. Nor does Spencer mention the various land tenure systems introduced by British government in India to which Marx refers in detail. However, both agreed that the land tax was oppressive and that there were undue extortions by the zemindars. As regards princely states, while Marx was of the view that owing to dual administration and the aristocratic living of princes they should be merged into British territory, Spencer felt that in some cases the princely states were better governed and that ryots when oppressed ran away to the princely states. Here, in our view, both were correct. The administration of about six hundred princely states varied from state to state depending upon the outlook of the local ruler. In the majority of these states the rulers were autocrats and there was no rational administration, while in some their rule was less oppressive and of a beneficial character.

We may conclude by saying that while Marx's study was more penetrating so far as modern India was concerned, Spencer's study of the ancient civilization, including that of the tribes, was deeper.

3   Max Weber (1864–1920) on general characteristics of Indian society

Weber's was a mind which continued to develop throughout his intellectually productive life.[1] With his background in law and economics he moved towards sociology.

> From the beginning of his academic career Weber addressed himself to two broad historical questions: The origin and nature of (1) capitalism in Antiquity, the Middle Ages and in modern times, (2) political domination and social stratification in the three ages. His dissertation of 1889 dealt with legal institutions of medieval capitalism, his Habilitation of 1891 (that is, the second doctorate required for academic teaching) with the relationship between Roman politics and capitalism.[2]

Unlike Marx who tried to demonstrate that modern capitalism developed only through material forces, his approach was eclectic. In the first meeting of the Sociological Association held in 1910, he remarked,

> I would like to protest the statement by one of the speakers that some one factor, be it technology or economy, can be the 'ultimate' or 'true' cause of another. If we look at the causal lines, we see them run, at one time, from technical to economic and political matters, at another from political to religious and economic ones, etc. There is no resting point. In my opinion, the view of historical materialism, frequently espoused, that the economic is in some sense the ultimate point in the chain of causes is completely finished as a scientific proposition.[3]

In this sense he was a great functionalist who, like Spencer and Durkheim, tried to point out the interdependence of various factors in explaining a particular social phenomenon.

Weber's three major works dealing with India

As Weber's approach was a comparative one, he studied the history of various civilizations to arrive at certain generalizations. To study the development of capitalism and the problems of domination in society, he studied those phenomena in earlier epochs and wrote a number of articles and books on the subjects, e.g. *Roman Agrarian History* (1895) and *Agrarian Conditions in Antiquity* (1909); yet we shall mainly be concerned with his later writings which are concerned with modern capitalism and domination. Among these, *Collected Essays in the Sociology of Religion* (three volumes), *Economy and Society* (three volumes) and *General Economic History* are of main concern to us. Before we deal with his views on Indian society it may be more appropriate to give a brief introduction to these works.

Economy and Society is his classic work.

> In his 1914 introduction to the series Weber spelled out the rationale of the project: The basic idea was to study economic development particularly as part of the general rationalization of life. In view of the systematic character of the work the addition of a general economic history has not been planned for the time being.[4]

The work is divided into two parts. Part I gives the conceptual exposition, while Part II, entitled 'The Economy and the Arena of Normative and *de facto* Powers', which was the original title of this work, emphasizes the functional importance of economic factors in social life even though, as already pointed out, Weber never believed in the economic determinism of social change as pointed out by Marx.[5] In the beginning of Part II Weber points out two facts:

(1) Most social groups in society engage in economic activities. However, the dividing line between groups with primary and secondary economic interests is fluid.[6] Strictly speaking, the first state of affairs prevails only in those groups that strive for profit by taking advantage of scarcity conditions. A special case of economically relevant groups consists of those whose norms regulate the economic behaviour of the participants but whose organs do not continuously direct economic activities through immediate participation, concrete instructions or injunctions. These are 'regulatory groups'. They include all kinds of political and many religious groups, and numerous others, among them those associated specifically for the sake of economic regulation (such as co-operatives of fishermen or peasants). Thus he deals with all types of groups which are economically relevant. Here he also stresses that one frequent economic determinant is the competition

65

for a livelihood—offices, clients and other remunerative opportunities. When the number of competitors increases in relation to the profit span, the participants become interested in curbing competition. Usually one group of competitors takes some externally identifiable characteristic of another group of (actual or potential) competitors—race, language, local or social origin, descent, residence, etc.—as a pretext for attempting their exclusion. Such group action may provoke a corresponding reaction on the part of those against whom it is directed. An interest group develops into a 'legally privileged group' and the participants have become 'privileged members'.

(2) He also deals with law (norms) as it is related to all social actions. Actually he begins Part II with chapter I as 'The Economy and Social Norms', where he says that,

> Law (in the sociological sense) guarantees by no means only economic interests but rather the most diverse interests ranging from the most elementary one of protection of personal security to such purely ideal goods as personal honor or the honor of the divine powers.[7]

Above all, it guarantees, political, ecclesiastical, familial, and other positions of authority which may be economically conditioned or economically relevant in the most diverse ways, but which are neither economic in themselves nor sought for preponderantly economic ends. Law, convention and custom belong to the same continuum with imperceptible transitions leading from one to the other.

However, here he also stresses that the means of coercion may be physical or psychological or they may be direct or indirect. He remarks,

> All we need to recall is that there exist non-violent means of coercion which may have the same or, under certain conditions, even greater effectiveness than the violent ones. Frequently, and in fairly large areas even regularly, the threat of such measures as the exclusion from an organization, or a boycott, or the prospect of magically conditioned advantages or disadvantages in this world, or of reward and punishment in the next, are under certain cultural conditions more effective in producing a certain behaviour than a political apparatus whose coercive functioning is not always predictable with certainty.[8]

Thus domination may be in rational, traditional or charismatic form. As Mr Roth rightly observes,

The Sociology of Domination is the core of *Economy and Society*. The major purpose of the work was the construction of a typology of associations, with most prominence given to the types of domination and their relation to want–satisfaction through appropriation. To be sure, religion and law were constituent parts of the work, irrespective of whether Weber planned the chapters to be as comprehensive as they finally came to be, but the 1914 outline and the proportions of the manuscript show the Sociology of Domination to be the central theme.[9]

Weber took it for granted that the economic structure of a group was one of its major, if variable, determinants and that the society was an arena for group conflicts. He did not believe, however, in the laws of class struggle, jungle or race; rather, he saw men struggle most of the time under created laws and within established organizations. 'Men act as they do because of belief in authority, enforcement by staffs, a calculus of self-interest, and a good dose of habit'.[10] With these assumptions in mind he deals with the general kinds of universal groups including household, neighbourhood, kin group, ethnic group, religious group, political community and the various kinds of rulerships.

In his book *General Economic History* he deals with aspects like household, neighbourhood, kin group, village, manor, etc., in historical continuity. The work is divided into four parts. Part I deals with household, clan, village and manor, Part II with industry and mining down to the beginning of the capitalistic development, Part III with commerce and exchange in the pre-capitalistic age and Part IV with the origin of modern capitalism.[11] Some of these topics he discusses in detail in his other works, i.e. *Economy and Society* and *Collected Essays in the Sociology of Religion*.

In his monumental work *Collected Essays in the Sociology of Religion,* in three volumes, he deals with the economic ethic of world religions. Besides he deals with the 'Sociology of Religion' in his major work *Economy and Society*. It may be mentioned here that Weber wrote this chapter on the 'Sociology of Religion' as part of his major work *Economy and Society* between the years 1910 and 1914. The rationale of this chapter as pointed out by Mr Roth, was to clarify his position on the controversy that had arisen after the publication of his two essays on the Protestant ethic in the *Archiv fur sozialwissenschaft* in 1904/5 and which has since continued unabated.

The exchange of critiques and anti-critiques between Weber and his adversaries lasted until 1910. Weber considered the exchanges 'pretty unrewarding' and decided on another positive statement, which became the present chapter. He left historical treatment of Protestantism to his friend Ernst Troeltsch, who was then working on 'The Social Teachings of the Christian Churches and Sects', and instead put the theme in a comparative perspective.... The last part (secs xii—xv) examines the influence of religious ethics on the 'world': the sphere of the economic, political, artistic, and sexual. The last extant section breaks off with yet another attempt to contrast Jewish rationalism, Puritan asceticism, Islamic this-worldliness, Buddhist other-worldliness and Jesus' indifference to the world—all with a look back toward 'The Protestant Ethic', but also in anticipation of the subsequent large-scale studies of the great world religions, to which Weber turned without completing Part Two of *Economy and Society*.[12]

In his introduction[13] to the three volumes (of which only the first had been prepared for the press by his own hand) he points out the rationale of these series.

The peculiar modern Western form of capitalism has been, at first sight, strongly influenced by the development of technical possibilities. Its rationality is today essentially dependent on the calculability of the most important technical factors. But this means fundamentally that it is dependent on the peculiarities of modern science, especially the natural sciences based on mathematics and exact and rational experiment. On the other hand, the development of these sciences and of the technique resting upon them now receives important stimulation from these capitalistic interests in its practical economic application. It is true that the origin of Western science cannot be attributed to such interests. But the technical utilization of scientific knowledge, so important for the living conditions of the mass of people, was certainly encouraged by economic considerations, which were extremely favourable to it in the Occident. But this encouragement was derived from the peculiarities of the social structure of the Occident. We must hence ask, from what parts of the structure was it derived since not all of them have been of equal importance.[14]

Among those of undoubted importance are the rational structures of law and of administration. But there was also required the rationalization of economic life.

For though the development of economic rationalism is partly dependent upon rational technique and law, it is at the same time determined by the ability and disposition of men to adopt certain types of practical rational conduct. When these types have been obstructed by spiritual obstacles, the development of rational economic conduct has also met serious inner resistance. The magical and religious forces and the ethical ideas of duty based upon them, have in the past always been among the most important formative influences on conduct. In the studies collected here we shall be concerned with these forces.[15]

In the first two essays of volume I, viz. 'The Protestant Ethic and the Spirit of Capitalism' (1904–5) and 'The Protestant Sects and the Spirit of Capitalism' (1906), as Professor Tawney points out, the question which Weber attempts to answer is simple and fundamental.

It is that of the psychological conditions which made possible the development of capitalist civilization. Capitalism, in the sense of great individual undertakings, involving the control of large financial resources, and yielding riches to their masters as a result of speculation, moneylending, commercial enterprise, buccaneering and war, is as old as history. Capitalism, as an economic system, resting on the organization of legally free wage-earners, for the purpose of pecuniary profit, by the owner of capital or his agents, and setting its stamp on every aspect of society, is a modern phenomenon. The moving spirits of modern capitalism are not possessed of a stronger economic impulse than, for example, an oriental trader. On the other hand it was the result of movements which had their source in the religious revolution of the sixteenth century. It was the change of moral standards which converted a natural frailty into an ornament of the spirit and canonized as the economic virtue habits which in earlier ages had been denounced as vices. The force which produced it was the creed associated with the name of Calvin. Capitalism was the social counterpart of Calvinist theology.[16]

Max Weber in the introduction adds,

Two older essays have been placed at the beginning, which attempt, at one important point, to approach the side of the problem which is generally most difficult to grasp; the influence of certain religious ideas on the development of an economic spirit, or the ethos of an economic system. In this case we are dealing with the connection of the spirit of modern economic life with the rational ethics of ascetic Protestantism. Thus we treat here only one side of the causal chain. The later studies on the Economic Ethics of the World Religious attempt, in the form of a survey of the relations of the most important religions to economic life and to the social stratification of their environment, to follow out both causal relationships, so far as it is necessary in order to find points of comparison with the Occidental development.[17]

In volume I along with these two essays and the introduction he includes 'The Religion of China' a study of Confucianism and Taoism. Volumes II and III which were published after his death, without the thorough revision which he had contemplated, deal with the religion of India and ancient Judaism respectively.[18]

Weber, in this introduction, also points out one great limitation of these studies: the fact that ethnographical material has not been utilized to anything like the extent which the value of its contributions naturally demands in any really thorough investigation, especially of Asiatic religions. This limitation was not imposed simply because human powers of work are restricted. It was because he was here necessarily dealing with religious ethics of the classes which were the culture-bearers of their respective countries. He was concerned with the influence which their conduct has had. Now it is quite true that this can only be completely known in all its details when the facts from ethnography and folklore have been compared with it. He hoped to contribute something to the closing of this gap in a systematic study of the 'Sociology of Religion'. This portion of his thought, as already stated, is included in his work *Economy and Society*.

With this background of his three major writings we may study his views on Indian society in the following pages. These views can be discussed under the following major heads:

1 General characteristics of Indian society
2 The Hindu social system
3 The main characteristics of Hinduism in early times
4 Jainism and Buddhism in India
5 Hinduism in the Middle Ages and after
6 General characteristics of Indian religion and other conclusions

The general characteristics of Indian society, as Weber observes, have been extracted mostly from his two works *Economy and Society* and *General Economic History*, though he also deals with some of these characteristics in his major work on Indian society, i.e. the *Religion of India*. His observations on other aspects, i.e. (2) to (5) above, have been mostly taken from his work *Collected Essays in the Sociology of Religion*, particularly volume II 'The Religion of India'. In this chapter we shall mainly be concerned with his views on the general characteristics of Indian society.

General characteristics of Indian society

In the general characteristics of Indian society, Weber expresses his views on aspects like marriage and family, kin groups, village communities, bureaucracy, etc. These views can be dealt under the following main heads:

1   The household and hypergamous marriages
2   Kin groups and property in land
3   Neighbourhood and village communities
4   Indian feudalism
5   The financing of political bodies
6   Bureaucracy in ancient and medieval India
7   The conflict between the priestly and the warrior castes
8   Prostitution in the temples
9   The organization of industries in villages
10 Craft work in urban areas on a caste basis
11 Trader castes and specialization in commerce
12 Difficulties in the growth of modern capitalism

The factors included in (12) were (a) the absence of rational law; (b) the lack of specific types of cities and citizenship; (c) caste exclusiveness and the absence of communes; (d) the lack of military and political strength in the bourgeois class; (e) and the absence of a rational spirit and rationalistic economic ethics.

(1) *The household and hypergamous marriages*

Weber observes that the relationships between father, mother and children, established by a stable sexual union, appear to us today as particularly 'natural' relationships. However, separated from the household as a unit of economic maintenance, the sexually based relationship between father and children is wholly unstable and tenuous.[19] Similarly today the house community of the family household is commonly a small family, that is, a community of parents and children. It is based on legitimate marriage, presumed to be permanent. However, the socialistic theory proceeds from the assumption of various evolutionary stages in the marriage institution, ranging from sexual promiscuity within the horde to group marriage and then legitimate monogamy connected with the origin of private property in an endeavour to secure legitimate heirs.

Endogamy within the house, or brother and sister marriage, is found as an aristocratic institution for maintaining the purity of the royal blood, as among the Ptolemies. Priority of the clan, under which the girl must be offered to members of her clan before marrying outside it, or their claim must be bought off, is explained by differentiation in wealth and is a defence against the dissipation of property. Levirate arises from the fact that the extinction of a male line was to be avoided on military and religious grounds.

Endogamy also takes the form of hypergamy, in the case where very intense class differentiation develops, as in the Indian caste system. While the man of a higher caste can enter into sex relations

71

or marry below his level at will, this is forbidden to women. As a result a woman of a lower caste may be sold for money while, on behalf of the girl of a higher caste, offers may be made to secure a man in exchange for money. The arrangements are made in childhood and the man may be married to a number of women and be supported by their parents, travelling from one household to another. In India, the English government put an end to this condition, enforcing the support of the women by the nominal husband. Wherever endogamy is found it is to be assumed that it is a phenomenon of retrogression, not a stage of progress.

Exogamy with regard to the household has obtained everywhere and always, with few exceptions. It arises from the effort to forestall the jealousy of the men within the household, and out of the recognition that growing up together does not permit a strong development of the sexual impulse.

In the case of domestic authority the belief in authority is based on personal relations that are perceived as natural. This belief is rooted in filial piety, in the close and permanent living together of all dependants of the household which results in an external and spiritual 'community of fate'. The woman is dependent because of the normal superiority of the physical and intellectual energies of the male, the child because of his objective helplessness, and the grown-up because of habituation. However, power and filial piety are not primarily based on an actual blood relationship, but on a master's power of disposition over property.

The above observations of Weber are mostly correct. The economic base of the family and household is well emphasized. Hypergamous marriages in India, the result of the caste system, led to the degradation of women and the dowry system. In spite of recent legislation by which men are prohibited to have more than one wife, the dowry system still prevails because of endogamy and hypergamy.

Disintegration of the household As regards the disintegration of the joint family system, Weber points out that, with the multiplication of life chances and opportunities, the individual becomes less and less content with being bound to the rigid and undifferentiated forms of life prescribed by the group. Increasingly he desires to shape his life as an individual and to enjoy the fruits of his own abilities and labour as he himself wishes. The function of the household has changed so radically that it is becoming increasingly inopportune for an individual to join a large communistic household. An individual no longer gets protection from the household and kinship groups but rather from political authority, which exercises compulsory jurisdiction. Furthermore, household and occupation become ecologically separated, and the household is no longer a unit of common production but of common consumption. Moreover, the individual receives his entire education increasingly from outside his home and by means which are supplied by various enterprises; school, book stores, theatres, concert halls, clubs, meetings, etc. He can no longer regard the household as the bearer of those cultural values in whose service he places himself.

So far as the joint family system in India is concerned, although some of these forces are working for the disintegration of the larger household, yet in peasant families, because of lesser opportunities for employment outside the village, this system still prevails.

(2) *Kin groups and property in land*

Weber observes that regarding property in land we can make only three generalizations. (a) Land may be primarily a place to work on. In this case all land and all yield belong to the women's kin group, as long as cultivation is primarily women's work. (However, in its pure form this case is rare.) (b) Conversely, land may be considered male property won and defended by force; unarmed persons, especially women, cannot have a share in it. Hence, the father's local political association may be interested in retaining his sons as military manpower; since the sons join the father's military group, they inherit the land from him, and only movable property from the mother. (c) The neighbourhood composed of a village or a 'rural commune', always controls the land gained through joint deforestation, that means, through men's work, and does not permit its inheritance by children who do not continuously fulfil their obligations towards the association. The clash of these practices, and possibly of even more complex ones, may have very diverse results.

When the members of a military caste were landowners living dispersed in the countryside, the patriarchal and agnatic structure of household and kin group usually became predominant. As far as our historical knowledge goes, the empire-building peoples of the Far East and India, the Near East, the Mediterranean and the European North developed patrilineal descent and exclusively agnatic attribution of kinship and property.

The major reason for this phenomenon is that great empires cannot be maintained in the long run by small monopolistic, staff-like groups of warriors who live closely together in the manner of 'men's houses'; in a natural economy, empire-building requires as a rule the patrimonial and seigneurial control of land, even if

73

this subjection proceeds from groups of closely settled warriors. This observation of Weber is mostly correct as the mahalwari (joint village ownership) system of land ownership in India, discussed by Weber at another place, is clear proof of this phenomenon.

(3) Neighbourhood and village communities

Weber observes that in a self-sufficient rural economy of early history the typical neighbourhood is the village, a group of households bordering upon each other. The household meets the everyday demands for goods and labour. In a self-sufficient agrarian economy a good deal of the extraordinary demands at special occasions, during national calamities and social emergencies, are met by social action that transcends the individual household: the assistance of the neighbourhood.

According to him the idea of a primitive agrarian communism at the beginning of all economic evolution was first suggested by investigations into the ancient German economic organization, especially by Hanssen and von Maurer.[20] These men originated the theory of the ancient German agrarian communism, which became the common property of scholarship. Analogies from other lands to the ancient German rural organization led finally to the theory of an agrarian communism as the uniform beginning of all economic development, the theory being developed especially by E. de Laveleye. Such analogies came from Russia and from Asia, especially India.

In India two different forms of village organization are met with. Common to the two is the common pasture and a garden area corresponding to the tract of arable on which in the German system wage labourers and cottagers lived. Here are settled craftsmen, temple priests, barbers, laundrymen and all kinds of labourers belonging to the village—the village 'establishment'. They hold on a 'demiurgic' basis; that is, they are not paid for their work in detail but stand at the service of the community in return for a share in the land or in the harvest.[21]

The villages differ in regard to land ownership. In the ryotwari village the land ownership is individual and the tax burden likewise. At the head of the village is a reeve. The peasants have no share in the common mark, which belongs to the king *(rajah)*. One who wishes to clear land must pay for the privilege.

Another type is represented by the village placed under a 'joint body', a community of a number of privileged nobles, a village aristocracy of full freeholders or hidemen without an individual head. These farmers ('Erbexen') grant out the land and to them belongs the common mark; thus they stand between the true cultivators and the rajah. Within this category two classes of villages may be further distinguished; one is the 'pattidari' village, where the land is definitely divided out and appropriated. On the death of the occupant his share goes to his descendants by blood and is redivided when it again passes by inheritance. The other is the 'bhayacharya' village. Here the land is distributed in accordance with the labour force, or the rank of the individual holders.

Finally, there are also villages in which an individual is in complete control as tax farmer and overlord. These are 'zemindari' villages, and the 'pattidari' villages also developed through the partition of feudal holdings. The special feature of Indian conditions is that a large number of rent collectors have intervened between the sovereign and the peasantry through the farming out and re-farming of the taxes.

He comes to the conclusion that all these examples do not prove the thesis of Laveleye, that at the beginning of the evolution agrarian communism existed in the sense of communistic husbandry and not merely that of joint ownership of the soil—two things which must be carefully distinguished. Husbandry was not originally common. In some primitive communities where hoe-culture predominates and the implement of tillage is a pointed stick, individual economy is found with no reason for assuming the previous existence of any other organization. The opposite extreme is the assembly of work in a large central dwelling, as in the long-house of the Iroquois. Here the women are herded together under the leadership of a head woman who apportions the work, and likewise the product, among the separate families. The man is warrior and hunter.

The two forms of village organization in India, as mentioned by Weber, were quite prevalent before the British came. The British government introduced the zemindari system under which a tax farmer was made the landowner of many villages. Later on many intermediaries came in between the zemindar and the actual tillers of the soil. This system could be abolished only after Independence in 1947, when the cultivator was made the owner of the land.

(4) Indian feudalism

Weber distinguished two types of feudalism, one based on fiefs *(Lehens feudalismus)* and the other based on benefices (prebendal feudalism), though he points out that these two types are connected by gradual, imperceptible transitions and that it is seldom possible to classify cases with complete definiteness under one category or the other. All other forms in which the use of land is granted in exchange for military service really has a patrimonial character and is therefore treated separately. The structure of domination in feudalism is different both from patrimonialism and from genuine or hereditary charisma. The fiefs are granted in return for specific services and are primarily of a military character, but they may also include administrative functions. Prebendal feudalism has a fiscal basis. This was typical of the Islamic Near East and of India under the Moguls. On the other hand, ancient Chinese feudalism before the time of Shi Huang-ti had, at least in part, a structure of fiefs, though benefices were also involved.

It is very common for the fief to originate in a system of want-satisfaction of the political group on the basis of a purely natural economy and in terms of personal obligations (personal services and military services). The principal motive is to replace the insufficiently trained popular levy, whose members can no longer equip themselves and are needed in the economy, with a well trained and equipped army of knights who are bound to their chief by personal honour.

Prebendal feudalism, on the other hand, usually originates in the reversion from monetary financing to financing in kind. The principal reason for such a policy may be the transfer of risk involved in fluctuating income to an entrepreneur, that is, a sort of tax farming. In addition to this, or alone, it may be established as a means of meeting the costs of administration and of securing tax payments for the royal treasury. In return for these services, in the first instance to enable those who undertook them to meet their obligations, an appropriation of governmental power in varying degrees and respect was permitted. Such appropriation has usually been for a limited period and subject to re-purchase. But when the means to do this have been lacking, it has often in fact been definitive. Those who hold such definitively appropriated powers then became, at the very least, landlords, as opposed to mere landowners, and often come into the possession of extensive political powers.

This process has been typical above all of India. It is the source of the powers over land of the zemindars, the jagirdars and the talukdars. It is also found in a large part of the Near East, as C. H. Becker has clearly shown—he was the first to understand the difference from the European fief.[22] He further adds that, though the manorial system has been abolished in many countries, in India it still persists.[23] English legislation protects the peasantry who formerly had no rights in the same way that Gladstone's laws protected the Irish in the possession of their holdings and against arbitrary increase in the traditional payments; but it has not in principle changed the established order. The observations made by

Weber are mostly correct. However, as stated before, this system has now been abolished.

(5) *The financing of political bodies*

In part I of *Economy and Society* Weber discusses the various types of political organization and how they finance themselves. He points out that an organization is one either when its social relationship is closed or the admission of outsiders is limited, and when its regulations are enforced by specific individuals, a chief and, possibly, an administrative staff, which normally also has representative powers. There is a most direct connection between the economic system and primarily non-economic organizations that lies in the way in which they secure the means of carrying on their corporate activity as such; that is, the activity of the administrative staff itself and that which is directed by it. The financing—that is, the provision of corporate activity with economically scarce means—may be organized in the following ways: (a) on an ad hoc basis (intermittent), which may be in the form of voluntary or compulsory contributions, or (b) on a permanent basis. In the former case the contributions may be (i) in the form of large gifts or endowments to charitable or scientific organizations which are primarily neither economic nor political; (ii) begging, which is typical of certain kinds of ascetic communities; (iii) gifts to persons recognized as politically or socially superior; these include gifts to chiefs, princes, patrons, feudal lords over land or persons and, because of the fact that they have become conventional, may in fact be closely approximated to compulsory payments; and (iv) compulsory contributions.[24]

(a) *Begging and robber castes* Begging (case (ii)), however, may be on a secular basis. In India we find secular castes of beggars and elsewhere, particularly in China, organized groups of beggars are formed. Begging may in these cases be extensively monopolized and systematized with territorial assignments. Also, because response is regarded as a duty or as meritorious, begging may lose its ad hoc character and in fact tend to become a tax-like source of income.

In the last case, i.e. compulsory contributions, financing is furnished by such organizations as the Camorra in southern Italy and the Mafia in Sicily. In India there have existed ritually separated castes of 'thieves' and 'robbers' and in China sects and secret societies with a similar method of economic provision.

(b) *Tax farming and military service in India* As stated above, financing may be organized on a permanent basis. The contributions may be in money or in kind and may be in the form of taxes, fees, customs, excise duties or sale taxes. The contributions may be collected by the organization itself, leased out (farmed), lent out or pledged. They may also be based on the existence of a productive establishment under the direct control of the organization. Or they may be organized 'liturgically' by means of burdens which are associated with privileges.

Examples of obligations to give personal services are obligations to military service, service in courts and on juries and all sorts of compulsory service for corporate purposes found in various types of organizations. Support by the granting of benefices is illustrated by the following cases: (i) in China, collectively to the body of successful examinees for official positions; (ii) in India, to the private guarantors of military services and tax payments; (iii) to unpaid *condottieri* and mercenary soldiers, as in the late Caliphate and under the regime of the Mamelukes; (iv) to creditors of the state, as in the sale of offices, common everywhere.

In China, India and Egypt, the countries with the earliest development of 'hydraulic' bureaucracy, liturgical organization was based on obligations to deliveries and services in kind. It is by no means out of the question that it might appear again in the modern world in this form if public provision by taxation should fall down and the satisfaction of private wants by capitalistic enterprise becomes subject to extensive regulation by the state.

The way in which political and hierocratic bodies provide for their corporate needs has very important repercussions on the structure of private economic activity. Historically, the most important case of obstruction of the development of market capitalism by turning public contributions into privately held benefices is China. The conferring of contributions as fiefs, which often cannot be differentiated from this, had the same effect in the Near East since the time of the Caliphs. Tax farming is found in India, in the Near East, and in the Western world in antiquity and in the Middle Ages. In India and the Near East it determined the development and distribution of wealth, notably of land ownership.

In India the jagirdar provided and equipped a military unit from the proceeds of his tax benefice. The use of land in return for military service is found throughout the orient since early antiquity. In India particularly it became an independent and highly developed practice. The usual arrangement was the granting of rights to these sources of income in return for the provision of military contingents and the payment of administrative costs.

The various systems of financing political bodies observed by Weber are really interesting. In India the begging and robber castes have existed since long. This has been noted by many Western scholars including Spencer. During the British period the government tried to restrict the movement of criminal tribes within certain areas by special legislation to control their anti-social activities. After Independence the government repealed the Criminal Tribes Act of 1871 in 1953 and allowed their free movement. Along with that, certain other measures have been taken for their rehabilitation. For example, efforts have been made to educate their children away from their families, to rehabilitate wandering families on new lands and provide them with other employment opportunities after the necessary training.[25] However, the programme of rehabilitation has not been very successful and it will take time to eradicate their anti-social activities completely. Similar measures are also being taken to rehabilitate beggar castes properly.

The jagirdari system of tax farming was prevalent during Muslim rule. The British government replaced the jagirdari system by the zemindari system which was ultimately abolished after Independence.

(6) *Bureaucracy in ancient and medieval India*

Weber observes that in the cultural evolution of Egypt, western Asia, India and China the question of irrigation was crucial. The water question conditioned the existence of the bureaucracy, the compulsory service of the dependent classes, and the dependence of the subject classes upon the functioning of the bureaucracy of the king. That the king also expressed his power in the form of a military monopoly is the basis of the distinction between the military organization of Asia and that of the West. In the first case the royal official and army officer is from the beginning the central figure of the process, while in the West both were originally absent. The forms of religious brotherhood and self-equipment for war made possible the origin and existence of the city in the Occident. It is true that the beginnings of an analogous development are found in the East. In India we meet with relations which verge upon the establishment of a city in the Western sense, namely, the combination of self-equipment and legal citizenship; one who could furnish an elephant for the army is, in the free city of Vaicali, a full citizen. In ancient Mesopotamia, too, the knights carried on war with each other and established cities with autonomous administration. But in the one case, as in the other, these beginnings later disappear as the great kingdom arises on the basis of water regulation.[26]

Bureaucracy might have existed in India in ancient and medieval times, but not to the same extent as in China. Local self-government in ancient India, as well as during medieval period, managed the water resources to a great extent, particularly in South India. Well irrigation in a rudimentary form was well developed in northern India. However, bureaucratic machinery for revenue collection in some parts of the country was well established. The bureaucracy established during British rule was quite different from the previous one.

(7) *Conflict between the priestly and the warrior castes*

Weber observes that everywhere state and society have been greatly influenced by the struggle between the military and the temple nobility, between the royal and the priestly following. This struggle did not always lead to open conflict, but it produced distinctive features and differences, whether we refer to the relationship between the priestly and warrior castes in India, the partly manifest and partly latent conflict between the military nobility and the priesthood in the oldest city-states of Mesopotamia, in Egypt and Palestine, or to the complete takeover of priestly positions by the secular nobility in the Hellenic *polis* and particularly in Rome. The clash of the two powers in medieval Europe and in Islam resulted in the greatest differences between the cultural development of the orient and the occident.

The extreme opposite of any kind of hierocracy, caesaropapism—the complete subordination of priestly to secular power—can nowhere be found in its pure type. Caesaropapist powers are wielded not only by the Chinese, Russian, Turkish and Persian rulers but also by the English and the German rulers, who are the heads of the churches in those countries; yet these powers are everywhere limited by autonomous ecclesiastic charisma. The Byzantine *basileus,* like the Pharaoh, Indian and Chinese monarchs and also the Protestant *summi episcopi,* attempted repeatedly, and mostly without success, to impose religious beliefs and norms of their own making. Such attempts were always extremely dangerous for them. In general, the subjugation of religious to royal authority was most successful when religious qualification still functioned as a magical charisma of its bearers and had not yet been rationalized into a bureaucratic apparatus with its own doctrinal system—two usually related phenomena. Subjugation was feasible, especially when ethics or salvation were not yet dominant in religious thought or had been abandoned again. But, wherever they prevail, hierocracy is often invincible, and secular authority must compromise with it.

As a rule, priestly charisma compromised with the secular power, most of the time tacitly but sometimes also through a concordat.

Thus the spheres of control were mutually guaranteed, and each power was permitted to exert certain influences in the other's realm in order to minimize collisions of interest.

(8) *Prostitution in the temples*

Weber points out that prostitution is not a product of monogamy and private property, but is of immemorial age.[27] There is no historical period and no stage of evolution in which it is not to be found. Prostitution, however, not only appears in the form of an unregulated sexual submission but is also met within the sacramentally regulated form of ritualistic prostitution, as for example, the hieroduli in India and the ancient East. There were female slaves who had to function in the temple in connection with the religious services, of which a part consists in sex orgies. The hieroduli are also found submitting themselves to the public for pay. The institution of the hieroduli goes back to sacerdotal sources, to animistic magic of a sexual character which has a way of running into sexual promiscuity in view of the progressive self-excitement of an ecstatic situation.

Copulation as a form of magic for stimulating fertility is widespread among agricultural people. The sexual orgy was even carried out on the ground itself with the expectation of increasing its productivity. Out of participation in this sacramental process arose in India the calling of the bayaderes which play an important role in the cultural life of India as free hetaerae, similar to the Greek women so designated. But in spite of the favourable conditions of their lives they ranked as outcasts and, as is shown by the Indian bayadere dramas, regarded it as the highest peak of good fortune to be elevated through a miracle to the class of married woman living under very degraded conditions.

Besides the hieroduli there are found in Babylon and Jerusalem the temple prostitutes proper, whose principal clients were the travelling merchants.

The struggle against this practice was carried by the prophets and priests of the great religions of salvation, Zoroaster, the brahmans, and the prophets of the Old Testament, partly on ethically and rational grounds; it was the battle of those who wished to deepen the inner life of man and saw in his subjection to eroticism the greatest obstacle to the triumph of the religious motive. Nevertheless, prostitution as such survived the discontinuance of the orgy.

Temple prostitution existed in India even during the British period. It was only after 1933 that certain steps were taken to

81

abolish this system through legislation, e.g. The Bombay Devadasi Protection Act (1934) and Madras Devadasi (Prevention of Dedication) Act (1947). Under these acts any ceremony or act intended to dedicate a woman as a *devadasi* was made an illegal act, because previously such devadasis had later on been exposed to prostitution as they could not marry.[28]

(9) *The organization of industries in villages*

Weber observes that from the economic standpoint industry—in the sense of transformation of raw material—developed universally in the form of work to provide for the requirements of a house community. In this connection it is an auxiliary occupation; it begins to be interesting when production is carried beyond household needs. This work may be carried on for an outside household, especially a seigneurial household by the lord's dependants; the needs of one household are covered by the products of other (peasant) households. Auxiliary industrial work may also be performed for a village, as in the case of India. Here the hand workers are small farmers unable to live from the product of their allotments. They are attached to the village, subject to the disposal of anyone who needs industrial service. They are essentially village serfs, receiving a share in the products or money products. This he calls 'demiurgical' labour. 'Here we find local specialization for self-sufficient production, with which an hereditary proprietorship of work places is regularly associated'.

The above observations of Weber are mostly correct, as in villages those who have very small farms or have no land may work as village artisans or as agricultural labourers.

(10) *Craft work in urban areas on a caste basis*

Weber remarks that the second mode of transforming raw materials, for other than the needs of a household, is production for sale—that is, craft work. By craft work we understand the case in which skilled labour is carried on to any extent in a specialized form, either through differentiation of occupations or technical specialization, whether by free or unfree workers, and whether for a lord, for a community, or on the worker's own account.

As stated above, the starting point of the development is house industry, producing for the requirements of a small or large household to supplement income. From this point the development may lead to tribal industry, which may arise in consequence of the possession by a tribe of a monopoly. This possibility leads to the establishment of castes as in India.[29] Through the combination of individual tribal groups under an overlordship, tribal industries which originally lay side by side horizontally have here become arranged vertically in a stratification, and the ethnic division of labour is now found among persons subjected to a common master. The original relationship of the tribes as mutually foreign is expressed in a system of castes whose members do not eat together or intermarry and receive only specified services at each other's hands. The caste system has had tremendous consequences for the whole social organization of India, because it is anchored in ritualistic and hence religious institutions. It has stereotyped all craft work and thus made impossible the utilization of inventions or the introduction of any industry based on capital. The introduction of any technical improvement whatever at any time would have presupposed the founding of a new caste below all the old series previously existing. When the Communist Manifesto says of the proletarian that he has a world to win and nothing to lose but his chain, the expression would apply to the Indian except that he can only get free of his chain in the after world, through the fulfilment to the last detail of his caste obligations in this.

Every Indian caste had its production process traditionally fixed; one who abandoned the traditional process lost caste and was not only expelled and made a pariah but also lost his chance in the future world, the prospect of reincarnation in a higher caste. Hence the system became the most conservative of possible social orders. Under English influence it has gradually broken down, and even here capitalism is slowly making its way.

Weber then explains the guild organization of India. He observes that a guild is an organization of craft workers specialized in accordance with the type of occupation. It functions through undertaking two things, namely internal regulation of work and monopolization against outsiders. It achieves its objective if everyone joins the guild who practises the craft in the location in question.

Guilds in the sense of unfree organizations were found in late antiquity and in Egypt, India and China. These were organizations for taking care of compulsory contributions to the state. They arose in connection with the fact that the function of supplying the political needs of a prince or of a community was laid upon the various industrial groups and to this end production was organized on occupational lines. It has been assumed that the castes of India also arose out of such guilds, but in reality they grew out of relations between ethnic groups. Already existing castes were utilized by the state, which carried out its financing in kind by requiring that the industry supply products for its needs.

In India the castes stood in the way of the complete

subjugation of the craftsman by the merchant. Down to recent times the merchant was unable to obtain possession of the means of production to the extent found elsewhere, because these were hereditary in the caste. Another reason for retarded development in these countries as compared with Europe is found in the presence of unfree workers and the magical traditionalism of China and India.

At another place he remarks that India once possessed a highly developed industrial technique, but here the caste stood in the way of development of the occidental workshop, the castes being 'impure' to one another. It is true that the caste ritual of India did not go to the extent of forbidding members of different castes to work together in the same shop; there was a saying 'the workshop is pure'. However, if the workshop system could not here develop into the factory, the exclusiveness of the caste is certainly in part responsible. Such a workshop must have appeared extraordinarily anomalous. Down into the nineteenth century, all attempts to introduce factory organization even in the jute industry, encountered great difficulties. Even after the rigour of caste law had decayed, the lack of labour discipline in the people stood in the way. Every caste had a different ritual and different rest pauses, and demanded different holidays.[30]

Most of the observations made by Weber are correct. The craft industries were generally organized on a caste basis and there was little intercourse among different craft workers on account of ritualistic defilement. The factory system was hindered by the exclusiveness of caste. Even at present the caste system stands in the way of rapid industrial development because of the resentment of certain castes towards manual work.

(11) *Trader castes and specialization in commerce*

Weber observes that in the beginning trade usually developed as an auxiliary occupation of peasants and persons engaged in house industry, and in general as a seasonal occupation. Out of this stage grew peddling and huckstering as independent occupations; tribal communities developed which soon engaged in commerce exclusively. In India trade is a monopoly in the hands of certain castes, especially the baniya caste, with ritualistic exclusion of others. Alongside this trade, conducted on ethnically restricted lines, is also found trade ritualistically restricted to sects, the magical-ritualistic limitations of the members of the sect excluding it from all other occupations. This is the case with the Indian sect of the dschaina. The dschaina is forbidden to kill any living thing, especially a weak animal. Consequently, he cannot become a soldier, or pursue a multitude of occupations—for example, those in which fire is utilized, because insects might be destroyed; he cannot make a journey in the rain because he might trample upon earthworms, etc. Thus no occupation is open to the dschaina except trade at a fixed location, and the honourable character of the occupation is as well established as that of the baniya caste.

In India we also meet with the differentiation of forms of trade according to various confessional sects. The dschaina sect is restricted by ritualistic considerations to trading at fixed points, the wholesale and distant trade based on credit is a monopoly in the hands of the Parsees, who are not restricted by ritualistic considerations and are distinguished by responsibility and truthfulness. Finally, the baniya caste carries on retail trade and is to be found in every connection where gain which is off-colour from an ethical standpoint is to be made. Thus its members engage in tax farming, official moneylending, etc.

The banking business which primarily consisted of exchanging money, wherever a plurality of kinds of money were in circulation, and money-disbursing business, especially that of making payments at a distance, is in its entirety strictly regulated by sects and castes. The functions of the banks in India are still limited to the business of making payments and small or occasional credit operations and they cannot make use of discount policy as in the West through bills of exchange.

Weber further observes that rational commerce is the field in which quantitative reckoning first appeared, to become dominant finally over the whole extent of economic life. The technical means of computation were crude, down almost to the beginning of the modern period. The system of characters, with values depending on their position, was an invention of the Hindus, from whom the Arabs took it over. It was perhaps brought to Europe by the Jews. But not until the time of the crusades was it really known generally enough to serve as a method of computation; yet without this system, rational planning was impossible.

Book-keeping grew up on the basis of the trading company. It is true that in this case the transactions concerned were not extensive and complicated like those of today, but were of a simple sort. It is characteristic that we hear nothing more of book-keeping either from Babylonia or Indian trading houses, although at least in India the position numerals were known. The reason apparently is that there, as in general in the orient and in China, the trading association remained a closed family affair and accountability was therefore unnecessary. The trading association extending beyond the members of a family first became general in the West.

The above observations of Weber that many trader castes

specialized in a particular branch of trade in the past are correct. However, with the expansion of industries the scope of commerce has widened. On the other hand with the expansion of modern education, with Western influence and with less vigour of caste organization, many trader castes have taken to new occupations. Some of them have established modern industrial enterprises. And Weber himself admits this at another place as stated in chapter 4.

(12) *Difficulties in the growth of modern capitalism*

Weber first defines modern capitalism, the factors involved in it and then enumerates difficulties which India has had to face in the development of modern capitalism. He observes that capitalism is present wherever the industrial provision for the needs of a human group is carried out by the method of *enterprise,* irrespective of what need is involved.

> More specifically, a rational capitalistic establishment is one with capital accounting, that is, an establishment which determines its income yielding power by calculation according to the methods of modern book-keeping and the striking of a balance. The device of the balance was first insisted upon by the Dutch theorist Simon Stevin in the year 1698.[31]

While capitalism of various forms is met with in all periods of history, the provision of everyday wants by capitalistic methods is characteristic of the occident alone and even there has been the inevitable method only since the middle of the nineteenth century. The factors involved in the development of modern capitalism are many, some of which are more important, some less important, while some are not important at all. Among the more important factors he mentions rational permanent enterprise, rational accounting, rational technology, rational law, and rational spirit.[32] Under rational spirit he includes the rationalization of the conduct of life and rational economic ethics. Among the less important factors he includes freedom of the market, free labour, commercialization of economic life, speculation, mass demand of goods, professional administration, specialized officialdom, better transport facilities, use of power and a specific concept of citizenship. The least important factor is colonialism, which has been very much emphasized by Sombart and other social scientists.

Let us explain some of these factors in brief before we discuss the factors which hinder the growth of modern capitalism in India. Weber observes that the most general presupposition for all large industrial undertakings which are concerned with provision for everyday wants is that of rational capital accounting. Such accounting involves the appropriation of all physical means of production—land, apparatus, machinery, tools, etc.—as disposal property of autonomous private industrial enterprises. Capitalistic enterprise is encouraged by freedom of the market, which means the absence of irrational limitations on trading in the market. It also means no special class consumption. Capitalistic accounting presupposes rational technology, that is, one reduced to calculation to the largest possible degree, which implies mechanization. This applies to both production and commerce, the outlays for preparing as well as moving goods. This is calculable or rational law. For a capitalistic form of organization to operate rationally, it must be able to depend upon calculable adjudication and administration. It is based on free labour. Persons must be present who are not only legally in the position, but are also economically compelled, to sell their labour on the market without restriction. Under this system the costs of products can be clearly determined by agreement in advance. There is commercialization of economic life. It means that there is the general use of commercial instruments to represent share rights in enterprise, and also in property ownership. There is allowed speculation. Speculation is an auxiliary to commercialization. It reaches its full significance only from the moment when property takes on the form of negotiable paper.

He further observes that the distinguishing characteristic of the modern factory is not the implements of work applied, but the concentration of ownership of workplace, means of work, source of power and raw material in one and the same hand. This combination was only exceptionally met with before the eighteenth century. Then he mentions that decisive factors in the modern enterprise are the mechanization and rationalization of work, which was possible because of the use of power and certain technical improvements (use of coal and iron through inventions, e.g. the steam engine and other iron machines), the expansion of transport, the recruitment of free labour and mass market demand. Here he refutes Sombart's argument that the standardized mass provision for war is among the decisive conditions affecting the development of modern capitalism. Nor does he share the argument that the demand of the court and the nobility for luxuries was responsible for modern capitalism. Though the demand from these two sources, namely war and luxury, were significant yet this did not lead to the modern factory system. For example, court luxury existed in China and India, on a scale unknown in Europe, and yet no significant stimulus to capitalism or capitalistic industry proceeded from the fact. The reason is that the provision for this demand was arranged liturgically through compulsory contributions. This system maintained itself so tenaciously that down to our own time the peasants in the region of Peking have been obliged to furnish to the imperial court the same objects as 3000 years ago, although they did not know how to produce them and were compelled to buy them from producers. In India and China the army requirements were also met by forced labour and contributions in kind. In Europe itself the liturgical contributions of the East are not unknown, although they appear in a different form. The decisive impetus toward capitalism could come only from one source, namely a mass market demand, which again could arise only in a small proportion of the luxury industries through the democratization of the demand, especially along the line of production of substitutes for luxury goods of the upper classes. This phenomenon is characterized by price competition; the luxury industries working for the court follow the handicraft principle of competition in quality.

Thus seeking of profit through cheapening production and lowering the prices was a great stimulus to capitalist enterprise. The tendency toward rationalizing technology and economic relations with a view to reducing prices in relation to costs, resulted in a feverish pursuit of invention. However, a positive innovation in connection with invention is the first rational patent law, the English law of 1623, which limits the protection of the invention to 14 years.

Weber does not share the view of many other social scientists that colonialism helped in the development of capitalism in Western countries on the one hand, and arrested the development of non-European colonies on the other. He observes that it is true that the acquisition of colonies by the European states led to a gigantic acquisition of wealth in Europe for all of them. The means of this accumulation was the monopolizing of colonial products, and also of the markets of the colonies, that is the right to take goods into them, and finally, the profits of transportation between motherland and colony; the last were ensured especially by the English Navigation Act of 1651. This accumulation was secured by force, without exception, by all countries. However, this accumulation of wealth brought about through colonial trade had little significance for the development of modern capitalism—a fact which must be emphasized in opposition to Werner Sombart. It is true that the colonial trade made possible the accumulation of wealth to an enormous extent, but this did not further the specifically occidental form of the organization of labour, since colonial trade itself rested on the principle of exploitation and not that of securing an income through market operations. Furthermore, in Bengal, as we know, the English garrison cost five times as much as the money value of all the goods carried thither. It follows that the markets for domestic industry furnished by the colonies under the conditions of the time were relatively unimportant, and the main profit was derived from the transport business.

In the end he again mentions the distinguishing characteristics of Western capitalism as the rationalization of labour, lifting of the barrier between external and internal economy, and external and internal ethics. It was also made possible by the concept of 'state' in the modern sense with a professional administration, specialized officialdom, and law based on the concept of citizenship. Only the Occident knows rational law, made by jurists and rationally interpreted and applied; and only in the Occident is found the concept of citizen, because only in the Occident again are there cities in the specific sense.

Among the specific factors which hinder the development of modern capitalism in India, Weber mentions many, some of which are very important. Among these he includes the absence of rational law, the absence of cities in a specific sense and citizenship, the exclusiveness of the caste system and the absence of communes, the lack of military and political strength among the bourgeoisie and the lack of rational spirit. Let us discuss these one by one.

(a) *The absence of rational law*   Weber observes that the state in the sense of the rational state has existed only in the Western world. Under the old regime in China a thin stratum of so-called officials, the mandarins, existed above the unbroken power of the clans and commercial and industrial guilds. But such an official performs no administrative work himself; administration lies rather in the hands of the chancery officials. As he does not understand the dialect of his province he cannot communicate with the public. A state with such officials is something different from the occidental state. In reality everything is based on the magical theory. The empire is an agrarian state; hence the power of the peasant clans who represent nine-tenths of the economic life—the other one-tenth belonging to commercial and trading guild organizations—is entirely unbroken. The officials do not rule but only interfere in the event of disturbances or untoward happenings. Very different is the rational state in which alone modern capitalism can flourish. Its basis is an expert officialdom and rational law. The rational law of the modern occidental state, on the basis of which the trained official renders his decisions, arose on its formal side, though not as to its content, out of Roman Law. The systematic legal doctrine was developed in the universities. The essential feature in the development, however, was the rationalization of procedure, free from spiritual and magical beliefs. The rational law was to be such that it could be counted upon, like a machine, and the creation of such a body of law was achieved through the alliance between the modern state and the jurists for the purpose of making good its claims to power. India had writers but no trained jurists.

The Vedas are the sacred books of Hinduism. They contain little 'law', even less than the Quran or the Torah. The Vedas are considered as *shruti* ('revelations'), while all derived sacred sources were viewed as *smriti* ('recollection' or 'tradition'). The most important categories of secondary literature, the prose Dharma-Sutras and the versified Dharma-Shastras (the last ranking entirely as *smriti,* while the former occupy a middle position), are, on the contrary, compendia of dogmatics, ethics, and legal teaching standing alongside the tradition of the exemplary lives and teaching of holy men.

The Dharma books, and specially one of the latest, viz. that of Manu, were important for a long time in the courts, as 'books of authority', i.e. private works of legal scholars, until they were displaced in legal practice by the systematic compilations and commentaries of the schools. This displacement was so complete that by the time of the British conquest legal practice was dominated by one such tertiary source, the *Mitakshara,* dating from the eleventh century.

Hindu legal erudition was to a great extent purely scholastic, theoretical and systematizing; it was the work of philosophers and theorists and strikingly possessed those features of a sacrally bound, theoretical, and systematizing legal thinking which has little contact with legal practice. In all these respect it differs from canon law. The treatises always present an abundance of casuistry about completely obsolete institutions. Examples are provided by Manu's treatment of the four castes. However, since the law is to serve holy ends, these law books are therefore compendia not of law but also of rituals, ethics and, occasionally, of social convention and etiquette. The consequence is a casuistic treatment of the legal data that lacks definiteness and concreteness thus remaining juridically informal and but moderately rational in its systematization.[33]

In India a dominant priesthood was able to regulate the whole range of life ritualistically and thus to a considerable extent to control the entire legal system.[34] According to prevailing Hindu theory, all law is contained in the Dharma Sutras. The purely secular development of law was confined to the establishment of particular systems of law for the various vocational groups of merchants, artisans and so forth. No one doubted the right of the vocational groups and castes to establish their own law, so that the prevailing state of affairs could be summarized in the maxim: 'Special law prevails over general law'. Almost all of the actually obtaining secular law came from these sources. This type of law, which covered almost the entire field of matters of daily life, was, however, disregarded in priestly doctrine and in the philosophical schools. Since no one thus specialized in its study and administration, it not only escaped rationalization, but also lacked a reliable guarantee of validity in cases of divergence from the sacred law. The latter was in theory absolutely binding, even though it was widely disregarded in practice.

Law finding represented that same characteristic intermixture of magical and rational elements. The courts were not of the type of popular justice. The rules that the king is bound by the decision of the chief justice and that the lay members (viz. merchants, scribes and guild masters) must be among the members of the courts are both expressive of rational tendencies.[35] Appeals from the organized tribunals of the consociations to the public courts were permitted as a general rule. The law of evidence is today primarily rational in character; resort is primarily had to instruments in writing and to the testimony of witnesses. Ordeals were reserved for cases in which the results of the rational means of evidence were not sufficiently clear. In those situations, however, they preserved their unbroken magical significance. This was especially true of the oath, which was to be followed by a period of waiting to determine the consequences of the self-curse. Similarly the magical means of execution, especially the creditor's starving himself to death before the door of the debtor, existed along with the official enforcement of judgment and legalized self-help. A practically complete parallelism of sacred and secular law existed in criminal procedure. But there was also a tendency towards the fusion of both these types of law, and on the whole sacred and secular law constituted an undifferentiated body, which obscured the remnants of the ancient Aryan law. This body of law was, in turn, largely superseded by the autonomous administration of justice of the consociations, especially the castes, which possessed the most effective of all means of compulsion, viz. expulsion.

The impediment to legal unification and consistency always existed as a natural consequence wherever the validity of sacred law or immutable tradition has been taken seriously, in China and India just as in the territories of Islam.

In the villages, the village communities had their own autonomy. Russian and oriental law, including Hindu law, have recognized liturgical collective liability and the corresponding collective rights of the compulsory organizations, especially of village communities, but also of craftsmen. Collective self-help is for the kin group the most typical means of reacting to infringements upon its interests.

The oldest procedures approximating to a trial are compulsory arbitration of conflict within the household or the kin group, either by the household head or the kin elder who best knows the customs, and mutually agreed arbitration between several households and kin groups.

For the development of a professional legal training and, through it, of specifically legal modes of thinking two different lines are possible. The first consists in the empirical training in the law as a craft: the apprentices learn from practitioners more or less in the course of actual legal practice. Under the second possibility, law is taught in special schools, where the emphasis is placed on legal theory and 'science', that is, where legal phenomena are given rational and systematic treatment. A fairly pure illustration of the first type is represented by the guild-like English method of having law taught by the lawyers. Modern legal education in the universities represents the purest type of the second way of legal training. Where only law-school graduates are admitted to legal practice, the universities enjoy a monopoly of legal education. At the present time it is supplemented by apprenticeship in legal practice and another examination; it is in this manner that legal education is nowadays everywhere combined with empirical training.

He concludes by saying that whatever form law and legal practice may come to assume under the impact of various influences, it will be inevitable that, as a result of technical and economic developments, the legal ignorance of the layman will increase. Inevitably the notion must expand that the law is a rational technical apparatus, which is continually transformable in the light of considerations of expediency and devoid of all sacredness of content.

(b) *The lack of a specific type of city and citizenship* According to Weber, the concept of rational law was related to citizenship, which was ultimately related to the cities of the Occident in the specific sense. Even the term citizenship is very complex and Weber gives three distinct significations. First, there is citizenship in the economic sense, where citizens are divided into two categories, i.e. greater citizens and lesser citizens; entrepreneurs and hand workers belong to this class. Second, in the political sense, citizenship signifies membership in the state, with its connotation as the holder of certain political rights. Finally, there is the case where among citizens are included persons of property and culture, i.e. entrepreneurs, recipients of funded incomes, etc. in contrast with the bureaucracy or the proletariat and others outside their circle.

As Weber points out, the concept of citizenship is very complex and so is the concept of city, so they are difficult to define. He makes an exhaustive study of different types of cities in the Occident, as well as in the Orient, in all periods. In the economic sense there may be the 'consumer' city, the 'producer' city and the 'merchant' city. Similarly there may be a political–administrative concept of the city. However, the castle or wall, normally were indispensable parts of the oriental as well as of ancient Mediterranean and medieval cities.[36] He points out that in the first stage of its development into a special political form, the fortified city either was itself a castle, or it contained or lay adjacent to a castle, the fortress of a king, a nobleman, or an association of knights. Such lords either resided in the fortress themselves, or they maintained a garrison of mercenaries, vassals, or bondsmen in it. The problem of the relationship between the garrison, the political citizenry of the fortress, on the one hand, and the civilian, economically active population, on the other hand, is frequently exceedingly complex; but it is always of crucial importance for the constitutional history of the city. However, a process that can be observed all over the world, but especially in coastal localities (not in 'cities' alone) where the trade middlemen are easily controlled, was that the interest of the resident warrior families in participation in the profits from trade would grow, and so could their power to assert this interest, until they eventually shattered the monopoly (if it had existed) of the local chieftain or prince of the castle. If this occurred, the prince was usually reduced to the position of *primus inter pares,* and perhaps ultimately to an approximately equal member of the urban *gentes,* elected for a short period only and with severely restricted powers, which he then had to share with the patrician 'families' owning urban land and participating either in peaceful commerce—in person or merely with their capital—or in the bellicose pursuits of piracy and maritime war.

However, not every 'city' in the economic sense, nor every garrison whose inhabitants had a special status in the political–administrative sense, has in the past constituted a 'commune'. The city-commune in the full meaning of the word appeared as a mass phenomenon only in the Occident; the Near East (Syria, Phoenicia and perhaps Mesopotamia) also knew it, but only as a temporary structure. To develop into a city-commune, a settlement had to be of the non-agricultural–commercial type, at least to a relative extent, and to be equipped with the following features: (i) a fortification; (ii) a market; (ii) its own court of law and, at least in part, autonomous law; (iv) an associational structure *(Verbandscharakter)* and, connected therewith, (v) at least partial autonomy and autocephaly, which includes administration by authorities in whose appointment the burghers could in some form participate. In the past, such rights almost always took the form of privileges of an 'estate' *(Stand);* hence the characteristic of the city in the political definition was the appearance of a distinct 'bourgeois' estate.

But, if the above definition were to be strictly applied, even the cities of the occidental Middle Ages would qualify only in part—and those of the eighteenth century only to the smallest part—as true 'city communes'. But the cities of Asia, with the possible exception of very isolated cases, would not, so far as he knows, fit this classification. It is true that they all had markets and that they also were fortresses. Separate court districts for the larger trade and craft towns of these countries were also quite frequent. The seat of the administrative authorities of the large political association was, in China, Egypt, the Near East, and in India, always in these towns—a statement which does not apply to precisely the most typical occidental cities of the early Middle Ages, especially those of northern Europe. However, the Asian cities did not know a special substantive or trial law applicable to the 'burghers' by virtue of their membership in the city-commune, or a court autonomously appointed by them. They experienced an approximation only in the case of guilds or (in India) castes which, if they primarily or exclusively inhabited a single city, might then develop a special law and their own courts. But from the point of view of the law, the urban seat of these organizations was purely accidental and of no significance. Autonomous administration of the city was unknown or merely vestigial. Most importantly, the associational character of the city and the concept of a 'burgher' (as contrasted to the man from the countryside) never developed at all or existed only in rudimentary form. The Chinese townsman was legally a member of his sib and hence of his native village, where the temple of his ancestor cult stood and with which he carefully upheld his association. Similarly, the Russian member of a village community who earned his living in the city remained a 'peasant' in the eyes of the law. The Indian townsman was, in addition, a member of his caste.

It is true that, as a rule, town dwellers were also members of local professional associations, of guilds and crafts with a specifically urban location, and they were members of the urban administrative districts, city wards, and blocks into which the city was divided by the local authorities—and that in these capacities they had definite duties and, at times, even certain rights. But a special status of the town dweller as a 'citizen', in the ancient and medieval sense, did not exist and the corporate character of a city was unknown. In strong contrast to the medieval and ancient Occident, we never find the phenomenon in the Orient that the autonomy and the participation of the inhabitants in the affairs of local administration would be more strongly developed in the city—that is, in non-agricultural–commercial and relatively large localities—than in the countryside. In fact, as a rule the very opposite would be true. In China, for example, the confederation of the elders was particularly all powerful in the village. In India, too, the village community had very far-reaching competencies, and the Russian *mir* ruled almost autonomously within its bailiwick until the bureaucratization under Alexander III. In the Asian city this could never occur, because it was usually the seat of the high officials or of the prince himself and thus directly under the cudgel of their military bodyguards. The Asian city was a princely fortress, hence it was administered by officials and military officers of the prince, who also held all judicial powers. The royal official always gained the upper hand in the bureaucratic monarchies. To be sure, he was not all-powerful; in fact, he often had to take account of popular opinion to an amazing degree. However, these limits were of a completely indeterminate kind. Guild or other occupational associations, on the other hand, had certain competencies, in China as well as in India, or at least claimed them in such a way that the officials had to reckon with them. The heads of these associations at times exercised far-reaching coercive powers, even over non-members. Normally, however, these were only competencies or factual powers of a particular association with respect to particular issues touching on its concrete group interests. But ordinarily, there existed no association which could represent the commune of burghers as such. The very concept of an urban burgher and, in particular, a specific status qualification of the burgher were completely lacking. It can be found neither in China nor in Japan or India, and only in abortive beginnings in the Near East.

In India the cities were royal seats or official centres of the royal administration as well as fortresses and market centres. We also find merchant guilds and castes, to a large extent coterminous with the occupational associations, both of which enjoyed considerable autonomy, above all in the fields of legislation and administration of justice. But the hereditary caste structure of Indian society, with its ritual segregation of the occupations, precludes the emergence of a 'bourgeoisie' as well as of a 'city commune'. Although several merchant castes and very many craft castes with innumerable sub-castes existed (and still exist), they cannot be equated as a group with the occidental burgher estate, nor could they themselves combine to form something corresponding to the medieval craft-ruled city, for caste barriers prevented all inter-caste fraternization.

However, Weber points out that in the period of the great religions of salvation we do in fact find in India the guilds, headed by their hereditary elders *(shreshtha)*, combining into an association in many cities; residues of this exist at present in some cities (Ahmedabad) which are led by a common urban *shreshth* corresponding to a Western lord mayor. There also existed, in the period prior to the large bureaucratic kingdoms, some cities which were politically autonomous and were ruled by a local patriciate recruited from those families who served in the army with elephants.[37] But all this later disappeared almost completely; the triumph of ritual caste barriers shattered the guild association, and the royal bureaucracy in alliance with the brahmans swept away all such budding developments except for the remnants which survived in north-western India.

After explaining the position in various countries he concludes by saying that all safely founded information about Asian and oriental settlements which had the economic characteristics of 'cities' seems to indicate that normally only the clan associations, and sometimes also the occupational associations, were vehicles of organized action *(Verbandshandeln)*, but never the collective of urban citizens as such. Transitions, of course, are fluid here too. But this statement holds precisely for the largest settlements, which sometimes embraced hundreds of thousands, and even millions, of inhabitants.

On the other hand the fully developed ancient and medieval occidental city was constituted, or at least interpreted, as a fraternal association, as a rule equipped with a corresponding religious symbol for the associational cult of the burghers: a city-god or city-saint to whom only the burghers had access. It is true that many Chinese cities also had a special god (often an apotheosized mandarin), but there he retained the character of a functional deity in the pantheon.

Thus one of the foremost factors responsible for the peculiarities differentiating the Mediterranean city of all periods from the Asian city is the absence of magical and animistic caste and sib constraints and of the corresponding taboos among the free townsmen. In China it has been the exogamous and endophratic sib, in India (since the victory of the patrimonial kings and the brahmans), in addition, the endogamous and exclusive caste with its taboos which has prevented any kind of fusion of city dwellers into an association of burghers based on religious and secular equality before the law, connubium, commensality, and solidarity against non-members. Because of the taboo-protected caste closure this applies to India even more strongly than to China; it is at least in part due to this factor that India had a population which, from the legal point of view, was 90 per cent rural, whereas in China the city played a considerably more significant role. While for the inhabitants of an Indian city a communal cult meal was an impossibility, the Chinese, owing to their sib organization and the overwhelming importance of the ancestor cult, had no need for one.

(c) *Caste exclusiveness and the absence of communes* Weber continues that the occidental city, especially the medieval one, was not only economically a seat of trade and the crafts, politically in the normal case a fortress and perhaps a garrison, administratively a court district, but beyond all this also a sworn confraternity. In antiquity the symbol of a confraternity was the joint election of the *prytaneis*. In the Middle Ages the city was a sworn *commune* which had the legal status of a corporation, although this was attained only gradually. The real home of the *coniuratio*, however, is obviously to be found in Italy.

> The immediate positive aim of the sworn confraternity was the unification of local landowners for protective and defensive purposes, for the peaceable settlement of internal disputes, and for the securing of an administration of justice in correspondence with the interests of the towndwellers. But there were further goals. One was the monopolization of the economic opportunities offered by the city: only the members of the sworn association were to be permitted to share in the commerce of the city. Another aim was the delimitation of the obligations owed to the city lord: the replacement of arbitrary taxation by fixed lump sum payments or by high (but determinate) annual payments. Finally, the city association took in hand the military organization for the purpose of expanding the political and economic power sphere of the commune against the outside.[38]

The purely personal and temporary *coniurationes* gradually developed into permanent political associations whose members were collectively, as urban citizens, subject to a special and autonomous law.

On the other hand, the development of an urban *confraternity*, and thus of a urban *commune*, was impeded in Asia by the magic ties of the sib associations and, in India, of the castes. In China the sibs were the bearers of the central religious concerns, the ancestor cult, and were therefore indestructible. In India the castes were carriers of a specific conduct of life, upon the observance of which the individual's fate in the next incarnation hinged; hence they were ritually exclusive *vis-à-vis* each other.

(d) *The lack of military and political strength in the bourgeoisie class*
The necessity of river regulation and an irrigation policy in the
Near East and in Egypt, and to lesser degree also in China, caused
the development of royal bureaucracies; initially these were charged
only with construction tasks, but from this core ensued the
bureaucratization of the entire administration which enabled the
king, through this apparatus and the revenues supplied by it, to take
the army administration under his own bureaucratic management.
The 'officer' and the 'soldier', an army recruited by compulsory
draft and equipped and fed from storehouses, became the
foundation of military power. The result was the separation
of the soldier from (ownership of) the means of warfare and the
military defencelessness of the subjects. On such grounds no political
commune of burghers independent from the royal power could arise.
The burgher was here simply the non-soldier. Things were quite
different in the Occident where up to the time of the Roman
emperors the principle of *self-equipment* of the armies prevailed.
The financial strength of his urban subjects forced the lord to turn to
them in case of need and to negotiate with them. To be sure, the
guilds of India and China and the 'money men' of Babylon also
possessed financial strength which compelled the king even there to
impose certain restraints upon himself in order not to scare them
away. But it did not enable the townsmen, however rich they may
have been, to unite and to offer a *military* check to the city lord.
By contrast, all *coniurationes* and city unions of the Occident,
beginning with those of early antiquity, were coalitions of the armed
strata of the cities. This was the decisive difference.

As regards the cities of the West, Weber further observes that
the Italian *popolo* was not only an economic category, but also a
political one. It was a separate political community within the
urban commune with its own officials, its own finances, and its
own military organization. In the truest sense of the word it was a
'state within the state'—the first *deliberately non-legitimate and
revolutionary,* political association. The causes of this phenomenon
must be sought in the fact that in Italy, much more than elsewhere,
knightly families settled in the cities themselves, owing to the much
stronger development of economic and political means of power of
the urban nobility.

Quite different was the fate of the city in the modern era.
The autonomy of the city was progressively taken away. The
English city of the seventeenth and eighteenth centuries had ceased
to be anything but a clique of guilds which could lay claim only to
financial and social class significance. Everywhere the military,
judicial and industrial authority was taken away from the cities.
In form the old rights were as a rule unchanged, but in fact the

modern city was deprived of its freedom as effectively as had happened in antiquity with the establishment of the Roman domination, though in contrast with antiquity they came under the power of competing national states in a condition of perpetual struggle for power in peace and war. This competitive struggle created the largest opportunities for modern Western capitalism. The separate states had to compete for mobile capital, which dictated to them the conditions under which it would assist them to power. Out of this alliance of the state with capital, dictated by necessity, arose the national citizen class, the bourgeoisie in the modern sense of the word. Hence it is the closed national state which afforded capitalism its chance for development, and as long as the national state does not give place to a world empire capitalism also will endure. Such conditions were absent in the East.

(e) *The absence of rational spirit and rationalistic economic ethics* Weber points out that it was neither the growth of population (as pointed out by Karl Marx, it provided the required labour, but, the population growth rate being the same in China, no growth), nor the importation of precious metals (as suggested by Sombart, because in the period of the Roman power India had imported an enormous quantity of precious metal) but certain other factors that were responsible for the development of capitalism. The external conditions are first geographical in character. In China and India the enormous costs of transportation, connected with the decisively inland commerce of the regions, necessarily formed serious obstructions for the classes who were in a position to make profits through trade and to use trading capital in the construction of a capitalistic system, while in the West the position of the Mediterranean as an inland sea, and the abundant inter-connections through the rivers, favoured the opposite development of international commerce. But this factor in its turn must not be overestimated (as such sources were available even before).

The factors responsible for the development of capitalism were rational permanent enterprise, rational accounting, rational technology and rational law. Necessary complementary factors were the rational spirit, the rationalization of the conduct of life in general, and a rationalistic economic ethic.[39]

At the beginning of all ethics, and the economic relations which result, is traditionalism, the sanctity of tradition, the exclusive reliance upon such trade and industry as have come down from forefathers. Primitive traditionalism may, however, undergo essential intensification owing to the material interests of privileged groups or because of some supernatural and magical beliefs. (Resistance may come from certain officials or landholders whose interests are threatened or because they fear loss due to change because of some supernatural evil.)

However, traditional obstructions are not overcome by the economic impulse alone (this element was present to a greater extent in oriental traders) but by the rational outlook of life which brought capitalism. A great part was played by the Reformation in changing this outlook, but it was Calvinism which played a crucial role in bringing capitalism. It was Calvinism which gave the idea that man was only an administrator of what God had given him; it condemned enjoyment, yet permitted no flight from the world but rather regarded working together, with its rational discipline, as the religious task of the individual. Out of this system of thought came the word 'calling', which is known only to the languages influenced by the Protestant translations of the Bible.[40] It expresses the value placed upon rational activity carried on according to the rational capitalistic principle, as the fulfilment of a God-given task. Here lay also, in the last analysis, the basis of the contrast between the Puritans and the Stuarts. The ideas of both were capitalistically directed; but in a characteristic way the Jew was for Britain the embodiment of everything repugnant because he devoted himself to irrational and illegal occupations such as war loans, tax farming and leasing of offices, in the fashion of the court favourite. In other words, Jewish capitalism was speculative pariah-capitalism while Puritan capitalism consisted in the organization of citizen labour.[41]

On the other hand other religions such as Hinduism, Buddhism, Confucianism, have been wanting in such teachings and were dominated by magical and other supernatural beliefs hindering capitalism. Magic involves a stereotyping of technology and economic relations. When attempts were made in China to inaugurate the building of railroads and factories a conflict with geomancy ensued. The latter demanded that in the location of structures on certain mountains, forests, rivers, and cemetery hills, foresight should be exercised in order not to disturb the rest of the spirits. Similar is the relation to capitalism of the castes in India. Every new technological process which an Indian employs signifies for him first of all that he leaves his caste and falls into another, necessarily lower. Since he believes in the transmigration of souls, the immediate significance of this is that his chance of purification is put off until another re-birth. He will hardly consent to such a change. An additional fact is that every caste makes every other impure. In consequence, workmen who dare not accept a vessel filled with water from each other's hands, cannot be employed together in the same factory room. Not until the present time, after the possession of the country by the English for almost a century, could this obstacle be overcome. Obviously, capitalism could not develop in an economic group thus bound hand and foot by magic beliefs. The other teachings of Hinduism goaded intellectuals to lead a life of asceticism and to become forest dwellers and poor monks. As this topic was of special interest to Weber, who made an extensive study of the various religions of the world to support his above contention, we shall study it in detail in the following chapters.

The factors for the development of modern capitalism in the West and the major difficulties which India has to face in bringing it about, as pointed out by Weber, are partly correct and partly wrong. The factors enumerated for the development of modern capitalism in the West, as pointed out by Weber, are mostly correct, except that of colonization. Weber contends that colonization was not an important factor in the development of modern capitalism. But so far as India is concerned, the British government deliberately exploited the country to the advantage of British industry, which crippled the indigenous industry, as pointed out by Marx and many Indian economists.[42] So far as the major difficulties, pointed out by Weber, in the development of modern capitalism in India, are concerned some of these would have been removed automatically once scientific education and industries started. Rational law would have developed with the expansion of modern education. Similarly the specific type of cities and citizenship would have developed with dissemination of ideas from the West. The barrier of caste would have broken with the expansion of railways and people working together in the factories. However, the development of the military and political strength of the bourgeoisie and rationalistic economic ethics would not have been possible in India owing to its different social structure and the religious teachings of this region. The major hindrance in the development of modern capitalism in India which Weber totally ignores, was its political subservience. Had India been politically independent at that period it would have developed industrially as did Japan, though not at the same rate (of course, it is doubtful whether India, had it not been conquered by the British and united into one country with the help of trained military personnel, a bureaucratic regime, a network of railways, etc., would have been politically one country or divided into different states fighting with each other). This is proved by the fact that after Independence, with a base prepared during the previous century, India has now made rapid progress in modern capitalism. But the progress has been hampered, partly because of idealogical conflicts in the world, but partly owing to the peculiar social structure and the religious outlook of the people. The caste system and the main religion of India, i.e. Hinduism, are closely interconnected. Both these phenomena have been examined in detail by Weber. We shall make

our comments on these issues after we have examined the views
of Weber on these topics in the following chapters.

4 The Hindu social system

It was pointed out in the last chapter that Weber's work 'The Religion of India—The Sociology of Hinduism and Buddhism', which contains his main views on Indian religion, was a part of his major work *Collected Essays in the Sociology of Religion* published in three volumes. Volume II of this series deals with Indian religion under the title cited above. In this work Weber deals with various aspects of the major Indian religions, i.e. Hinduism, Jainism and Buddhism, and how they affected Indian society. However, his central theme in this work remains the same as that which he had taken up in his first famous essay 'The Protestant Ethic and the Spirit of Capitalism' (published in 1904–5), i.e. how the economic ethics of different religions have affected the development of modern Capitalism and the social stratification of their environment.

He divided this work 'The Religion of India' into three parts: (1) the Hindu social system, (2) orthodox and heterodox holy teachings of the Indian intellectuals and (3) the Asiatic sects and the redemption religions. Part I dealing with the Hindu social system is most important as it studies the relation of Hinduism with the general social structure, i.e. its political structure, the social classes, particularly the caste system, family structure, the development of law, etc. But as most of these aspects have already been touched on in the foregoing chapter we shall not repeat them here, with the exception of the caste structure, which is exhaustively dealt in this part. However, from the philosophical point of view the other two parts are as important as the first one. With this background we shall study his findings in this work under the following heads: (1) The Hindu social system, (2) The main characteristics of Hinduism in early times, (3) Jainism and Buddhism in India, (4) Hinduism in the Middle Ages and after, and (5) General characteristics of Indian religion and other conclusions. In this chapter we shall be concerned with the Hindu social system.

The Hindu social system has been dealt with by Weber under the following heads:

1 The Indian social system in the past
2 The general pattern of the caste system
3 Diffusion patterns of Hinduism or the process of Hinduization
4 Caste dharma and sects
5 Attributes of the caste system
6 The social rank order of castes
7 The origin and formation of castes
8 The formation of new castes
9 The caste system as a hindrance to industrialization
10 Complex factors leading to the caste system

1 The Indian social system in the past

In part I of the book where he deals with the Hindu social system, Weber first depicts the Indian social system in the past and then tries to explain how various factors, particularly the caste system, hindered the development of modern capitalism. He says, India, in contrast to China, has been and remains, a land of villages and of the most inviolable organization by birth.[1] But at the same time it was a land of trade, foreign, particularly with the Occident, as well as domestic. Trade and credit usury appeared in India from ancient Babylonian times. In the north-west, Indian commerce was under constant perceptible Hellenic influence. At an early period the Jews settled in the south while Zoroastrians from Persia settled in the north-west. Under the great Moguls, and also repeatedly before them, all or almost all of India for generations was formed into one political unit. Such periods of unity were interrupted, however, by long periods of disintegration with the country divided into numerous, constantly warring political dominions.

Princely methods of warfare, politics and finance were rationalized, made subject to literary and, in the case of politics, even to quite Machiavellian theorizing. Knightly combat and the disciplined army equipped by the prince appeared. While, as is occasionally maintained, the use of artillery did not develop here for the first time, it appeared early. State creditors, tax farming, state contracting, trade and communication monopolies, etc., developed in the fashion characteristic of occidental patrimonial logic. For centuries urban development in India paralleled that of the Occident at many points. The contemporary rational number system, the technical basis of all 'calculability', is of Indian origin. The 'positional' number system has existed for an undetermined time. The zero was invented and used sometime after the fifth or sixth century A.D. Arithmetic and algebra are considered to have been independently developed in India. For negative magnitudes the term 'debts' (*ksaya*) was used. In contrast to the Chinese, the Indians cultivated rational science (including mathematics and grammar). They developed numerous philosophical schools and religious sects of almost all possible sociological types. For the most part the schools and sects developed out of the basic need for rational consistency which was expressed in the most varied spheres of life. For long periods tolerance toward religious and philosophic doctrines was almost absolute; at least it was infinitely greater than anywhere in the Occident until most recent times.

Indian justice developed numerous forms which could have served capitalistic purposes as easily and well as corresponding institutions in Western medieval law. The autonomy of the merchant stratum in law-making was at least equivalent to that of Western medieval merchants. Indian handicrafts and occupational specialization were highly developed. From the standpoint of possible capitalistic development, the acquisitiveness of Indians of all strata left little to be desired and nowhere is to be found so little antichrematism and such high evaluation of wealth. Yet modern capitalism did not develop indigenously before or during the English rule. It was taken over as a finished artefact without autonomous beginnings. One factor among many which prevented capitalistic development (in the occidental sense) was Indian religion (i.e. Hinduism) in the form of the caste system.[2]

2   The general pattern of the caste system

Weber observes that the national form of Indian religion is Hinduism. The term 'Hindu' was first used under the foreign domination of the Mohammedans to mean unconverted native Indians. It is the official designation of the English census for the religious complex also described in Germany as 'brahmanism.' The term 'brahmanism' refers to the fact that a definite type of priest, the brahman, was the leader of the religion. It is known that the brahmans constituted a caste and that, in general, the institution of the castes—a system of particularly rigid and exclusively hereditary estates—played and continue to play a role in the social life of India. Also, the names of the four main castes of classical learning as represented in the Laws of Manu are known: brahmans (priests); kshatriyas (knights); vaishyas (free commoners); shudras (serfs).

The general public is quite unfamiliar with the details of the castes, with the possible exception of vague ideas about the transmigration of souls. These ideas are not false, they merely require clarification in terms of the abundant sources and literature.

Under the heading 'religion' the tables of the Census of India for 1911 list in round numbers, 217·50 million people as 'Hindus', i.e. 69·39 per cent of the population. Among the imported faiths there are: Mussulmen (66·6 million, or 21·26 per cent); Christians, Jews, Zoroastrians and 'Animists' (10·29 million, or 3·28 per cent). The following non-Hindu religions are listed as native to India: Sikhs (around 3 million, or 0·86 per cent); Jains (1·2 million, or 0·40 per cent); Buddhists (10·7 million, or 3·42 per cent). However, all but a third of a million of the Buddhists reside in Burma (which since early times has been almost nine-tenths Buddhistic); the remainder live in the bordering territories of Tibet.

A part of the decrease of Hindus since 1881 (when the first census was taken) is to be ascribed to single conversions to Islamism and Christianity, the converts being mainly people from the lower castes bettering their social position. Formal conversions to Hinduism do not officially exist; according to the theory of Hinduism they are impossible. However, like most generalizations about Hinduism this is true only with qualifications. Quite apart from the exclusiveness of the upper castes, as reported by the Census, there are important processes in some of the lower castes. Some of these castes not only recruit excommunicated former members of other castes but occasionally do so quite indiscriminately. For example, the impure caste of the bhangi of Bombay Province is partially made up of out-castes from higher castes. However, the bhangi of the 'United Provinces' were recruited by admitting voluntary applicants and hence were often identified, as Blunt does in the Census Report of 1911, with the tshandala, the lowest unclean caste of the ancient law books. Several other castes, in principle, allow individuals to affiliate. In general, the more completely Hinduized in the classical pattern, the more exclusive the caste. And genuine old Hindu castes hold that the affiliation of an individual with a caste is impossible. However, people from tribes were taken into the fold in a special way.

3 Diffusion patterns of Hinduism or the process of Hinduization

Weber observes that Hindu propaganda in the grand manner occurred in the past and is still of considerable importance. In the course of about eight hundred years the present Hindu system has spread from a small region in northern India to an area containing over 200 million people. This missionary propagation was accomplished in opposition to 'animistic' folk belief and in conflict with highly developed salvation religions, i.e. Buddhism and Jainism. The system is still expanding from census to census.

Ordinarily, the propagation of Hinduism occurs in approximately the following way. The ruling stratum of an 'animistic' tribal territory begins to imitate specific Hindu customs in something like the following order: abstention from meat, particularly beef; the absolute refusal to butcher cows; total abstinence from intoxicating drinks. To these certain other specific purification practices of good Hindu castes may be added. The ruling stratum gives up marriage practices that may deviate from Hindu custom and organizes itself into exogamous sibs, forbidding the marriage of their daughters to men of socially inferior strata.... The assumption of additional Hindu customs follows rapidly: restrictions are placed upon contact and table community; widows are forced into celibacy; daughters are given into marriage before puberty without being asked; the dead are cremated rather than buried; ancestral death sacrifices (sraddha) are arranged; and native deities are rebaptized with the names of Hindu gods and goddesses. Finally, tribal priests are eliminated and some Brahman is requested to provide and take charge of ritual concerns and thereby also to convince himself and provide testimony to the fact that they—the rulers of the tribe—were of ancient, only temporarily forgotten, knightly (kshatriya) blood.[3]

It is not always easy to find true brahmans ready to accept such spurious propositions, and neither in the past nor nowadays would a high-caste brahman accept them. However, numerous brahman sub-castes were and are still to be found. There in substance is the typical way in which Hinduism has been extensively propagated in new territories since its full development. In fighting for the significance of their national culture today, the representatives of Hinduism seek to define Hinduism as broadly as possible. They claim as a Hindu anyone who passes one of the possible tests of Hinduism defined by the census authority, thus also a Jain, Sikh or Animist.

The motives working for the reception were and are two. The brahmans, serving as intermediaries, primarily have a material interest in opportunities for expanding income, ranging from service fees for the casting of horoscopes to prebends and the gifts due to house and sacrificial priests.[4] The 'tribes' which would be transformed into 'castes', particularly their ruling stratum, assume an enslaving yoke of rituals hardly duplicated elsewhere in the world. Integration into the Hindu community endowed the ruling stratum of the barbarians with recognized rank in the cultural world of Hinduism. Their transformation into castes also secured their superiority over the subject classes with an efficiency unsurpassed by any other religion. (In ancient times it was the kings who took the lead in the struggle for Hinduization.) Similar to the legitimation interest of the ruling groups are the interests of pariah peoples who only acquire the humiliating position of an inpure caste. It is however, advantageous to secure a monopoly over their work opportunities by being recognized as a legitimate 'caste', however underprivileged, rather than remaining an alien people. Also by borrowing an organization peculiar to Hinduism (e.g. the caste *panchayat*) the assumption of caste status can be given practical significance. Islam, too, succumbed in India to the engulfing tendency toward caste formation.

Weber also mentions about ritualistic duty of a caste (*dharma*) and the doctrine (*mata*) followed by them. For example the father may be a Shivaist while the son may be a Vishnuist. In practice this means that one of them was instructed by a guru of the Shiva sect, the other by one of the Vishnu sect. Thus one may observe the general rites of the caste and the special rites of his sect.

4 Caste dharma and sects

According to Weber, *dharma*, that is, ritualistic duty, is the central criterion of Hinduism. Here he means by *dharma* the caste *dharma*, which is, from a Hindu's point of view, a narrower concept. He remarks,

> *Dharma* differs according to social position and, since it is subject to 'evolution', which is not absolutely closed and completed, *dharma* depends upon the caste into which the individual is born. With the split of old into new castes *dharma* is specialized. Through the advance of knowledge *dharma* can be further developed.[5]

Dharma depends first on sacred tradition, the adjudication, the literary and rationally developed learning of the brahmans. The everyday *dharma* of the caste derives its content, in large measure, from the distant past with its taboos, magical norms and witch-crafts.

He further adds that officially, Hinduism, like the other religions, has a holy book—the Vedas. They are, however, only a collection of hymns, prayers and formulae. They contain nothing about the divine and human affairs fundamental to Hinduism. The three great gods of Hinduism, even their names, are hardly mentioned. The Vedas have nothing to say about the specific character the Hindu gods acquired later. The gods of the Vedas are functional and hero gods, externally similar to those of Homer. The two great Vedic gods, especially the two greatest in their opposed characteristics are Indra and Varuna. Indra, the god of the thunderstorm, was (like

Jahvweh) a passionately active, war and hero god, and thereby god of the irrational fate of heroes. Varuna was the wise, omniscient, functional god of eternal order, particularly legal order. Both these gods have almost disappeared from Hinduism. No cults are built around them. The Vedas rather defer the *dharma* of Hinduism. To a Christian, the official recognition of the Vedas might appear to be a 'formal principle' of Hinduism in the manner of the Protestant recognition of the Bible—always with the reservation that it is at least not absolutely indispensable. With similar reservations the sacredness of the cow, and hence the absolute prohibition against killing cows, if anything, might be considered among the ritualistic, substantive principles of Hinduism forming part of the universal Hindu *dharma*. Whoever does not accept them as binding is not a Hindu. The worship of the cow had extensive economic and ritualistic implications. Even today rational animal husbandry fails, because, in principle, the animals must not die an unnatural death and hence are fed although their use value is long gone. A beef-eater is either a barbarian or of low caste. The source of these Hindu conceptions is of no concern to us here; the point is that the Vedas supply no evidence for such attitudes towards cattle and take beef-consumption for granted. Moreover, if we look beyond the ritualistic prescriptions to the structured core of Hindu ideas, we fail to discover in the Vedas a single trace of such fundamental conceptions as the transmigration of souls and derived *karma*-doctrine (of compensation). These ideas can only be interpretatively read into some ambiguous and undatable passages of the Vedas. Thus the Vedas contain incipient and preliminary steps of the later development and classical form of Hinduism.

Some of the observations made above by Weber about caste *dharma* and other rituals followed by Hindus are correct. However, Weber does not clearly mention two sets of dharma among Hindus and lays emphasis on caste *dharma* only. As pointed out by Mrs Dasgupta, in Hinduism there are

> two sets of Dharmas, one which is universal in their application, to be followed by persons of all castes (varna) or ranks and stages (asrama) aspiring to a moral regeneration, and the other to be adhered to by people belonging to a particular caste or stage. This first is known as *sadharana* dharma, the second as varnasram-dharma. The first group involves, non-injury, truthfulness, nonstealing, purity of the body and mind, sense control, charity, control of inner mental states, helping the distressed and tranquillity in the midst of distress and troubles, and these are to be observed by the higher and lower caste people alike. The second group involves particular duties

determined by the caste, such as, a Brahmin should teach and study the Vedas, the Ksatriyas should fight for their country, and the like.[6]

5   Attributes of the caste system

Weber observes that perhaps the most important gap in the ancient Veda is its lack of any reference to caste. The Veda refers to the four later caste names in only one place, which is considered a very late passage; nowhere does it refer to the substantive content of the caste order with the meaning it later assumed and which is characteristic only of Hinduism. (The specialists see in the Purisha Sukta of the Rig-Veda the 'Magna Carta of the caste system'. It is the latest product of the Vedic period.) Caste, that is, the ritual rights and duties it gives and imposes, and the position of the brahmans, is the fundamental institution of Hinduism. Before every-thing else, without caste there is no Hindu. But the position of the Hindu with regard to the authority of the brahmans may vary extraordinarily, from unconditional submission to the contesting of his authority. This may seem to contradict the fact that 'castes' and 'brahmans' belong together in Hinduism. But as a matter of fact, if caste is absolutely essential for each Hindu, the reverse, at least nowadays, does not hold, namely that every caste is a Hindu caste.[7]

From the above account we may infer that according to Weber caste is a social rank group and this social rank is determined with reference to brahmans. Caste gives and imposes certain ritual rights and duties upon the group. Weber does not give any definition of caste, but started with its negative attributes. However, among Hindus 'caste' is, and remains essentially social rank, and the central position of the brahmans in Hinduism rests primarily upon the fact that social rank is determined with reference to brahmans.

What is caste then? (The term is of Portuguese derivation. The ancient Indian name is *varna*: 'colour'.) As stated above, instead of defining caste Weber starts with its negative contents. What is not a caste? Or, what traits of other associations, really or apparently related to caste, are lacking in caste? First, he com-pares caste with tribe, then with guild and status group. Whereas a tribe usually has a fixed territory, a genuine caste does not. In any case the caste does not form a local, territorial, corporate body. Secondly, a tribe is, or at least originally was, bound together by obligatory blood revenge, whereas a caste never has anything to do with such blood revenge. Thirdly, whereas a tribe can pursue all possible occupations, the kinds of pursuits for a caste are limited. Fourthly, normally a tribe comprises people of every social rank, whereas a caste is bound up with social ranks. Of course these may be sub-castes within the caste with different social ranks. Fifthly, whereas it is decisive for a tribe that it is originally and normally a political association, a caste is never so. By its very nature the caste is always a purely social and possibly occupational association, which forms part of, and stands within, a social community. Sixth, with regard to the social norms, the exogamy of the totem or of the village coexist with the exogamy of the sibs in a tribe. Endogamy has existed only under certain conditions in a tribe but, for the caste, endogamy forms its essential basis. Similarly, dietary rules and rules of commensality are always characteristic of the caste but are by no means characteristic of the tribe.

Then he explains the difference between a guild and a caste. In the case of merchant, trade or craft guilds there may be factual barriers restricting the connubium between differently esteemed occupations; but there were no ritual barriers, such as are essential for caste. Within the circle of the 'honourable' people, ritual barriers to commensalism were completely absent; but such barriers belong to the basis of caste differences. Furthermore, caste is essentially hereditary. On the other hand, the guild of the Occident, at least during the Middle Ages, was regularly based upon the apprentice's free choice of a master. Another difference between guild and caste is of even greater importance. The occupational associations of the medieval Occident were often engaged in violent struggles against themselves, but at the same time they evidenced a tendency towards fraternization. Such organizations seized political power, either legally or illegally. Often they had common meals, common drinking rooms and common processions to the church. At least in the Lord's Supper there was commensalism with one another in the most festive form. Fraternization at all times presupposes commensalism; it does not have to be actually practised in everyday life, but it must be ritually possible. The caste order precluded this.

Differentiating 'class' and 'caste' Weber points out that whereas 'classes' are groups of people who, from the standpoint of specific interests, have the same economic position, ownership or non-ownership of material goods, or possession of definite skills constitutes a class situation. 'Status', however, is a quality of social honour or lack of it and is in the main conditioned as well as expressed through a specific style of life. There is close association between the two, but they may not coincide. A status group can be closed (status by descent), or it can be open. A caste is doubtless a closed status group. There is extraordinary complexity of the rank relationship of the caste system (e.g. the system of hypergamy, dietary rules, etc.). The caste order is orientated religiously and ritually to a degree not even partially attained elsewhere.

6 The social rank order of castes

Weber observes that according to the Census of India (1901) the caste groups were to be distinguished on the following basis. First come the brahmans and following them, a series of castes which claim, rightly or wrongly, to belong to the two other 'twice born' castes of classical theory: the kshatriya and the vaishya. Throughout the system a third group of castes follow. They are counted among the satshudra, the 'clean shudra' of classical doctrine. They are the Jalacharaniya, that is, castes who may give water to a brahman and from whose *lota* (water bottle) the brahman accepts water. Close to them are castes whose water a brahman would not always accept (that is, acceptance or non-acceptance would possibly depend upon the brahman's rank). The high-caste barber does not serve them unconditionally, and the laundryman does not wash their laundry. But they are not considered absolutely 'unclean' ritually. They are the shudra in the usual sense in which the classical teachings refer to them. Finally, there are castes who are considered unclean. All temples are closed to them, and no brahman and no barber can serve them. They must live outside the village district, and they may infect either by touch, or even by their presence. All these restrictions are related to those castes, which according to the classical doctrine, originated from ritually forbidden sexual intercourse between members of different castes.

Within these groupings one could proceed with further gradations of caste rank, but such gradation would present extremely varied characteristics: among the upper castes the criterion would be correctness of life practices with regard to sib organization, endogamy, child marriage, widow celibacy, cremation of the dead, ancestral sacrifice, foods and drinks, and social intercourse with unclean castes. Among the lower castes one would have to differentiate according to the rank of the brahmans who are still ready to serve them or who will no longer do so, and according to whether or not castes other than brahmans accept water from them. In all these cases, it is by no means rare that castes of lower rank raise stricter demands than castes who otherwise are considered to have a higher standing. The extraordinary variety of such rules of rank order forbids any closer treatment here. It is difficult to establish a list of castes according to rank because rank differs absolutely from place to place, as only some of the castes are universally diffused. Furthermore, great rank differences appear between sub-castes of a single caste, especially among the upper castes but also among some of the middle castes. One would often have to place individual sub-castes far behind another caste, which otherwise would be evaluated as lower. In general, the brahmans to this day, are theoretically, the final authorities on questions of rank, though in the past, as now, were in no position to settle the problems alone.

As already stated, Weber stressed that in the beginning there were no castes. The two lower so-called 'castes' of the law books were perhaps never castes at all in the present-day sense of the term, but, even in classical times, were rank-classes of castes. Originally there were simply status groups. An occasional passage of the literature observes: 'The vaishya and shudra were there before the Brahmans and Kshatriyas ever existed'.[8] The vaishyas were the ancient freemen who were surpassed by the noble sibs—the noble sibs being war nobles, hence chieftains, and later knightly *gentes* and partially, also, priestly nobles as found elsewhere. The status inferiors of the freemen were 'helots' (shudras). The brahmans and kshatriyas engaged in certain, prescribed, exclusive activities which implemented their styles of life as status group: for the brahmans—sacrifice, study of the Vedas, receipts of gifts (particularly land grants), and asceticism; for the kshatriyas—political rule, knightly feats of valour. The occupation of a vaishya—tillage and trade and, particularly, the lending of money at interest—were considered by both upper castes as unbecoming to their rank and station. However, in time of need, when it proved impossible to earn one's living conventionally, it was temporarily permissible, with some reservations, to take up the occupations of a vaishya. In contrast to this, the way of life of the shudra signified 'menial service'.

7   The origin and formation of castes

Weber first traces the origins of castes within the four major groups, i.e. the brahmans, the kshatriyas, the vaishyas and the shudras. He then discusses the splits, i.e. schisms within the castes, which turn into separate castes, and also the formation of castes from tribes and pariah groups. In the end he discusses a number of the factors leading to the development of the caste system.

Weber observes that the general stages in the development of the brahmans into a caste are clear but that the causes of the development are not. Obviously, the priesthood of the Vedic period was not a closed hereditary status group, even though the clan charisma of certain priestly sibs was established in the eyes of the people along-side the personal charisma of the ancient magician. Among the functionally specialized priests the *hotar*, or fire priest, played the chief role in the cult practices. The historical ascendancy of the brahmans seems to have several reasons. Perhaps the older assumption holds that the increasingly stereotyped cult practices and magical formulae made the master of sacrificial ceremonies, that is, the brahman, more and more the decisive leader. The main cause, however, may have been the increasing significance of family priests of nobles and princes as opposed to those administering the community sacrifices.

The kshatriyas were and remained kings, sub-kings, and in the lowest stratum, village notables with special economic privileges. The ancient kshatriyas *gentes* rivalled the brahmans in education and were, as we shall see, the supporters of anti-brahmanical salvation religions (such as Buddhism). The rajputs, on the other hand, had to submit to the superior brahmanical education, and, in common with patrimonial kinship, supported the Hindu restoration.[9] The peculiar, unclassical segregation of the rajputs into exogamous subdivisions indicates their derivation from a tribe of mercenary knights.

As they appear in classical learning, the vaishyas suggest somewhat a comparable status of free commoners in Europe. Viewed negatively, i.e. in contrast to the higher castes, the vaishyas lacked the ritualistic, social and economic privileges of a priestly and lay nobility. Viewed from below, in contrast to the shudra, the most important privilege of the vaishyas—though it is never expressly mentioned—was their right to own land, a right clearly denied to the shudras. In classical sources the vaishya is, first, a peasant. Even in the law books, however, the lending of money for interest and trade are recognized as permissible occupations for this class.

In post-classical times, and at present, the conception of the vaishya as a peasant has completely vanished. Even in early historical times trade was held to be the true occupation of the vaishya, vaishya and *vanik* (trader) being considered identical. A caste claiming vaishya rank today seeks to prove that it always was a trader caste. The removal of the peasantry from status equality with urban propertied and income groups was determined by a number of factors. Feudalization was doubtless the first, patrimonial fiscalization and prebendalization the second.

Since the time of Mogul rule, and even earlier, fiscal interest was decisive for the position of the peasants with respect to others. Here Weber discusses the various forms of land settlement to which we have already referred in the foregoing chapter. For example when each field is separately assessed and each village land owner is liable for the tax on his property the village is a ryotwari village. When a circle of owners has joint liability to the state for the tax levy, the village is known as pattidari village (joint village). Generally the members of the privileged associations (joint villages) of rent-receiving landlords claim their partnership and a birthright, derived from membership in a charismatic (princely) clan. However, such landlords formed classes which, even when they did the managing themselves, refused as long as possible to lay a hand on the plough, thus to avoid the ritualistic degradation that occasionally occurred among impoverished rajputs and other distinguished landowners. However, there were groups of villagers who maintained their place as 'independent' peasants. Among these may be included the Khumbhi in the west and north and the Vellalar in the south. In general, among the relatively high-ranking castes are to be found a number of Hinduized tribes, such as the Jat, Gujar and Koch. Some extremes of settled landowners derived from castes of former professional soldiers; the scattered remainder represent non-noble landlords who are considered relatively distinguished. In short, the caste-fate of the peasants bore traces of the social changes which resulted from the fiscalism of the bureaucratic state. A series of conditions, in part quite general, in part specifically Indian, co-operated to bring this about.

The shudras

Among the industrial castes two groups are outstanding. First is the ritualistically degraded caste which was able neither to give water to brahmans nor employ them as house priests. These included village craftsmen, i.e. artisans and workers who had no full right to the land. Such workers and artisans received garden land, and wages in kind or money. Among these may also be included the blacksmith, carpenter, tailor, potter, part of the pedlar trade, the liquor dealers, oil presser and the numerous castes of farmhands and smallholders.

Ranking just above this ritualistically degraded stratum is another substantially less degraded stratum which is considered to be 'pure'. In addition to the whole series of peasant castes, which vary in rank in the different regions, which contain the mass of this class, there is typically to be found in this stratum a qualitatively important category of castes, the so-called *nabasakh*—or nine-part-group. The nine-part-group obviously forms the kernel of the so-called *satshudra* (pure shudra). The occupations of this group are urban industries and trades: betel, perfume and oil vending, pastry-making, gardening and, at times, the making of pottery. An equal or superior position is occupied by the goldsmiths or silversmiths, lacquer-workers, masons, carpenters, silk-decorators and a series of similarly specifically luxury or city occupations. However, these classifications were in no way systematized. At times practical necessity played a role in the elevation of an occupation. A man rendering personal service, who is forced, while caring for the patron's person, to touch him—a butler or barber, for example— could hardly be assigned to an impure caste.

The lowest caste stratum was considered to be absolutely defiling and contaminating. First, this stratum comprised a number of trades which are almost always despised because they involve physically dirty work: street-cleaning and others. Furthermore, this stratum comprised services which Hinduism had to consider ritually impure: tanning, leather work, and some industries in the hands of itinerant guest workers.

Having surveyed the origin and development of various castes in the four main *varnás* Weber concludes that the caste-groups are not holding any permanently social rank in the hierarchy of caste structure. There are various reasons for the ascent or descent of a caste or sub-caste. This depends upon the conditions determining the origin, developments, or change of castes and sub-castes. These he considers in detail in the subsequent pages.

8 The formation of new castes

According to Weber there are two basic types of caste, tribal and professional. As stated earlier, a multitude of castes developed historically from Hinduized tribal and guest peoples. Their caste rank was generally irrational. For, other things being equal, a tribe which at the time of Hinduization was settled on its own land achieved and maintained higher rank than pure pariah tribes which have been Hinduized. Moreover, a tribe which supplied mercenaries and soldiers of fortune fared still better. Generally the purely professional castes are the more inflexible.

Apart from the reception of tribes, caste formation and change in status could be incurred by the split of castes into sub-castes. This was expressed by the complete or partial denial of connubium and commensalism. This may result from various factors. (1) Migrant members may be separated from the caste because they are suspected of having offended against ritual caste duties. (2) The renunciation of former ritual duties or the assumption of new ones may cause caste schism. For example, propertied members may assume the ritual obligations of higher castes to claim a higher rank and then ultimately break away from the major caste. (3) Occupational changes may lead to caste schism. (4) Sometimes a mere change of work technique may be sufficient reason for the followers of tradition to consider the group as broken. (5) New castes may originate from illicit inter-caste marriages.

Weber also observes that today the Hindu caste order is profoundly shaken. Many norms have practically lost their force. The railway, the taverns, the changing occupational stratification, the concentration of labour through imported industry, colleges, etc. have all contributed their part. Owing to the impact of Western education all caste relations have been shaken, and the intellectuals bred by the English are here, as elsewhere, bearers of a specific nationalism. They will greatly strengthen this slow and irresistible process. For the time being, however, the caste structure still stands quite firmly.

Weber also points out that all historical signs indicate that the truly strict caste order was originally based on the professional castes. This is indicated in the first place by the geographical distribution of tribal and professional castes. However, sometimes ethnic differences also led to the formation of new castes.

9   The caste system as a hindrance to industrialization

Of great interest to Weber were the economic reasons for caste and sub-caste origin: property differentiation, occupational mobility and technological change.[10] The stability of caste order could not hinder property differentiation, but it at least blocked technological change and occupational mobility, which from the point of view of caste were objectionable and ritualistically dangerous. Today, the very fact that new skills and techniques actually lead to the formation of new castes or sub-castes strongly handicaps innovation. It sustains tradition, no matter how often the all-powerful development of imported capitalism overrides it.

The rigid traditionalism of these professional castes is expressed in their still tenacious attachment to their customary pursuits—they are second in this only to a few very ancient pariah tribes. As one would expect, the devastating competition of European and now Indian capitalist industry had completely eliminated quite a number of professions or at least their handicraft basis. Where this is not the case, the ratio of professional caste members who continue their traditional pursuits despite basic transformation of the economy still remains extraordinarily high. In big industrial cities like Calcutta the majority of these workers for specifically 'modern' job opportunities, particularly big industry, are recruited, not from the ancient industrial castes, but predominantly from rural migrants, declassed and pariah castes, and declassed members of certain higher castes. Modern capitalist businessmen (if Indian at all) and commercial and administrative employees are largely recruited from certain ancient trade castes. However, owing to the educational prerequisites of modern office work, recruitment also occurs from literati castes, which earlier had a wider occupational choice than the industrial castes. Among these he mentions castes like Prabhau (ancient caste of officials), mahars (village officials), brahmans, kayasthas (scribes), etc.

However, not only do the ancient occupational castes sustain a rigid traditionalism, but also, in general, they uphold the strictest ritualistic caste exclusiveness. Nowhere are endogamy and the exclusion of commensalism more rigidly observed than by the occupational castes. The extreme caste traditionalism of many industrial and indeed lower castes (apart from an important religious ground to be examined later) is determined by their frequently strict caste or, as a rule, sub-caste organization known as caste panchayat.

Occupational issues, however, in no way form the centre of gravity; at present the caste or sub-caste does not function primarily as a guild or trade union. On the other hand, most issues involve questions of ritual. Among the issues adjudged by the panchayat are, in order, adultery and other offences against inter-sexual ritualistic etiquette and atonement for their ritualist offences of the members, including especially the offence against the rules of intermarriage and commensalism or against purity or dietary laws. Problems such as these always played an important role because tolerance of magical offenders by the caste could draw evil magic upon the whole caste. However, professional problems play a significant role among some ancient and traditionally stable middle and lower castes. In such cases the shift of some members to ritually degrading or suspect pursuits, be they new professions or new techniques may draw their immediate attention. Against outsiders the sanction of the caste is boycott: against members its sanctions are the imposition of money fines, judgments of ritualistic expiation and, in the case of obstinacy and grave cases of the violation of caste norms, excommunication (*bahishkara*).

From the above account Weber draws certain generalizations about the effects of the caste system on the economy. He concludes that this order, by its nature is completely traditionalistic and anti-rational in its effects. The bases of this are, however, not in one particular factor as alleged by Marx (Marx has characterized the peculiar position of the artisan in the Indian village—his dependence upon fixed payment in kind instead of upon production for the market—as the reason for the specific 'stability' of the whole system). He agrees with Marx that one of the factors responsible for the slow change in occupations was the dependence of the village artisan upon fixed payments instead of upon production for the market. But, in addition to the ancient village artisan, there were the merchant, urban artisan and others who worked for the market. On the other hand the ritual law, in which every change of occupation, every change in work technique, may result in ritual degradation is certainly not capable of giving birth to economic and technical revolutions from within itself, or even of facilitating the first germination of capitalism in its midst. The artisan's traditionalism, great in itself, was necessarily heightened to the extreme by the caste order. Commercial capital, in its attempt to organize industrial labour on the basis of the putting-out system, had to face an essentially stronger resistance in India than in Occident. The traders themselves in their ritual seclusion remained in the shackles of the typical oriental merchant class, which by itself has never created a modern capitalist organization of labour. This situation is as if none but different guest peoples, like the Jews, ritually exclusive toward one another and toward third parties, were to follow their trades in one economic area. Some of the great Hinduist merchant castes, particularly, for instance, the vania have been called the 'Jews of India', and, in this negative sense, rightly so. They were, in part, virtuosi in unscrupulous profiteering. Moreover, modern capitalism undoubtedly would never have originated from the circles of the completely traditionalist Indian trades. Modern industrial capitalism, in particular the factory, made its entry into India under the British administration and with direct and strong incentives. But, comparatively speaking, how small is the scale and how great the difficulties. In addition the recruitment of labour is difficult, even in those manufacturing industries with the highest wages. (In Calcutta, labour often has to be recruited from the outside.) Only the most recent acts for the protection of labour have made factory work somewhat more popular.

The Indian factory work-force shows some traditionalist traits. An increase in the wage rate does not mean for them an incentive for more work or for a higher standard of living, but the reverse. They then take longer holidays because they can afford to do so, or their wives decorate themselves with ornaments. To stay away from work as one pleases is recognized as a matter of course, and the worker retires with his meagre savings to his home town as soon as possible. He is simply a mere casual labourer. 'Discipline' in the European sense is an unknown idea to him. Hence, despite a four-fold cheaper wage, competition with Europe is maintained easily only in the textile industry, as two-and-a-half times as many workers and far more supervision are required. One advantage for the entrepreneurs is that the caste division of the workers has so far made any trade union organization and any real 'strike' impossible.

The partial employment of tremendous native wealth as investment capital in modern business was of relatively minor importance for a long time. In the jute industry it is lacking almost completely. 'Bad experiences' not only with entrepreneurs and *associés*, but also with foremen was at the back of this. Even now, for example, in the Indian jute industry only the overseer—and almost no other technical or commercial functionary—is of Indian descent.

To all these difficulties is added the religious promise of the caste system, which does not allow much change in the social structure. As noted earlier, Hinduism is unusually tolerant of doctrine (*mata*) while placing emphasis on ritual duties (*dharma*). Besides, Hinduism has certain dogmas which it is considered heretical to deny. Among these, the two most important are the belief in the transmigration of the soul and the doctrine of *karma*. Weber observes,

> All Hindus accept two basic principles: the *samsara* belief in the transmigration of souls and the related *Karman* doctrine of compensation. These alone are the truly 'dogmatic' doctrines of all Hinduism, and in their very interrelatedness they represent the unique Hindu theodicy of the existing social, that is to say, caste system.[11]

The belief in the transmigration of souls (*samsara*) grew directly out of universally diffused representations of the fate of the spirit after death. It appears elsewhere in the world, for example, in Hellenic antiquity. In India the fauna and coexistence of different coloured races may have facilitated the origin of the idea. Originally the departed soul was as little viewed 'as immortal' in India as elsewhere. The death sacrifice was intended to put the souls at rest and allay their envy and wrath against the fortunate living. The residence of the 'fathers' remained problematical. When the Brahmans began to speculate about their fate, there gradually appeared the teaching of a 'second death' leading the dying spirit or god into another existence. The idea that this existence was also on earth was joined to the concept of 'animal souls' which probably existed in India as elsewhere.

The connecting of the doctrine of transmission of souls with that of compensation for good and evil deeds in the form of a more or less honourable rebirth is not exclusively Indian, but it is found elsewhere, for example, among the Hellenes. However, two principles are characteristic of brahman rationalism which determined the pervasive significance of the doctrinal term. (1) It was believed that each single ethically relevant act has inevitable consequences for the fate of the actor, hence that no consequence can be lost—the doctrine of *karma*. (2) The idea of compensation was linked to the individual's social fate in the societal organization and thereby to the caste order. All (ritual or ethical) merits and faults of the individual formed a sort of ledger of accounts; the balance irrefutably determined the fate of the soul at rebirth, and this in exact proportion to the surplus of one or other side of the ledger.

In India, belief in destiny, astrology and horoscope-casting were widely diffused for a long time. On closer inspection it seems that the horoscope might well indicate man's fate, but that *karma* determined the good or evil significance of the constellation for the individual. There could be no 'eternal' reward or punishment for the individual; such, indeed would be entirely out of proportion to finite doings. One can stay in heaven or hell only for a finite period. That man was bound in an endless sequence of ever new lives and deaths and that he determines his own fate solely by his deeds—this was the most consistent form of the *karma* doctrine.

This doctrine meant that the very caste situation of the individual is not accidental. In India the idea of the 'accident of birth' so critical of society is almost completely absent. The idea of the accident of birth is almost common to traditionalistic Confucians and occidental social reformists. The Indian views the individual as born into the caste merited by his conduct in a prior life. It means that in this life there is no escape from the caste, at least no way to move up in the caste order. The inescapable on-rolling *karma* causality is in harmony with the eternity of the world, of life, and, above all, the caste order.

Karma doctrine transformed the world into a strictly rational, ethically-determined cosmos; it represents the most consistent theodicy ever produced by history. The devout Hindu was accursed to remain in a structure which made sense only in this intellectual context; its consequences burdened his conduct. The Communist Manifesto concludes with the phrase 'they [the proletariat] have nothing to lose but their chains, they have a world to win'. The same holds for the pious Hindu of low caste. He too can 'win the world', even the heavenly world; he can become a kshatriya, a brahman, he can gain heaven and become a god—only not in this life, but in the life of the future after rebirth into the same world pattern.

Order and rank of the castes is eternal (according to doctrine) as the course of the stars and the difference between animal species and the human race. To overthrow them would be senseless.

Weber also observes that Hinduism is characterized by a dread of the magical evil of innovation. Even today the Indian jute peasant can hardly be moved to fertilize the land because it is 'against custom'. In addition to this, Hinduism places its supreme premium upon caste loyalty. In the often cited principle of classical teaching: 'It is better to fulfil one's [caste] duty even without reward than someone else's no matter how excellently, for therein always lies danger'.[12] The neglect of one's caste duties out of high pretensions unfailingly is disadvantageous in the present or future life.

It is difficult to imagine more traditionalistic ideas of professional virtues than those of Hinduism. So long as the *karma* doctrine was unshaken, revolutionary ideas or progressivism were inconceivable. The lowest castes, furthermore, had the most to win through ritual correctness and were the least tempted to innovations. Thus it was

121

impossible to shatter traditionalism, based on caste ritualism anchored in *karma* doctrine, by rationalizing the economy.

10 Complex factors leading to the caste system

Having discussed the origin and formation of the various castes, Weber tries to summarize the various complex factors leading to the caste system. He observes that in view of the numerous disagreements, even among the most distinguished Indologists, only guesses are possible. Obviously, mere occupational differentiation *per se* could not give birth to such sharp segregations. That ethnic factors alongside status and economic factors were important for the formation of castes is beyond doubt. However, to equate caste stratification with racial differences is not correct. Originally, the transition between the warrior and priestly (rishi) *gentes* was free. In the early Middle Ages—pre-Buddhistic times—the knightly community who conquered certain areas in the north (the present-day Bihar) did not think of recognizing the brahmans as their peers.

At first the great patrimonial Hindu kingdoms used the brahmans in support of their legitimation interests. Then the Islamic conquest smashed the politico-military power of the kshatriya but sustained the brahmans as an instrument of social control. The pretensions of the brahmans in classical literature and the law books were then stereotyped.

There were a number of reasons for the channelling of priestly power into the caste system. Ethnic antagonism takes form with respect to contrasts in the external bearing and way of life of various social groups. The most striking contrasts in external appearance simply happens to be different skin colour. Although the conquerors replenished their insufficient supply of women by taking women from among the conquered, colour differences still prevented a fusion in the manner of the Normans and Anglo-Saxons.

As noted earlier, under the sway of animistic beliefs positions are usually linked to the possession of magical charisma, particularly power positions of a sacerdotal and secular nature. But the artisan's craft in India soon tended to become clan charismatic; finally it became 'hereditary'. The phenomenon—found elsewhere—nowhere appears so strongly as in India. This was the nucleus of the caste formation for those positions and professions. In conjunction with a number of external circumstances this led to the formation of true castes. Charismatic sibs and phratries occupied the conquered land, settled in villages, reduced the conquered to rent-payers or village artisans, agricultural or industrial workers, referred them to the outskirts and *Wurthen*, or into special helot and craftsmen villages.

At the time of guild power the princes were financially quite dependent on them. However, the unmilitary urban stratum was in no position to resist princely power. With the aid of the brahmans, princely patrimonialism successfully mastered the guild citizenry which was at times powerful. Brahmanical theory served in an unequalled manner to tame the subjects religiously. The invasion and domination of foreign conquerors benefited the power monopoly of the brahmans. The foreign conquerors divested the most important competitors of the brahmans of all their power, because it conceived them to be politically dangerous. Thus the knighthood and the residue of urban guilds were reduced.

With the increasing stabilization of economic conditions the ritually segregated guest and pariah tribes were more and more integrated into the expanding caste order which thus became the dominant system. For a thousand years, from the second century A.D. to the beginning of Islamic rule, we find the caste system in an irresistible and ever-continued expansion, slowed down through the propaganda of Islamism. As a closed system, the caste order is a product of consistent brahmanical thought.

Ancient Indian conditions, however, provided the structural elements for the caste system; the inter-ethnic specialization of labour, the development of innumerable guest and pariah peoples, the organization of village crafts on the basis of hereditary artisan cotters, the monopoly of internal trade by guest traders, the small extent of urban development, and the flow of occupational specialization into the channels of hereditary status segregation and monopoly of patronage. Likewise the secondary beginnings of liturgical and fiscal organization of occupations by the princes, and their strong interest in legitimacy and domestication of the subjects, encouraged an alliance with the brahmans and the joint preservation and stabilization by prince and brahman of the established sacred order of Indian society.

All factors important for the development of the caste system operated singly elsewhere in the world. Only in India, however, did they operate conjointly under special Indian conditions: the conditions of a conquered territory within ineffable, sharp, 'racial' antagonisms made socially visible by skin colour. More strongly than anywhere else, magical as well as social rejection of communion with strangers was called forth. This helped preserve the charisma of distinguished sibs and established insurmountable barriers between strange ethnic subject tribes, guest and pariah peoples and their overlords, even after definitive integration of guest and pariah peoples into the local economic community.

Individual acceptance, for apprenticeship, participation in market deals, or citizenship—all these phenomena of the West—either failed to develop in the first place or were crushed under the weight first of ethnic, later of caste fetters.

> We repeat, however: this well-integrated, unique social system could not have originated, or at least could not have conquered and lasted without the pervasive and all-powerful influence of the Brahmans. It must have existed as a finished idea long before it conquered even the greater part of North India. The combination of caste legitimacy with *Karma* doctrine, thus with the specific Brahmanical theodicy—in its way a stroke of genius—plainly is the construction of rational ethical thought and not the product of any economic 'conditions'. Only the wedding of this thought product with the empirical social order through the promise of rebirth gave this order the irresistible power over thought and hope of members and furnished the fixed scheme for the religious and social integration of the various professional groups and pariah peoples.[13]

Although caste order is prevalent among Muslims too, it lacks the 'vocational ethic' similar to that of the Hindu professional castes. Missing too is the authority of the brahman. The ritualistic defilement through commensalism with non-members is also lacking even though commensalism and social intercourse among different social strata may be avoided.

Appraisal

As shown in the foregoing pages Weber very ably summarizes the characteristics of the Hindu social system. In the past the Indians cultivated rational science and developed numerous philosophical schools and religious sects of almost all possible sociological types. For centuries urban development in India paralleled that of the Occident at many points. Indian justice developed numerous forms which could have served capitalistic purposes. Indian handicrafts and occupational specializations were highly developed. In spite of all these achievements modern capitalism could not develop in India because of its peculiar religion in the form of caste system.

There is no reference to caste in the Vedas and the four later caste names referred to only in one place is a very late passage. The vaishyas and shudras were there even before the brahmans and kshatriyas existed. However, in due course the 'caste' became the fundamental institution of Hinduism, as without caste there was no Hindu. Caste was a social rank group having certain rights and duties, and this social rank was determined with reference to brahmans. Here Weber distinguishes clearly between caste and other associations like tribe, guild and status group. The caste was a close group and caste order was oriented religiously and ritually to a degree not even partially attained elsewhere. In a hierarchical position the castes could be divided into five major groups. First come the brahmans, then twice-born castes, kshatriyas and vaishyas. In the third group come the shudras which are again divided into two groups sat-shudras and ordinary shudras. In the lowest rank come the 'unclean castes' to whom all temples are closed and no brahman or barber can serve them. Multitudes of castes developed from Hinduized tribes and guest peoples, but many a time caste formation and change in status could be incurred by the split of castes into sub-castes. Although the railway, the tavern, the changing occupational stratification, concentration of labour in factories, Western education, etc. have shaken the roots of caste system, yet the caste structure still stands quite firmly. The professional castes continue to stick to their old customary pursuits and this blocked technological change. The occupational castes also uphold the strictest ritualistic caste exclusiveness. The ritual law, in which every change of occupation, or work technique may result in ritual degradation could not give birth to economic and technical revolutions from within itself. Even the traders in their ritual seclusion confined their trade to one particular branch and partial employment of tremendous native wealth as investment capital in modern business was of relatively minor importance for a long time.

To all these difficulties was added the religious promise of a caste system which does not allow many changes in the social structure. The two basic principles of Hinduism were the *samsara*—belief in the transmigration of souls—and the related *karma* doctrine of compensation. It was believed that each single ethically relevant act has inevitable consequences. This meant that the very caste situation of the individual is not accidental. Thus the idea of the 'accident of birth', so critical of society in the West was almost completely absent. It meant that in this life there is no escape from the caste, at least no way to move up in the caste order. However, one can 'win the heavenly world' or can become a kshatriya, a brahman, but only in the life hereafter. For this, Hinduism placed supreme premium upon caste loyalty. In such a situation revolutionary ideas or progressivism were inconceivable. In the end Weber explains in detail how the caste system developed in India as the result of the interconnection of various factors which operated singly elsewhere in the world. The above analysis of Hindu social structure given by Max Weber is quite exhaustive and penetrating. However, it must be emphasized that Weber completely ignored the political situation of the country at that time when modern capitalism was developing in the West. It is admitted that the caste system was a great hindrance in the development of new technology or new industrial enterprises, but even where some enterprising members of the trader community tried to establish modern industries in the different fields, their initiative was killed by the British government. On the other hand, in Germany and Japan the national governments helped the industrialists in many ways by giving up the *laissez faire* policy, which only suited an industrially advanced country like Britain. After the First World War when the British government on the recommendations of the Fiscal Commission (1921) gave discriminating protection to certain industries in India, these developed at a faster pace, though the progress was still slow owing to limited protection.[14] It was only after Independence that industries could develop at a rapid pace. Nor did the British government help in the expansion of education, particularly scientific education. It did not change the personal laws of the Hindus and Muslims. On the other hand it encouraged casteism by establishing the zemindari system giving more economic power to the upper castes. The Bhakti movement started during fourteenth century preached against ritualism and favoured the idea of equality, yet this was checked by the rigid social structure imposed from above by the British government. Thus Weber's findings were valid only to a limited extent.

5   The main characteristics of Hinduism in early times

In part II of his book *The Religions of India* Weber deals with the holy teachings of intellectuals, both of the orthodox Hindu religion and of heterodox religions, i.e. Jainism and Buddhism. In this chapter we shall mainly deal with his views on the teachings of intellectuals of the orthodox Hindu religion, while the teachings of the other two religions will be discussed in the next chapter. Among the teachings of intellectuals belonging to orthodox Hindu religion he confines his study in this portion to their teachings in the ancient period before the coming of Jainism and Buddhism. Among these he specially refers to the following teachings: (1) the anti-orgiastic and ritualistic character of brahmanism; (2) the position of Brahmans and other holy intellectuals in society; (3) vashisha dharma and the absence of the concept of natural law; (4) rights and duties of the king; (5) the development of knowledge, asceticism and mysticism; (6) yoga and the development of religious philosophy; (7) salvation doctrines; (8) six schools of religious philosophy; (9) the professional ethics of Mahabharata; (10) the holy teachings of the Bhagavad-Gita.

1   The anti-orgiastic and ritualistic character of brahmanism

Weber observes that the brahmanical priestly stratum was a distinguished and cultivated nobility, later a class of genteel literati, that determined the religiosity of Hindu religion. As in comparable cases, e.g. the Confucians, orgiastic and emotional ecstatic elements of ancient magical rites were not taken over, and for long periods were either completely suppressed or were permitted only as unofficial folk magic. As Mr V. Schroder has demonstrated, in individual instances residues of ancient orgiasticism are to be found in the Vedas.[1] Indra's drunkenness and dance, and the sword dance of the *maruts* (corybants) stem from the intoxication and ecstasy of heroes. Moreover, it is obvious that the great priestly soma-sacrifice was originally a cult-tempered intoxication orgy. The much-discussed dialogues of the Rig-Veda are presumably the slender residues of cult drama. However, the official ritual of the Vedas, with all their hymns and formulae, rest upon sacrifice and prayer and not on typical orgiastic technique—dance emotionality, sexual or alcoholic intoxication, meat orgiasticism—all of which were rather carefully eliminated. Ritualistic copulation in the fields as a means of securing soil fertility and the lingam cult with its phallic hobgoblins, the *gandharvan*, are very ancient in India. But the Rig-Veda is mute with respect to them. In the Vedas the ancient fertility god Rudra, with its orgiastic cults of sex and meat, has a diabolical character. Later he was worshipped as Shiva, one of the three great Hindu gods. While in the Vedas Vishnu is a secondary figure, in the later triad he appears as Shiva's rival and is honoured in pantomimes as a great celestial and fertility god, as patron of the dance drama and erotic orgies of the Krishna cult. At the sacrifice, in the Vedic period, the laity was 'denied the cup'— only the priest drank soma. The same held for sacrificial meat. While female deities were extremely important for ancient and modern Asiatic folk beliefs, in the Vedas they were completely eclipsed as fertility demons of primarily orgiastic sex cults. In details the Atharva-Veda is not completely cold toward figures of folk belief (for example, the *gandharvan*). But in it, too, ritual formulae, not orgiasticism and ecstasy, are magical implements. Brahmanical literature ever inclined towards formalistic ritualism. Alongside the brahman, as in China beside the official with his state cult, we find the house father (*grihastha*) performing important ritualistic duties, thoroughly regulated by the Grihya-Sutra. The Dharma-Sutras (law books) then drew all the social relations of the individual into their compass. Thus, the whole of life became enmeshed in a net of ritualistic and ceremonial prescriptions. Punctiliously to observe them all became, at times, well-nigh impossible.

2 The position of brahmans and other holy intellectuals in society

Whereas in China the mandarins form a stratum of officials and candidates for office, in India the brahmans represent a status group of literati partly comprising princely chaplains, partly counsellors, theological teachers and jurists, priest and pastors. In both cases only a portion of the status group occupied the characteristic positions. The typical prebends of the distinguished brahmans were not state-paid salaries and profit opportunities from tax collections and extortion in patrimonial state offices, but fixed land and tribute rent. Unlike the prebends of the mandarins which were subject to recall and at best granted for a short term, the brahman's rents were permanent grants for life, or for several generations, or forever in individuals and organizations (monasteries, schools). The highest brahman station in ancient times was that of court chaplain; later, and on to the time of British rule, the senior rank and consulting jurist, that is, the brahmanical chief *pandit*, was the first man of the land. In India the Hindu intellectuals (including kshatriyas and others during the Buddhist period) largely constituted a stratum of men educated in literature and philosophy and dedicated to speculation and discussion of ritualistic, philosophical and scientific questions.

3 Vashisha dharma and the absence of the concept of natural law

Weber observes that the power relation between brahmans and kshatriyas was quite unstable for a long time. However, even after the status superiority of the brahmans was theoretically established, the prerogatives of the great kings, who had meanwhile risen to power, remained independent and essentially secular. Indeed, the duties of the kings as against the brahmanical hierocracy, like those of any status group, were determined by their *dharma*, which formed part of brahmanically regulated holy law. But this *dharma* differed for every status group, hence also for the kings.

There was no universally valid ethic, but only a strict status compartmentalization of private and social ethic, disregarding the few absolute and general ritualistic prohibitions (particularly the killing of cows). This was of great moment. The doctrine of *karma* deduced from the principle of compensation for previous deeds of the world, not only explained the caste organization, but the rank order of divine, human and animal beings of all degrees. Hence it provided for the coexistence of different ethical codes for different status groups which not only differed widely but were often in sharp conflict.

Thus there was no 'natural' order of men and things in contrast to positive social order. There was no sort of 'natural law'. All the problems which the concept of 'natural law' called into being in the Occident were completely lacking. There simply was no 'natural' equality of man before any authority, least of all before a super-worldly god. This is the negative side of the case. Most important, it excluded forever the rise of social criticism of rationalistic speculation, and the abstraction of the natural law type, and hindered the development of any sort of idea of 'human rights'.

129

It may be stated here that Weber later on mentions the universal ethic in the form of non-injury to living beings, truthfulness, not stealing, living purely, controlling the passions, etc. Weber had already discussed this aspect in detail in his essay on 'Sociology of Law' in *Economy and Society* to which we have referred in chapter 3. As regards inequalities in society, it was not a peculiar feature of Indian society. Even in Europe certain privileges were enjoyed by the aristocracy for a long time and it took time to establish equal rights for all human beings irrespective of birth.

4 Rights and duties of the king

As patron of the *rayat* (client), the kshatriya had the ascribed *dharma* of 'protection' essentially in the sense of defence against the outside. The kshatriya was also responsible for the administration of justice and integrity of trade and related matters. Such ethical commandments were his *dharma*. For the rest it was the primary duty of the prince, as for others, but particularly for the prince, to support and further the brahmans, especially by sustaining their authoritarian regulation of the social order according to holy right, not to tolerate attacks upon the brahman's station. The struggle against anti-brahman heterodoxy is clearly required and it did occur. But this in no way altered the place of the prince, and politics retained its autonomy in a peculiarly significant manner.

The problem of a 'political ethics' has never preoccupied Indian theory and in the absence of ethical universalism and natural right, it could hardly be otherwise. The *dharma* of the prince was to conduct war for the sake of pure power *per se*. He had to destroy his neighbour by cunning and fraud by no matter what crafty or unknightly ruses, by surprise attack, when in distress through the instigation of conspiracies among his subjects and by bribing his trusted friends. All political theory was a completely oral technology of how to get and hold power. It went far beyond what was familiar and normal practice for the *signores* of the early Italian Renaissance in these respects and was completely devoid of all 'ideology' in our sense of the word. However, it may be mentioned here that Weber later on points out that in the Mahabharata emphasis was laid on the ethics of just war.[2]

5 The development of knowledge, asceticism and mysticism

(a) *The development of special sciences and philosophies*

It is typical of Hinduism, in contrast to the anti-professionalism of

Confucianism, to do justice in their own terms to the informing spirit of the most varied spheres of life and knowledge, promoting the development of special sciences. Thus it was that, alongside important mathematical and grammatical contributions, they developed especially a formal logic as the technology of rational proof. A special philosophical school, Nyaya (founded by Gotama) occupied itself with the technology of the syllogism and the Vaisesika school (recognized as orthodox), by applying these formal aids to cosmology, arrived at the theory of atomism. Indian natural science in many areas arrived at a level which Western science had attained about the fourteenth century. There are noteworthy contributions to anatomy, medicine, (excepting surgery, but including veterinary science) and music (*tosolfa*). Historical science, however, was altogether lacking. In all disciplines, including astronomy, developed for ritual purposes, and in mathematics (outside of algebra), Indian science measured by the standards of occidental science has essential achievements to its credit. It had the advantage of not having to contend with certain prejudices of Western religious ideas, i.e. the belief in resurrection which blocked the dissecting of corpses, and of an interest in the sophisticated control of the psychosomatic apparatus implementing the technique of contemplation. Western science did not raise such questions or have such interests. In India all science of social life remained in the form of a policing and cameralistic technology. This can well compare with the contributions of our seventeenth- and early eighteenth-century cameralism. Considering natural science and technical philosophy, however, one has the impression that noteworthy developmental beginning were somehow hindered. Unlike Hellenic science it did not even come near the beginnings of rational experimentation.[3]

The socially anchored unshakeability of certain metaphysical presuppositions pushed all philosophy in the direction of individual salvation-striving. For example the Vedanta school conceived of the empirical world as a cosmic illusion (*maya*). And the philosophic position taken on all problems was dominated by salvation interests. This served as a barrier to the development of special sciences as well as to a framing of the problem of thought in general. It produced terminologies for special callings and spheres of life and furnished no principles for an ethical universalism which would raise general demands for life in the world.

Such literature of India as one can pose as parallel with the philosophical ethic of the West was—or, better, became— something quite different, namely a metaphysically and cosmologically substructured technology of the means to achieve salvation from this world. This is the final, general anchorage point of all philosophical and theological interest in India.

(b) *Asceticism and mysticism* [4]

While the brahmans, like the mandarins enhanced their status by their knowledge of the social order, there remained, nevertheless, this vast difference: the Chinese literati constituted a political bureaucracy which renounced magical techniques as the scorned arts of sorcerers while the brahmans were by background and nature priests, i.e. magicians. This was the historical condition of the very different place asceticism and mysticism held for both.

Confucianism scorned magic as a parasitical humbug contrary to the distinguished man's sense of dignity. In contrast the brahmanhood was never able completely to shake off the historical relation to ancient magical asceticism out of which it had grown. The name of the novice (*bramacharin*) is derived from magical novitiate chastity and the stipulation of a contemplative forest life, so to speak, a form of retirement for the aged. In classical literature they are extended to the two other status groups of the 'twice-born' but were originally characteristic only of magician asceticism. Both prescriptions (novitiate chastity and contemplative forest life) are today and have indeed long been obsolete. However, their place in classical literature remains. And, finally, contemplative mysticism as a type of gnosis remains the crown of the classical brahmanical style of life, the goal of every well-educated brahman; though the number of those who actually pursue it was as small in the medieval past as today.

Requiring closer examination are the place of brahmanical culture with respect to asceticism and mysticism and, as far as the context makes it indispensable, also certain related philosophical representations growing out of the culture. The Hindu salvation religions, including Buddhism, arose on the basis of such philosophical conceptions, partly in typical apposition to them, but, in any case, only in close relation to them.

Technically, Indian asceticism was the most rationally developed in the world. There is hardly an ascetic method not practised with virtuosity in India and often rationalized into a theoretical technology. Often in India have some forms been pushed to their final—and, to us, often grotesque—conclusions. The *urdhamukti-sadhu's* downward suspension of the head and live burial (*samadh*) were still practised in the nineteenth century. Alchemy appears at present. The student of an alchemist who had once committed a sexual sin was immediately repudiated, for magical charisma adhered to a correct life.

The origin of classical asceticism was in the ancient practice of magical ecstasy with its various functions and with the usual purpose of achieving magical power. Ascetic magical potency (*tapas*) was conditioned through a sort of (hysterical) brooding intensity. With sufficient asceticism man could achieve anything, an idea still accepted as self-evident in classical Sanskrit drama.

The charismatic attainment of magical potency was highly personal and bound to no status group. Hence these magicians in earliest times were certainly not recruited only from official priestly or magician castes, as were the brahmans. While this continued to be possible, it was difficult, and becoming more so, as the brahmanhood turned into a status group of genteel experts, resting its claims on knowledge and genteel cultivation. The more this was the case the less was brahmanhood able to encompass all forms of magical asceticism. Thus the status pride of cultured men resisted undignified demands of ecstatic therapeutic practices and the exhibition of neuropathic states. Some magical practices, the acute-pathological, emotionally ecstatic—in this sense 'irritational'—were either explicitly rejected as unclassical and barbarian or actually not practised within the status group and precluded by its way of life. The magical elements retained were more systematically rationalized the more the brahmans turned into genteel literati. The brahmanical philosophy could not be understood without consideration of the importance of rationalized asceticism and ecstasy for all basic elements of correct brahmanical living.

The bramacharin (novice) was personally subordinate to the strict authority and household discipline of the teacher. He was enjoined to chastity and mendicancy and his life was ascetically ordered throughout. Retirement to the forests (as *vanaprastha*) was thought to be an ideal way of life for the aging brahman, leading finally to heart-searching in eternal silence as a hermit (the fourth *asrama*) and the attainment of the qualification as a *yati* (an ascetic, inwardly free of the world). Not only were these things present, but in a large measure the inner-worldly life-conduct of the classical brahman himself as *grihastha* (householder) was ascetically regulated. Alongside the avoidance of plebeian forms of profitable pursuits, above all trade, usury, and personal tillage, stood numerous proscriptions which later appeared again in the world-denying Hindu salvation religions.

The intensification of vegetarianism and abstinence from alcohol clearly developed out of opposition to meat orgies; the very strong tabooing of adultery and the admonition to control the sexual impulse in general has similar anti-orgiastic roots. Anger and passion were here, as in China, taboo because of the belief in the demonical and diabolic origin of all emotions. The commandment of rigid cleanliness, especially in eating, stemmed from magical purity rules. The commandment of veracity and liberality and the prohibition against laying hands on other peoples' property, in the last analysis, were but a sharpening of the universally valid (for the possessor) basic features of the ancient neighbourhood ethic.

However, he adds, that one should not, naturally, exaggerate the ascetic elements in the worldly way of life of the brahmans in historical times. For example in classical literature as well as in the *Puranas* there are repeated recommendations that one say what is true and pleasing, not what is untrue and pleasing, but possibly also not what is true and unpleasing.

Alongside the relative 'ascetic' features of the brahman's regulated workaday life stands the rational method for the achievement of extraordinary holy states. Indeed, there was a school (Mimamsa, founded by Jaimini) held to be orthodox, which acknowledged ceremonial good work *per se* as the holy path. But this is not the case for classical brahmanical teaching. In classical times the following was fundamental: ritual and other virtuous deeds alone could merely help improve rebirth chances, they could not lead to salvation. This last is always dependent on extraordinary behaviour qualitatively extending over and beyond the duties in the world of the castes; namely, ascetic flight from the world and contemplation.

Weber here also points out that classical literature contains repeated instances of brahmans instructed by wise kings in basic philosophic questions. That the ancient knighthood was well educated in literature, that the classical kshatriya, before the appearance of the great kingdoms, had participated in philosophical thought is beyond all doubt. In India, discussion of natural and religious philosophy reached a high point around the beginning of the seventh century B.C.[5] During this period, cultured laymen appear among the most important participants in the controversies. Certainly the brahmans never played a secondary role in this.

The brahmans were as little able to maintain the monopoly of personal mystic holy-seeking as that of philosophy and science. They certainly claimed it. This was because mystical holy-seekers, especially the anchorites, in India as elsewhere, were considered to be possessors of holy charisma, and even revered as saints and wonder-workers giving them a power the brahmans wished to monopolize for themselves. Until the present, official theory wished to recognize as full *sramana*, or *samana*, (hermit) among *sadhu* (monks) only the *sannyasi* in the early sense of the word, that is, those who transferred out of the brahmanical caste to the life of the monk. Orthodox teaching always rigorously reaffirmed this brahmanical monopoly, most sharply, of course, against the lower strata.

In the Ramayana an ascetic of great miraculous powers has his head cut off by heroes because he is a shudra and has nevertheless dared to assume these superhuman capabilities. This very passage indicates, however, that even according to orthodox learning in the time of the epics the shudra was capable of achieving magical powers through asceticism. And the monopolistic claim, never given up officially, was never completely effective in practice.

The brahmanical hermit upon achieving the quality of *yati* (full-ascetic) always appeared (1) as teacher and (2) as magical helper in time of need, gathering scholars and lay admirers around him. The bonds of piety which bound such a holy teacher and spiritual adviser, the *guru,* or *gosian,* to his students and clients was in Hindu ethics so extraordinarily strong that these relations could have and must have been basic to almost all religious organizations. Each guru enjoyed an authority over his students superior to that of a father. If he lived as a *sramana* the guru was an object of worship by the laity (hagiolatry). At least in the time of the Upanishads, it was assumed that only a guru could impart proper wisdom. Hence quite a few identifiable founders of philosophical schools and sects have left behind them hierocratic dynasties, which often for centuries elaborated the founder's learning and technique of gnosis. The monk's way of life represented an intensification of routine brahmanical asceticism, partly simply in degree, partly however, also in nature and meaning. The last was determined by the interrelation with brahmanical holy doctrine as developed in the Brahmanas and Upanishads.

The following represent merely intensification of routine asceticism: the command of chastity; abstinence from sweet nourishment (confining nourishment to fallen fruit); owning no property; prohibition from storing goods; living from begging (later usually under the restriction to accept only the remains of the donor's meal); the commandment to wander (later often intensified by the injunction to sleep only one night in a village or not to sleep there at all), the restriction of clothes to basic necessities.

The transformation of classical brahmanical asceticism from magical to soteriological ends was consummated in the religious literature in the wake of the Veda collections, namely, the Brahmanas which deal interpretatively with sacrifice and ritual, and especially the following Aranykas 'works created in the forest'. They are the products of contemplative, elderly brahmans living in the retirement of forest retreats. The speculative sections, the Upanishads, 'secret teachings' comprise the decisive soteriological parts of brahmanical wisdom. (They represent *jnanakanda,* that is, gnosis, in contrast to *karma-kanda,* the knowledge of ritual.) The Sutra literature contains the ritual prescriptions for practical use: the *srautacastra,* the holy ritual, the *smartacastra,* the ritual of everyday life (*grihyasutra*) and the social order (*dharmacastra*). The ancient rhapsodists were succeeded by the *vyasas* (compilers) on the one side, and by the speculative brahmans on the other. Both were later replaced by poets and reciters who elaborated the *kavaya* forms, combining story-telling with instruction. These poets were partially *pauranikas* and *acthiasikas,* story-tellers of edificatory myths, myths for an essentially intellectualized urban public; partially, they were *dhamapatakas,* the reciters of the law books, who probably took the place of the ancient law speaker (and with Manu and in the epics had a stake in commissions for expert opinions on doubtful cases).

A difficult journey is in store for the Western reader once he leaves the world of the Rig-Veda and popular fable, which are gathered in the *Panchatantra* and are the sources of almost all the fables of the world, or when he leaves the world of secondary art drama and lyric to enter the field of religious poetry and philosophical literature. Most of the Upanishads not expected, the Western reader will find a mass of quite implastic, because rationally intended, symbols and images alongside inwardly dry schematism; and only at long intervals may he chance upon the fresh source of a true, and not apparently dead, insight. This peculiarity of brahmanical thought contributed its part to those internal impediments which prevented further development.

The most important restriction which issued from the focus of attention of Indian thought was that it was indifferent to the actualities of the world, and through gnosis, sought the one thing needful beyond it—salvation from it. The perspective was formerly determined by the techniques of contemplation of the intellectual strata.

6 Yoga and the development of religious philosophy

Weber observes that like all methodologies of apathetic ectasy, technologies of contemplation were based on the same theoretical principle the Quakers[6] formulated, that 'God only speaks in the soul when the creature is silent'. In practice this doubtless rests on the ancient magical experience of auto-hypnosis and related psychological states, and is induced by physiological effects of controlled regulation and temporary stoppages of breathing and its reaction upon brain functions. The emotional states resulting from such practices were valued as holy and cherished as blissful removal of the soul. They formed the psychological basis of the philosophical speculations which sought rationally to establish the significance of these emotional states.

Among the varieties of techniques for inducing apathetic ectasy, the yoga technique was championed by the Hindu philosophic school of yoga. According to this school, yoga signifies exertion and asceticism, and represents the rationalization of ecstatic practice (of ancient sorcerers). It is said that originally it was Krishna Hero who imparted this technique to Vivasvat, the tribal god of the kshatriya caste and he in turn to the old sages of the warriors. It is necessary to mention this here because variations of yoga appear in orthodox as well as heterodox teachings. It gained greater influence than any other equivalent technique and represents the characteristic holy techniques of the intellectuals. Whether it actually had its main origin inside or outside brahman circles can hardly be decided. Historically it was diffused beyond these circles.

The yoga technique places central emphasis upon controlled breathing and related means of inducing apathetic ecstacy. In this connection it concentrates the conscious psychic and mental functions upon the partly meaningful, partly meaningless flow of inner experiences. They may be endowed with an indefinite emotional and devotional character, but are always controlled through self-observation to the point of completely emptying consciousness of anything expressible in rational words, by gaining deliberate control over the inner motions of heart and lungs and, finally, auto-hypnosis. Intellectually, yoga technique presupposes that the grasp of the godly is an irrational psychic experience available by irrational means which allegedly have nothing to do with rational, demonstrable knowledge.

However, Weber also observes that the classical brahmanical intellectualism has never completely accepted this view, for it places knowledge *per se* in the centre of all holy means. In the first place, this includes knowledge of rituals peculiar to the brahman guild. The salvation-seeking brahman, however, beyond this, sought the metaphysical, practitional gnostic interpretation of their cosmological meaning. This conceptual goal developed gradually out of the rationalization and sublimation of holy practices. As in other religions the right (ethical) intention displaces mere externally correct thought, so that in brahmanism, corresponding to its specific prestige of wisdom and thought, the right idea became paramount. Right thought and right knowledge were held to be the sources of magical power. Here, as elsewhere, such knowledge did not retain the character of ordinary common sense. The supreme good could be achieved only through a higher knowledge: a gnosis.

Yoga technique, on the other hand, sought primarily to achieve magical states and miraculous power. Thus, for example, one sought the power to suspend gravitation and to gain the ability to float around. Moreover, one sought to gain omnipotence with power directly to realize imagined events without external action by virtue of the magical will-power of the yogin. Finally, omniscience was sought, that is, clairvoyance, especially of other men's thoughts.

Two purposes of yoga

Classical brahmanical contemplation sought the blissful rapture of a gnostic comprehension of the godly. All intellectualized holy techniques had one of two purposes: either (1) through the emptying of consciousness they attempted to make room for the holy, which then is more or less clearly felt because it is incommunicable; or (2) by combining internally isolating techniques, which concentrated meditation, they sought to achieve a state experienced not as feeling, but as gnostic knowledge. The opposition is not sharp, but classical brahmanical contemplation in agreement with the nimbus of wisdom, was inclined to the second, so much so that the Nyaya school could even consider its pursuit of empirical knowledge as the holy path. This, of course, hardly corresponded to the classical brahmanical type which is firmly convinced of the metaphysical nature of gnosis. Hence it cherished mechanical meditation techniques of achieving 'institution' as a psychic experience never to be gained via empirical proof. It, therefore, never completely rejected yoga practices. In fact, yoga was, in its way, also a supreme form of a specific, intellectualistic, conquest of the godly. For the feelings intended through ever higher levels of concentration (*samadhi*) first had to be experienced with the greatest possible consciousness. To achieve this the sentiments of friendship (to God), sympathy (for creatures) beatitude and, finally, indifference (toward the world) were methodically and rationally pursued in the self thought meditative exercises. Thus only the highest step is catalepsy.

Classical yoga rejected irrational mortification, the *hatha yoga* of pure magical asceticism. It was, for its part, a rationally systemized form of methodical, emotional asceticism, and therein somewhat comparable to the spiritual exercises of St. Ignatius Loyola. Its systematization essentially represented a level of rationalization superior to that of contemplation. The latter, however, was more rational with regard to the intended 'set', namely, knowledge, not feeling, was sought.

7 Salvation doctrines

Among salvation doctrines Weber discusses the concentration techniques which free a man from the bondage of *karma* and help in the attainment of *moksha*; *purusha* and *prakriti* tinged with the three *gunas, satva, rajas* and *tamas,* and *moksha,* through gnosis and mysticism; *moksha* by following rituals and universal ethic of life through progeny. The knowledge may be conceived by two different paths which may be monistic or dualistic.

Concentration techniques

Weber observes that the historical origin of devout concentration upon the sacred prayer—syllable 'Om'—cannot be ascertained. The mechanical repetition of this magically efficacious word assists in emptying the consciousness of worldly thoughts. In addition to this technique there are others with similar functions. The purpose is always to free one's self from the world of the senses, from anxieties, passions, drives and striving, and the purposeful considerations of everyday life, thereby preparing one's self for a final state signifying eternal rest (that is, the salvation (*moksha, mukti*) from these pressures) and unison with the godly.

All salvation technologies of India stemming from the intellectual strata, involve a withdrawal, not only from everyday life but from the world in general, including also paradise and the world of the gods. Thus in the classical form brahmanical salvation is always absolute salvation from the world. The world is an eternal, meaningless 'wheel' of recurrent births and deaths steadily rolling on through all eternity. Only two non-temporal realities are discoverable in it: the eternal order itself, and those beings who, through escape of on-going rebirths, must be conceived as their subjects. They are the souls.

The central concern of all Hindu philosophy was with the structure and relation of these beings to the world and the godhead. The one and only one question of Hindu philosophy was: how could souls be disentangled from the web of the *karma*-casuality tying them to the wheel of the world? An absolute presupposition of Hindu philosophy after the full development of the *karma* and *samsara* doctrines was that escape from the wheel of rebirth could be the one and only conceivable function of a 'salvation'.

This conclusion, so fraught with consequence, was, of course, only gradually attained and, even then, it was by no means universal. Even though the *karma* and *samsara* doctrine have become the general property of Hindu thought, the concept of an impersonal godhead and the un-createdness of world have not. Indeed, as a rule, the last was accepted even where people believed in personalized gods of the world.

The later cosmologies, such as are contained in the Puranas, ordinarily visualized the world as evolving through a series of ages. In the Vishnu Purana the various ages designated as Krita, Treta, Dvapara and Kali unceasingly follow one another. In the Kali-age the upper castes disintegrated, the shudra and the heresies come to the fore, for Brahma is asleep. Vishnu then assumes the form of Rudra (Shiva) and destroys all existent forms: the twilight of the gods sets in. However, then Brahma awakens in the form of Vishnu, the merciful god, and the world begins anew.

The early cosmologies either do not know such supreme deities or recognize them under different names and plural forms in a way of no interest here. Of more importance is the change of thought pattern. Very slowly the early, personal god-father and creator of the world (*prajapati*) has been displaced by the impersonal brahman principle, originally the magical prayer formula, then a magical world potency. There was, however, a growing tendency for this potency, in turn, to be endowed with the traits of a personalized, super-worldly god-Brahma, who, according to classical learning, no longer has created the world out of nothing. The world, rather, has emanated from him or appeared by individualizations. His supra-divine nature was perhaps established for theory by the fact that as the functional god of prayer, he could not himself be subject to the magical compulsion of prayer. Below the circles of philosophically schooled brahmanical intellectuals, in fact, in their very midst, there always reappeared in some form the actually unclassical belief in a supreme, personal-creator God, over and above the crowd of local and functional deities—the *ekantika dharma*—(we would say monotheism). With this appeared belief in saviours and salvation in paradise.

Yoga, particularly, with its irrational asceticism and the personal emotional character of its holy states did not, at least in the form given it by Patanjali, eliminate the personal supreme god (Isvara, 'ruler'). Of course, in strict logic his existence was hardly consistent with *karma* and *samsara*. Indeed, the question properly arose as to the consistency or the ideas of creation and reign of this world belaboured with suffering, torment, and vanity and a supreme god. Alongside less consistent solutions to this question (in the Maitrayana-Upanishad) the answer appears as follows: the supreme being called this thing to life for his own diversion and enjoyment.

On the other hand, the orthodox assumption of a possible salvation of souls from the wheel of rebirth would certainly have led to the concept of a temporarily finite world. If not in this form, it would have led to the conception of an end to the process of unceasing rebirths under the assumption of a finite number of souls. Actually, to escape this conclusion the most consistent school posited an infinitude of souls.[7] Thus the redeemed ones who had attained beatitudes were not only, as in Christianity, a remnant, but this number became infinitesimally small. In polar opposition to the belief in election by divine grace, this doctrine left it entirely to the individual soul to work out its own fate.

Two basic doctrines

As already stated the basic teaching of the entire theory of salvation, namely, transmigration of souls and ethical compensation, were gradually developed. In the Brahmanas the first was still quite undeveloped. The second only made its appearance in the Upanishads. Once conceived, these teachings isolate the transitory nature of earthly things as the essential reason for the devaluation of the world. They also established the idea that the manifold nature of the world, its forms and individuals, is the decisive sign of its apostasy or at least remoteness from Brahma (and no longer, as it once was, his creation). Consistent extension of these ideas imparts to Brahma the quality of impersonal oneness and—as this vanished behind the phenomenal pluralism of things—at the same time, the hidden negation of the world.

Indian philosophy essentially represents a theory of metaphysical structure of the soul as the vehicle of individuation. According to a widely-held version, the breath was originally considered to be the substance, so to speak, of the immaterial, of the 'psychic' and 'mental' in man. The originally related concept 'atman', therefore, represents the sublimation of such ideas into the concealed, immaterial, magical unity of the 'self', In the Mudeka-Upanishad, the inner self still consists of 'breath' which also in the Khandogya-Upanishad is conceived as something special in contrast to all other organs indispensable to life. In these sources it is already incorporeal. In this last source there is also found the 'astral' body of a spiritual self. In the Maitrayana-Upanishad it becomes simply 'what a man thinks that he is'. Thoughts alone cause the cycle of rebirth when orientated to the world rather than to the Brahma. The famous passage in the Khandogya-Upanishad (1, 1, 10) in which the teacher conducts the student through the realm of the living from the seed of grain to man, unceasingly calling attention to the inwardly turned 'fine essence' of life, 'by virtue of which all exists that has a self' (the Indian conception of 'entelechy') with the

141

constant refrain—'that is the essence that is the self—and that, Osvetakatu, is thou (*tat tyam asi*)'—belongs to the most striking formulations of old brahmanical wisdom.

The close relation of classical brahmanical thought to magic hindered the transformation of the concept of the highest world potency into a 'substance' as occurred in Hellenistic philosophy. From this vantage point one can readily understand why all materialistic speculation was sharply rejected as heterodox. It would have led in a similar direction.

On the other hand, the rationalization of apathetic ecstasy into meditation and contemplation, as the (yoga) technique of self-concentration, once carried out consistently awakened special and unsurpassed capacities among virtuoso-like, consciously intellec-tualistic Indians, for various psychic processes of the self, particularly feeling states. The habituation of one's self, to an interest in the events and processes of one's psychic life at the same time that the self is turned into a disinterested observer was achieved through yoga technique. This must have quite naturally led to conception of the 'I' as an entity also standing outside all 'spiritual' processes of consciousness, and, indeed, outside the organic depository of consciousness and its 'narrowness'.

Purusha and prakriti

Similar to the Chinese dualism of *yang* and *yin,* the duality of world potencies appears therefore in the early Upanishads as sources of individuation. The masculine spirit principle, the *purusha,* is entangled with the feminine principle, primordial matter, the *prakriti.* Therein the undeveloped, materially conceived psychic and mental powers of the empirical world are slumbering. They include, particularly, the three basic powers of the soul, the three *gunas*: *satva*, namely, divine brightness and benevolence; *rajas*, human striving and passions; and *tamas*, bestial darkness and stupidity. All conceivable modes of internal behaviour in the usual schematism and pedantic–fantastic manner were reduced to the operation of mixtures of these three powers. More important is the fact that already in the Upanishads, *purusha* appears as the spectator who takes no active part in the business of the world and the soul as conjured up by the *prakriti.* Of course, as soon as he attains wisdom and views the *prakriti* and her doings for what they are, she will behave 'like a woman from a good family, when seen naked': she will withdraw and leave him at liberty for that eternal, immobile tranquillity peculiar to his nature.

Universal ethic of life

With these conclusions brahmanical speculation found itself faced with several important difficulties which adhere to mysticism in general, but especially to gnostic mysticism. For one thing, from such mysticism no ethic for life within the world could be deduced. The Upanishads contain nothing or almost nothing of what we call ethics. For another, salvation through gnostic wisdom alone came into sharpest tension with the traditional content of holy writing. The gnostic doctrines led to the devaluation not just of the world of the gods but, above all, of ritual. But the orthodox remedied the situation through 'organic' relativism. There is no universal 'ethic', but only a status—and professionally—differentiated *dharma* according to caste. But also one should not forgo all and every formulation of a general teaching of virtue for the gentleman (*arya*). The law books particularly (the books of house ritual, the Grihya-Sutras) could hardly dispense with such. The eight virtues, once ten in number, are unusually colourless. Forbearance, patience, freedom from envy, purity, tranquillity, correct life, freedom from desire, and freedom from covetousness are the eight good qualities of the soul in Gautama's law book (the oldest perhaps pre-Buddhistic). The virtues listed by Manu are given somewhat more positive turn: contentment, patience, self-control, non-stealing, purity, control of desire, piety, knowledge, truthfulness, and freedom from anger. These were also condensed into five commandments for all castes: to injure no living being, to tell the truth, not to steal, to live purely, to control the passions. Quite similar commandments appear as the first step of yoga.

However, the tension between this concept of salvation and Vedic ritual was not settled by such commandments. And for the layman in search of salvation who did not qualify for training in gnostic wisdom, the Vedic ritual and house ritual (Grihya-Sutras) remained all-important. For the law books, too, the Vedic gods and sacrifices, the heavens and hells as means of compensation and punishment remained the decisive and most ultimate realities of man's life. For the layman who did not qualify in gnostic wisdom Ancestor worship remained a central concern.

Continuation of progeny

In agreement with the significance of ancestor worship and, thus, of progeny for the death peace and ancestral bliss, an especially delicate question was posed: whether one could be permitted to be a *sramana* without having first produced progeny. Even if one believed it to be no longer needful to perform ancestral sacrifices on behalf of one's self, one must not leave his forebears unprovided for by successors. Thus the law books generally take as self-evident the fact that the individual must pass through all the marital stages to attain merit in the beyond. With this emerged the conception that continued life or 'immortality' consists in nothing else but continued existence in one's own progeny.

Different ways of holy-seeking: knowledge versus rituals

The philosophical holy teaching, known as *cruti,* that is, 'salvation', in contrast to *sriti,* i.e. 'traditional ritual', has accepted the relativization of the holy paths according to intent and the personal charisma of the holy-seeker. The gods are present and they are powerful. However, their heavenly world is transitory. By means of correct ritual the laity may join them. So, too, may he who properly studies the Vedas, because his mental power does not suffice for more. However, whoever has the charisma of gnosis can escape this world of ephemeral things. If gnosis is the highest soteriological means, its substance may develop along two separate courses.

The concept of maya

Knowledge may be of the material-psychic-mental processes of reality as a world of the qualitatively particular, which is the forever becoming and passing away, in contrast to the eternally unchangeable and quality-less self: the heterogeneous, but actually existing, from which the self turns away. Then, the dualism of the knowing self and known matter (including the so-called 'mental processes') is taken as the basic metaphysical fact. Or knowledge may be 'gnosis' in a much more specific sense: the world of reality of eternal growth and decay simply cannot be 'true'. It is an appearance (*maya*), a phantasmagoria presented through the enchantment of knowledge by a daemonical creature, the demi-urge (Isvara). Thus *maya* 'creates' the world. Reality is an attribute not of this apparent growth and decay, but of a being, which, in this semblance of change, remains self-identical. Naturally, this is a transcendant reality, it is a divine being; it is Brahman. By means of the organs of knowledge (belonging to the realm of semblances) this Brahman issues through individuation in the individual mind. When, by means of knowledge, this cosmic illusion is destroyed, emancipation from suffering under this illusion is consummated. Once having attained gnosis the mind is no longer needful. The mind can be brought to this state only by suitable means, for the gnosis is no ordinary knowledge but a 'possession'.

144

Monistic versus dualistic

This peculiar religious difference of both conceptions which is in practice more important than the theoretical contrasts, thus rests upon this conception of the illusory nature of reality. Liberating knowledge can be attained only by a mystical reunion of the spirit, which has been individualized only through its cosmic illusion, with the divine, All-One, Brahman. For the *dualistic* points of view, recognizing reality as true, a Brahman is, in the last analysis, superfluous for the successful holy-seeking attained through systematic schooling of knowledge in the sense of yoga practice. Thus the dualistic doctrine does not concern itself with the Brahman and is, in this sense, *'atheistic'*: the soul sinks into eternal dreamless sleep, but it does not vanish. Monistic brahman doctrine might be called 'pantheistic', if one intends this rather inappropriate term to cover adequately the quite specific metaphysical 'superworldliness' of the Brahman as the truly real opposite for cosmic semblance.

The dualistic doctrine of reality was elaborated by the Samkhya school, which Kapila first systematically established. The monistic doctrine of cosmic illusion is known under the name of 'Vedanta'. Samkhya teaching is already anticipated in the Upanishads and is without doubt older and prior to the Vedanta doctrine. This is proved by its relation to yoga, which technique furnished the preconditions for its constructions.

Vedanta which was written down in the Brahma-Sutras of Badarayana, and later commented upon by Gankara, the pre-eminent philosopher of the school, later became the classical system of orthodox brahmanical Hinduism. This is certainly not astonishing. The proud denial of any form of belief in God, and the acknowledgment of the reality of being in Samkhya doctrine were inevitably more congenial to a stratum of cultured brahmans and lay intellectuals drawn from knightly circles in the time before the development of the great kingdoms. However, to the priestly caste which stood for the great partimonial kings, the existence and mystical access to godly power was of central interest. It was able to bring its teachings easily into harmony with the presuppositions of Vedic literature, a goal which can be seen from its very name (Vedanta means 'end, conclusion of the Veda'). As a truly fundamental emotional disposition, it is first found in the late Upanishads, though some traces of it were also seen in old Vedic literature.

8 Six major schools of philosophy

The great Indian doctrinal systems represented proud and rather rational conceptions of thinkers who were consistent in their ways.

THE MAIN CHARACTERISTICS OF HINDUISM IN EARLY TIMES

The mystic nature of the holy, so strongly determining their teachings, resulted from the internal situation of a stratum of intellectuals who as thinkers face life and ponder its meaning but do not share its practical tasks as doers. This kind of orientation, sensitivity, and 'world feeling' that resulted was only in part derived from their rational image of the world. It was in part also determined by striving after holiness through contemplation. When in one of the Upanishads[8] the three cardinal virtues of the Indian were named as self-control, generosity and compassion, the second may be seen to be of knightly, the first of brahmanical origin. 'Compassion', however, was clearly the product of a worldly euphoria typically bound up with apathetic mystical ecstasy and later elevated to universal ethical significance in Buddhism.

Among the six official orthodox Veda schools were Jaimini's Mimansa, Kapil's Samkhya, Vyasa's Vedanta, Gotama's Nyaya, Kanada's Vaicesika and Patanjali's Yoga. Vedanta was the old Mimansa. Mimansa was divided into two: Purva (early) Mimansa ant Uttara (later) and it is Purva which is near to Vedanta. Among the six schools Samkhya and Vedanta were so outstandingly important that the metaphysics of the rest can be ignored here. Also we are concerned with the doctrines of both great schools only in so far as they determine practical ethics in a manner important for our context.

Their basic principles

The 'orthodoxy' of all six schools was expressed in the fact that they recognized the authority of the Vedas, that is to say, they did not dispute the binding character of ritual duties developed in brahmanical literature and did not attack the position of the brahmans. The orthodox philosophic schools have always recognized the pluralism of holy paths (*marga*). Ritual works, asceticism, and wisdom were the three they recognized as classical from the beginning. However, only the last two led beyond the bounds of the *karma*-chain. This holds above all for wisdom. This wisdom was gnosis, 'illumination', for which the expressions, 'bodhi' and 'Buddha' occasionally appear. Its soteriological significance lay in its capacity for dissolving the unfortunate linkage of spirit and matter, the 'materialization' (*upadhi*) of the 'I'. The state of complete dematerialization or elimination of all 'material basis' (*upadhi*) was designated later as *nirvana,* a psychic state which sets in when all relation with the world has been severed. But this state is not necessarily other-worldly in the sense that it can be entered upon only after death.

Vedanta particularly placed decisive emphasis on this earthly joy attained through unison with Brahma. It also meant a this-worldly emancipation from the *karma*-chain. Through perfect knowledge the redeemed *jivanmukta* escapes the ethical compensation mechanism. No act clings to him. Ritual no longer binds him. Both the main schools, i.e. Samkhya and Vedanta (e.g. see the Taittireya-Upanishad) had this conclusion. As a result of this the ritual suffered devaluation and the great ascetic became a guru.

'Corresponding to the organically graded holy statuses there were: redeemed ones (*jivanmukta*); other-worldly aspirants to salvation by means of asceticism or contemplation; the ritually correct and Veda-educated Brahmans; and further, the simple laity'.9 In accord with this the attempt was naturally made to bring the steps of extra-worldly, soteriological, *karma*-free holy-seeking and the inner-worldly *karma*-ethic together into organic relation. In the Samkhya soteriology, for example, the following stages, from lower to higher, were held to be means of perfection: (1) liberality—corresponding to the ancient Vedic virtue; (2) intercourse with wise friends, (3) personal studies; (4) instructing others; and finally (5) meditation or deliberation of reason (*uha*). Whoever truly strove for the supreme goal should strive for unconditional physical detachment (*virage*). Desire and grief destroy receptivity. One should, therefore, give up possessions and above all, withdraw from the company of all men save those possessing wisdom. According to pure Samkhya doctrine social acts were valueless for salvation. Vedanta teaching on the other hand has always esteemed rites and 'work', i.e. traditional social duties as valuable for .salvation-striving. However, here the idea was that the correct fulfilment of external duties of ritual, and particularly sacrificial duties, indirectly facilitated the attainment of right wisdom and not that they were themselves a path to salvation. According to Vedanta, only he who has attained perfect wisdom and therewith bliss has no more use for the rites.

9 Professional ethics of Mahabharata

If everyday duties and the holy path to brahmanical understanding thus had been brought into a reasonably satisfactory mutual relation of organic stages, this solution was not satisfactory for the needs of the educated laity, particularly the knighthood. While the brahman could pursue meditation alongside his ritualistic everyday profession, the warrior could hardly do so. His status *dharma* was irreconcilable with any sort of escape from the world. However, he was hardly disposed to see himself treated as religiously inferior.

147

The tension between everyday-*dharma* and holy striving partly contributed to the establishment of those heterodox salvation religions to be discussed later, and partly, however, to a further development of soteriology within the orthodoxy.

Its classical literary source is, of course, the Mahabharata (non-definitive edition dating from about the sixth century B.C.), and especially one of the philosophical dialogue insertions with which this work abounds. On the one hand we encounter residues of the belief in 'fate' and an arbitrary play of chance with men, a belief close to all warrior heroism. It is a belief which can hardly be harmonized with the *karma*-doctrine without difficulty. Further, especially in the conversations of King Yudhischthira with his heroes and with the Draupadi, we encounter discussions of the 'justice' of the fate of the individual hero and of the 'right' of war. Many of them indicate that the purely autonomous (Machiavellian) conceptions of the *dharma* of princes resulted only in part from the political conditions of the later *signores*-epoch and partly from consistent brahmanical ratiocination. In detail, King Yudhischthira of the epic in his blameless misfortune discusses with his spouse the reign of God. The woman comes to the conclusion that the great God only plays with men according to his whims. It is by the grace of God that the good receive immortality. This has quite a different ring from the philosophy of the Upanishads which knows nothing of such a world regime by a personal God. It is taken over from the ancient father-God of the brahmans, who stands above the unethical deities of the Vedas. The Vedic gods also are all to be found, but they are powerless. The hero does not fear them. They cannot help him, they can only cool his forehead and admire him.

Arjuna is convinced of the meaning of 'fate', also he externally commits himself to the philosophy of the brahmans. The ancient Valhalla, India's warrior heaven, is, it seems, his true goal, and death on the field of honour, death which here as elsewhere is amenable. At least in one place it is stated that this is better than asceticism and the land attainable through ascetism. Action is better than doing nothing. Since the hero also practised asceticism, and since the power of the ascetic and the significance of holy knowledge is completely fixed for him as well, this pure heroic ethic can only be one aspect of the matter. So it is in fact. The Mahabharata, as a whole, represents a peculiar mixture of features of an ancient, humanistically intellectualized ethic of proud knights. 'Nothing is nobler than being human', says the epic,[10] with the bourgeois need for assurance in the grace of a God guiding man's fate according to his will and with priestly, mystical indifference to the world.

10 The holy teachings of the Bhagavad-gita

The question of the ethical implications of hero dharma and war is discussed at length in the very famous episode, known by the name of Bhagavad-gita. Externally it represents a discussion directly preceding the bloody battle between opponents related by blood, between the hero Arjuna, who is concerned during the battle about the justice of killing such close relatives, and his chariot master Krishna, who successfully disputes such worries. Krishna, however, is viewed already by the poet as a human incarnation (avatar) of the supreme divine being, the Bhagavat (the majestic), and we already find ourselves on the ground of these epiphanies which dominated the unclassical, folk-saviour religiosity of later Hinduism. The characteristic emotional traits of this religiosity, so important for the India of the Middle Ages—to be discussed later—were still in their beginning. In the central points we meet the product of the genteel intellectual stratum of ancient times.

The historical status of the figure of Krishna is disputed. While occasionally he has been held to be an ancient sun god, outstanding scholars have maintained that he was, rather, the deified author of the Bhagavata religion. (There was an ancient community of Bhagavata worshippers who championed the kind of soteriology rendered by the Bhagavad-Gita.) Without going into this controversy let us discuss the essential features of the Bhagavad-Gita.

Under close inspection it may be seen that to Arjuna's thoughts against fighting close relatives in battle, Krishna answered with several rather heterogeneous arguments. Firstly, the death of these enemies was decided anyway and could occur even without Arjuna's doings. Moreover, Arjuna's kshatriya nature would drive him into battle even without his will, this being beyond his control. Here 'causality' is read into the determinism of caste-*dharma*. However, the question remains why then should Arjuna fight at all? Because in the eyes of the warrior the fight is good and so especially is the 'righteous' war. To avoid a battle is shameful. Whoever falls in battle goes to heaven.

However, action has to be taken without wishing for reward. In action this is achieved by performing everything without ever seeking success and giving up all and every wish for the fruits of endeavour. Such desires would lead to entanglement in the world, hence the emergence of *karma*.

One cannot dispense with works so long as one has a body (such works include spiritual functions materially conceived by Samkhya doctrine), but one may well dispense with the fruits of such works.[11]

The derivation of the Bhagavata religiosity from the kshatriya ethic makes it probable that it is older than the official ethic which, in reverse gives a higher place to meditation as the business of charismatic saints. However, both holy paths are acknowledged to be correct. *Jnana-yoga* (right knowledge) and *karma-yoga* (right action), each corresponding to the respective caste-*dharma* are ordered alongside one another. Also in the education of the cultured laity the place of methodical contemplation as the classical path to gnosis was no longer to be shaken. The derivation from the stratum of cultured intellectuals is clear throughout. This is obvious in the absolute rejection of orgiastic ecstasy and all active asceticism. In the Bhagavad-Gita, senseless asceticism full of desire, passion, and defiance is of daemonic character[12] and leads to ruin. Over and against that, the intimate relation of Bhagavata piety to classical yoga is quite obvious and fully in agreement with the Samkhya dualism of known spirit and known content of consciousness evinced in numerous passages of the poem.

The *yogin* is more than an ascetic and—characteristic of the original attitude of classical brahmanical teaching—also more than a 'knower'.[13] Yoga technique, the regulation of breath and perception are extolled.[14] General Hindu principles find their correspondence in the commandments of world indifference: the avoidance of lust, rage and greed as the three gates of hell,[15] the inner emancipation from attachment to home, wife and children and absolute ataxia[16] are here again bidden to the redeemed. The statement that he who knows spirit and matter will not be reborn 'no matter how he has conducted his life' is opposed at least to the classical principles of yoga and is also non-Vedantic, representing, rather, an extreme Samkhya formula. The anomic consequence which we have come to know in classical Hinduism, in the last analysis, as resulting from the position of the redeemed believer (*jivan-mukti*), in the Bhagavata religion, however, was brought into relation to a theme we have not previously encountered, and one which also actually represents an alien element in classical teaching; 'lay down all duties in me, your refuge',[17] Krishna says occasionally. Even a miscreant who truly loves Krishna became holy. Dying with the syllable 'Om' on one's lips and in thought of Krishna gives assurance against ruin in the future life.[18]

Here a type of religion of 'faith' emerges. For 'faith' in the typically religious sense does not necessarily intend facts and teachings to be true—such belief in dogmas can only be fruit and symptom of the actual religious sense. A religion of faith implies the religious devotion, the unconditional trust and obedience and the orientation of one's entire life to a god or redeemer. Krishna here appears as such a redeemer. This concept which, except perhaps for weak traces in some of the Upanishads, is lacking in ancient classical Hinduism because it presupposes the super-worldly god and, at bottom, signifies also a disruption of *karma* causality or, at least, of the ancient principle that the soul should alone be responsible for its own peculiar fate. Originally, the concept of dispensing grace *per se* is not foreign to Hindu religion. The hagiology-worshipping magicians, dispensing grace by virtue of their charisma and the grace of the super-mundane, personalized God or deified hero—suggested itself as the transposition of the human into the divine. However, the thought that salvation from the world be available along this path is a new phenomenon. The first scriptural mention of the Bhagavata religion would seem to date from the second century B.C. (the cult of Bhagavat Samkarshana, also Vasudeva) and to this we shall refer in the next chapter.

However, the Bhagavata religion also preserved its character as religion of intellectuals in its unconditional retention of gnosis hence of the holy aristocracy of knowledge. Only the wise were holy. In fact, it carried these conceptions to their logical conclusion by relativizing the paths of salvation along organic status-group lines. All honestly and zealously pursued holy paths lead also to the goal, namely, the particular goal sought by the aspirant. One should not disturb the ignorant 'who are attracted to action' that is to say, who never free themselves from striving for the fruits of action and do not attain indifference to things worldly. The knowing man, indeed, acts in an elevated state (yoga) of indifference to the world, but he calls the work of the ignorant 'good'.[19] This is quite similar to the Chinese mystics who leave the masses with their material pleasures and personally strive for Tao. The reason is the same in both cases, namely that people vary in receptivity to religious experience, as every virtuoso knows.

The inner-worldly ethic of the Bhagavad-Gita is 'organismic' in a sense hardly to be surpassed. Indian 'tolerance' rests upon this absolute relativizing of all ethical and soteriological commandments. They are organically relativized not only according to caste membership, but also according to the goal or end sought by the individual.

Appraisal

In the above few pages Weber sketches the main characteristics of Hinduism from early times to the Middle Ages when the Bhagavata religion in the form of personal God appears. The religion prevalent during the period 1500 to 500 B.C. is popularly known as Vedic religion, when brahmans alone had the privilege of studying Vedas and other sacred books and performing sacrifices.[20] Buddhism starts from 600 B.C. and it becomes more popular after 200 B.C. in the reign of Asoka. The main sacred books of this period are the Vedas, Brahmanas, Aranyakas, Upanishads and Sutras.[21] Then there are Itihas, Puranas and Kavyas. Among the Itihas are included two epics Mahabharata and Ramayana, including Bhagavad-Gita. Connected with the above literature is the Indian philosophy based on Upanishads. This was in a chaotic condition and they were systematized in a manual from the first century A.D.

Weber's analysis of Hindu religion of this period is quite penetrating and incisive in certain respects but quite shallow in other aspects. Weber rightly points out that the Vedic religion in the beginning laid more emphasis on ritualism than on the orgiastic and ecstatic element, as was done in China. Similarly, whereas in China the mandarins formed a stratum of officials paid salaries by the state, the brahman literati, some of whom were princely chaplains, theological teachers, jurists, priests and pastors, were paid permanent grants for life or for generations or forever by individuals or organizations. Generally the Hindu intellectuals (including kshatriyas and others) were educated in literature and philosophy and dedicated to speculation and discussion of ritualistic, philosophical and scientific questions. There was no concept of natural law and rather strict compartmentalization of private and social ethic, the caste organization and rank order based on karma doctrine. There was no natural equality of men before any authority. Here it may be mentioned that such was the position in Western countries for a long time and it was after certain revolutions in France and England that the position changed gradually in this respect. As regards the duties of the king, it was his duty to protect the subject, administer justice and to preserve the integrity of trade and other matters. It was the right of the king to conduct war for the sake of pure power *per se*. But Weber himself contradicts this later on and says the ethic given in Mahabharata was quite different.

The Hindus developed many special sciences including mathematics, astronomy, logic, medicine, music, etc. However, noteworthy developmental beginnings were hindered because of certain metaphysical suppositions which pushed all philosophy in the direction of individual salvation-striving.

The brahmans enhanced their status by their knowledge of the social order and, most of them being priests, also laid emphasis on magical techniques in the form of asceticism and mysticism. The Bramacharin's life of chastity, ascetism and mendicancy, and the contemplative forest life of vanaprastha were important parts of a brahman's life. Similarly emphasis was laid on contemplative mysticism as a type of gnosis. In the Upanishads emphasis was laid on *jnanakanda*, that is, gnosis, in contrast to *karmakanda,* the knowledge of rituals. However, the charismatic attainment of magical potency through ecstatic therapeutic practices was not much liked by brahmans as they rested their claim on knowledge and genteel cultivation. A hermit achieving the qualities of *yati* (full ascetic) was a teacher and magical helper gathering scholars and lay admirers around him. The asceticism and mysticism was combined in the technique of contemplation known as yoga. Among the techniques for inducing apathetic ecstasy this (yoga) technique was championed by the Hindu philosophic school of yoga. It places emphasis upon controlled breathing and related means of inducing apathetic ecstasy. Intellectually yoga technique presupposes that the grasp of the godly is an irrational psychic experience available by irrational means which allegedly have nothing to do with rational, demonstrable knowledge. However, the classical brahmanical intellectualism placed knowledge *per se* in the centre of all holy means. The supreme good could be achieved only through a higher knowledge: a gnosis. All intellectualized holy techniques had one of two purposes: either (1) through the emptying of consciousness they attempted to make room for the holy, which then is more or less clearly felt because it is incommunicable or (2) by combining internally isolated techniques with concentrated meditation, they sought to achieve a state experienced not as feeling, but as gnostic knowledge. However, even the gnostic doctrine led to the devaluation not only of the world but also of the gods, and above all of the rituals. The opposition is not sharp but classical, Brahmanical contemplation, in agreement with the nimbus of wisdom, was inclined to the second. Classical yoga rejected irrational mortification, the *hatha yoga* of pure magical asceticism.

Therefore, for the layman in search of salvation who did not qualify for training in gnostic wisdom, the Vedic ritual and house ritual remained all important. Ancestor worship remained a central concern. However, here Weber does not give a correct description of the *atman* as it was stated in certain important Upanishads and also depicted by many other Western writers. For example, Mr Barth points out that the essence of the philosophy proper of the Upanishads is as follows:

They appear to have started from the idea that the principle of life which is in man, the atman, or self, is the same as that which animates nature. This principle in man appeared to them to be the prana, the breath; the air, or something more subtle than air, the ether, being the atman in nature. Or else the atman was a small being, a homunculus, a *purusha,* which had its seat in the heart, where it was felt stirring, and from which it directed the animal spirits. Here it sat at its ease, for it was not larger than the thumb. It could even make itself still smaller, for it was felt making its way along the arteries, and could be distinctly seen in the small image, the pupil, which is reflected in the centre of the eye. A purusha quite similar, appeared with dazzling effect in the orb of the sun, the heart and eye of the world. This was the *atman* of nature, or rather it was the same atman which thus manifested itself in the heart of man and the sun; an invisible opening at the top of the skull affording a passage for it to go from the one dwelling place to the other . . . . They have never for once, even when they must have seemed to them perplexing, given up those old popular ideas, of which pre-intimations occur already in the hymns,[22] and to which assent was given without reflection from mere force of habit. Up to the last they will go on speculating about the *atman* breath and ether, the atman-purusha of the heart, the eye, and the sun.

The point at which they have arrived is this: the atman is the one, simple, eternal, infinite, incomprehensible being, assuming every form, and itself without any, the only, yet immovable and immutable agent, the cause of all action and all change. It is both the material and efficient cause of the world, which is its manifestation, its body. This is drawn from its own substance, and again absorbs into it, not by necessity, however, but by an act of its own will, as the spider spins forth and draws back into itself the thread of its web . . . . More subtle than an atom, greater than the greatest of existences, it has nevertheless a dwelling, the cavity of the heart of every man. It is there that it resides in its fulness, and that it rests rejoicing in itself and its works. By intense meditation, aided by operations in which a fanciful physiology plays a prominent part (for there is not a little materialism at the bottom of all these conceptions), he has only to make his soul literally re-enter his heart again in order to bring it into contact with the supreme unity, and enable it to be conscious of itself in that unity.[23]

As Barth points out here, it is true, there arose some puzzling questions. What room would there be for his soul, this individual *atman,* this *jivatman* identical with the *paramatman,* the supreme *atman,* and yet distinct, capable of self-consciousness in it and yet ignorant of it? These are difficulties, and there are others besides, which the authors of the Upandishads are not alone in having had to face; and it is not astonishing that they have not resolved them. It is only in the philosophy of the sects, in what may be called the new Vedanta, in certain Upanishads of more recent date, in the Bhagavad-Gita and in the Vedantasara, that an attempt will be made to formulate with any exactness a radical solution. In this system, the finite world does not exist; it is the production of the *maya,* of the deceptive magic of God, a mere spectacle where all is illusion, theatre, actors, and piece alike, a 'play' without purpose which the Absolute 'plays' with himself. The ineffable and the inconceivable is the only real.

Here Barth also mentions the ecstatic state and the means of inducing it as described by Weber.

> There is in the Upanishads, especially in those of the less antiquity, a complete theory given of the ecstatic state and the means of inducing it; such as a protracted bodily stillness, a stupefying fixity of look, the mental repetition of strange sets of formulae, meditations on the unfathomable mysteries contained in certain monosyllables, such as the famous *Om*, which is the brahman itself, suppression of the breath, a succession of sleep-inducing exercises, by which they fancied they charmed the vital spirits into the thought, the thought into the soul, concentrated this last entirely in the brain, and thence conveyed it back into the heart, where the supreme atman holds his seat.[24]

These processes have been collected and expounded *ex professo* in the system which more particularly bears the name of yoga.

Weber further points out that very slowly the early personal god-father and creator of the world (*prajapati*) has been displaced by the impersonal brahman principle and then this was endowed with the traits of a personalized super-worldly god-Brahma. With this appeared belief in a saviour and salvation in paradise.[25]

Here Weber also refers to six major schools of philosophy. All these schools recognize the pluralism of holy paths. These included ritual works, asceticism and wisdom. Among these wisdom (gnosis) was the best, as through perfect knowledge the redeemed *Jivan-mukta* escapes the *karma-* chain. According to Vedanta the performance of rites and the traditional social duties were valuable for salvation-striving but they were not a path to salvation. It was the Mahabharata and particularly the Bhagavad-Gita which laid stress on social duties as the way to salvation. This path suited the warriors better; while the brahman could pursue meditation alongside his ritualistic everyday profession, the warrior could hardly do so. His status-*dharma* was irreconcilable with any sort of excape from the world. We encounter here residues of the belief in 'fate' and an arbitrary play of chance with men. It is by the grace of God that the good receive immortality and here comes the concept of a personal God. The ancient Valhalla, Indian's warrior heaven is his true goal, and death on the field of honour. This is better than asceticism. However, in Bhagavad-Gita, Krishna points out that action has to be taken without wishing for reward. In the Gita both holy paths, i.e. *jnana-yoga* (right knowledge) and *karma-yoga* (right action) are acknowledged to be correct. Similarly the place of methodical contemplation (with moderate asceticism) as the classical path to gnosis was not shaken. And last there was the faith in God—the redeemer will emancipate a man from future life. Bhagavata religion relativizes the paths of salvation along organic status-group lines. All honestly and zealously pursued holy paths lead to the goal sought by the aspirant.

Here we agree with the analysis given by Weber that all four paths i.e. gnosis, *karma-yoga, dhyana-yoga* (contemplation) and *bhakti* or faith in God, the redeemer, will emancipate a man from bondage. But his view that the God-the-redeemer in personal form was not seen in earlier Vedic literature is not wholly correct. It is true that God in a personal form may not be seen in the earlier literature but God in an impersonal form who is merciful, kind and benevolent is quite evident in the Vedas. As Barth points out,

> The connection between man and the gods is conceived in the hymns as a very close one. Always and everywhere he feels that he is in their hands, and that all his movements are under their eye. They are masters close at hand, who exact tasks of him, and to whom he owes constant homage. He must be humble, for he is weak and they are strong; he must be sincere towards them, for they cannot be deceived. Nay, he knows that they in turn do not deceive, and that they have a right to require his affection and confidence as a friend, a brother, a father. Without faith (*craddha*) offerings and prayers are in vain.[26] These are so many strict obligations due to the gods, on which the hymns insist in a variety of passages.[27]

However, it cannot be denied that at that time emphasis was more on rituals than on prayer and faith.

Nor does Weber say anything about the Nastika or Carvakas philosophy when referring to the other six schools. As Barth points out, in the course of those idle, barren discussions, rugged good sense has at times had its revenge, and to such day-dreams it has been able to reply with scepticism, scoffing and cynical negation. As early as the Rig-Veda, we find mention of the people who denied the existence of Indra.[28] In the Brahmanas the question is sometimes asked if there really is another life;[29] and the old scholiast Yaska, who is ordinarily supposed to have lived in the fifth century B.C., finds himself obliged to refute the opinion of teachers of much more ancient date than himself, who had pronounced the Veda to be a tissue of nonsense.[30] The most ancient designation we find applied to them is that of Nastika (a derivative of *na asti, non est*), 'those who deny'.[31] They appear to have formed associations, more or less avowed, under the title of Carvakas (from the name of one of their teachers) and Lokayatas, or 'secularists'. Like other sects, they had their Sutras, ascribed, doubtless in derision, to Brihaspati, the guru or preceptor of the gods. Their doctrine is represented as absolute scepticism, and their morality, which has been preserved to us in certain clokas, or couplets, written with much verve, and ascribed to the same Brihaspati, is a simple call to enjoyment: 'So long as life lasts, delight thyself and live well; when once the body is reduced to ashes, it will revive no more'.[32]

6   Jainism and Buddhism in India

Weber observes that Jainism and Buddhism are historically important forms of belief because they had their origin in India and succeeded for several centuries in winning recognition as the dominant competitors of Hinduism. Buddhism diffused to all areas of India; Jainism to considerable portions of India. However this was only transitory. Although Buddhism later completely disappeared from India, it developed into a world religion which partly exerted a culturally revolutionizing influence from Ceylon and India across Tibet to Siberia including China, Korea and Japan. Jainism remained essentially restricted to Indian territory and was confined to a small sect which often is claimed by the Hindus as belonging to their community. Of the two, which were in sharpest competition with one another and which emerged in classical kshatriya times (in the seventh and sixth centuries B.C.), Jainism is the older and more exclusively Indian and for reasons of expedient presentation shall be discussed first.

Jainism

According to tradition the author of Jain asceticism Inatriputra (Nataputta), named Mahavira (died around 600 B.C.) was a kshatriya noble. According to Jainism the *arhats* (holy men) always stem from a royal family of pure lineage and never from lower families. This is in sharp opposition to Vedic-brahmanical education on the part of the *sramana* (hermit monk), who originated in lay circles. The ritualistic commandments and teachings of the Vedas, as well as the holy language, are emphatically rejected. They have not the slightest significance for salvation which depends solely on the asceticism of the individual. The teaching rests solidly on the general presupposition that salvation consists of freedom from the wheel of rebirth attainable only by detachment from this world of imperfection, from inner-worldly action, and from *karma* attached to action.

Contrast between Buddhism, Jainism and Hinduism

In contrast to Buddhism, Jainism accepted the essentials of the classical *atman* doctrine. Like ancient Samkhya, however, it bypassed the brahman doctrine, the concept of the divine soul of the universe. It was heterodox particularly because of its rejection of Veda education, of rituals and of the brahmans. The absolute atheism of the doctrine, the rejection of any supreme deity and of the total Hindu pantheon would have been no absolutely compelling reason for the charge of heterodoxy, since other ancient philosophies of the intellectuals, particularly the Samkhya doctrine, were of the same bent. Of course, Jainism rejected all orthodox philosophies, not only the Vedantic but also the Samkhya doctrine. Yet it was close to the last in certain metaphysical presuppositions. This holds especially for its view of the nature of the soul. All souls, i.e. the actual, ultimate I-substances of the Ego, are alleged to be equal and eternal essences. These and only these, not an absolute divine soul are *jiva,* the carriers of life. And indeed they are (in sharpest contrast to Buddhistic teaching) a kind of soul-monad which is capable of infinite wisdom (gnosis). The soul is no mere passive, receptive spirit, as in the case of orthodox Bhagavata religion, but an active principle of life to which the inertia of matter is opposed as a contrast (*ajiva*).

Jainism in place of the world of completely dethroned deities gives divine honours to great virtuosi of asceticism: the *arhat*, the *jina*, and, as supreme, the *tirthankara*. They are worshipped during their lifetimes as magicians and after death as exemplary helpers in virtue. From a total of twenty-five *tirthankaras*, Parsvanatha (allegedly in the ninth century B.C.) was the next to the last, Mahavira being the last. With them the 'prophetic age' came to a close. After them no one has attained the stage of omniscience or the penultimate stage (*manahparyaya*).

As the quality of brahmanical gnosis increases by steps, so Jain charisma is graded into seven statuses according to the stages of knowledge: from knowledge of the writings and holy traditions to the stage of enlightenment concerning the things of this world (*avadhi*), the first stage of supernatural knowledge; then the ability to have visions (*hellsehens*); then to the possession of magical powers and the ability of self-transformation; then (fifth step) to the knowledge of the thoughts of all living beings (*manahparyaya,*

the second stage of supernatural wisdom); and freedom from all
suffering (sixth step); and, therewith, finally, (seventh step) to the
certainty of the 'last birth'.[1] Therefore, says the Acharanga-Sutra,
the soul of the perfectly redeemed is qualityless, bodyless,
soundless, colourless, tasteless, without feeling, without resurrection, without contact with matter, knowing and perceiving
'without analogy', hence directly and without imagery, leading an
'unconditional' existence.[2]

Whoever in life has attained the proper intuitive knowledge sins
no more. He sees, like Mahavira, all deities at his feet, and is all-
knowing. Mahavira's is the (earthly) final state which the perfect
ascetic enters and is also called *nirvana* (in this case identical with
the later *jivan-mukti*). This state of Jainistic *nirvana* means,
however, in contrast to Buddhist *nirvana* not salvation from
'existence' in general, but 'salvation from the body', the source of
all sin and lust and of all limitation of spiritual power. In addition
to study and meditation, asceticism has a great part to play in
attaining *nirvana*. Indeed, with the Jains, asceticism has been
pushed to an extreme point. He achieves supreme holiness who
starves himself to death. 'Homelessness' is the basic holy concept.
It signifies the break with all worldly relations, thus, above all,
indifference to all sense perceptions and avoidance of all action
based on worldly motives. It aims at seeking to cease to 'act', to
hope and to wish. A man who only feels and thinks 'I am I' is
'homeless' in this sense. He yearns neither for life nor for death.

Professional monks and two sects

The reception of the novitiate into the community of monks in
classical times took place under a tree, after the laying aside of all
jewels and clothes as a sign of the renunciation of all possessions,
and it consisted of tearing of the hair and smearing the head, and
ended with the communication of the *mantra* by the teacher into
the ear of the novitiate.

A schism of the order occurred through innovation in the first
century A.D. when one part of the monks followed the commandment of absolute nakedness, at least for holy teachers, and another
part, indeed the majority declined. The former Digambara (those
clothed with the width of the world) separated themselves from the
Swetambara (white-clothed) and ended by excluding women
completely from the possibility of salvation. A further split
occurred when Islam carried the struggle against idols into the
community and led to the emergence of an *anti-idolatrous* sect.
Naturally, the Swetambara sect composed the bulk of the Jains.

During the nineteenth century the Digambara were driven from public life by the British police.

The classical rules of Jainism laid upon the monk the duty of restless wandering from place to place, lest he be entangled in personal or local relationships. A painstaking casuistry regulated the manner of his mendicancy such that the voluntary nature of giving and the avoidance of all *karma*-engendering action of the giver (for which the monk could become answerable) seems to have been secured. The commandment of wandering homelessness quite naturally gave the order a strong missionary power. In fact, propaganda was expressly recommended.

In complete reversal of the duty to wander for the monks was the rule for the laity against travel, for travel puts them in danger, uncontrolled and ignorant as they are, of falling into sin. For any trip the guru had to give permission and instructions to determine in advance the route of travel, maximum duration of travel as well as the permissible maximum of travel expenses. These prescriptions are characteristic for the position of the Jain laity in general. They were treated as incompetent minors and held under disciplinary control by means of inspection trips of the clergy and the guardians of morality.

Gems of Jainism

In addition to 'correct knowledge' the second 'gem' of Jainism was 'correct insight', which meant blind submission of the laity to the insight of the teacher. The holy was achieved through a series of steps—according to the most widely diffused Jain doctrine—after eight rebirths reckoned from the time one set out upon the proper path.

The laity also was required to meditate for a definite time (forty-eight minutes) daily. On definite days (usually four times a month) they were required to lead a full monkish existence. The lay individual was also compelled to take upon himself special austerity on definite days, not to leave the village, and to eat only one meal a day. Lay *dharma* could only mean a possible approach to the *dharma* of monks. Hence, above all, the laity by special vows should take up obligatory duties. Thus, the Jain confession acquired the typical character of a 'sect' into which one was specially received.

The commandments of Jain asceticism, the third 'gem' 'right practice' placed supreme importance on *ahimsa*, the absolute prohibition of the killing (*himsa*) of living beings. This principle originated in the rejection of the meat sacrifice which the brahmans had illogically preserved out of ancient Vedic sacrificial ritual.

However, some safety valve had to be provided with respect to military service, in this case similar to ancient Christianity. Thus, according to the revised doctrine, the conduct of the king and the warriors was just in 'wars of defence'. The ancient proscription was now reinterpreted to mean that for the laity it precluded only the killing of 'weaker' beings, that is, unarmed enemies. In this form the *ahimsa* of the Jains has been pushed to the extreme. During the dark season the correct Jain will burn no lights as it might burn moths. He kindles no fire, because it would kill insects. The Jain goes about with his mouth and nose covered with a cloth to prevent the inhalation of insects. Lest he kill lice with the scissors he does not cut the hair on his head or body (instead, he plucks the hair out by the roots). He never goes through water lest he step on insects.

The practice of *ahimsa* led to the exclusion of the Jain from all industrial trades endangering life, hence from all trades which made use of fire, involved work with sharp instruments (wood or stonework); from masonry; and, in general, from the majority of industrial callings. Agriculture was, of course, completely excluded: ploughing endangered the lives of worms and insects.

The second most important commandment for the laity was the limitation of possessions. One should have no more than 'necessary'. Personal effects in some Jain catechisms are restricted to twenty-six definite articles. Moreover, the possession of riches in general beyond those necessary for existence is dangerous to the holy. One should give his surplus to the temple or the veterinary in order to gain service merit. This occurred in Jain communities famous for their charitable institutions.

It may be noted that the acquisition of considerable wealth was in no way forbidden, only the striving after wealth and attachment to riches; this was rather similar to the ascetic Protestantism of the Occident. As with Protestantism 'joy in possessions' (*parigraha*) was the objectionable thing, but not the possession or gain in itself.

This similarity extended further; a Jain commandment forbids saying anything false or exaggerated; the Jains believed in absolute honesty in business life, all deception (*maya*) was prohibited, including especially all dishonest gain through smuggling, bribery, and any sort of disreputable financial practice (*adattu dama*). All this excluded the sect, on the one side, from typical oriental participation in 'political capitalism' (accumulation of wealth by officials, tax farmers, state purveyors) and, on the other, it worked among them in terms of the dictum (of early capitalism) 'honesty is the best policy'. The honesty of the Jain trader was famous. Their wealth was also famous: formerly it had been maintained that more than half the trade of India passed through their hands.[3]

That the Jains, at least the Swetambara Jains, nearly all became traders was due purely to ritualistic reasons—a case similar to the Jews. Only the trader could truly practise *ahimsa*. That they remained confined to commercial capitalism and failed to create an industrial organization was again due to their ritualistically determined exclusion from industry.

The commandment to retain no more than is 'necessary' (parigraha viramana vrata) provided but a very elastic restriction to their extensive accumulation of wealth. As with the Puritans, the strict methodical nature of their prescribed way of life was favourable to such accumulation. Abstinence from intoxicants and from the enjoyment of meat and honey, absolute avoidance of any sort of unchastity and strict loyalty in marriage, avoidance of status pride, of anger, and all passions are, among them as among all cultured Hindus, self-evident commandments. Among merits their social ethic counts the feeding of the hungry and thirsty, the clothing of the poor, the forbearance of and care for animals, care for the monks (of their own confession), saving another's life, and kindness toward others.

The discipline of the monks was severe. The *acharya* (superior) of the monastery was ordinarily designated by age. Originally, however, he was chosen because of his charisma, by his predecessor, or by the community. He accepted confessions of the monks and imposed penance. The competent monastic superior controlled the life of the laity, which for this purpose was divided into *samghas* (dioceses), these further into *ganas* (sub-dioceses) and these, finally, into *gachchas* (parishes).

The five great vows of the monks contain, in addition to *ahimsa, asatya tyaga* (prohibition of dishonesty), *ashaya vrata* (prohibition against taking anything which is not freely offered), *brahmacharya* (chastity), and *aparigraha vrata* (the renunciation of love for anyone or anything). Love must be eliminated for it awakens a desire and the processes of *karma*.

Despite these ritualistic commandments there is completely lacking the Christian conception of 'neighbourly love', as well as any equivalent to the 'love of God'. For there is no grace and forgiveness, no repentance which wipes out sins, and no effective prayer. The well-reasoned redemptory advantage which the act yields to the doer is the lodestar of action: 'The heart of Jainism is empty'.

It was the laity—here as in Buddhism—which for want of cult objects introduced hagiolatry and idolatry. The origin of the sect was closely contemporaneous with the rise of the Indian city. Anti-urban Bengal, on the other hand, was least receptive to Jains. One must, however, guard against the notion that it was a 'product' of

163

the 'bourgeoisie'. It stemmed from kshatriya speculation and lay asceticism. Its doctrine, especially the demands addressed to the laity, and its ritualistic prescription formed a workable routine of the everyday life only for a stratum of merchants.

Causes of its rise and fall

Doubtless, the rise of Jainism like all orthodox and heterodox Hindu communities was due to the favour of princes. It would seem very likely that one of the most important (political) motives for supporting the Jains was that it was the wish of these princes to be free of brahman power. The great flowering of Jain religion does not occur in the time of the rising bourgeoisie but coincides precisely with the decline of city politics and guild power, somewhere between the third and thirteenth centuries B.C.—a time also of the flowering of Jainist literature, which gained especially at the expense of Buddhism. In some southern Indian areas and in the realm of the Western Chalukaya kings it was, at times, accepted as the state religion. In the West the main sects of practising Jains have continued to exist right down to the present.

After the Hindu restoration, Jainism to a large extent submitted to the fate of Hinduization. At the beginning it had ignored the castes. The castes had no relation, even indirectly, to Jainist soteriology. This changed even as, under the influence of the laity, the temple and idol assumed even greater dimensions.

The genuine Jain monk could not possibly take care of temples and idols since the practice produced *karma*. The task of taking care of temple idols thus fell into the hands of the laity. We find the peculiar phenomenon that the temple cult was preferentially placed into the hands of brahmans, for they were trained for such tasks. However, these brahmans were of somewhat degraded ranks.

The caste order now overpowered the Jains. In south India the Jain sects are completely organized into castes, while in the north, Hinduistic theory is inclined—according to the familiar type—to treat them as sect castes—which they have always expressively denied. The modern representatives of Hinduism are inclined to claim them for their own. The Jains themselves have given up propaganda proper.

The services of Jains comprises a sermon in which no 'God' appears and only the exegesis of sacred scriptures. The belief of their laity seems inclined to the view that there is indeed a God but that he does not trouble himself with the world and has contented himself with revealing how to redeem oneself from this world. There were certain contradictions in the teaching; while it was asserted that an initial stage was available only through contemplation, its specific holy path was asceticism. At least, radical ascetic means had equal standing with meditation and con-templation. The Jains themselves have always viewed themselves as a specifically ascetic sect. The number of believers is relatively declining.

Buddhism

Like Jainism, but even more clearly, Buddhism presents itself as a product of the time of urban development, of urban kingship and the city nobles. The founder of Buddhism was Siddharta, the Sakya Muni, called Gautama, the Buddha, who was born in Lumbini in the present-day Nepal territory at the foot of the Himalayas. He belonged to the noble (kshatriya) sib, the Sakya of Kapilavastu.

In the ancient literary documents of the Buddhists, just as with the Jains, guild leaders play an important role. Oldenberg drew attention to the fact that rural surroundings, cattle and pasture, were characteristic of the ancient brahmanical teachers and schools, at least in the early times of the Upanishads; whereas the city and the urban palace with its elephant-riding kings were characteristic of Buddha's time. Moreover, the dialogue form reflects the advent of city culture. Early Buddhism, like Samkhya teaching and the Jain sect knew nothing of Brahman. In opposition to both, however, it also denies the *atman* and, in general, the problems of individuality which had been the preoccupation of philosophical, school soteriology.

The opposition to *atman* doctrines occurs, partially, in so pointed a form against the whole complex of problems that it must have been thoroughly worked over before it could be dismissed as vain and without substance. The feelings of competitiveness among Buddhists were combined with feelings that arose from the inner opposition of Buddhistic holy striving not only against the classical brahmanical path, but also and especially, against the Jainistic.

Ancient Buddhism

'Primitive' or 'ancient Buddhism—whether this term is understood to mean the teaching of the master or the practice of the oldest community—represents in almost all, practically decisive points the characteristic polar opposite of Confucianism as well as of Islam. It is a specifically unpolitical and anti-political status religion, more precisely, a religious 'technology' of wandering and of intellectually-schooled mendicant monks. Like all Indian philo-sophy and theology it is a 'salvation religion', if one is to use the

165

name 'religion' for an ethical movement without a deity and without a cult. More correctly, it is an ethic with absolute indifference to the question of whether there are 'gods' and how they exist. Indeed, in terms of the 'how', 'from what' 'to what end' of salvation, Buddhism represents the most radical form of salvation-striving conceivable. Its salvation is a solely personal act of the single individual. There is no recourse to a deity or saviour. There is no religious grace. There is, moreover, no predestination either. According to the *karma* doctrine of the universal causality of ethical compensation, which replaces the theodicy, and which Buddhism does not doubt, man's ultimate fate depends entirely on his own free behaviour. And *karma* doctrine does not take the 'personality' for its points of departure, but the meaning and value of the single act. No single world-bound act can get lost in the course of the ethically meaningful but completely cosmic causality.

One might think that an ethic based on these premises must be one of active conduct, be it within the world (like those, each in its particular way, of Confucianism and Islam), or in the form of ascetic exercises, e.g. Jainism, its main competitor in India. Early Buddhism, however, rejected both alike because its salvation 'from what?' and 'for what?' precluded both alternatives. Buddha even in his first address after the 'illumination' drew the ultimate conclusion that the basic cause of all illusions inimical to salvation is belief in a 'soul' as a lasting unit. From this the doctrine concludes that it is senseless to be attached to all or any inclinations, hopes or wishes connected with belief in this-worldly, and above all, other-worldly life. To Buddhistic thought an 'eternal life' would be a *contradictio in adjecto.* What is sought is not salvation to an eternal life, but to the everlasting tranquillity of death. The basis of this salvation-striving for Buddhism, as for the Indians in general, was not any sort of 'satiety' with the 'meanness of life' but 'satiety' with 'death'. The solace is sought in the flight from home into the solitude of the woods. The absolute senselessness of ephemeral beauty, happiness, and joy in an everlasting world is precisely that which in the end devalues the goods of the world. Certainly there were sins for Buddhistic monks and they only required penance. However, everything that hinders salvation is by no means a 'sin'. In fact, sin is not the final power inimical to salvation. Not 'evil' but ephemeral life is the obstacle to salvation; salvation is sought from the simply senseless unrest of all structures of existence in general.

All 'morality' could only be a means, hence, could have meaning only in so far as it is a means to salvation. The concept of neighbourly love, in the sense of the great Christian virtuosi of brotherliness, is unknown. Like a mighty wind the blessed one blows over the world with the wind of his love, so cool and sweet, quiet and delicate. Only this cool temperance guarantees the internal detachment from all 'thirst' for the world and men. The mystic, acosmic love of Buddhism (*maitri* or *meta*) is psychologically conditioned through the euphoria of apathetic ecstasy.

This love and 'unbounded feeling' for men and animals like that of a mother for her child give the holy man a magical, soul-compelling power over his enemies as well. His temper, however, remains cool and aloof in this.

In Buddhism, too, salvation is achieved through 'knowledge'. Naturally this is not in the sense of broad knowledge of earthly or heavenly things. On the contrary, early Buddhism demanded an extreme restriction of the quest for knowledge, namely, the conscious renunciation of the search for what will occur after the death of the saved. A concern for knowledge is also a 'desire', a 'thirst', and does not benefit the holiness of the soul. But salutory 'knowledge' is exclusively the practical illumination by the four great truths of the nature, origin, conditions, and means of destroying suffering. The Buddhist flees passion by all means. The illumination definitively liberating one from passion is solely secured through meditation, through the contemplative absorption in the simple practical truths of life. 'Knowledge' which is denied to active men and available only to the aspirants of enlightenment, hence is also practical in nature.

Problem of individuality

What is it that establishes the unit? What is a 'chariot'? Clearly, it is not any one of its single component parts (wheels, etc.). And, obviously, the chariot cannot be thought of as all its parts together as a simple sum. Rather, we experience the whole as a chariot by virtue of the unity or 'meaning' of all the single parts in interrelation. Exactly the same holds for 'individuality'. Of what does it consist? Certainly not of the single sensations; also not of all of them together; but of the unity of purpose and meaning governing these sensations, as the meaningful purpose of the chariot constitutes the object. But wherein is the purpose and meaning of individuality? In the unified will of the existing individual. And the content of this will? All individual wills are in hopeless, manifold striving against and from each other and only in one single point is there unity: the will to exist, or the will to life. This will in its metaphysical meaninglessness is what ultimately holds life together. It is this which produces *karma*. The task is to destroy the will if one wishes to escape *karma*. The illumination, however, is not a free, divine gift of grace, but the wages of incessant meditative absorption by the truth for the sake of giving up the great illusions from which spring the thirst for life. Whoever achieves that illumination enjoys—note this—bliss here and now.

The arhat *or emancipated person*

The tone to which the hymns of ancient Buddhism are attuned is triumphant joy. The *arhat* who has reached the goal of the methodical, contemplative ecstasy is *karma-free* and feels himself replete with a strong and delicate (objectless and desireless) experience of love, free from earthly pride and Philistine self-righteousness, but possessed by an unshakable self-confidence which guarantees a lasting state of grace, free from fear, sin and deception, free from yearning for the world and—above all—for a life in the hereafter. The master's message rejects mundane pride and self-righteousness. It did so in favour, not of edifying self-humiliation or emotional love of man in the Christian sense, but in favour of manly clarity about the meaning of life and the ability to draw the conclusion with 'intellectual honesty'.

Buddha and his mission

According to Buddha, salvation is an absolute personal performance of the self-reliant individual. No-one, and particularly no social community, can help him. Thus Buddha was quite aloof from forming a 'church' or even a 'parish'. According to legend the Buddha did not commit himself to preach his redemptory doctrine because he wished to, but he took it upon himself at the special request of a deity.

For salvation from the endless struggle of eternally renewed individuality in order to achieve everlasting tranquillity could be achieved only by giving up every 'thirst' linking man to the world of imperfection and the struggle for existence. Naturally, such salvation was accessible only to the 'homeless' status group, or the wandering disciples who in later times were called monks, *bhikkshu*. The 'house-dwelling people' existed only for the purpose of sustaining by alms the Buddhist disciple who aspires for the state of grace until he has reached it. Wandering homelessly, without possessions and work, absolutely abstemious as regards sex, alcohol, song, and dance, practising vegetarianism, shunning spices, salt, and honey, living from door to door by silent mendicancy, for the rest given to contemplation, the Buddhist sought salvation from the thirst for existence. Material support of the holy seekers fell on the laity and ultimately this alone constituted the highest merit and honour available to the *upasaka* (adorer).

The ten commandments

In their original substance the advisory counsels were roughly in agreement with the *Decalogue*, but with a broader understanding of the prohibition against killing (*ahimsa*), extending it to all injury of live beings, the commandment of unconditional truthfulness (in the *Decalogue* it applied only to court witnesses), and the express prohibition of drunkenness. For the loyal observance of these commandments of lay morality (especially of the five cardinal prohibitions: not to kill, steal, commit adultery, lie or get drunk), prospective worldly goods are held out to the pious laity such as riches, a good name, good company, death without fear, and betterment of rebirth opportunities. Thus, in the best case, one may be reborn into one of the (to be surely transitory) godly paradises scorned by those entering *nirvana*. However, this morality does not lead—this is the decisive point—to increasingly rational asceticism (extra- or inner-worldly) or to a positive life method. Every satisfaction of work (*kriyavada, karmavada*) is and remains heretical. Rather the opposite holds; active virtue in conduct recedes more and more into the background as against *cila,* the ethic of nonaction, for the purpose of eliminating *rajas* (drives) in the interest of pure contemplation.

The noble eight-fold path

The basis for Buddhistic soteriology in rational form is based on his sermon in Benares concerning the four holy truths. The four holy truths are concerned with (1) suffering; (2) the basis for suffering; (3) the end of suffering and, finally, the means thereto (4) the noble eight-fold path.

(1) Suffering and grief are attached to transitoriness *per se*, bound up with imperfection as such, which is, in turn, bound to individuation. All the splendour of life is not only transient but rests upon the struggle with other lives and originates only at the cost of these.

(2) The basis of all life and therewith all suffering is the senseless 'thirst' (*trishna*) for life, for the preservation of individuality even beyond death in an 'eternal' life. The belief in the 'soul' and its duration is only the consequence of this unquenchable thirst with all the meaninglessness this brings with it. It is also the source of the belief in a 'god', who hears our prayers.

(3) The end of thirst for life is the end of the suffering in imperfection and in life.

(4) The way thereto, however, is the noble eight-fold path. Its steps are: *sammadi* (correct insight), namely, first rational understanding, then, however, insight permeating one's entire

being to the effect that all constitutive elements of life by nature bear the predicates of suffering, transitoriness, and the absence of any 'eternal' kernel in the way of the brahmanical *atman*, the 'soul'. The second step is *sammarsankappa*, (right will), the compassionate wise renunciation of all pleasures of life, which generally are only possible at the expense of others. The third step is *sammavaca* (right speech), the avoidance of untruths and loveless speech through mastery of one's own passionate nature. The fourth step is *sammakammanta* (proper life conduct), the elimination from conduct of all impurities and particularly all interest in the results or fruits of one's own correct action. Whoever fully attains this, wins the fifth step, which, in Christian terms, provides *certitudo salutis*, the no longer alienable holiness of life: *sammoajivo*. The tremendous exertion of all his powers in the service of the holy goal gives him a spiritual power of the holy will, which surpasses by far what is attainable for others: *sammavayano* (the right 'power of will'), the sixth step. He had this power over himself not only while waking but also when sleeping; he knows who he is or was. And this inner attitude of holy knowledge leads him to the seventh step of perfection, *sammasati*, in which he is no longer available to anything but holy thoughts and feelings. And through this ability for exceeding normal consciousness he inwardly reaches the 'shores wrested from death', *nirvana*, in the right concentration, *sammasamadhi,* the last and highest step.

In this holy teaching there is complete elimination of any form of inner-worldly motivation to conduct or rational purpose in nature. For all rational action (goal-directed action) in compliance with the principle is expressly rejected. Thus, there is lacking an element which in occidental monkhood increasingly developed and signified so much, namely, the strain toward rational method in life conduct in all spheres except that of the pure intellectual systematization of concentrated meditation and pure contemplation. This has been increasingly developed to that level of sophistication, also otherwise characteristic of things Indian. The later development took many aids from yoga technique with which the master was certainly acquainted. These techniques varied from breath regulation to the submergence of thought step by step through the forty *karmasthanas*; all means were methodologically rationalized to the successive attainment of the four degrees of salvation.

In the beginning Buddhism persisted in an unstructured state which was dangerous to the uniformity of the community and which actually soon led to heresies and sect formation. The single countervailing means—the calling of councils—soon failed, and the unity of the community was apparently possible only through the support of secular authorities. It looks as if even the few, finally created elements of organization and discipline, hence the establishment of an order, and likewise the fixing of the teaching, occurred only after the death of the founder and against his own intentions.

The orthodox teaching of the community, as it continues to live a thousand years later in the Hinayana-Buddhism, recognized, besides seniority, only one absolute and highly efficient element of structural cohesion, the teacher–disciple relationship. The novice had to abide by the strict rule of piety of the Indian *bramacharin* toward his guru. The ancient Buddhism, which rejected the later development of cloisters into landlordships and of the salvation doctrine into a lay soteriology, was recruited from the outset, not exclusively but predominantly, like the founder himself, from among great noble families and from rich burghers. Also brahmans appear to have been taken up; but they were the distinguished representatives of a cultured laity—a secular strata of nobles who formed the majority of Buddha's disciples. Buddha's disciples were never a horde of uncivilized beggars. In contrast to other sects, not only was dress regulated from the beginning, but it was also subject to planned provision. The attractiveness of Buddhism, especially for the upper strata, is to be explained, in part at least, exactly in terms of its concern for decorum. This suggests the inner peculiarity of the teaching of Buddha. The typical form of his teaching is the Socratic dialogue, by which the opponent is led through a considerable argument to a *reductio ad absurdum* and then forced into submission.

A 'struggle' against the brahmans, somewhat in the manner of Christ against the Pharisees and scribes, cannot be traced in Buddha's preaching. He left aside the question of the gods as well as the meaning of the castes. According to tradition he would insist, after the energetic quizzing of a brahman, only that not birth but right acts make a true brahman. Likewise there is to be found no true struggle against sacrifice, such as was peculiar to the Jains. It simply had no value for the goal pursued by the strong and wise. As a whole, early Buddhism was the product not of the underprivileged but of very positively privileged strata. Its devaluation of brahmanical knowledge of ritual and of brahmanical philosophy made the princes and patricians sympathetic to its teachings. The kind of salvation which was promised to the mendicant monk certainly was not one to the taste of the socially oppressed strata, which would have rather demanded compensation in the hereafter or this-worldly hopes for the future.

However, Buddhism became one of the greatest missionary religions on earth. That must seem baffling. Viewed rationally,

171

there is no motive to be discovered which should have destined Buddhism for this. What would cause a monk who was seeking only his own salvation and was therefore utterly self-dependent to trouble himself with saving the souls of others and engaging in missionary work? For a long time Buddha was uncertain whether or not, at the request of Brahma, he should preach salvation to man.

Nevertheless, this was but a dogmatic interpretation. There were two motives or factors which led to this missionary zeal. First, for the most part there is a compassionate acosmic love which almost always goes with the psychological form of a mystical holy state, the peculiar euphoria of god-possessed tranquillity. This drove the majority of them, as over and against the rational consequences of mystical holy-seeking, on the road toward saving souls. But this was a general phenomenon of all soteriologies of the time. Second, and decisive for the success of the propaganda, as with the Jains, was the appearance of the 'professional monks' in the form of communities. The motive for the propaganda activities was the material interests of the monks in the increase of the givers of subsistence, the *upasaka*. And this interest was shared by the competing monkish associations, the Buddhists and especially the Jains. In addition the weaknesses of orthodox Hinduism helped in the expansion of Buddhism.

Yet Buddhism would hardly have been able to embark upon its career of international conquest without the historical accident that one of the first great kings, ruling almost over the entire Indian cultural area, became its ardent adherent.

The transformation of ancient Buddhism

Ancient Buddhism was a most consistent religion and, to that extent, presents the perfection of the soteriology of the distinguished Hindu intellectuals. Externally, Buddhism became the official religion of all India under the Maurya dynasty for the first time. Soon after the expedition of Alexander had brought about the first, albeit transient, contacts between north India and Hellenism, there arose a great king in India in the dynasty of the Maurya. The standing army and the officers, the kingly bureaucracy and its many bureaus of scribes, the kingly tax farmers, and the kingly police then formed the ruling powers. The patrimonialism of the great king took the place of the ancient petty kingdoms. Therewith the situation of nobles and bourgeois patricians was unavoidably changed.

The brahmanical tradition ascribes a low origin to the members of the Maurya dynasty, and, at least in the bureaucracy and officers' corps, a patrimonial prince must have been inclined to give the lower strata opportunities to rise. At first, this was in perfect agreement with the circumvention of status barriers by the Buddhistic salvation religion, and actually the great king Asoka of the Maurya dynasty who first succeeded in uniting the entire cultural area of India into a unified empire, changed over to Buddhism first as a lay person, then even formally as a member of the order.

Religious needs of the masses

The relative levelling of the political power of the distinguished status groups, and especially the apparent elimination of the ancient kshatriya stratum with its numberless small castles as independent centres of an eminent knightly culture, must have had profound ramifications for the social conditions of the competing religions. The souls of the laity for whom these religions struggled were no longer made up exclusively of educated nobles, but of courtiers, the literate officials and the petty bourgeois and peasants. Princes, priests and monks alike had an interest in how religious needs were met. The holders of political power saw in it an instrument to domesticate the masses. The champions of religion saw an opportunity to win pillars of spiritual power and a source of prebends and casual fees. Thus opened a plebeian epoch of orthodox Indian soteriology or, more correctly speaking, an epoch aimed at satisfying plebeian religious needs.

In early Buddhism, court society missed the distinguished literary culture and opportunity for artistic stylization. It also missed the means for the domestication of the masses. The petty bourgeois or peasant could as little think of yearning for *nirvana* as he could of uniting with the Brahman. Above all, he did not have the means at hand to attain these holy objects; it required leisure for the meditation necessary to achieve the gnosis. He had no such leisure and, as a rule, saw no reason for gaining such leisure by living as a penitent in the woods.

To some degree both orthodox and heterodox soteriology had prepared for this contingency: orthodoxy through holy promises of caste ritualism; heterodoxy through a secondary lay morality, for which premiums in this and the future life were promised.[4] However, all this was essentially negative and ritualistic in nature. It in no way satisfied the specifically religious need for emotional experience of the super-worldly and for emergency aid in external and internal distress. Such unsatisfied emotional needs were and are always decisive for the psychological character of religion for the masses, in contrast to the rational character of all soteriologies of intellectuals.

For emotional mass religiosity there have been and are but two possible types of soteriology: magic or a saviour; both may occur together. In its relation to the laity, ancient Buddhism was relatively inimical to magic as well as to images. The Buddhist prohibition against pictorial representation is reliably transmitted and reformers introduced into church art a certain reliable Puritanism. The religion was also apolitical. In the last point appears the first change.

Ancient Buddhism reached its acme in India under the reign of the great Maurya king Asoka, the first monarch who in the Egyptian and Assyrian manner saw to it that his deeds and arrangements were carved forever in countless mountain caves.[5] They report that the king received the opportunity to be a novice, then an official member of the order. The king was not considered to be an ordinary monk, but he accepted a special position. With this, for the first time in Buddhism, the beginnings of political theory emerge. The power of the world monarch (*tshakravati*) must necessarily supplement the spiritual power of Buddha, which necessarily leads away from all worldly action. The monarch is patron of the Church somewhat in the sense claimed by the Byzantine monarchs.

Asoka's edicts indicate some of the peculiar ramifications of a semi-theocracy. The conversion of the king took place after the bloody conquest of the Kalinga realm. The king declared that forthwith it would not belong to the *dharma* of his descendants to conquer by the sword and more important to him than even these peaceful conquests was the salvation of the soul in the next world. With this pacifistic religious turn from the traditional kingly *dharma* came, as could not be otherwise, the development towards a patriarchal ethical and charitable ideal of a welfare state. The king who has to care for country and people must work for the public welfare in order that the subjects be 'happy' and 'attain heaven'.[6] Allowance is made for reports to him at any time of those of his affairs which require speed. He personally conducts an exemplary life, forswears war and the hunt, which was until then, as everywhere, propaedeutically linked to war service, taking the place of it in peacetime. Instead of this, in his journeys he will engage in the propaganda of piety. Corresponding to *ahimsa*, he prohibits slaughtering in the capital city of Pataliputra and on festivals (*samaja*) bound up with meat orgies; and he announced that in the royal kitchen forthwith no cattle would be slaughtered. Hospitals for men and animals, as well as the required apothecaries, should be established. Fruits and shade trees should be planted on the streets.

The most important peculiarity in this case was the 'tolerance' which results from the ancient Buddhistic prohibition against violence. The king declared that all his subjects, regardless of what belief, were his 'children' and—with a turn of phrase which reminds us of the Bhagavad-Gita—that only the honesty and the earnestness of piety matter; the practical conclusions drawn from their teaching was that ceremonies and external rites are of little avail.[7] He supported all of the sects by foundations. Especially in the early edicts he expressed reverence of the brahmans. The sects should desist from debasing one another which under all circumstances is wrong, and turn to the cultivation of the ethical substance of their teaching. These are essentially the same in all confessions, although it is most perfectly contained in the *dharma* of Buddha. He summarized these generally binding rules as 'laws of piety' and reportedly enumerated them as: (1) obedience to parents (and the aged as such); (2) liberality towards friends, relatives, brahmans, ascetics; (3) respect for life; (4) avoidance of bad temper and excesses of all sorts. Not everyone can fulfil the whole law. Each sect, however, can endeavour to control the senses, cultivate and spread purity of heart, thankfulness and loyalty. Each good deed bears its fruit in the next world, often already in this one. To control and carry out these ideas the king created special officials, usually called 'censors' (*dharmaraharatra*). Apparently their first duty was to watch over the kingly and princely harems.

Thus, Buddhism is quite intentionally treated here as a specific levelling and, in this sense, a 'democratic' religion, especially in connection with the very derogatory treatment of ritual, including caste ritual. Such purposeful opposition to the ruling strata was thoroughly lacking in ancient Buddhism.

However, formally, the greatest innovation, which most likely goes back to this king, who presumably first changed over to systematic administration by scribes and to the Church council (allegedly the third) under him, was the fixing in writing of the two-and-a-half century long, orally-transmitted tradition. The Chinese pilgrim Fa-Hien, sent out by the Emperor to procure authentic copies of the holy books found in all India, written scriptures only in the monasteries of Pataliputra (the seat of the kings and, allegedly, of the council) and in Ceylon and elsewhere only oral traditions. It is clear how much the writing-down meant for the preservation of the unity of the Church, likewise, however, what it meant for the mission. In a land of literati like China, Buddhism could gain a footing only as a book religion.

Next the wild tribes were to be converted. Ambassadors were sent to foreign powers, particularly to the great Hellenistic powers of the West, to Alexandria, to make known the pure teaching in all the world; and a mission with the support of the king went to Ceylon and outlying Indian territories. The great international expansion of Buddhism in Asia in any case had its ideal beginnings at that time. It has become and has remained the official confession of Ceylon, Burma, Annam, Thailand and other outlying Indian states, of Korea and, in the later changed form, of Tibet; and, for quite some time, Buddhism held sway over China as well as Japan. In order to qualify for this role the ancient soteriology of the intellectuals had to undergo deep transformations.

Changes in Buddhism

These changes took place at various levels. (1) In the first place, it constituted a completely new situation for the order that a worldly ruler as such took its legal affairs into his hands. In certain states, the king appoints or (at least) confirms a 'patriarch' of the Buddhistic territorial Church (in Siam he is called *Sanharat,* in Burma *Thatanabiang*, and he is always an abbot of a charismatically distinguished cloister). It is, of course, quite contrary to the tradition, possible that this dignitary first emerged under Asoka; previously, it appears, simply, that seniority (of the monastery and within it of the monk) was decisive. Besides, the king granted titles (as in Siam) to distinguished monks. Obviously this has developed out of the position of the king's chaplain. He had the monasteries and their discipline supervised by secular officials and called monks to account for offences. Thus Asoka had an official position at least in matters of church discipline. In fact, the king himself donned the monkish garb. However, it is said that he was himself dispensed by his guru from the full content of the vows. It later led to the general practice in orthodox (Hinayanistic) territories of temporarily joining the monkish community, considered to be a custom of social distinction, as a part of the education of young people; temporarily or partially, the fulfilment of monkish duties by the laity became a specifically meritorious work, furthering rebirth chances. Thereby a certain external approximation of lay piety to monkish holy-seeking was brought about.

Education of the laity Elementary popular education, which in connection with the cloister education of gentility and in imitation of it had been set up by the monks for the mass of the laity, might have had more extensive ramifications had it been rational in nature. For at least in Burma popular education was almost universal. There, and in Ceylon, it included, corresponding to its purpose, reading and writing and religious instruction. Thus Asoka's missionary zeal had given the first push toward this work with the laity, which was by no means close to ancient Buddhism.

The concept of the welfare state   For the first time in the Hindu culture area there appeared the idea of the 'welfare state' of the 'general good' (the promotion of which Asoka regarded as the duty of the king). 'Welfare' was, however, partially understood to mean spiritual welfare (as the furtherance of salvation chances), and partially to mean charities, but also rational and economic action. The tremendous irrigation works of the Ceylonese kings, however, like those of northern India (Tschandragupta) even, were throughout fiscal in orientation, i.e. intended to augment the number of taxpayers and the capacity to pay taxes, not to implement welfare politics.

The relaxation in the rules for monkhood   The transformations of the ancient Buddhistic monkhood was not exhausted with these theocratic ramifications. Given the momentum of the masses who took to the ancient monk community, it had first to soften the austere, world-fleeing character and to make extensive concessions to the abilities of the average monks, and also to the requirements of cloisters, which were not places established for the holy-seeking of eminent thinkers but centres of religious mission and culture. For the rest, Buddhism had to meet half-way the needs of the laity, which in ancient Buddhism, given its nature, had essentially played an incidental role. Hence, soteriology had to be bent in the direction of faith in magic and saviours.

The division of Buddhism into two sects   Owing to the difficulties involved in making Buddhism a popular religion it split into two branches, i.e. Hinayanistic and Mahayanistic. According to Mahayanistic tradition the great schism first broke out in the council (*sanghiti*) of Vaicali, (allegedly the second) which is supposed to have occurred 110 years after the death of Buddha. (This was during Asoka's period.) The famous 'ten theses' of the Vajji monks, over which agreement was not reached, were throughout disciplinary rather than dogmatic in nature. Along with some details of monastic conduct, all aimed at relaxing the discipline, an organizational question formed the prelude of the schism. There was one fundamentally important point at issue and this was an economic one. The statutes of the founder forbade any sort of money possession, hence, also, the acceptance of money donations. A strict observant rejected money donations. The majority of the monks declared this to be an insult to the laity. According to the Hinayanistic tradition, the council presumably confirmed the orthodox tradition. Agreement, however, was not secured.

Dogmatic controversies Along with the problems of discipline there also appeared dogmatic controversies. In the first council held under Asoka three questions were raised by the chairman: (1) whether an *arhat* could fall from grace; (2) whether the existence (of the world) was real; (3) whether *samadhi* (gnosis) could be attained by way of continuous thought. The later councils concerned themselves with dogmatism. (These changes are discussed later on). In the course of time, the parties were essentially distributed geographically, in such a way that ancient Buddhist strict observance prevailed in southern India, the lax direction (Mayayana, the 'great ship', i.e. the universal Church) since the first century A.D. dominated in the north.

The tradition suggests, as is probable, that the laity, either from the beginning or later, stood on the side of a more lax form of Buddhism, which was originally called Mahasamghika (great community). A speciality of the Mahasamghika was the cooperation of the laity in the councils. Of course, this did not concern the 'lower' classes— who never were or could be spoken of as an active driving element—but, precisely, the ruling strata. Also, distinguished ladies are said to have excelled as partisans of the Mahayana school. Literary interests demanded simply the pursuit of science and of the five *vidya*: grammar (always most important), medicine, logic, philosophy and also, the theoretical pursuit of 'fine arts'. Monastic schools for the laity and primers for children were created. There was express recognition of the caste organization, which had previously been ignored. The influence of the cultured strata is also shown by the external circumstance that the Mahayana school participated in the renaissance of Sanskrit which had Kashmir as its point of departure. Its holy scriptures were written in the ancient scholarly language. The Pali-canon remained in possession of the southern Buddhists.

Fa-Hien (around 400 A.D.) wrote that the teaching had spread as far as Turkestan. The kings there arranged for the five-year assemblies as was done during the time of Asoka. In Nagrak (near Jelladabad) the king attended divine service each morning; similarity, in Takshasila. A century later, accounts indicate that the kings in Punjab, partly as late as the sixth century, continued to live as strict vegetarians and did not mete out capital punishment.

Asoka's empire had long since disintegrated. However, relatively pacifistic principalities prevailed in northern India. In Oude (between Kashmir and Kabul), as well as in Kanouj, the

Hinayanistic school held sway. In the ruins of Asoka's capital city Pataliputra (Patna) were monasteries of both schools. Buddhistic brahmans are described as gurus of the kings in the neighbourhood of Pataliputra. Sung Yun even stated that, whereas a conquering king in Gandhara scorns Buddha, the people 'belonged to the Brahman Caste' and have the greatest respect for the laws of Buddha.[8]

Buddhism was and continued to be the doctrine of genteel intellectuals. The pilgrim Hiuen-Tsang (628 A.D. and the years following) reported that there was the opposition of the Mahayana school against the Hinayanistic orthodoxy. Actually Mahayana is discussed and he thought it was not necessary to go to Ceylon where the orthodox school still prevailed. In addition, there was a growing interpenetration of specifically brahmanical elements into the increasingly dominant Mahayana doctrine. India was called by Hiuen-Tsang the 'Kingdom of the Brahmans' (*To-lo-man*).

Image worship Statues of Brahma and Indra stood in the holy temples of the Ganges Valley beside the statue of Buddha.[9] The Vedas (*Wei—ho*) are termed 'sabaltern', that is to say, lay literature; but they were read. The king of Kosala was honoured beside Buddha, however, in the brahmanical temple, the Hindu Devas. Although there were still kings (*ciladitya*) who yearly called the great councils of Buddhistic clergymen, this is clearly not the rule. The Hinayana in northern India are pushed back, but Buddhism generally is declining.

For the sharpening of the antagonism between Mahayana and Hinayana the ancient disciplinary differences were no longer decisive. In Hinayana, too, lay representatives received money and managed it for the monks.

Causes of decline Monastic landlordism and permanent monastic residence (not, as originally, restriction of monks to the cloister in the rainy season), appeared here and there, and for a time quite extensively. This occurred even in Ceylon, the seat of strict observance.

Idol worship In the Mahayana Church the religious needs of the laity became paramount. They had no wish for *nirvana* and could not be satisfied with an exclusively exemplary prophet of self-salvation such as Buddha. The laity demanded helpers-in-need for life here and now and paradise in the hereafter. Thus the process began which is usually described as the replacement of *pratyeka-Buddha* and *arhat*

179

(self-salvation) with the *bodhisattva* (redeemer) ideas. While the Hinayana school divided its adherents into *cravakas* (laity) and *pratyeka-Buddhas* (self-savers) and *arhats* (the saved) as religious status groups, the *bodhisattva* idea became the peculiar and common characteristic of the Mahayana sect.

Changes in salvation theory This presupposed an inner transformation of the salvation theory. As indicated earlier the controversy over this issue had arisen in the council during the time of Asoka. The old school maintained Buddha's human quality. The Mahayanists developed the *'Trikaya'* theory, the doctrine of the supernatural character of the Buddha. He had three appearances: first, the *nirmana kaya,* the 'transformed body' in which he wanders on earth; then he might take the form of the *sambhoga kaya,* somewhat like the 'Holy Ghost' the all-pervasive 'ethereal' body constituting the community; and, finally, Buddha appears as the *dharma kaya,* of which more below.

Thus the typical Hindu deification process took its course first with regard to the person of Buddha. To this was joined the Hindu incarnation apotheosis. Buddha was represented as an embodiment of (impersonal) divine grace, which appeared ever anew on earth in a series of rebirths and for which, often, also an *adi-buddha* was thought to exist. From there it was no great step to fashion the Buddha into a type, the representative of the saint who had fully achieved salvation and is thereby deified and who could have appeared and still may appear in as many copies as one wishes. 'Self-deification' was the ancient Indian meaning of asceticism and contemplation, but with these conceptions, the living redeemer had entered the belief. However, the living redeemer is the *bodhisattava.* Formally, the *bodhisattava* was bound up with the Buddha, first through the theory of rebirth and the concept taken over from the Hindu philosophy of world epochs.

The historical Gautama Buddha of the present epoch had passed through 550 rebirths before his entrance into *nirvana.* With the penultimate rebirth as the saintly *arhat,* who in the next rebirth would be Buddha, the state of *bodhisattva* (whose nature, *sattva,* is illumination, *bodhi*) is attained. He dwells in *tuschita,* heaven, where even now the future Buddha, Maitraya is sojourning as *bodhisattva.* By a miraculous incarnation in the body of his mother, *maya,* the historical Gautama Buddha himself had come from the *tuschita* to his last journey on earth in order to bring his teaching to man before his entrance to *nirvana.* Clearly, with his 'blowing away', interest had to turn to the coming saviour, the *bodhisattva.*

A *bodhisattva* was, ideally, a saint who has attained 'perfection', and who with the next birth can be a Buddha and arrive at *nirvana.*

When this does not happen and he remains, rather, a *bodhisattva* it was held to be an act of grace which he dispenses so that he may work as a helper-in-need to the believer. Hence he became the peculiar object of Mahayanistic hagiolatry. It is clear this change went a long way towards meeting lay interest in the holy.

Active goodness (*paramita*) and grace (*prasada*) are the attributes of the *bodhisattva*. He is not only there for his own salvation but at that same time and primarily for the sake of man. He is not only a *pratyekabuddha* but also a *sammasambuddha*. He could not possibly resolve to achieve his own salvation alone from this world of suffering so long as there were still others left there to suffer. *Upaya* (the duty, actually, in characteristic ceremonial terminology 'propriety') hindered him. The speculative doctrine of a trinity which had emerged in this school made this easier for the *bodhisattva*. He had experienced *nirvana* only in the first of his forms of existence, the *nirvana kaya*. The Buddha becomes a man in order to save men. He saves them, however, not by suffering, but through the mere fact that now he, too, is transient and as a goal has only *nirvana* before him.

In addition to adaptation to economic conditions, and adaptation to the needs of the laity for a helper in time of distress, there was adaptation to the needs of brahmanically-schooled intellectuals. The simple banning of all speculation on things useless for salvation, as Buddha had consistently done, could not be upheld. A whole religious-philosophical literature came into existence, increasingly and exclusively employing the classical language (Sanskrit), establishing universities, holding debates and religious disputations, and developing, above all other things, a somewhat complicated metaphysics in which all ancient controversies of classical Indian philosophy were revived. With this, the rift between knowledgeable theologians and philosophers and the illiterates was, in a quite brahmanical manner, imported into Buddhism.

Concept of soul In ancient Buddhism the denial of the 'soul' concept had been one of its essential peculiarities. But this idea was soon given up. As the 'metempsychosis' of Buddhism turned into the brahmanical concept and did not retain the ancient pure doctrine, so too was the case of the concept of divine potency. As in Vedanta, it is the conception of the 'pan-psychic' and the extreme spiritualization of the world, conceived as an emanation closely approaching the *maya* doctrine which occasionally appears explicitly. Everything is but subjective appearance; supreme knowledge dissolves it. Finally, the beginnings of a revival of an organic relativism of ethics is reminiscent of the Bhagavad-Gita.

181

The *bodhisattva* appears, like Krishna, ever anew on earth and can, corresponding to the *trikaya* doctrine, according to the ethical needs of the world, appear in any form and profession according to demand. Hence he appears also, above all, as a warrior. According to his nature he would fight only just and good wars. But when he does fight he will be unhesitatingly free of scruples. This theory, in practice, represents the most extensive adaptation to the needs of the world. Theoretically, these accommodations were predicted on the introduction of some sort of super-worldly divine being.

Acosmic love as in Bhagavata

In the Mahayana school one can also observe the crossing of gnostic and practical elements of acosmic love. Besides the absolute escape in *dharma kaya* with death, there were dis--tinguished two kinds of this-worldly *nirvana*: (1) *Upadhisesa nirvana*, the freedom from passion which, however, has not yet been freed from *samsara* because intellectual gnosis was lacking—always the characteristically relational element in Buddhism; and (2) *Anupad-hisesa nirvana*: *Upadhi*-(materialization)-free *nirvana*, which through full gnosis is a this-worldly state of bliss of the *jivan-mukti*, freed from *samsara*. However, the concept of inner-worldly *nirvana* is not thereby exhausted.

Besides world-fleeing mysticism there is found (3) the inner-worldly mysticism of a world-indifferent life, which proves itself precisely within and against the world and its manipulations. Inwardly it escapes from the world and death and accepts birth and death, rebirth and renewed death, life and action with all their apparent joys and apparent griefs as the eternal forms of being; it is in this that the mysticism maintains its assurance of salvation (*certitudo salutis*).

The Buddhist turn of the scholarly form of inner-worldly world indifference, which appears in the Bhagavad-Gita represents the wisdom and feeling of the absolute nothingness of those events over and against the timeless value of the conscious unity with *dharma kaya,* and thereby with all creatures who are encompassed with acosmic compassionate love. Traces of this point of view extend far back and it is understandable that this approach should be represented at present as the truly authentic Mahayanistic one, for it allows for the interpretation of the *bodhisattva* idea in the sense of a very modern mysticism.

Bodhicitta is the capacity slumbering in each human heart for 'knowing love' which awakened wakes *pranidhana,* that is, the unshakable will to work as *tathagata* (redeemer) through the whole sequence of one's own births for the salvation of the brethren. In this way the theoretical basis was won for satisfying the religious needs of the nonliterary lay strata which ancient Buddhism had been unable to offer, namely, living redeemers (*tathagatas* and *bodhisattvas*) and the possibility of dispensing grace, self-evidently and primarily magical grace for the here and now, and only secondarily grace for the future, for rebirth and the hereafter.

The middle way of attaining holiness and folk magic   While the spiritualistic form of the Mahayana doctrine existed, yet in the practice of religious life the ubiquitous, customary, lay representations gained the upper hand. Nagarjuna, who founded the Mahayana teachings in the first century A.D. had in his *prajana paramita* (transcendental wisdom which has attained the shore of the future) indeed taught the 'void' as the specific form of existence (*sattva*) of the saved. Besides a combination of all means of self-alienation described as the 'middle way' (*madhyamika*, including particularly alms-giving and readiness to die for the suffering creature), he held continuous meditation and knowledge (*prajna*) as the last and highest means of achieving the holy. However, even he considered the sage to be endowed with magical power. With verbal spells (*dharani*) and mystical finger-placing he compels men and natural spirits. Finally, with Vasubandhu's teaching, four hundred years later *tantra* folk magic, namely, the attainment of the ecstatic *samadhi* state imparting magical power (*siddhi*) was introduced alongside the Hindu pantheon. With this the development was completed; Vasubandhu was held to be the last *bodhisattva*.

The lack of rational ethics   A rational inner-worldly conduct was not to be established on the basis of this philosophically distinguished, spiritualistic soteriology of Mahayana. The elaboration of the ancient lay ethic does not go beyond recommending the customary virtues and the special Hinduistic–Buddhistic rituals—elements which in our context it is not worthwhile to analyse in detail. For obedience to the superhuman miraculously qualified *bodhisattvas* and magic was, of course, the dominant trait. Magical therapy, apotropaic and magical homeopathic ecstasy, idolatry and hagiolatry, the whole host of deities, angels, and demons made their entrance into Mahayana Buddhism. Above all, it accepted heaven, hell and a messiah. In the seventh heaven enthroned on high, beyond 'craving' for life, and for 'name and form' (individuality), dwells the Bodhisattva Maitreya, the future saviour, the bearer of a specific Buddhistic messianic belief.

Merits of Buddhism   However, in this development we must not overlook those traits of inwardness and charitable compassion for all creatures which Buddhism and, in Asia, Buddhism alone wherever it went has incorporated into the sensitiveness of peoples. In the case of Hinayana Buddhism monastic schools for lay needs in the form of elementary schools existed, presumably since Asoka. While the actual doctrine of salvation of Buddhism represented the soteriology of genteel intellectuals, one cannot deny that its indifference to the castes also had practical ramifications. Some of its ancient schools are expressly recorded as having been founded by shudras. These schools, as reported by Chinese pilgrimages, were located in the bordering lands of northern India and represented the ancient Church.

Outside missions and the decline of Buddhism

A direct foundation of Hinayanism, perhaps more rightly, of the pre-schismatic ancient Buddhistic orthodoxy is to be found in the Singhalese (Ceylonese) Church. This occurred a few centuries after the Aryan conquest (345 A.D.) when (presumably) Malinda, a son of Asoka, made his appearance as a missionary. In spite of frequent reverses, repeated conquest by Malabars and especially the South Indian Tamils, the rule of the Buddhist monastic hierarchy has yet been permanently maintained. This was supported by kingship based upon a magnificent irrigation system and the requisite bureaucracy which made Ceylon the granary of southern Asia. Very extensive land grants and the inculcation of the reader with the authority of the monastic hierarchy fill up almost the entire epigraphic and chronistic legacy of the time of the Ceylonese rulers. (There was an expansion of this school also in Burma, Siam, etc.)

However, the truly great missionary religion of Asia, as stated before, was not the Hinayana but the Mahayana Church. Mahayana Buddhism, too, like the Hinayana school first won its missionary tendency through a king, Kanishka of Kashmir and north-west Hindustan, shortly after the beginning of our era. Under him the presumably third and last of the canonical councils which Mahayana Buddhism recognizes took place in Kashmir.

The main expansion of Mahayanism took place in the time up to the seventh century A.D. Ever since the fifth century A.D. the star of Buddhism in India has been slowly paling. In addition to the reasons already adduced, perhaps one of the factors is also the prebendalizing process which, in one sense, sets in with all religions and which the Mahayana school could promote. Settled hierocrats dispensing grace, i.e. prebendaries, appeared in the place of wandering mendicant monks. It appears, too, that later Buddhism, like Jainism, often and preferentially employed ritually schooled and devoted brahmans for the temple services proper. Given the original enmity to the brahmans, these play a surprising role in many of the legends. Hence, in India too, there rather soon appears a Buddhistic secular priesthood composed of individuals who are married and are hereditarily appropriating the monastic prebends. As soon as a strictly disciplined organization with missionary purposes came onto the scene in competition, not only the external but the internal weakness of Buddhism became apparent. This was the lack of a firmly outlined lay-ethic such as that represented by brahmanical caste ritualism and also Jainistic parish organization. Obviously, the renaissance of Hinduism found an easily tillable field and has eliminated almost every trace of the ancient Buddhist Church. However Mahayanism expanded beyond India to China, Korea and Japan and became a world religion from the time of the king Kanishka. There it encountered dynasties which were more firmly bound up either with a non-Buddhistic stratum of literati (China and Korea) or with a non-Buddhistic state cult (Japan) and therefore the secular power in general there assumed more the role of a 'religious police' than that of a 'patron saint' for the Church, hence, theocratic clericalization was very slight.

It should be mentioned here that the decisive opponents of Buddhism in China were the Confucian literati. Their views were that duty, and not fear and hope of transcendental reward and punishment, should be the source of virtue and that devotion for the sake of obtaining remission of sins was no expression of true piety. Finally they thought that *nirvana* idealizes inactivity. To these views the apologists of Buddhism rejoined that Confucianism showed consideration only for the present world, or, at best, for the happiness of descendants, but not for the future hereafter. They argued, furthermore, that heaven and hell are the only effective disciplinary means to human virtue. Especially this last argument may have made an impression on the emperor. In addition to this was the belief as well in the magical power of the Buddhist genteel literati, which made this religion popular among the Chinese. Thus, in spite of opposition, Buddhism penetrated the Chinese masses. Whatever inwardness, charitable feeling for man and animals, and sensitivity are at all to be found in China had to some degree been promoted by the mass of translated and familiarized Buddhistic legendary literature. However, Buddhism never won a controlling influence over conduct.

In Asia as a whole there was free competition of religions and there was reasonable 'tolerance' except for certain restrictions for reasons of state. Where some political interests in any way came into question, they had religious consequences in the grand style.

They were greatest in China, but they also appeared in Japan and, to some extent, in India.

Appraisal

As far as Weber's study of Jainism is concerned most of his observations are correct, but there are some inconsistencies which need to be pointed out. Weber rightly observes that Jainism is older than Buddhism, though some of the writers do not agree with this view. They hold that Jainism is not just younger, it is a sect of Buddhism. The supporters of this view are A. Barth, A. Weber, Lassen, etc., while Jacobi supports Max Weber.[10] Weber rightly points out that Jainism laid more emphasis on asceticism than Buddhism. Both denied God. Whereas Jainism believed in Atma, Buddhism did not. However, even in Buddhism, the Mahayana sect had some sort of belief in Atma, which changed its form after the death of a person.

However, Weber is not correct when he mentions that there were twenty-five *tirthankaras,* Mahavira being the last. According to most of the scholars there were twenty-four *tirthankaras,* Mahavira being the last.[11] His contention that the Digambara separated themselves from the Swetambara is also not correct. Actually it was the Swetambara who formed a new sect, after separating themselves from the Digambara. Barth rightly observes that the Digambara or 'those who are clothed in air', that is to say, who go naked, appear to be more ancient as this title already occurs in the inscriptions of Asoka.[12]

His contention that the Digambara were driven from public life during the nineteenth century by the British police is also untanable. His statement that there were severe restrictions on the travel of laity and they had to obtain the permission of the guru in advance is also not correct.

Although Weber rightly mentions the three gems of Jainism, i.e. right knowledge, right faith and right conduct, and refers to certain steps to achieve holiness, he does not mention clearly the fourteen steps which are the essential ingredients of Jainism. Neither does he mention the twelve vows and eleven pratimas which raise the householder to the stage of an ascetic. His interpretation of the Jains' vow of *ahimsa* is also not correct. His contention that the practice of *ahimsa* led to the exclusion of the Jains from all industrial trades endangering life does not appear to be wholly valid as many of the Jains were agriculturalists. As Barth rightly observes,

> They still always collect, however, in remarkable groups in the south, where they in general practise agriculture, and in western

Hindustan, where they prefer to devote themselves to commerce, and where communities of them, which are for the most part wealthy, hardly present any traces of their primitive asceticism.[13] His contention that there were some contradictions in Jain's teaching about the importance of contemplation and asceticism in attaining *moksha* is also not tenable. Between the two, i.e. contemplation and asceticism, which is more important for attaining holiness, may be confusing for a Westerner, but an Orientalist knows very well that both are equally important and are complementary to each other.

As stated above, Weber failed to mention some of the important characteristics of Jainism. So it will be appropriate to give a more clear exposition of those tenets which Weber's writings lack. The five important elements of Jainism are (1) the three gems (*ratnatraya*), (2) the fourteen steps or *Cauda gunasthanaka*, (3) the twelve vows, (4) the eleven *pratimas* (or steps), and (5) the five different ranks an ascetic may hold before he finally attains *moksha*. As stated before the three gems of Jainism are: right knowledge (*samyak jnana*), right faith (*samyak darsana*) and right conduct (*samyak caritrya*). Before stating the fourteen steps to liberation from *karma* and attaining *moksha,* by the laity as well as by the ascetic, it may be mentioned here that the number of vows and the extent to which they are to be followed differ for different classes and also for the laity and the ascetic.[14] Out of the twelve vows to be followed by the laity, the first five great vows are the same both for the laity and the ascetic, though their contents for the two differ. For example in case of *ahimsa* whereas the laity promise never intentionally to destroy a *jiva* that has more than one sense and they would not prevent a king leading an army in defence of his kingdom, an ascetic must be careful never to run the risk of breaking the vow in walking. For instance he must walk the trodden paths, in which the presence of any insect could be detected.[15] Now let us discuss the fourteen steps. The Jains believe that the soul, while on the first step (*mithyatva gunasthanaka*), is completely under the influence of *karma* and knows nothing of the truth. At the second step, the soul, whirled round and round in the cycle of rebirth, loses some of its crudeness and ignorance, and attains to the state called *granthibheda* when it begins to distinguish a little between what is false and what is true. It is on rare occasions that he has some faint remembrance of what is true. A soul that mounts to the third step is in an uncertain condition, one moment knowing the truth and the next doubting it. A man at the fourth stage has, either through the influence of his past good *karma*, or by the teaching of his guru, obtained true faith. However, the soul is still unable to take vows which help in the fight against *karma* and so the step is called *avirati*. Although the man at this stage has destroyed excessive anger, pride and greed, he has not yet entirely escaped from their influence. On the fifth step, the step of merit, as it is often called, one realizes the great importance of conduct, for up till now the faith has exercised the thoughts of the climbers. He can now take the twelve vows which deal largely with questions of behaviour. This step has three parts. First a man promises not to drink intoxicants or to eat flesh and constantly repeats the *magadhi* salutation to the Five Great Ones (*panca paramesvara*). Secondly, he tries to follow the twelve vows. Thirdly, he eats only once a day, maintaining absolute chastity and finally forms the determination to become a *sadhu*. This is the highest step that a layman can reach as such, for if it be successfully surmounted, he will become a *sadhu*. At this stage, too, moderate anger, deceit, pride and greed are controlled, and sometimes destroyed.

The next nine steps are for the professed ascetic. At the sixth step even slightest passions are now controlled or destroyed. These include pride, enjoyment of the senses, *kasaya*,[16] sleep, gossip, etc. The Jains believe that if a soul is to mount the next step, he must never indulge in any of these for more than forty-eight minutes at a time. At the seventh step anger is absolutely destroyed, but pride, deceit and greed remain. The soul's power for meditation increases, for the bad qualities which lead to sleep are absent. At the eighth stage called the *apurvakarana* the man experiences such joy as he has never known before in his life. (Among the Digambara some say that women can only mount as high as the fifth stage, others believe they can reach the eighth step.) As anger disappears at the seventh step, so does pride now. A man at this stage increases his powers of meditation of yoga. At the ninth stage not only does the man attain freedom from deceit, but he becomes practically sexless. At the tenth step the advanced ascetic loses all sense of humour, all pleasure in beauty of sound or form, and all perception of pain, fear, grief, disgust and smells. Some slight degree of greed still remains to the ascetic at this stage.

At the eleventh stage the greed of the ascetic is completely destroyed and he becomes an *anuttaravasi deva*. He knows that he will become a *siddha* after he has undergone one more rebirth as a man. When a man is on the twelfth step, he has not only won freedom from greed but also from all the *ghatin karmas,* which prevent him from acquiring true knowledge, true faith and true happiness, from speaking the truth, from controlling his passions, etc. If a man reaches the thirteenth stage, he preaches and forms a community or *tirtha,* he becomes a *tirthankara*. He first obtains 'eternal wisdom, illimitable insight, everlasting happiness and unbounded prowess'. When this absolute knowledge is acquired, Indra, Kubera and other heavenly beings meet to hear eternal wisdom from the *kevali*. After prayers have been offered, the *kevali* goes about preaching truth, until, when the day of deliverance approaches, he takes to the third part of the pure contemplation (*Sukladhyana*). Here the soul reaches every part of the universe and is yet contained within the body. It is the *tirthankara,* the man at this stage, that the people worship. The moment a man reaches the fourteenth stage, all his *karma* is purged away, and he proceeds at once to *moksha* as a *siddha*. The *siddha* alone know exactly where every one is on the heavenward road, but they have lost all interest in this question. Thus as a soul passes from stage to stage, it gains the three gems, and the possession of these ensures the attainment of *moksha*.

We have mentioned above the qualities which an ascetic possesses as he moves along the fourteen steps. However, the different ranks which the monks hold in a Jain community need brief discussion before we conclude, as Mrs Stevenson rightly remarks,

> We have traced the journey of a *jiva* along the upward path that leads through the destruction of karma, by way of the fourteen upward steps and the keeping of the twelve vows and the eleven Pratimas, to monkhood. It only remains to us to note the different ranks a man may hold as an ascetic before he finally attains *moksha*.[17]

As mentioned above there are five ranks among Jain monks and collectively they are known as *panca paramesvara*. At the initial stage a Jain monk is just an ordinary ascetic or *sadhu* roaming from place to place, immersed in meditation and eating only once a day. The next step to which he can rise is that of a *upadhaya* or instructor. He is expected to study the scriptures and teach them to his fellow monks. He should have a standing of at least one year before he is chosen as an instructor. A still higher rank is attained when a monk becomes an *acharya* or superior. In many sects the *acharya* is chosen simply by seniority but in others an *achara* is selected for ability, or powers of leadership. The power of excommunication for religious offences lies with the *acharya* acting with the Jain community or *sangha* and it is to the *acharya* that, whenever possible, the monks of his *sangha* should make confession. The goal of every monk is to become at last an *arihanta* or *tirthankara*, the being who has attained perfection of know-ledge, perfection of speech, perfection of worship, and absolute security, for no danger or disease can ever come where he is. Literally a *tirthankara* is one who finds a ford (*tirtha*) through this world (*samsara*) to *moksha*, or one who attains a landing on the other side. A *tirthankara* has still four *karma* left which bind him, and he has not yet reached his final goal. And it is by austerities that these last *karma* are destroyed, then the soul loses its body and becomes a *siddha*. The *siddha* has the following characteristics: absolute knowledge, faith, insight, righteousness and prowess. He also has the power of becoming minute and gigantic at will, and of moving anywhere unhindered; he is unaffected by anything, so that neither death, disease, rebirth, nor sorrow can any longer touch him. He is also without a body; and this is the reason why Jains feel that they never pray to a *siddha*.

As far as Buddhism is concerned Weber's knowledge was better than his knowledge of Jainism. He rightly points out that Buddhism in the early stages denied both God and atma, to distinguish itself from Jainism and laid more emphasis on contemplation than on asceticism. He rightly stresses that salutary knowledge in Buddhism meant the practical illumination by the four great truths of the nature, origin, conditions and means of destroying suffering. However, his version that its five commandments not to kill, steal, commit adultery, lie or get drunk, and even its noble eightfold path (right understanding, right thought, right speech, right action, right livelihood, right effort, right mindfulness and right concentration) did not lead to rational asceticism or a positive life method is not very convincing. Gard, on the other hand, rightly observes that Buddha gave a middle path which was conducive to rational living. Once when Buddha was dwelling near Benares in the Deer Park he said,

> Monks, these two extremes should not be followed by one who has gone forth as a wanderer. What two? Devotion to the pleasures of sense, a low practice of villagers, a practice unworthy, unprofitable, the way of the world (on the one hand); and (on the other) devotion to self-mortification, which is painful, unworthy and unprofitable.[18]

The Aryan eight-fold way is, to wit: right view, right aim, right speech, right action, right living, right effort, right mindfulness, right concentration. Weber's contention that the emphasis was on non-action, to have pure contemplation, is too exaggerated. It was meant mostly for the monks, and not for the laity.

Weber describes some of the causes which led to the rapid expansion of Buddhism. These include (1) compassionate acosmic love (which always goes with the psychological form of mystical holy state), (2) the appearance of professional monks in the form of a community and in this the motive for the propaganda activities was the material interest of the monks in the increase of

the givers of subsistence, the *upasaka*, (3) the weakness of the
orthodox Hinduism which laid too much emphasis on sacrifices,
and (4) the adoption of the religion by great kings particularly
Asoka. Although Weber mentions these four factors for the
expansion of Buddhism, his emphasis is on the second and fourth
ones, while from the historical point of view the first was more
important. Not only did he fail to emphasize the role of the first
factor correctly, he also forgot to mention two other important
factors, viz. (1) the role of Buddha's personality, which was deified,
and (2) that preaching, as instructed by Buddha, was done in local
dialects. As Barth rightly points out,

> Besides its doctrines and precepts, Buddhism had its institutions
> and its spirit of discipline and propagandism, a quite new art of
> winning and directing souls; it had, especially, Buddha himself,
> and his memory, which remained a living one in the Church. . . .
> Brahmanism, in which everything is impersonal, whose most
> revered sages have left behind them only a name, has nothing to
> oppose to the life of Buddha, which however imperfectly
> historical as regards facts, has certainly preserved to us the
> physiognomy of the Master, and the ineffaceable image of him
> transmitted by his disciples. These narratives, drawn up as they
> are in that frightful Buddhist style, the most intolerable of all
> styles, form, nevertheless, one of the most affecting histories
> which humanity has ever conceived. . . .
>   In any case, these have gained more souls for Buddhism than
> its theories respecting existence and Nirvana. To meditate on the
> perfections of Buddha, to admire him, to love him, to confess
> and feel one's-self saved by him, were new sentiments unknown
> to Brahmanism; and singular it is that it was thus a religion
> without God which first introduced India to a sense of the inner
> delights of devotion. So long as Buddhism preserved the
> monopoly of these sentiments, it grew and multiplied, and its
> existence will be threatened from the day when the neo-
> Brahmanic religions, particularly Vishnuism, shall in their turn,
> take advantage of these sentiments, and turn them against it.[19]

He further adds that we have also to see the legend of Buddha in
this context.

> The ideal of the Brahman, elevated as that is, is egoistical; it is
> to save himself, and to save himself alone, that he aspires at
> perfection. It was to save others that he who was one day to be
> Gautama disdained to tread sooner in the way of Nirvana, and
> that he chose to become Buddha at the cost of a countless
> number of supplementary existences. The Brahman has got the

length, too, of in theory professing goodwill towards all other creatures; but among his own fellows there are many whom he spurns with horror, and contact with whom defiles him. Buddha knows that man is defiled only by sin, and the very Candala, who is less than a dog, is received by him as a brother.[20]

He further adds its weapon of war was that which the Master had already employed, preaching in the vulgar tongue. To that, besides its legends and biographies, was added by degrees quite a popular literature, of collections of parables and semi-religious, semi-profane stories, the subject of which is often taken from the earliest existences of Buddha, and which form one of its most original creations. Mr Gard observes, 'Buddha made a radical departure from the ancient Indian custom of recording the scriptures in a particular language, and this can well be pointed out as one of the causes of the success of Buddhism'.[21] About its service to others Mr Gard observes that in Buddhism the first four principles of progress towards enlightenment included four sublime states (*brahma-viharas*) included loving-kindness or benevolence (*maitri* or *metta*), compassion (*karuna*), joyous sympathy or gladness in others' well-being (*mudita*) and equanimity (*upekha*). When there is suffering in others it causes good people's hearts to be moved, thus it is compassion. Gladness is characterized as gladdening (produced by others' success). Its function resides in being unenvious. Equanimity is characterized as promoting the aspect of neutrality towards being. Its function is to see equality in beings.[22]

Weber rightly points out some of the changes brought about in the ancient religion whether in both the branches or in one of them. For example the practice of receiving money by the monks, idol worship and the concept of *bodhisattva* (redeemer), the concept of soul, *tantra* folk magic and less emphasis on good conduct by monks, which ultimately led to its downfall. But Weber also discusses changes which brahmanism brought about in its own practices to fight Buddhism (see the next chapter). According to Barth some of these changes were the introduction of personal deities of legendary character such as of Mahadeva, Krishna, Rama, etc., the gradual discontinuance of sacrifice to the advantage of alms giving, pious deeds, and the worship of *latreia*, especially that aversion to the shedding of blood which has more and more restricted the practice of animal sacrifice, and which ended up eventually in the whimsical exaggeration of charity towards brute beasts in the erection of hospitals for them in a country where there were none for men.[23]

Max Weber refers to the ten commandments of Buddhism and the eight noble principles but does not discuss these clearly in spite of the fact that they are the heart of Buddhism. These, along with certain other essential elements of Buddhism, have been discussed in detail by Gard and we would like to mention them in brief here before we close. Gard points out that the 'middle way' given by Buddha indicates two important points:

> The Eightfold Path is an amplification, or an exemplification, of the Middle Way, a course of 'right doing'; and the Eight-fold Path is stressed particularly by the Theravada Pali tradition—it has been largely supplanted by the six or ten Paramitas (perfections) of the Bodhisattva in the Mahayana and Vajrayana traditions.
>
> The Eight-fold Path consists of eight interdependent categories or aspects of proper Buddhist practice, both mental and physical.[24]

These eight principles have already been mentioned in the foregoing pages. But the last two, i.e. *right mindfulness* and *right concentration*, need further elaboration. The following description is attributed to the Buddha.

> And what, bhikkhus, is right mindfulness? Herein, O bhikkhus, a brother, as to the body, continues so to look upon the body, that he remains ardent, self-possessed and mindful, having overcome both the hankering and the dejection common in the world. And in the same way as to feelings, thoughts and ideas, he so looks upon each, that he remains ardent, self-possessed and mindful, having overcome the hankering and the dejection that is common in the world. This is what is called right mindfulness.
>
> And what, bhikkhus, is right rapture? Herein, O bhikkhus, a brother, aloof from sensuous appetites, aloof from evil ideas, enters into and abides in the *First Jhana*, wherein there is cogitation and deliberation, which is born of solitude and is full of joy and ease. Suppressing cogitation and deliberation, he enters into and abides in the *Second Jhana*, which is self-evoked, born of concentration, full of joy and ease, in that, set free from cogitation and deliberation, the mind grows calm and sure, dwelling on high. And further, disenchanted with joy, he abides calmly contemplative while, mindful and self-possessed, he feels in his body that ease whereof Aryans declare 'He that is calmly contemplative and aware, he dwelth at ease'. So does he enter into and abide in the *Third Jhana*. And further, by putting aside ease and by putting aside mal-aise; by the passing away of the happiness and of the melancholy he used to feel, he enters into and abides in the *Fourth Jhana*, rapture of utter purity of

mindfulness and equanimity, wherein neither ease is felt nor any ill. This is what is called right rapture.

This bhikkhas is the Aryan Truth concerning the Way leading to the cessation of Ill.[25]

He further adds that an understanding of the threefold training is essential for an understanding of Buddhist principles and practices which form an integrated way of life. The threefold training is called *ti-sikkha* in Pali and *tri-Siksa* in Sanskrit, in which *sikkha* means 'study, instruction, discipline'. It comprises (1) *adhisila-sikkha:* virtuous conduct (nos. 3, 4, 5, i.e. right speech, right action, and right living of the eight-fold path); (2) *adhicitta-sikkha*: training in *samadhi*, concentrative absorption, i.e. higher thought (nos. 6, 7, 8, i.e. right effort, right mindfulness and right concentration of the eight-fold path); and (3) *adhipanna-sikkha*: training in panna, transcendent comprehension and understanding for enlightenment (*bodhi*) i.e. higher insight (nos. 1 and 2, i.e. right understanding and right thought of the eight-fold path). Thus the threefold training provides instruction and guidance for those who would progress toward enlightenment.

Ten commandments and the principles of progress towards enlightenment

The principles of progress toward Enlightenment—other than the middle way, the eight-fold path, and the threefold training to which they may be related—are sets of training rules which become self-imposed vows and disciplines for the *sangha* and valued guidances for the laity.

> They are the four *Parajikas*, the ten *Sikkhapadas* and related ten *Silas,* and the ten *paramitas* in the Theravada tradition; the thirty-seven *Bodhipakkhiya dhammas* in the so-called Hinayana tradition; and the ten *Parajikas* (first four identical with the Theravada tradition) and six or (later) ten *Paramitas* in the Mahasanghika and Sarvastivada schools and the Mahayana and Vajrayana traditions.[26]

The ten *sikkhapadas* also known as *dasa-sikkhapadani* are training rules or precepts (but not 'commandments') for the monks. These are (1) training in aversion/abstinence from destroying life, (2) abstinence from taking what is not given, (3) abstinence from sexually immoral conduct (chastity for the monk or nun, non-adultery for the laity), (4) abstinence from false speech, (5) abstinence from occasions for the use of intoxicating liquor, (6) abstinence from eating at the wrong hour, (7) abstinence from dancing with singing and instrumental accompaniment and travelling shows or fairs, (8) abstinence from occasions for adorning oneself with garlands, perfumes, and unguents, (9) abstinence from the use of high, large (comfortable) beds, and (10) abstinence from accepting gold and silver (money).[27]

The so-called *dasa-sila* (ten requisites of good behaviour) are of more concern to the laity. They are undoubtedly influenced by the *dasa-sik khapadant*: (1–4) are the same but thereafter, (5) abstinence from slander, (6) abstinence from harsh or impolite talk, (7) abstinence from frivolous and senseless talk, (8) abstinence from covetousness, (9) abstinence from malevolence and (10) abstinence from heretical views. The first five *silas* are regarded the most important for the *sangha* and laity and are commonly called the *panca-sila* which are recited in ceremonies as the 'Pansil' by the *Sangha* and laity, either separately or together in assembly.

Another set of principles, the *paramitas* (perfections, virtues, requisites), for the training of the *bodhisattva* toward enlightenment arose with the Mahayana, possibly as an attempt to combine monastic and lay Buddhist practices, and provided its characteristic approach. These are:

(1) *Dana-paramita* (perfection, etc. of giving) according to which a *bodhisattva* must know and practise (a) whom to give to, (b) what to give, (c) how to give, (d) why to give, (e) *karuna* (universal compassion), and (f) transfer his *punya* (merit) to others.
(2) *Sila-paramita* (perfection, etc. of virtuous conduct), which is comparable to the *dasa-sila* of the Theravada Pali tradition listed above.
(3) *Ksanti-paramita* (perfection, etc. of forbearance, endurance, and acceptance of the truth).
(4) *Virya-paramita* (perfection, etc. of 'energy') in which there is the *virya* of practice and activity, and hence a threefold activity of moral development, textual study and general education,. and altruism.
(5) *Dhyana-paramita* (perfection, etc. of meditative concentration). These are almost the same as nos. 7 and 8 of the eight-fold path.
(6) *Prajana-paramita* (perfection, etc. of transcendent comprehension and understanding for enlightenment). In this, *prajana* depends upon hearing the teaching from another person and on the study of Scripture to have realization.

To these six *paramitas* four more have been added to make them ten. These are:

(7) *Upaya-paramita* (perfection, etc. of beneficial expediency), according to which the *bodhisattva* exercises 'skilfulness or wisdom

in the choice and adoption of the means or expedients for converting others or helping them'.

(8) *Pranidhana-paramita* perfection, etc. of the profound resolution to produce the thought of enlightenment, *bodhi-citt-otpada*).

(9) *Bala-paramita* (perfection, etc. of the ten powers which are differently listed in the *Dharma-sangraha* and the Mahavyutpatti)

(10) *Jnana-paramita,* (perfection, etc. of transcendent understanding and knowledge).

In the Theravada tradition the ten *paramis* (cf. *paramitas*) are slightly different. Having thus fulfilled the (ten) perfections, these (divine abidings) then perfect all the good states classed as the ten powers, the four kinds of fearlessness, the six kinds of knowledge not shared (by disciples) and the eighteen states of the 'enlightened one'. This is how they bring to perfection all the good states beginning with giving.[28]

The stages of progress towards enlightenment   In following the principles of progress toward enlightenment, irrespective of their particular formulation in the Theravada, Mahayana and Vajrayana traditions, and the various schools, the Buddhist must be mindful of the threefold training (*tri-siksa*)—that virtuous conduct (*sila*), concentrative absorption (*samadhi*) and transcendent comprehension and understanding (*prajna*) for enlightenment (*bodhi*) are interrelated and interdependent. He should objectively know and subjectively experience that he is in the process of development towards enlightenment. Such a process is conceived and described in all major Buddhist traditions as 'stages of progress towards enlightenment' in categories of (a) the four *brahma-viharas,* (b) the four *caryas* and (c) the seven, ten or thirteen *bhumis* (cf. *viharas*).

(a) *The four brahma-viharas* (sublime states) are (1) *metta* (or *maitri*), loving-kindness or benevolence; (2) *karuna,* compassion; (3) *mudita,* gladness in others' wellbeing; and (4) *upeksa*, equanimity. These have already been stated in the foregoing pages.[29]

(b) *The four caryas*: When the *stravaka* has made a profound resolution (*pranidhana*), which becomes a prediction (*vyakarana*) of his success, and undertakes the production of the thought of enlightenment (*bodhi-citt-otpada*), then he is ready to train as a *bodhisattva*. Then according to Mahayana tradition his career will be in four stages (*caryas*). These are the 'natural' career (*prakreti-carya*), the 'resolving' career (*pranidhana-carya*), the 'conforming' career (*anuloma-carya*) and the 'preserving' career (*anivartana-carya*).

In the first stage it is the nature of *bodhisattvas* in this world to respect mother and father, to be well-disposed to recluses and brahmans, to honour their elders, to practise the ten right ways of behaviour, to exhort others to give alms and acquire merit, and to honour contemporary Buddhas and their disciples. But as yet they do not conceive the thought of winning the unsurpassed perfect enlightenment.

In the 'resolving' career, apprehending the remorseless force of impermanence, (Sakya Muni) as soon as he had worshipped (a Buddha), resolutely exerted himself to destroy that power.

In the 'conforming' career, the great being, the *bodhisattva,* is established in conformity with his (future) enlightenment.

In the 'preserving' career, *bodhisattvas* fall away and go again through the round of rebirths.

(c) *Bhumis*: A *bodhisattva's* entire career has been divided into several parts and stages. He rises and advances from one stage to another till he attains enlightenment. These stages have been called *bhumis*, and also *viharas*. *Bhumi* has thus become a philosophical term, meaning 'stage' (of spiritual progress). Almost all the (Sanskrit) Buddhist treatises divide a *bodhisattva's* career into *bhumis*, but the *bodhisattva-bhumi* also discusses thirteen *viharas* (states, stations). There are at least four different schemes of division in the principal Sanskrit treatises combining different numbers of *bhumis* and *viharas* in different ways. The titles of the ten *bhumis,* commonly recognized by the Mahayana and Vajrayana traditions are as follows:

1 Pramudita (the Joyful One)
2 Vimala (the Pure, Immaculate One)
3 Prabhakari (the Illuminating One)
4 Arcismati (the Radiant, Flaming One)
5 Sudurjaya (the One Difficult to Conquer)
6 Abhimukhi (the One Which is Present)
7 Durangama (the One Which goes Far)
8 Acala (the Unmovable One)
9 Sadhumati (the One Having Good Discrimination)
10 Dharmamegha (the Cloud of Dharma)

To these sometimes are added:

11 Tathagata (the Buddha) or Samantaprabha
    (the Universally Luminous One)
12 Nirupama (the Incomparable One)
13 Jnanavati (the One Possessing Knowledge)

Mr Gard concludes by saying,

Knowledge, morality and concentration (panna, silam, samadhi) are the pillars of the Buddha-sasana. Morality has no meaning or value without knowledge. Therefore knowledge is placed before morality. Concentration on the other hand without morality is like a house without foundation. Morality is the discipline in the outer life on which concentration, the discipline of the inner life, is built up. Morality thus has to precede concentration. Concentration again is of no value in itself; it is an instrument for the attainment of insight (vipassana) and wisdom (panna), which in its turn produces a higher form of morality and concentration until by this spiral-like progression (in which the same elements re-appear on each higher stage in greater intensity) Boddhi or enlightenment is attained.[30]

7 Hinduism in the Middle Ages and After

It was pointed out in the last chapter that Buddhism began to emerge as a great religion after the death of Buddha and it actually became so near 200 B.C. when King Asoka adopted it as a state religion. He himself became a convert. The various reasons which led to its expansion along with princely patronage were: (1) an organized monkish community with certain rules and regulations; (2) its opposition to sacrifices; (3) the abolition of caste distinction; (4) its literature being available in the people's language; (5) its accessibility to all; (6) its magic power; and (7) Buddha as its saviour. But after the reign of Kanishka it began to decline and was wiped out of India by 1000 A.D. The reasons for its decline, as stated by Weber, have been discussed in the last chapter. Here we shall study what happened to Hinduism after the emergence of Buddhism and Jainism in India and the factors which led to its restoration gradually.

The beginning of various cults and sects in Hinduism

Weber points out that the impersonality of the godly has been the truly classical conception but presumably it has never consistently been the only one, even among the intellectual strata and the brahmans. This held least for lay circles, particularly the strongly developed, cultured, but unmilitary citizenry in the time of emergent Buddhism.

With a universalism based on the religious depreciation of the world and an organic relativism of 'world affirmation' we find ourselves on the true grounds of the classical viewpoint of the Indian literati, as developed by the intelligence during the ancient epoch of nobles and petty princes. Yet there always existed that massive popular orgiasticism against which the intellectuals had closed the doors and which they detested and scorned. Alcoholic, sexual, and meat orgies, magical compulsion of the spirit, personal deities, living and apotheosized saviours, ardent cultist love of personalized helpers-in-need, conceived as incarnations of great merciful gods-all, these were familiar elements of popular religiosity. The Bhagavata religion, although in structure still native to the cultured stratum, nevertheless made extensive concessions to the redemption belief of the laity with its need for grace and help in distress. These were also affected by Buddhism and Jainism as we shall see later on.

In the Middle Ages Shiva and Vishnu were not new creations. Shiva was only eliminated by silence in the literature of the ancient Vedic brahmanhood because of the orgiastic character of the ancient Shiva cults. That the individual could find refuge with a redeemer as with a divine incarnation was a concept which was at least current in the heterodox soteriology of the intellectuals, particularly the Buddhistic, from the beginning. It was hardly invented by the Buddhists. The position of the magical guru, with his absolutely authoritative and personalized character, is already known to us in the Upandishads. What was first lacking in the classical Bhagavata religion or, if it already existed, was not taken up by the strata of cultured literati, was the ardent love of the redeemer of the later Krishna religion.

The Buddhism which for certain reasons (discussed in the last chapter) had become predominant in India and elsewhere from 200 B.C. onwards was pressed back step by step in the first one thousand years and finally was almost completely exterminated.

The restoration took place with the decay of the heterodox intellectual soteriologies, on the one side, in the stereo typing of caste ritualism, namely in the form in which it appears in the law books of the first century of our time calculations. On the other side, the restoration occurred in the propagation of the ancient classical Hindu sects dating to the epoch of prior great kingdoms. And indeed it took place through the same means to which the heterodox communities owed their success: an organised professional monkdom.[1]

It is to these sects that Weber turns now. The soteriological interests of the ancient intellectual strata, i.e. the kshatriya, had receded and the brahmanhood had to reckon only with the non-literary strata of 'rajputs' who were indeed different from the ancient kshatriya, their namesakes.

Literarily the brahmanical restoration manifested itself in the final editions of the epics. In practice, however, it appeared as a mission, in the rise of Purana literature. The final editions of the epics are the products of eminent brahman editors. Quite the contrary is the case for Puranas. It was no longer the ancient, scholarly, pre-eminent brahman families who composed this species; ancient bardic poets, it appears, left the material. It was procured by temple priests and wandering monks (concerning whom more follows) eclectically organized, and contained the holy teaching of the particular sects; the epics, however, above all the Mahabharata, were still a kind of interconfessional, ethical paradigm. And as such it was recognized by all great sects.

Like the learned rewritten sections of the epics, which in their latest editions are already developing into this genre of literature, so are the Puranas, above all, the Bhagavata Purana, even now an object of recitation for the broad Hindu public.[2] What then were the new elements of content? There are two new personal gods—in themselves ancient, but at last accepted into the official intellectual culture for the first time grown to influence—Vishnu and Shiva. There are some new holy values. Finally, the construction of the hierarchical organization of the sect development of medieval and contemporary Hinduism had made its appearance. We now turn to the holy values.

Tantra *magic*

The ancient, cultivated, intellectual soteriology ignored and banned all orgiastic–ecstatic and emotional elements, together with the correlated magical practices belonging to original folk belief. However, the brahmans, in the interests of their power positions, could not completely ignore the influence of this magic and the need for rationalizing it, as, indeed, had been accomplished already in the Atharva-Veda with its concessions to unclassical magicians. In *tantra* magic folk ecstasy made its entrance into brahmanical literature, and the *tantra* writings were viewed by many as the 'fifth Veda'.

Tantra magic was originally a form of orgiastic–ecstasy called forth through common indulgence of the five *nukara* (known in later terminology as the 'holy circle' (*purubhishaka*)), the five things beginning with the letter 'M': *madia,* alcohol; *mamsa,* meat; *matsya,* fish; *maithura,* sexual intercourse; *mudra,* holy finger gestures (presumably originally pantomines). The most important was alcohol bound up with sexual orgies, and next, the bloody sacrifice beside the concluding meal. The goal of the orgy was doubtless ecstatic self-deification for magical purposes. He who has attained possession of god, *bhairava* or *vira,* has magical power; he is united with the feminine creative power of Sakti, which later appears under the names Lakschmi, Durga, Devi, Kali Sana, etc., represented by a naked woman eating meat and wine (*bhairavi* or *nayika*).

In some of its forms this cult was certainly ancient. As everywhere, here also the orgy as a form of holy-seeking of the lower strata, especially also the Dravids, remained for a long time, particularly in South India where the brahmanical caste order only developed late. The Jagannath festival in Pali was an occasion, until the very threshold of the present, when all castes still ate together. Even the very energetic moral policy of the British was only able with difficulty to control the sexual orgies and at most suppress their public manifestation.

The symbol of the ancient fertility spirit with which the sexual orgies were homeopathically tied was here as everywhere else in the world the phallus (*lingam,* actually the combination of male and female genital parts). In all India it is lacking in almost no village. The Vedas deride the cult as an evil custom of the underprivileged.

In the course of amalgamation the ancient feminine fertility spirits were first elevated to the status of wives of the brahmanical gods. A particular godly form illustrating this process is the ancient Vedic fertility god, Shiva (the Vedic Rudra). Ranged beside him was Vishnu as sun and fertility god. The feminine fertility demons came to be ordered beside one of the three orthodox gods, or better, subordinate to them. So, for example, Lakschmi was located beside Vishnu, Parvati to Shiva, Sarasvati (as patroness of lovely music and writing) to Brahma. Other goddesses followed. Many gods and, above all, goddesses not even represented in ancient literature now appear, and the Puranas are their literary expression.

The driving motive of the brahmans in this reception and accommodation process was in part quite grossly material. They wished to protect the many prebends and incidental fees which were available if one accepted the services of these ineradicable folk deities. There also was the force of competition against the powerful salvation confessions of Jainism and Buddhism which had managed to get into the saddle only through adaptation to the folk tradition. The important parts of tantristic, magical-esoteric literature, formed its literary expression. The religious–philosophical connecting point was sought in the teaching of Samkhya philosophy of the *prakriti* and in the Vedanta concerning *maya*, which they conceived monistically as the original material, or dualistically as the feminine principle in opposition to masculinity, represented through Brahma as world creator. The intellectual spiritualization of the orgy was developed into meditative worship of the holy circle (instead of the feminine sexual organs). The urban Sakta cult also developed into the adoration of the naked woman as representative of the goddess cult act. Bound up with the alcoholic and sexual orgy of the folk cult was often the specifically Sakta cult form of blood sacrifice, the *puja*—originally, and until the threshold of the present, a human sacrifice and a meat orgy. Such cults negative to the rationalization of conduct are also found, in eastern North India (Bihar and Bengal), to be bound up with the middle classes. Such was the kayastha (scribe) caste which for a long time was predominantly tantristic. However, the distinguished strata of brahmanhood always remained remote from this accomodation, although they too had to seek a relation to folk cults.

Shivaism and the lingam cult

The brahmans succeeded in concealing the alcoholic and sexual orgiastic character of the adoration of the phallus (*lingam* or *linga*) and transformed it into a pure ritualistic temple cult which was diffused throughout the whole of India. This cult commands the interest of the masses because of its cheapness, as water and flowers serve for the normal ceremonies. In characteristic opposition to the ancient sexual orgiasticism, the god was happy when the lingam remained chaste. The *tantra* literature, corresponding to its orgiastic origin, consists almost completely of dialogues between Shiva and his wife.

The brahman and mimamsa teacher Kumarila Bhatta, named Bhattacharya, in the seventh century A.D. is the first great polemicist against the Buddhist heterodoxy. The first-established, extensive and lasting workable solution, however, the renaissance of brahmanhood in the sense of a joining of the ancient philosophical tradition of intellectual soteriology with the propaganda needs, took place under an (apparently) Malabar brahman half-breed and learned commentator on classical Vedanta writings of Sankara, named Sankaracharya, in the eighth or ninth centuries. He presumably died at the early age of thirty-two years (in truth, thirty-two years after the beginning of his reformation). He appears to have been the first to have systematically developed the particularly incongruous Vedanta doctrine that Brahma-Para-Brahma was the personally highest and, at bottom, single god.

All other divine beings were appearance-forms of Brahma. Of course, though he was himself regent of the world he was not its final basis. In the Hindu system this must unavoidably remain super-personable and inscrutable. In the Hinduistic hagiolatry Sankara stands at the peak. All orthodox Shivaistic sects consider him leader and many conceive him as an incarnation of Shiva. In the most eminent brahman school of India, the Smarta (from *smriti*, tradition), especially in the south with the famous monastic school in Shringerie and in the north primarily with the monastic school in Sankeshwar, Sankara is made central to doctrine and the schools adhere rigidly to his teaching. Since his work, each new brahmanical reform movement has had to acknowledge a personal god as world regent and the syncretistic orthodoxy has then formed Brahma with both folk gods Shiva and Vishnu into the classical Hindu trinity. Of course, Brahma himself remained an essentially theoretical figure and in the nature of the case subordinated to both other deities. A cult was organized around him only in a few temples for distinguished brahmans. Actual sect relations considered either Shiva or Vishnu to be the highest and, particularly in fact, the single God.

The peculiar classical neo-brahmanical soteriology develops almost completely in the name of Shiva. Sankaracharya proposed a monastic reform in the grand style, with the conscious intention of fighting the heterodox Buddhist and Jainist monastic orders. This monastic order, according to official tradition divided into ten schools, he headed as '*dandi'*, the name taken from the pilgrim's staff. Only a family-less brahman (without parents, wife or children) could be taken into the order. This was different from the ancient classical hermit, i.e. *vanaprastha*. It was his *dharma* in the time of wandering not to stay more than one night in a village. The rules of ethical conduct were bound up with the traditional brahmanical soteriology: 'self-control', controlling the word, body and soul in action, and thought was basic. For each of the four great monasteries, which Sankara himself founded a 'novitiate' was established. After twelve years as monks the *dandi* and sannyasi achieved the dignity of 'Para Hamsa'. Only the deified full monk was originally permitted to serve the laity as guru. Each monk and also each correct lay person who belonged to a sect had his guru. Generally only 'twice-born' castes could be received into the sect, only brahmans into the order. The monks at present designated *sannyasi* are often illiterate, serving member castes not 'twice-born', taking money, and conducting an empirical (in general not workable) therapeutic which they propagate as a secret teaching.

The chastity asceticism generally known from the epics was transformed by Shivaism into a mass phenomenon within the sect as well as for the laity. However, their holy practices are of an irritative type—in opposition to yoga contemplation—often pure, nervous virtuosity performances. The most frightful spirits and the fertility god were represented as powerful magical virtuosi thirsting for sacrificial blood. With these things, gradually freed from its symbolic origin, the phallic lingam-fetish came to play a major cultic role for the masses. The eminent Smarta school considered itself to be the representative of the ancient tradition because it retained in its purest form the Vedantic holy value of self-negation through unification with the deity and the Vedantic holy path: contemplation and gnosis. The ancient Hindu teaching of the three *gunas—satva, rajas, tamas—*lived on in the sect. So did the impersonality of the divine spirit in the three forms—being, wisdom, holiness—live. Within the *maya* world of cosmic illusions, they could be manifested as a personal god and as an individual spirit which could be conscious (*viraj*). The wakeful spiritual state of the individual soul is the profundity of divinity—dreamless removal of the highest type because the holy object is approached.

With this teaching, the popular lingam cult had only slight relation. For the simple worshipper of the lingam, in general it was not Shiva but the lingam-fetish, and in all cases the ancient masculine or, more often, feminine and strongly animistic local deity which was familiar to him as the object of the cult. In this the ancient Shiva cult and, particularly, the ancient Sakti cult, in a manner originally peculiar to his wife the goddess Durga, received the orgy and blood sacrifices as an unclassical form of folk cult.

The introduction of the entire unclassical lingam cult into classical ritual which knew nothing of it was, of course, difficult in practice. The greatest Shivaist festival on the twenty-seventh of February is even now purely the worship of a decorated lingam bathed in milk. The entire 'spirit' of this cult was in tension with the tradition of intellectual soteriology as well as with that of classical Vedic ritual. In fact the danger of a breach always remained, as the split between orgiastic and ascetic orientation in Shivaism today indicates. It resulted in a large number of controversies, above all, in the heresy of Basava, the founder of the Lingayat sect, which in the general view is the most bigoted of all Hindu religious communities. The denial of Vedic ritual by Basava resulted in a breaking loose from the brahmans and a splitting of the caste order.

The religious equality of all men, and also of women, was preached. They not only rejected *tantra*, but belonged, at least in their beginnings, to the few sects which doubted the *samsara* teaching. The holy objective of the intellectuals consisted of meditation on the theory and symbols of the supernatural potency of Shiva's spiritualized lingam, leading to complete indifference to the world and the highest achievement of grace (*prasada*). However, Shiva was worshipped in magical-ritualistic form. They carried the lingam as an amulet (*jangama-lingam*). The loss of this object was held to be highly dangerous to one's luck. Besides the adoration of this amulet and the temple-phallus (the *sthavara-lingam*, that is to say, the firmly fixed, non-portable lingam), they recognized the devotion to the holy word and syllable (Om). Its priesthood, the Jangama, were in part wandering and monastic ascetics, in part lingam-temple priests. The latter belonged at times to an 'establishment' of Lingayat villages. In general they served as gurus for the laity.

In the beginning they first adhered to the ancient castelessness. However, later on, with the general fate of the sects, the Lingayat was pressed into the caste order, on the basis of professions or traditional castes.

Vishnuism and Bhakti piety

In spite of all contrary influences and nuances a significantly different type of religion (or group of religions) of the Hindu renaissance, different from that of genuine Shivaism, is indicated by Vishnuism. Orthodox brahmanical Shivaism reduced the orgiastic ritualism of the lingam cult to chastity. It took over the ancient classical Vedanta soteriology and introduced a personal world-regent into the system. In its inwardly highly heterogeneous form it won adherents, on the one hand from distinguished brahmans as a new orthodoxy; on the other hand, among the masses of peasants it appeared as a village temple cult. In truth, of course, though not recognized by the orthodoxy, blood, alcohol, and sexual orgies remained the domain of the actual folk cult of Shiva.

Vishnuism, on the other hand, tempered orgiasticism through passionate devotion and, indeed, primarily in the form of the love of the redeemer. The bloody sacrifice of ancient Shivaism and the radical virtuosity of chastity were strange to it. Vishnu, as an ancient sun god, a vegetation deity, was celebrated by a non-bloody cult, rather than with sexual (fertility) orgiasticism. The specific saviour religiosity found its basis primarily in the middle-class burgher strata of Indian society.

It was primarily the Krishna cult, which provided the basis from which this development could proceed. Vishnuism was the religion of 'avatars'. It was the religion of the incarnation of highest gods come down to earth. Krishna was not alone: ten, then twenty, then twenty-two, then even more deities were found. Ranking beside Krishna appeared a second important and highly popular incarnation of Vishnu: Rama. Rama was perhaps a victorious historical king, the hero of the second great Indian epic, Ramayana. He was occasionally represented as the brother of Krishna. He was even occasionally (in the Mahabharata), described as one of Krishna's appearance forms and in three different figures, all held to be the incarnations of the same hero, as benefactor and saviour. In contrast to Krishna, who in all his acts is throughout unethical, Rama is far more moralistically accoutered. The relation to the ancient cult of the sun, Surya, was far more strongly retained in his cult than in that of Krishna. We have already indicated how the 'belief' in a personal inner relation of trust came to the foreground, e.g. in the Bhagavat religion. Further development led to the concept of an all-powerful personal god, Vishnu, the ancient Vedic sun and fertility god, with whom the ancient deity of the Bhagavat was identified. Krishna was held to be the most important incarnation of the mythical redeemer. The main point, however, was that a new quality of piety already appears in late interpolations in the Mahabharata. Holy knowledge and gnosis, ritual and social fulfilment of duty, asceticism and yoga meditation are in no case the decisive means of holiness. This was obtained through *bhakti*, the passionate inward devotion to the redeemer and his grace.

It is possible that this meditative piety was peculiar to a sect, the Bhaktas, who were different from the Bhagavats already in earlier times. In the last edition of the epics meditative piety is bound up with the doctrine of grace. The orgiastic, and indeed sexual-orgiastic origin of Bhakti ecstasy, is clear beyond all doubt, for the sexual orgies of the Krishna worshippers persisted even after the brahmanical sublimation to god-contemplating devotion, remaining until the present. The youthful adventures of the hero who was, according to the legend, a shepherd (Gobinda) with the shepherdess (Gopis) stood from early times at the centre of the Krishna myths and also, indeed, of the Krishna mimes. The famous Gitagovinda, first made available to the West in Ruckert's translation, was a glowing, erotic, poetic representation of these adventures.

Bhakti versus other holy paths

In contrast to the *certitude salutis* which this salvation circumstance provided, all the other holy paths receded. The *advaita* salvation of the Vedantists, as well as Mimamsa justification by work, are minimized while the 'cool' wisdom of the Samkhya salvation did not even come into the consideration of the Bhakti practitioners. All ritualistic or other holy practices of Hindu piety only had value so far as they were addressed to the redeeming god or saviour. This had already been taught by the Bhagavata religion. Such religious manifestations were important, finally, only as technical devices, subordinate to the single decisive holy circumstance.

In this interpretation, anything, at least so long as the right attitude is present, may serve as a religious means. The theory of the *gratia irresistibilis*, being saved as the young are carried in the mouth of the cat stood over and against that of *gratia cooperativa*, in which grace operates like the ape mother whose young hang about her neck.[3] Once again the 'sacrifice of the intellect' was demanded. The individual is required 'not to doubt the command-ments of the Vedas with human reason'. 'Works' are valuable only if—corresponding to the teaching of the Bhagavad-Gita—they are disinterested (*niskama*). 'Interested' (*sakama*) works cause *karma*, the 'disinterested' works lead to *bhakti*. According to the sublimated form of Bhakti theory, the true Bhakti adherent preserved himself in the love of god finally in the absence of impure thoughts and drives, particularly anger, envy and desire. Beside *karma-marga*, the holy path of the ritualistic brahmans, and *inana-marga*, the holy way of the contemplative Brahmans, and beside *yoga-marga*, the holy path of the (increasingly) non-literary ecstatics, appeared also *bhakti-marga* as an independent holy means. Meanwhile the most sublimated and ethically rationalized forms were opposed to one another which the *bhakti*-state essentially crudely included. For *bhakti* became a form of holiness which was diffused in all strata of Vishnuistic Hinduism—and partially also beyond these. And of the non-ritualistic, pure forms of holy-seeking, it is even today, in general, the most broadly diffused in India. This is true even though by the classical brahmanical tradition each of its forms is held only to be an unclassical holy path.

The Rama cult

As a form of emotional redemption religion *bhakti-marga* quite naturally became the primary form of holy-seeking among the non-literary middle classes. Almost all Hindu reformers of Vishnuistic preference have in some way or other seized upon the crypto-erotic sublimation, or, in reverse, the popularization of Bhakti holy-seeking and its combination with ancient Vedic ritualism. In South India the professional teachers of Bhakti, the alvar, distinguished themselves from the teachers of disputation, the *acharya*. Parti-cularly to them belong Ramanuja (twelfth century) and Raman-anda (fourteenth century), the most significant founder of Vishnuist sects based on the Rama cult. Both these founders were brahmans who led wandering lives as teachers and who conducted the organization and instruction of mendicant monks, quite in the manner of Sankaracharyas.

The Ramanuja sect and dwaitawadi

Ramanuja is supposed to have left behind him seventy-four (or indeed eighty-nine) gurus as personal disciples and *directeurs de l'âme*. And it appears that the stability of his organization essentially rested on the fact that it was a hereditary hierarchy. In addition to the *dandis* and *sannyasins*—names which forthwith were used for the Shivaistic mendicant monks—there appeared the vairaghis as (most) of its Vishnuist competitors were described.

The doctrine which Ramanuja constructed out of the Vedanta system of Sankara held that behind the personal god belonging finally to the *maya* world is the inscrutable, attribute-less Brahman. The personal God (*parabrama*) is reality and world regent, not a part of the *maya* world but substantially different. In fact he is as much different from the spiritual (*chit*) as from the non-spiritual (*achit*). *Maya* and impersonal divinity were held to be products of 'love-less' doctrine. Accordingly, as a holy value, immortality and not reception in the divine was promised. The influence sphere of the sect was called 'dualistic' (*dwaitwadi*) because it taught the substantial difference of God from the soul substance and thereby the impossibility of reception in God (the Vedantic *nirvana*). Among Vishnuists there were two schools: the adherents of the *gratia cooperativa* which characterized the Sanskrit-educated monks (Vadagala) and the adherents of the *gratia irrestibilis* (Tengala). The last-named school inclined to strong indifference towards caste distinctions. However, according to the genuine teaching of Ramanuja the achievement of the true *bhakti* was connected with *upasana*, the ancient classical meditation, also with Vedic education. Consequently, it was not immediately available to the shudra. *Bhakti* could be achieved only through *piapatti*, unconditional devotion to God out of a feeling of complete helplessness; therefore, holiness was available only through the guidance of the Vedic-cultured guru. Thereby the lower strata who were drawn to it, in consequence of the lack of sentimental motives, were turned toward pure, prayer-formula ritualism combined with all sorts of animal cults (such as the holy ape of the epics). The competition against the Shivaists was at times very sharp and bitter, with counter-persecutions and expulsions, religious disputes, competing monastic establishments or monastic reforms. The discipline of the Vishnuist gurus was partially anomalous and on the whole less ascetic than that of the Shivaists. Ramanuja's reform consisted of actions counter to the phallus (*lingam*) cult. In place of these practices, which in his eyes were unclassical fetishism, he advanced forms of sublimated orgiasticism, namely, the cult meal often practised as the Arkan discipline. The *mantra,* the invocation formula consisting of a few words, occasionally acquired a great significance. Here the feminine deity is the true goddess, in opposition to the Krishna cult with its orgiastic eroticism and preoccupation with Krishna's lovemaking.

The Ramananda sect and the abolition of caste distinctions

On the other hand, an important social innovation was that to be found for the first time as a principle in the mission of Ramananda. This was the disruption of the castes. Such disruption did not concern everyday social organization and everyday ritual. In this, with some exceptions, all sects accepted the caste restrictions without question. However, the question was opened as to the possibility of lower castes achieving guru status. The ancient wandering and teaching philosophers, sophists and holy wise men of the kshatriya epoch, as we saw, were largely eminent lay persons. Very often they were old men who had for the first time taken up the life of the ascetic and wandering teacher, as others who had assumed it temporarily. The heterodoxy, namely, Buddhism, had principally ignored the caste membership of those whom it took into the order and had created the 'professional monk'. The brahmanical restoration took these over, indeed, but once again required for reception into the philosophical schools and monasteries brahman caste membership as a prerequisite to becoming a guru. The Shiva sect, at least officially, on the whole adhered to this.

Ramananda, for the first time, expressly rejected this. Here, indeed, a role was played by the Islamic foreign domination. With Muslims as rulers the spiritual power of the brahmans was multiplied, but the external means of their power decayed. As a result of this founders of the sects sought more than ever to join forces with the masses. All eminent founders of Hindu sects until Ramananda were brahmans and, so far as is known, accepted only brahmans as students and teachers. Ramananda broke with this principle. Among his immediate students—according to tradition—alongside a rajput, Pipa; and a jat, Dhuana was a weaver, kabir; and a chamar (leather-worker), Rai Das. Finally, and more important than this, however, was a phenomenon not without consequences for the infiltration of mendicancy with non-brahmanical elements. Henceforth sects developed in all on the basis of status and professionally diverse non-literary strata. The sect which stemmed from Ramananda and bore his name (the Ramanandi) in a characteristic reaction to the 'democratic' tendencies of his reform, later appeared to have restricted admission to members of the aristocratic caste—the brahmans and those classed as kshatriyas. The esteemed Ramaistic mendicant strata—the Achari—were even recruited exclusively from brahmans.

On the other hand, the Rai Das Panthi sect founded by his

student the chamar, Rai Das, had, corresponding to its social situation, developed social, charitable acosmic love out of bhakti piety; out of opposition to the brahmans it had developed a denial of priestly power and idolatry.

Other sects and Bhaktas

Congruent with the social situation of these despised professional castes is traditionalism and a conviction of the unchangeable nature of the order of the world. It is the basic attitude of many sects. The Maluk Dasis developed the consequences of quietism, while the Dadu Panthi, a Ramanandic sect of cotton-washers established in the seventeenth century, drew extremely deterministic consequences from the doctrines of the Bhagavad-Gita. One should not intentionally seek either heaven or hell, for everything is pre-established and only the capacity for spiritual love of Rama is a guarantee of grace, freedom from illusion and pride, and the suppression of a desire.

In addition to the mendicant monks (virakata), believers in strict possessionlessness, was a stratum which the Indians class as rajas, soliders (nagas), and a third, (bhistu dhari), which pursues bourgeois callings. This cult restricted itself almost completely to formal invocation of Rama. Finally, the sect widely diffused among the weaver castes—the Kabir Panthi, established by Ramananda's student Kabir—came to deny brahmanical authority and all Hindu deities and ritual. It was strongly pacifistic, suggesting the Quakers. It advocated ascetic techniques of holy-seeking—displaying forbearance to all forms of life, avoiding lying and shunning all worldly lust. Here, as in the Occident, textile handwork, with its relation to the household and opportunity for meditation, appears to have demanded such almost completely non-ritualistic religiosity. Here devout worship of the founder as a helper-in-need, and unconditional obedience toward the gurus were cardinal virtues.

The militaristic trend in sects

A great number of Hindu sects developed the naga type of outright weaponed propaganda of their ideas under the strict control of an ascetic guru or gosain. In caste affiliation they were rather 'democratic', however, some like the nagas of the Dasu Panthi sect, were exclusively restricted to the 'twice-born' castes. They made the role of the English difficult, but also have fought each other in bloody feuds. So, for instance, in 1790 under Hindu dominion a battle occurred between the Shiva nagas whom the *vairaghis* had excluded from the great market of Hardwar; the Shivas nagas gave battle, leaving numerous dead on the field. As well, they have repeatedly attacked English troops.

The most significant example of this development of orders of propaganda fighters were the Sikhs ('students', of the founder of the sect and his guru successors), which for a time until the defeat of 1845, retained sovereignty over the Punjab, having established there a kind of pure warrior state. (We shall not pursue further this very interesting development.)

Vallabha

Besides the Vishnuistic sects mentioned above there were certain others which had their teachings on the basis of Vishnuistic salvation religiosity. Among these the two most important are Vallabha's and Chaitanya's. All were renaissances of orgiasticism against the single dominion of brahmanical contemplation as a holy technique. Both display in the turning away from brahmanical ritualism and world-fleeing contemplation not an active, inner-worldly asceticism but an inflaming of irrational holy-seeking—and this despite the introduction of a super-worldly god.

The sect founded at the beginning of sixteenth century by brahman Vallabha, the Vallabhachari or Rudra Samperadaya, is still active among the merchants and bankers of north-west India. It adheres to the Krishna cult and seeks the holy, not in asceticism or contemplation, but in refined, sublimated Krishna orgies, together with a rigid ceremonialism. The founder taught that not abstinence, loneliness or scorn of beauty, but enjoyment of the beauties of the earth and achieving community with him (the *pushui-marga,* doctrine of the holy dinner) led to becoming worthy of the honour of God.

He left his son Vittala Nath as leader, from whose sons the dynasty of gurus ramified. The most distinguished were the successors to Gokula Nath, the Gokulas *gosains*. The temple Steri Nath Dwar in Ajmer is the central holy place of the sect to which each believer must make a pilgrimage once in his life.

The power of the gurus over the laity is great. A scandalous trial in 1862 in Bombay brought to light the fact that occasionally the *jus primae noctis* was practised on the wives of the members and that holy conception, according to ancient orgiastic custom, is still realized among the community members in the present.

The meat and alcohol orgies were sublimated into chaste culinary dinners; and similar changes took place in sexual orgies. It is self-evident that the plutocracy—the richest Hinduistic trader castes, above all, the baniya—was able, in such terms, to find a taste for the service of God. It is strikingly evident here that ascetic religiosity absolutely does not, as, is generally maintained, develop out of the imminent 'nature' of bourgeois capitalism and its professional representatives—quite the contrary. The baniyas, 'the Jews of India', represent indeed the main contingent of these outspoken, anti-ascetic, partly hedonistic, partly ceremonial cults. The holy object and holy path were graduated. Corresponding to the Bhakti principle, grace (*pusti*), becomes the single principle.

The exclusion of the lower castes from the Vallabhachara sect, however, apart from the great expenditure which its *pushui-marga* required, gave this essentially moralistic sect, founded by Swami Narayand, the possibility of doing considerable damage in the lower and also in the middle strata.

The Chaitanya sect and Sankirtan

Exactly the opposite phases of Krishna-orgiasticism to those of the Vallabhacharis were developed in north-east India in a number of sects which had their origin at about the beginning of the sixteenth century with the brahman Chaitanya. He was himself apparently, an epileptic and ecstatic. He taught the identity of Krishna with Parmaturu, the uncreated spirit of the world, which endlessly manifests itself in countless temporary appearances. His important new innovation was Sankirtan, the great singing procession which, particularly in the great states, was elevated to the first rank as a folk festival. Pantomimic or dramatic dances appeared therewith. Vegetarianism and abstinence from alcohol was retained at least among the upper strata, to which the kayasatha (scribes) and the satscudra belonged in Orissa. The principle of hereditary guruhood was also retained by this reform sect. It is the most popular, at least in North India, primarily in Bengal. In mass religion crass sexual orgiasticism dominated. The adherents recruited from the lower-caste Chaitanyatic sect formed the numerically most significant strata of Vishnuists and practised jointly the orgiastic invocation of Krishna (Hari, Hari, Krishna) and Rama. At least for most of them, the sexual orgy was the primary means of self-deification, the device by which they sought absolution. During the sexual orgy each man was Krishna, each woman Radha (his favourite). There is an account of the love life of Radha in the tenth book of the Bhagavata Purana as a symbol of reciprocal mystic love of the divine and central point of the human soul. These rituals are celebrated with song, dance, mimicry, confetti and some orgiastic sexual freedom.

213

The Madhava sect and inner purity

The estimation of pure, inner-worldly behaviour as a holy technique appears only in some small disappearing Vishnuist communities. This was perhaps the case in the sect of Madhava whose adherents were drawn from the brahman Madhava (and minister of King Vijayanagar), abbot of Shringerie, founded the doctrine in the thirteenth or fourteenth century. He was a Vishnuist, an opponent of the Vedanta and an adherent of the unclassical Ramaistic *dwaita* (dualistic) doctrine. Naturally for him dualism was not the opposition between 'good' and 'evil', or between 'god' and 'creatures', rather it lay between temporary life and eternal being. It was not eternal being alone that, for human striving at least, is real, but exactly the opposite life. It is eternal and irreversible. An absorption in formal eternal 'being' in the sense of the brahmanical doctrine, namely, the Vedanta, holds nothing for man.

Thus all presuppositions of brahmanical soteriology are cast aside. Within this life man has to create his own holiness. A self-deification is unattainable, an attainment of unity with the godly impossible, for the eternal god is absolutely super-worldly and super-human. Yoga and all the exercises of intellectual soteriologies are meaningless; God dispenses his grace with correct behaviour. With this the way was clear for an ethic of active, inner-worldly behaviour in the sense of the Occident. Meanwhile, meditation as the highest holy path and 'disinterested' behaviour were held alone to be free from sin. There remained only the general presuppositions of Hindu theodicy—*samsara* and *karma*. Beyond this there was also retained the absolute authority over the believers of the knowledge of those soul helpers equipped with the holy (Vedic) wisdom. The unconditional dependence on the guru was held to be indispensable for lay salvation; only from him, not from books, could one win knowledge.

The sects and the gurus

The place of the guru with respect to the believers was, in general, most widely extended in the Hindu community after the brahmanical restoration. The position of the guru was modelled on the original absolute authority of the distinguished teacher of the Veda (guru) over the scholar (*bramacharin*). At that time, however, this held only for conduct within the school. Moreover these Vedic gurus were employed as house chaplains by kings and nobles and as tutors for their sons. They imparted the genteel culture of the kshatriya time. On the other hand the gurus of the Middle Ages and even of modern times were essentially plebeian and less literary mystagogues and soul helpers, though Sankaracharya did not favour such gurus. He had laid down certain qualifications for the gurus as indicated before. Most of these mendicants and gurus were brahmans, but some were non-brahman too. The income which the gurus obtained from the mass sects led to the sharp resistance of the brahmans to the usurpation of these positions. Not new doctrines but the universality of the guru authority symbolized the restoration of Hinduism. Quite apart from the Krishna and Rama cult which it embodied, it was a 'redeemer' religiosity in a special sense. It offered the masses the corporal living saviour, the helper-in-need, confession, magical therapeutic, and, above all, an object of worship in the form of a dignity-bearing guru or gosain—whether it be through the designation of successors or hereditary. All sect founders were deified and their successors became and are objects of worship. The guruhood now constituted the typical role of the brahman. As a guru the brahman is a living god (*thakur*). No correct shudra would fail to drink water in which a brahman had touched his toe or fail to eat the left-overs procured from his table. The eating of the excrement of the gurus in the Gayatri-kriya sacrament (presumably by the Satnami sect established by a kshatriya in North India) and still practised for short periods, was only an extreme case. Each sect-believer had his guru who imparted religious instruction to him, and who taught him the *mantra* (prayer formulae). The guru took the believer into the sect with the drawing of the sect signs through branding or painting. The believer turned to his guru for advice in all life situations. In the Krishna sect children were brought to the guru in their sixth or seventh year and a crown of roses was placed on them. Confirmation took place in their twelfth to thirteenth year with corresponding (*samupana*) ceremony, for which the ancient form of girdling with the holy belts (the *samavartana* ceremony) supplied the rite. However, in terms of its significance it represented consecration of the particular body to Krishna.

Religiously, among the masses the worship of the gurus replaced all other forms of redemption religion. The living saviour or god among the believers displaced all transcendent objects of worship. The authority of the guru was most extensive among the specifically plebeian sects. The institution also offered heterodox mystagogues the chance to represent themselves as soul leaders and to gather adherents to themselves—especially since exclusive political support of the brahmans was lacking. In the days of the Islamic foreign dominion and persecution, the gurus at times were the fixed support of the masses of Hindus in all inner, and consequently also external needs.

215

The position of brahmans

The aristocratic brahman of the early times was the house chaplain of a king (*purohita*), or a noble, as they remain, for instance, in Rajputana. Of equivalent honour to the *purohita* was the position of independent teacher of descendants of brahmans. Ranking after these was the position of teacher of nobles compensated by *dakshina*. A brahman of high caste was and is permitted to receive *dakshina* only from the aristocratic castes. On the other hand, the distinguished caste which, according to rank, was aristocratic and Vedic-cultured (vaikika) claimed a monopoly in the taking of *dakshina* (therefore named 'dakshinacharas'). All temple priests were degraded (in Bengal they were called *madhya*). This was for two reasons. (1) They did not have Vedic schooling; (2) they often lived on the gifts of impure castes.

. Among the full brahmans the highest-ranking individual, according to his own claims, took the ranked position of *pandit*. They were responding jurists and judges; the highest among them in the time before the foreign domination was often held to be the first man of the land.

In all these ancient, historical, brahmanical power positions, it was the possession of holy wisdom which constituted the quality which decisively lent a monopoly to the spiritual prebends. Profane juridical wisdom and the literary schooling constituted properties affording a claim to worldly place.

The increasing number of small burghers and proletarian masses, and the increase of wealth among the burgher strata in the city, raised the chances of a fee for the guru demagogue who was oriented towards them. Eminent brahmans' deep suspicion of this competition could not spare them the bitter experience of developing out of their circles the inclination to incorporate elements from tantristic and other such esoteric elements of Vishnuism. The authority of the *pandits*, even the use of eminent Sanskrit-cultivated and other Brahmans held to be completely classical, declined before that of the non-literary (i.e. non-Sanskrit-cultivated) hierarchies of the masses.

The slow capitilistic development furthered by the English dominion demanded this transformation. The old address '*thakur*', god, for the brahmans was not only given up, but in general, also depreciated by the fact that it is the guru of the plebeian sect who is earnestly and really honoured as a god. Such a divine or godlike place of the guru appears most strongly in precisely the kind of Hindu sect which radically set aside all idolatry and irrational, ecstatic, orgiastic, or ritualistic cult means. Adoration of the living saviour was the last word in Hindu religious development.

Under the Hindu princes this manner of instituting new cults could hardly prevail. However, under the alien beliefs of foreign dominions they were almost exclusively the external form of the propaganda of sect-cults. These developed in greater number under the dominion of the bourgeois occupational strata. For the first time they achieved the possibility of emancipating themselves economically from official orthodox brahmanism or of forcing this brahmanism to accommodate itself to them.

It is established that apparently the most extreme forms of guru veneration were first realized in the last part of the fifth and sixth centuries. And this is understandable. So long as the kings had an interest in the brahmanical secular priesthood, the power of mystagogues and magicians and of monkhood in general could not become excessive. The kings were not inclined to permit the power of sect heads, even where their domestication of the masses exceeded their own. It was first the foreign domination of Islam which shattered the political power of the distinguished Hindu castes, which gave the development of guru power free rein, permitting it to rise to grotesque heights.

Religious faith and economic development

In addition to the ritualistic and traditional inner relation anchored through the caste order to the *samsara* and *karma* teaching (undermined by none of the sects), there also appeared the religious anthropolatry of the Hindu laity against the naturally strong, traditionalistic, charismatic clergy of the gurus. These hindered the rationalization of life conduct throughout. It is quite evident that no community dominated by inner powers of this sort could out of its substance arrive at the 'spirit of capitalism'.

Here Weber also mentions the 'spiritual' elements which outside the caste order and the guru domination of the masses served to fix the economic and social traditionalism of Hinduism. In addition to authoritative fixity, within the intellectual strata there was above all the dogma of the unalterability of the world order, common to all orthodox and heterodox Hindu thought forms. The devaluation of the world which each salvation religion brought with it could here only become absolute flight from the world. Its highest means could be nothing other than mystic contemplation, not active ascetic conduct. Always the extraordinary quality and irrationality of the holy means remained. Either they were of an orgiastic character and linked quite immediately in an anti-rational manner to the course of each alien life methodology, or they were indeed rational in method but irrational in goal. The professional fulfilment, however, which was demanded for example, in highest measure by the Bhagavad-Gita was 'organic'. That is to say, it was rigidly traditionalistic in character and thereby mystically oriented as an activity in the world but yet not of the world. At any rate, it would occur to no Hindu to see in the course of his economic professional integrity the signs of his state of grace or—what is more important—to evaluate and undertake the rational con-stitution of the world according to empirical principles as a realization of God's will.

Allowance must be made for the thinness, past and present, of the Indian intellectual strata proper and, in general, the strata interested in 'salvation' in some sort of rational sense. The masses, at least of contemporary Hindus, know nothing about 'salvation' (*moksha, mukti*). They hardly know the expression, let alone its meaning. Except for short periods, it must have always been so. Quite crude and purely this-worldly holy interest, gross magic, along with the betterment of rebirth chances were the values for which they did and do strive. Moreover the sects, at least today, do not address themselves to the real 'masses'. If one takes as a standard the public membership of a sect (through imparting of the *mantra*, and painting and branding), they comprise scarcely more than 5 per cent of the people. There are probably even fewer Vishnuists, Shivaists, Jains and Buddhists.[4]

The mass of the Hindus sometimes do not even know the names of Shiva and Vishnu. By 'salvation' (*mukti*) the mass of the Hindus understand all events affecting rebirth which is precisely, correspond-ing to old Hindu soteriology, according to the individual's own work, not that of the god. From his local village god the Hindu expected the dispensation of rain and sunshine. From his family god, the Mailar Linga or Kedar Linga (fetish), he expected other everyday needs. From his 'confessional' relation to the guru, whom he consulted as an adviser, hardly anything could be expected, for the guru indeed, beside ritualistic formulae had learned a brahmanical theology quite meaningless for the mass of the laity. Precisely here is the cleft between intellectual religion and the everyday needs of the masses.

The sects and their redemption religiosity were and are an opportunity, mainly for the middle strata advised by intellectuals, to achieve salvation through the power of contemplation in the same manner as the intellectual strata. Wherefrom, to be sure, the point has well been made, that perhaps it does not follow that the peculiarity of intellectual religion and its promise does not have the most enduring indirect influence on the conduct of the masses. However, in its effects, this influence never operates in the sense of an inner-worldly, methodological rationalization of the life conduct of the masses but generally exactly the reverse. Riches, and expecially money, enjoy an almost overwhelming valuation in

Indian proverbial wisdom.[5] However, beside the alternatives self-enjoyment or giving of gifts there stands a third loss. Instead of a drive toward the rational accumulation of property and the evaluation of capital, Hinduism created irrational accumulation chances for magicians and soul shepherds, prebends for mystagogues and ritualistically or soteriologically oriented intellectual strata.

Modern reform movements

Essentially, an opportunity is provided in the modern reform movement within Hinduism for the intellectual strata and indeed, in this case, the modern, European-educated or influenced intellectuals. This appears in the community of 'Brahmo Samaj' much discussed by us, and perhaps still more importantly in the 'Arya Samaj'. Their history belongs in our study as little as that of the Anglo-Indian university-educated, political and journalistic bearers of the gradually developing modern Indian nationalism. Such is emerging in this land of schisms into countless bitter enemy castes, sects, speech and blood groups. This is an appearance which is necessarily foreign to the basic Indian character here portrayed. It grows only on the basis of a unified bourgeois class in connection with a national literature base and above all a press. In general, it establishes a sort of unified (external) life conduct. Historical Hinduism is in precise opposition to all this.

Appraisal

Although most of the observations made by Weber regarding the position of Hinduism from 200 B.C. to the beginning of nineteenth century are correct, yet he misses some of the links in the emergence of neo-Hinduism and the details of various sects under Vedantism. Weber points out that massive popular orgiasticism in the form of alcoholic, sexual, and meat orgies, magical compulsion of the spirit, personal deities, living and apotheosized saviours and ardent cultist love of personalized helpers-in-need were familiar elements of popular religion in the past and were revived in a modified form during the Middle Ages. Similarly the Bhagavata religion advocated by Krishna made extensive concessions to the redemption belief of the laity with its need for grace and help in distress. But he does not mention the other factors, pointed out by Barth and other scholars, which led to the personal worship of Vishnu, Shiva, Brahma and other deities. Barth points out,

219

Almost all ancient literature was esoteric, or became so at
length.... The art of writing having become general, and regard
being had, perhaps, to the practice common among the sects,
attempts were made, without trespassing on the sacred domain
of the Veda, to reproduce under a more accessible form such
doctrines as were of more general interest than others. We think
we must instance the majority of the Upanishads as the first
attempt that was made in this direction, particularly the small
ones, which were of a character specially adapted to the common
intelligence. Other monuments of this literature have perished,
or have only come down to us very materially altered, such as
the old epic and legendary collections, the ancient Itihâsa and
the ancient Purana.... At a later period the numerous
Dharmacastras, or codes of laws, such as those of Manu, of
Yajnavalkya, and others, were drawn up with this very object.
These are compilations comparatively modern, very few of
which date before our era, and some of which are much more
recent, though all are very old in respect of the foundation they
rest on. In this way there arose a purely Brahmanical literature,
without any sectarian admixture, accessible to everybody, and
kept alive uninterruptedly to our day,... It is in these books (i.e.
Smritis particularly Manusmriti) that the most decided stress is
laid on the role of Brahma (mas.), the creator, the father of gods
and men, a figure majestic indeed, but somewhat pallid, as all
the products of speculation are, and ill qualified to dispute the
supremacy with his formidable rivals that had their origin in the
popular beliefs. Unknown to the ancient cultus—although his
prototype, Prajapati, filled a pretty large space in it—he does not
appear to have occupied more space in the new systems of
worship; and many sanctuaries that there are in India, we know
of only one of these that of Pushkara, near Ajmer, in Rajasthan,
which is exclusively dedicated to him. It is likewise in these
books that the theory of four ages of the world (yuga), and of
the gradual triumph of evil, as well as that of the successive
creations and destructions of the universe, following each other
in the lapse of immense periods, is expounded for the first time
in any exact manner.... Besides, no effort is made to raise again
the old deities after the many blows dealt at them in succession
by ritualism, theosophy, and sectarian devotionalism.

Through their eclectic and monotheistic tendency, these books
contributed to the formation of a certain orthodoxy in the
bosom of Brahmanism. On the other hand, the Veda was
accepted more than ever as an absolute authority, which was the
less to be challenged in theory that it was so slightly troublesome
in practice; on the other hand, the recognition of a personal god

and a divine providence, with which the Brahmanas and Upanishads at time dispensed so easily, became by degrees a settled dogma. Under whatever name he might be worshipped, and whatever metaphysical explanation might be given of his nature, it was necessary to confess an Icvara, a lord, and humble one's self before him. The Sankhya, which denied this notion, was pronounced guilty of impiety. The Mimamsa, which ignored it, was also looked upon with suspicion, in spite of its severe traditionalism; and it was obliged to introduce it at the beginning of its creed.... Thanks to that elasticity of Vedanta which enabled it to satisfy all kinds of piety, this system ended by absorbing into itself all the others in the religious domain.... The cultus of Brahmanism never merged in any of the sectarian systems.... The cultus of these new religions was never more than a special devotion, a rendering of a system of acts of homage, a *puja*, which was radically different from the *yajna*, the sacrifice of tradition. The doctrines were intermingled; the rites remained distinct.[6]

Neither does Weber mention clearly the various branches of Vedanta to which he refers. As Professor Varadachari points out

The *Vedanta* system is based on the *Upanishads* which represent the latter portion of the Vedas or their *jnanakanda* portion. Hence this is called as *Vedanta* or *Uttaramimamsa*. This system discusses the nature of God in relationship to the world and the individual souls. Therefore this system is also called the Brahmamimamsa the Supreme Being denoted by the word Brahman.... The main principles of this system are expounded in the *Vedantasutras* also called the *Brahmasutras* in four chapters. Tradition tells that there were in existence the *sutras* of *Sankarsanakanda* in four chapters. They were in continuation of the *Mimamsasutras* and were followed by the *Brahmasutras*. This *Sankarsanakanda* dealt with the deities who were to be worshipped by means of the rites enjoined and dealt with in the *Mimamsasutras*. These sutras which were composed by Jaimini are now lost. The *Brahmasutras* are attributed to the authorship of *Badarayana*. Some scholars identify him with Vyasa son of Parasara while others are opposed to this identity. The date of the *sutras* is placed in 500 B.C. It has four chapters or adhyayas called (1) *Samanvaya* according to which the Upanishads prove the nature of the Brahman, (2) *Avirodha* refuting the views of the other schools of thought, (3) *Sadhana* dealing with the means to get *moksa* and (4) *Phala* stating the results achieved by these means.[7]

The basic texts on which each school of Vedanta is based are the Upanishads, the Brahma-Sutras and the Bhagavad-Gita. Almost all the schools have commentaries on all these texts written to represent their views. Each school seeks to support its doctrines and the lines of interpretation by citing lines from the epics Ramayana, and Mahabharata and to some extent the Puranas. Some of the systems of philosophy and of religion base their authority on the Agamas in addition to these three texts and some are based mainly on the Agamas. The Agamas, which are also known as *tantras* in some cases, prescribe the mode of worshipping a particular deity and a way of life in conformity with the nature of that worship. They must have taken their rise from the influence of the Brahmana portions of the Vedas exercised on those men who preferred the *bhakti* course to that of *karma*. The principles of life and modes of worship prescribed in these, run counter to those established by Vedic tradition in some cases and agree with them in others. They deal in general with *jnana* (knowledge), *yoga* (concentration on one object), *kriya* (action) and *craya* (daily rites). All the Agamas admit that the world is real, and consists of the supreme being, individual souls and material objects. The supreme deity is the lord of the worlds. The Agamas are of three types according to the deities worshipped. Thus there are Vaisnava Agamas, Saiva Agamas and Sakta Agamas.

The main schools of Vedanta are Dvaita, Advaita, Visistadvaita and Suddhadvaita. The minor schools are those of Nimbarka, Bhaskara, Yadavaprakasa, and Caitanya and Sivadvaita.

The founder of the Dvaita school was Anandatirtha, commonly known as Madhva. He attacked the Advaita doctrine and established the Dvaita system. They lend support to the main doctrine of dualism (*dwaita*). Matter (*prakriti*), souls (*jivatman*) and God (*paramatman*) are eternal and different from each other. There is difference also within matter and among the souls. The supreme being is Vishnu whose body is not made up of matter (*aprakrta*). At his will, matter changes into world. The souls are atomic in size. They are of two groups, viz. male and female, which distinction continues to exist even in the released state (*Moksa*). The relationship between God and souls is that of a master and servant. Among the courses prescribed in the Bhagavad-Gita, the course of *bhakti* is adopted by the followers of this school.

According to the Advaita school, the Brahman alone exists. The world which appears to exist does not really exist. It is like mirage, that it appears to exist. Owing to the screen of *maya*, the Brahman's real nature is not understood and therefore the world is found to exist. The Brahman is existent, conscious and is bliss itself. Existence, consciousness and bliss are not the attributes of the Brahman. They are identical with it. The Brahman has no quality. It is *nirguna*. This school admits the reality of the world till this truth of monism is realized. Souls are required to worship the gods. Through this worship and the doing of obligatory rites (*nitya karma*) without expecting any reward in return, a soul gets liberated. There is identity established between the soul and the Brahman and this is the truth (*tattva*) taught in the Upanishads. On account of this identity, this school came to be called Advaita. This experience of identity could be had during one's lifetime and this stage is called *jivan-mukti*. Among the courses prescribed, the path of knowledge is to be pursued to get the final release. Among the earlier writers of this school, were Bhartrprapanca and Gaudapada. Sankara was the pupil of Gobindabhagavatpada, whose preceptor was Gaudapada.

The Visistadvaita school recognizes three realities: supreme being, individual souls and matter. However, Brahman is the only one reality which exists having for its modes the animate beings and the inanimate objects. Among the courses mentioned in the Bhagavad-Gita, this school recognizes the path of devotion and the path of resignation unto God (*prapatti*). Self-surrender is therefore the easiest and surest way to get *moksha*. Vishnu with Lakschmi is considered as the Brahman. In addition to the Upanishads, Brahma-Sutras and Bhagavad-Gita, this school treats the Vaisnava Agamas as authoritative texts. The Vaisnava Agamas are of two types, viz. Pancaratra and Vaikhanasa. The Pancaratra Agamas lay down the way of life for one who follows this school of thought. The Pancaratra Agamas are of as high authority as the Vedas. Aniruddha, one of the incarnations of Vishnu preached these doctrines and they were revealed to Narada, Sanaka, Sandilya and others. Hence these are called Bhagavachhastra. Ramanuja was the main figure who preached the doctrines of Visistadvaita.

According to Suddhadvaita the Brahman is both *saguna* and *nirguna*. It is the cause for the origin, maintenance and destruction of the world. It has *sat, chit* and *ananda* as its attributes which are real. The difference which is found to exist between the individual souls and the Brahman is not natural but due to the will of the supreme being. This is not due to nescience (*maya*) as in Advaita and therefore this school is called Suddhadvaita. By his free will God would give the individual souls a divine body as his own to sport with him eternally. The relation between God and the soul is one of the lord and the lady. Devotion and self-surrender are the means to get his grace. The God worshipped in this system is Krishna under the name of Gopijanavallabha or Sri Nathaji. The preceptor (guru) on earth is regarded as divine and gets divine honours. This school takes as authorities, the Vedas, Bhagavad-Gita and Upanishads and also the Bhagavata. Vallabhachari was the founder of this school.

Among the five minor schools of Vedanta, four are of Vaisnavism, i.e. Nimbarka, Bhaskara, Yadavaprakasa and Caitanya. Among these the last is considered to be most important. His cult places *bhakti* over *jnana* and yoga. Devotion is treated as a sentiment which is felt while adoring Krishna and Radha. Jayadeva's Gitagovinda and the Bhakti cult of the Visistadvaita school appear to have moulded the doctrines of this cult.

The Sivadvaita school holds Shiva as the highest god and except for this it is similar to the Visistadvaita school. Strikantha is considered as the earliest authority on this school. The development of this school is closely connected with Saivism. It may be mentioned here that some of the religious schools of Saivism are wholly based on the Agamas. Among these three, i.e. the Pasupata, Saiva and Kashmirian Saivite schools are based on the Saiva Agamas, while Saktaism is based on the Sakta Agamas. The Saiva Agamas are said to be twenty-eight in number and the Sakta, seventy-seven. The Saiva Agamas believe in the worship of Shiva as the highest deity and the Sakta Agamas in that of Sakti regarded as the world mother. Saktaism recognizes the worship of Sakti. In this school, stress is laid on the powers of sounds, the presence in the human body of a number of threads of occult force (*vadi*) and six great centres of occult force (*cakra*) each resembling a lotus. Faith is laid in the mystic forms of yoga, magic power of diagrams (*yantra*) and gestures made with the fingers (*mudras*). The Sakti-Sutras and the Sakta Agamas are held as the most authoritative texts of this school.[9] Some of them believe in gruesome practices like offering animals and human beings to the deities. Saktaism influenced the Buddhists to a great extent, making them take to tantric practices.

8 General characteristics of Indian religion and other conclusions

In the beginning of the last chapter of *The Religion of India* Weber observes that, for Asia, China played somewhat the role general observations about the Asiatic religions as a whole, including those of China which he studied earlier in detail in a separate volume under the title *The Religion of China* (Confucianism and Taoism). He also studied the main features of these religions *vis-à-vis* other world religions in comparative perspective in his work *Economy and Society* under the head 'The Sociology of Religion'. As we are mainly concerned with Weber's observations on Indian society we shall confine ourselves here to his views on the general characteristics of Indian religion as expressed in the above cited works and where necessary we shall also refer to his views on the general character of Asiatic religion as a whole. In the last chapter of his work *The Religion of India* he also mentions certain other basic features of Indian society which are indirectly related to Indian religious teachings, such as the caste system, the mysterious and secretive character of Indian intellectuals, the lack of national feeling etc., and these we shall also discuss here.

Three main characteristics of Indian religion

In the beginning of the last chapter of *The Religion of India* Weber observes that, for Asia, China played somewhat the role of France in the modern Occident. All cosmopolitan 'polish' stems from China and spreads to Tibet, to Japan and outlying Indian territories. Against this, India has a significance comparable to that of antique Hellenism. There are few conceptions transcending practical interests in Asia whose source would not finally have to be sought there. Particularly, all orthodox and heterodox salvation

225

religions that could claim a role in Asia similar to that of Christianity are Indian.

As regards the chief characteristics of Indian religion he points out its three significant features: (1) toleration of different faiths and sects, (2) salvation through exemplary promise based on knowledge, and (3) salvation to be achieved not by ethical conduct but by grace.

(1) Toleration of different faiths and sects

In the first case Indian religions differed from other great religions, i.e. Christianity, in that, apart from local and pre-eminent exceptions, none of them succeeded in becoming the single dominating confession, as was the case in Northern Europe in the Middle Ages after the Peace of Westphalia. Asia was, and remains, in principle, the land of the free competition of religions, 'tolerant' somewhat in the sense of late antiquity. On the whole various cults, schools, sects and orders of all sorts adapted to each other as in occidental antiquity. Of course, the competing directions could hardly have been valued equally by the majority of ruling strata of the time, nor very often by the political powers. Different social strata cherished different forms of soteriology. The same religions dispensed different forms of holy values and in terms of these they made demands of variable strength on the different social strata. How they did so has been explained by him in *The Sociology of Religion*. He points out,

> As the masses increasingly became the object of the priests' influence and the foundation of their power, the priestly labours of systematization concerned themselves more and more with the most traditional, and hence magical, forms of religious notions and practices. Thus, as the Egyptian priesthood pressed towards greater power, the animistic cult of animals was increasingly pushed into the centre of religious interest, even though it is most likely that the systematic intellectual training of the priests had grown by comparison with earlier times. And so too in India, there was an increased systematization of the cult after the displacement by the Brahmins of the *hotar*, the sacred charismatic singers, from first place in the sacrificial ceremonial. The Atharva Veda is much younger than the Rig Veda as a literary product, and the Brahmanas are much younger still. Yet the systematized religious material in the Atharva Veda is of much older provenance than the rituals of the noble Vedic cults and the other components of the older Vedas; indeed, the Atharva Veda is a purely magical ritual to a far greater degree than the older Vedas.[1]

226

The process of popularization and transformation into magic of religion which has been systematized by the priests continued even further in the Brahmanas. The older Vedic cults are indeed, as Oldenberg has emphasized, cults of the propertied strata, whereas the magical ritual had been the possession of the masses since ancient times.[2]

(2) Exemplary promise and emphasis on mystical knowledge

With very few exceptions the Indian soteriologies knew only an exemplary promise. The exemplary promise takes two forms: either in improving one's chances in the next incarnation by following certain norms or, if the senseless struggle for mere existence is ever to be ended, in the elimination of rebirth as such.[3] Most of these were only accessible to those living monastically but some were valid for the laity. The bases of both phenomena (i.e. different strata have different soteriologies and exemplary promises) were equivalent and were closely interrelated. Once and for all, the cleft between the literary 'cultivated' and the non-literary masses of philistines rested on this. Hanging together with this was the fact, that all philosophies and soteriologies of India finally had a common presupposition: that knowledge, be it literary knowledge or mystical gnosis, is finally the single absolute path to the highest holiness here and in the world beyond. This is not a knowledge of the things of this world or of the everyday events of nature and social life and the laws that they hold for both. Rather, it is a philosophical knowledge of the 'significance' of the world and life. Such a knowledge can evidently never be established by means of empirical occidental science and, in terms of its particular purpose, should by no means be confused with it. It lies beyond science. Asia, and that is to say India, is a typical land of intellectual struggle, each person singly and alone seeking for a *Weltanschauung*, in the particular sense of the word, for the 'significance' of life and the world. Each according to the nature of his own apprehension, unavoidably found gnosis to be the single way to the highest holiness, and at the same time, however, the single way to correct practice. Therefore, in no way is the proposition so close to all intellectualism more self-evident: that virtue is 'teachable' and right knowledge has quite infallible consequences for right practices. According to the circumstances, only wisdom provides ethical or magical power over the self and others. Throughout the 'teaching' this 'knowledge' is not a rational implement of empirical science such as made possible the rational domination of nature and man as in the Occident. Rather it is the means of mystical and magical domination over the self and the world: gnosis. It is attained by an intensive training of body and spirit, either through asceticism or, as a rule, through strict, methodologically ruled meditation. This had two important consequences. (1) The capacity for mystical gnosis is a charisma not accessible to all. (2) Correlated therewith it acquired an asocial and apolitical character. Mystical knowledge is not, at least not adequately and rationally, communicable. This soteriology leads those seeking the highest holy objectives to an other-worldly realm of the rationally unformed; and even because of this lack of form alone available, to a godlike beholding, possession, property, or obsession of a holiness which is not of this world and yet can, through gnosis, be achieved in this life. It was conceived by all the highest forms of Asiatic mystical belief as an 'emptying'. This is an emptying of experience of materials of the world. It is the meaning-content of mystical holy possession which rationally cannot be further explained. The devaluation of the world and its drives is an unavoidable psychological consequence of this.

This mystically experienced holy circumstance, rationally interpreted, takes the form of the opposition of peace to restlessness. The first is 'God', the second specifically creature-like, therefore, finally, either illusory or still soteriologically valueless, bound by time and space and transitory. Its most rational interpretation, of the experientially conditioned inner attitude to the world was conditioned by the Indian *samsara* (belief in the transmigration of souls) and *karma* (compensation for actions) teachings.

Through these two doctrines the soteriologically devalued world of real life won a relatively rational meaning. From *karma* there was no escape other than flight, by means of gnosis, into that other-worldly realm. Thereby the fate of the soul could simply take the form of an 'extinction', or as a circumstance of eternal, individual rest the form of a dreamless sleep, the form of a circumstance of an eternal peaceful state of holy feeling in the countenance of God, or a reception into divine individuality.

Similarly, the idea that for transitory deeds of transient beings on this earth 'eternal' punishments or rewards in the future could be assigned. Therewith disappeared the powerful emphasis which the soteriology of the occidental doctrine of the beyond placed upon the short span of this life. This Weber explains in detail in his essay, *The Sociology of Religion*.

Salvation: this-worldly and other-worldly In his *Sociology of Religion* Weber explains that salvation is related to eschatology, i.e. to the doctrine of death and rebirth and also to the relation of God to the world and to man. Salvation is of two types—this-worldly and other-worldly.

Only a few religions of salvation have produced a single pure solution of the problem of relation of God to the world and to man, from among the various possible pure types. Wherever a pure type was produced it lasted for only a little while. Most religions of salvation have combined various theories, as a result of mutual interaction with each other, and above all in attempt to satisfy the diverse ethical and intellectual needs of their adherents. Consequently, the differences among various religious theories of god's relation to the world and to man must be measured by their degree of approximation to one or another of these pure types.

Now the various ethical colorations of the doctrines of god and sin stand in the most intimate relationship to the striving for salvation, the content of which will be different depending upon what one wants to be saved from, and what one wants to be saved for. Not every rational religious ethic is necessarily an ethic of salvation. Thus, Confucianism is a religious ethic, but it knows nothing at all of a need for salvation. On the other hand, Buddhism is exclusively a doctrine of salvation, but it has no god. . . . Sometimes religious activities which are regarded as distinctively sacred and which promise their participants some salvation have merely utilitarian expectations. . . . In the catalog of goods in the *Shih Ching*, the highest rewards promised to the Chinese subjects for their correct performances of the official cult and their fulfillment of personal religious obligations are wealth and long life, while there is a complete absence of expectations in regard to another world and any compensation there. Again, it is wealth that Zoroaster, by the grace of his god, principally expects for himself and those faithful to him, apart from rather extensive promises relating to the world beyond. As rewards for the ethical conduct of its laity, Buddhism promises wealth and a long and honorable life, in complete consonance with the doctrines of all inner-worldly ethics of the Hindu religions. Finally wealth is the blessing bestowed by god upon the pious Jew.

But wealth, when acquired in a systematic and legal fashion, is also one of the indices of the certification of the state of grace among Protestant ascetic groups e.g., Calvinists, Baptists, Mennonites, Quakers, Reformed Pietists, and Methodists. To be sure, in these cases we are dealing with a conception that decisively rejects wealth (and other mundane goods) as a religious goal. But in practice the transition to this standpoint is gradual and easy.[4]

It is difficult to completely separate conceptions of salvation from such promises of redemption from oppression or sufferings as offered by the religion of the Jews, and also by the doctrines of Zoroaster and Mohammed. For the faithful these promises might include world dominion and social prestige as promised by Islam. In addition to such economic and political salvation, there is the very important factor of liberation from fear of noxious spirits and bad magic of any sort.

The distinctive content of other-worldly salvation may essentially mean freedom from the physical, psychological and social sufferings of terrestrial life. On the other hand, it may be more concerned with a liberation from the senseless treadmill and transitoriness of life as such. Finally, it may be focused primarily on the inevitable imperfection of the individual, whether this be regarded more as chronic contamination, acute inclination to sin, or more spiritually, as entanglement in the murky confusion of earthly ignorance.

He also observes that

> Our concern is essentially with the quest for salvation, whatever its form, insofar as it produces certain consequences for *practical behaviour in the world*. It is most likely to acquire such a positive orientation to mundane affairs as the result of a conduct of life which is distinctively determined by religion and given coherence by some central meaning or positive goal. The goal and significance of such a pattern of life may remain altogether oriented *to this world*, or it may focus on the world beyond, at least in part. In the various religions, this has taken place in diverse fashions and in different degrees, and even *within each religion* there are corresponding differences among its various adherents. Furthermore, the religious systematization of the conduct of life has, in the nature of the case, certain limits insofar as it seeks to exert influence upon economic behaviour.[5]

Having the two theories of salvation in view, i.e. the this-worldly and the other-worldly, Weber comes to the conclusion that Hindu religion as well as the other Asiatic religions were mostly other-worldly religions. The devaluation of the world and its drives is an unavoidable psychological consequence of the Indian religious philosophy stated above. The theory of rebirth, *samsara* and *karma* and finally the gnostic and mystical character of these soteriologies offered no foundation for the development of an adequate, rational methodology for inner-worldly life conduct.

Weber further observes that 'the decisive historical difference between the predominantly oriental and Asiatic types of salvation religion and those found primarily in the Occident is that the former usually culminate in contemplation and the latter in asceticism'.[6] (Of course, the distinction is a fluid one and the heterogeneous elements may combine, as in the monastic religiosity of the Occident.) This distinction has great consequences for the empirical consideration of religions so far as human conduct is concerned. In India, even so ascetical a planned procedure for achieving salvation as that of the Jain monks culminated in a purely contemplative and mystical ultimate goal. In the Occident, on the other hand, apart from a few representatives of a distinctive quietism found only in modern times, even religions of an explicitly mystical type regularly became transformed into an active pursuit of virtue, which was naturally ascetical in the main.

Asceticism and mystical character of Indian religion   Weber points out that asceticism is of two types, i.e. world-rejecting and inner-worldly. The attitude toward salvation, which is characterized by a methodical procedure for achieving religious salvation may be termed as 'ascetic'. Religious virtuosity, in addition to subjecting the natural drives toward a systematic patterning of life, always leads to a radical ethico-religious critique of the relationship to society, the conventional virtues of which are inevitably unheroic and utilitarian. Not only do the simple 'natural' virtues within the world not guarantee salvation, but they actually place salvation in hazard by producing illusions as to that which alone is indispensable. The 'world' in the religious sense, i.e. the domain of social relationships, is therefore a realm of temptations. The world is full of temptations, not only because it is the site of sensual pleasures which are ethically irrational and completely diverting from things divine, but even more because it fosters in the religiously average person complacent self-sufficiency and self-righteousness in the fulfilment of common obligations, at the expense of the uniquely necessary concentration on active achievements leading to salvation.

Concentration upon the actual pursuit of salvation may entail a formal withdrawal from the 'world': from social and psychological ties with the family, from the possession of worldly goods, and from political, economic, artistic and erotic activities—in short, from all creaturely interests. One with such an attitude may regard any participation in these affairs as an acceptance of the world, leading to alienation from God. This is 'world-rejecting asceticism'.

On the other hand, the concentration of human behaviour on activities leading to salvation may require participation within the world (or, more precisely, within the institutions of the world but in opposition to them) on the basis of the religious individual's piety and his qualifications as the elect instrument of God. This is 'inner-worldly asceticism'. In this case the world is presented to the religious virtuoso as his responsibility. He may have the obligation to transform the world in accordance with his ascetic ideals, in which case the ascetic will become a rational reformer or revolutionary on the basis of a theory of natural rights.[7] The person who lives as a worldly ascetic is a rationalist, not only in the sense that he rationally systematizes his own conduct, but also in his rejection of everything that is ethically irrational, aesthetic, or dependent upon his own emotional reactions to the world and its institutions.[8]

He further observes that the distinctive content of salvation may not be an active quality of conduct, that is, an awareness of having executed the divine will, it may instead be a subjective condition of a distinctive kind, the most notable form of which is mystic illumination especially through contemplation. For the activity of contemplation to succeed in achieving its goal of mystic illumination, the extrusion of all everyday mundane interests is always required. According to the experience of the Quakers, God can speak with one's soul only when the creaturely element in man is altogether silent. All contemplative mysticism from Lao Tsu and the Buddha to Tauler is in agreement with this notion, if not with these very words.

These beliefs may result in absolute flight from the world. Such a contemplative flight from the world is characteristic of ancient Buddhism and to some degree characteristic of all Asiatic and Near Eastern forms of salvation. In contrast to asceticism, comtemplation is primarily the quest to achieve rest in God and in him alone. It entails inactivity, and in its most consistent form it entails the cessation of thought, of everything that in any way reminds one of the world, and of course the absolute minimization of all outer and inner activity. By these paths the mystic achieves that subjective condition which may be enjoyed as the possession of, or mystical union with, the divine. This is a distinctive organization of the emotions which seems to promise a certain type of knowledge. For the ascetic too, the perception of the divine through emotion and intellect is of central importance, only in his case feeling the divine is of a 'motor' type, so to speak. This 'feel' arises when he is conscious that he has succeeded in becoming a tool of his god, through rationalized ethical action completely oriented to his god. But for the contemplative mystic, who neither desires to be nor can be the god's 'instrument', but desires only to become the god's 'vessel', the ascetic's ethical struggle, whether of a positive or a negative type appears to be a perpetual externalization of the divine in the direction of some peripheral function. For this reason ancient Buddhism recommended inaction as the precondition for the maintenance of the state of grace, and in any case Buddhism enjoined the avoidance of any type of rational, purposive activity, which it regards as the most dangerous form of secularization. On the other hand, the contemplation of the mystic appears to the ascetic as indolent, religiously sterile and ascetically reprehensible self-indulgence—a wallowing in self-created emotions prompted by the deification of the creaturely.

From the standpoint of a contemplative mystic, the ascetic appears to be forever involved in all the burdens of created beings, confronting insoluble tensions between violence and generosity, between matter-of-factness and love. The ascetic is therefore regarded as permanently alienated from unity with God, and as being forced into contradictions and compromises that are alien to salvation. But from the converse standpoint of the ascetic, the contemplative mystic appears not to be thinking of God, the enhancement of his kingdom and glory, or the fulfilment of his will but rather to be thinking exclusively about himself. Therefore the mystic lives in everlasting inconsistency, since, by reason of the very fact that he is alive, he must inevitably provide for the maintenance of his own life. This is particularly true when the contemplative mystic lives within the world and its institutions. This is a sense in which the mystic who flees from the world is more dependent upon the world than is the ascetic. If he has to live consistently according to his theory, he must maintain his life only by means of what nature or men voluntarily donate to him. This requires that he lives on berries in the woods, which are not always available, or on alms. This was actually the case among the most consistent Hindu *sramanas* (and it accounts also for the very strict injunction in all *bhikshu* regulations against receiving anything that has not been given freely).[9]

As a rule, the more the genuine mystic remains within the world, the more broken his attitude towards it becomes, in contrast to the proud aristocratic feeling with respect to salvation entertained by the contemplative mystic who lives apart from the world.

However, Weber concludes, 'By itself the finally gnostic and mystical character of these soteriologies offered no foundation for the development of an adequate, rational methodology for innerworldly life conduct'.[10]

(3) Salvation by grace

The third distinctive feature of Hindu religion was that, besides gnosis or contemplation, salvation was available by the grace of living saviours. Weber observes, 'So far as its religiosity was sublimated under the influence of the saviour doctrines the religion was transposed into a different form'.[11] The saviour religiosity assumed the form of hagiolatry and indeed a hagiolatry of living saviours, the gurus and their equivalents, be it as mystagogues or as magical dispensers of grace. This gave the religiosity of the non-literary middle classes its decisive stamp.

A charismatic stratum established the practical life conduct of the masses and dispensed magical salvation for them. The gift of the 'living saviour' was the characteristic type of Indian piety. In *The Sociology of Religion* Weber explains the effect of 'soteriology' or salvation from outside. This may be attained either by grace or faith. In the first case the individual's own labour is considered completely inadequate for the purpose of salvation.

> From this point of view, salvation is accessible only as a consequence of the achievement of some greatly endowed hero, or even the achievement of a god who has become incarnate for this very purpose and whose grace will redound to the credit of his devotees, *ex opere operato*. Grace might become available as a direct effect of magical activities, or it might be distributed to men out of the excess of grace which had accumulated as a result of the human or divine saviour's achievements.[12]

According to another view, the god might not be content with one single act of incarnation, but as a result of the permanence of the world, which is practically axiomatic in Asiatic thought, he might become incarnated at various intervals or even continuously as seen in the idea of *bodhisattva* or the *avtara* concept.

Of an essentially magical nature is the view that one may incorporate divine power into himself by the physical ingestion of some divine substance, some sacred totemic animal in which a mighty spirit is incarnated or some host that has been magically transformed into the body of a god. 'Now the means of acquiring these divine blessings may take either a magical or a ritualistic form, and in either case they entail not only belief in the saviour or the incarnate living god, but also the existence of human priests or mystagogues'.[13]

Institutional grace, by its very nature, ultimately and notably tends to make obedience a cardinal virtue and a decisive precondition of salvation. In India for example the guru may on occasion exercise unlimited authority. In such cases the resulting pattern of conduct is not a systematization from within, radiating from a centre which the individual himself has achieved, but rather is nurtured from some centre outside the self. The content of the pattern of life is not apt to be pushed in the direction of ethical systematization, but rather in the reverse direction.

In this pattern, salvation may also be linked with faith.

A completely anti-rational effect upon the conduct of life is generally exerted by religions of faith when the relationship to the god or the saviour exhibits the trait of passionate devotion, and consequently whenever the religion has a latent or manifest tinge of eroticism. Its most striking manifestation occurs in the characteristically Hindu religiosity of love (*bhakti*), particularly in the soteriological forms of Vishnuism. In this Hindu religiosity of love, devotion to Krishna, who has been apotheosized from the *Mahabharata* to the status of a saviour, and more especially devotion to the Krishna child, is raised to a state of erotically tinged devotion.[14]

Besides the unbroken character of magic in general and the power of the sib appears the impregnability of charisma in its oldest form: as a pure magical power.... Not the 'miracle' but the 'magical spell' was the core substance of mass religiosity in India. This was true not only for the peasants and laborers, but also for the middle classes. The 'miracle' in terms of its meaning always appears as the act of some sort of rational, world-linked, godly gift of grace, seen and practised, thus inwardly motivated as a 'spell'; in terms of its sense it stands as a manifestation of magical potencies manipulated by irrational, operational arts and by charismatically qualified beings.[15]

In *The Sociology of Religion* he observes that magical spells and the worship of a functional god were the origin of salvation religion and these continued, because the most elementary forms of behaviour motivated by religious or magical factors are oriented to *this* world.[16]

This most highly anti-rational world of universal magic also affected everyday economics. There is no way from it to rational, inner-worldly life conduct. There were spells not only as therapeutic means, but especially as a means aimed at producing births and particularly male births. The undergoing of examinations or endurance tests was contemplated for achieving all conceivable sorts of inner-earthly values—spells against enemies, erotic or economic competition, spells designed to win legal cases, spiritual spells of the believer for forced fulfilment against the debtor, spells for the securing of wealth, for the success of undertakings. All this was either in the gross form of compulsive magic or in the refined form of persuading a functional god or demon through gifts. With such means the great mass of the non-literary and even the literary sought to master everyday life.[17]

The lack of a rational practical inner-worldly ethic

Weber observes that a rational practical ethic and life methodology did not emerge from this magical garden which transformed all life within this world. Certainly the opposition of the sacred and the secular appeared—that opposition which in the West historically conditioned the systematic unification of life conduct, describable in the usual manner as 'ethical personality'. But the opposition in Asia was by no means between an ethical god and the power of 'sin', the radical evil which may be overcome through active life conduct. Rather the aim was to achieve a state of ecstatic godly possession through orgiastic means, in contrast to everyday life, in which god was not felt as a living power. Also, it involved an accentuation of the power of irrationality, which the rationalization of inner-worldly life conduct precisely restricted. Or the aim was the achievement of apathetic–ecstatic godly possession of gnosis in opposition to everyday life as the abode of transient and meaningless drives. This, too, represents an orientation that is both extra-worldly and passive and thereby from the standpoint of inner-worldly ethics it is irrational and mystical, leading away from rational conduct in the world.

In *The Sociology of Religion* Weber observes,

> At the opposite extreme from systems of religious ethics preoccupied with the control of economic affairs within the world stands the ultimate ethic of world-rejection, the mystical illuminative concentration of authentic ancient Buddhism (naturally not the completely altered manifestation of Buddhism assumed in Tibetan, Chinese and Japanese popular religions). Even this most world-rejecting ethic is 'rational' in the sense that it produces a constantly alert control of all natural instinctive drives, though for purposes entirely different from those of inner-worldly asceticism. Salvation is sought, not from sin and suffering alone, but also from ephemeralness as such; escape from the wheel of *karma*-causality into eternal rest is the goal pursued.[18]

All rational purposive activity is regarded as leading away from salvation, except of course the subjective activity of concentrated contemplation, which empties the soul of the passion for life and every connection with worldly interests. The achievement of salvation is possible for only a few, even of those who have resolved to live in poverty, chastity and unemployment (for labour is purposive action), and hence in mendicancy. Those chosen few are required to wander ceaselessly—except at the time of the heavy rains—freed from all personal ties to family and world, pursuing the goal of mystical illumination by fulfilling the injunctions relating to the correct path (*dharma*). When such salvation is gained, the deep joy and tender, undifferentiated love characterizing such illumination provides the highest blessing possible in the existence, short of absorption into the eternal dreamless sleep of nirvana, the only state in which no change occurs.

There is no path leading from this only really consistent position of world-flight to any economic ethic or to any rational social ethic. The universal mood of pity, extending to all creatures, cannot be the carrier of any rational behaviour and in fact leads away from it. The same Buddhism when it became a missionizing popular religion, duly transformed itself into a saviour religion based on *karma* compensation, with hopes for the world beyond guaranteed by devotional techniques, cultic and sacramental grace, and deeds of mercy. Naturally, Buddhism also tended to welcome purely magical notions.

In India itself, Buddhism succumbed, among the upper classes, to a renascent philosophy of salvation based on the Vedas; and it met competition from Hinduistic salvation religions, especially the various forms of Vishnuism, from tantristic magic, and from orgiastic mystery religions, notably the *bhakti* piety (love of God).

At all events, no motivation toward a rational system for the methodical control of life flowed from Buddhist, Taoist or Hindu piety. Hindu piety in particular, maintained the strongest power of tradition, since the presuppositions of Hinduism constituted the most consistent religious expressions of the organic view of society. The existing order of the world was provided absolutely with unconditional justification, in terms of the mechanical operation of a proportional retribution in the distribution of power and happiness to individuals on the basis of their merits and failures in their earlier existences.

The lust for gain on the basis of magic and not rational character

Weber observes that the laity to which the gnosis and also the highest holiness is denied or which it refuses itself, is handled ritually and traditionally in terms of its everyday interests. The unrestricted lust for gain of the Asiatics in large and in small is notoriously unequalled in the rest of the world. However, it is precisely a 'drive for gain' pursued with every possible means including universal magic. It was lacking in precisely that which was decisive for the economics of the Occident: the refraction and rational immersion of the drive character of economic striving and its accompaniments in a system of rational, inner-worldly ethic of behaviour, e.g. the 'inner-worldly asceticism' of Protestantism in the West. In *The Sociology of Religion* Weber observes that

All these popular religions of Asia left room for the acquisitive drive of the tradesman, the interest of the artisan in sustenance

237

and the traditionalism of the peasant. These popular religions also left undisturbed both philosophical speculation and the conventional status-oriented life patterns of privileged groups. These status-oriented patterns of the privileged evinced feudal characteristics in Japan; patrimonial-bureaucratic, and hence strongly utilitarian features in China; and a mixture of knightly, patrimonial and intellectualistic traits in India. None of these mass religions of Asia, however, provided the motives or orientations for a rationalized ethical transformation of a creaturely world in accordance with divine commandments. Rather they all accepted this world as eternally given, and so the best of all possible worlds.

'Capitalism' existed among all these religions, of the same kind as in Occident Antiquity and the medieval period. But there was no development toward modern capitalism, nor even any stirrings in that direction. Above all, they evolved no 'capitalist spirit' in the sense that is distinctive of ascetic Protestantism. But to assume that the Hindu, Chinese, or Muslim merchant, trader, artisan, or coolie was animated by a weaker 'acquisitive drive' than the ascetic Protestant is to fly in the face of the facts. Indeed, the reverse would seem to be true, for what is distinctive of Puritanism is the rational and ethical limitation of the quest for profit. Only ascetic Protestantism completely eliminated magic and the supernatural quest for salvation, of which the highest form was intellectualist, contemplative illumination. It alone created the religious motivations for seeking salvation primarily through immersion in one's worldly vocation. (Beruf)[19]

Protestant ethics

Here it may be pertinent to point out some of the religious ideas of ascetic Protestantism and their connection with everyday economic conduct, which Weber explains in his first essay 'The Protestant Ethic and the Spirit of Capitalism'. For example Richard Baxter, one of the leaders in Calvinism advocates that, on earth man must, to be certain of his state of grace, 'do the works of him who sent him, as long as it is yet day. Not leisure and enjoyment, but only activity serves to increase the glory of God, according to the definite manifestations of His will'. Waste of time is thus the first and, in principle, the deadliest of sins. The span of human life is infinitely short and precious to make sure of one's own election. Loss of time through sociability, idle talk, luxury, even more sleep than is necessary for health, six to at most eight hours, is worthy of absolute moral condemnation. Inactive contemplation is also valueless, or even directly reprehensible if it is at the expense of one's daily work. For it is less pleasing to God than the active performance of His will in a calling. Besides, Sunday is provided for that and, according to Baxter, it is always those who are not diligent in their callings who have no time for God when the occasion demands it.

Accordingly Baxter's principal work is dominated by the continually repeated, often almost passionate preaching of hard, continuous bodily or mental labour. It is due to a combination of two different motives. Labour is, on the one hand, an approved ascetic technique, as it always has been in the Western Church, in contrast not only to the Orient but to almost all monastic rules the world over. 'Work hard in your calling' is a moral virtue. But the most important thing was that even beyond that labour came to be considered in itself the end of life, ordained as such by God. 'He who will not work shall not eat' holds unconditionally for everyone. Unwillingness to work is symptomatic of the lack of grace.

Baxter further holds that wealth does not exempt anyone from the unconditional command. Even the wealthy shall not eat without working, for even though they do not need to labour to support their own needs, there is God's commandment which they, like the poor, must obey. For everyone without exception God's providence has prepared a calling, which he should profess and in which he should labour. And this calling is not, as it was for the Lutheran, a fate to which he must submit and which he must make the best of, but God's commandment to the individual to work for the divine glory. This seemingly subtle difference had far-reaching psychological consequences. What God demands is not labour in itself, but rational labour in a calling. In the Puritan concept of the calling the emphasis is always placed on this methodical character of worldly asceticism, not, as with Luther, on the acceptance of the lot which God has irretrievably assigned to man. Hence the question whether anyone may combine several callings is answered in the affirmative, if it is useful for the common good or one's own, and not injurious to anyone, and if it does not lead to unfaithfulness in one of the callings. Even a change of calling is by no means regarded as objectionable, if it is not thoughtless and is made for the purpose of pursuing a calling more pleasing to God, which means, on general principles, one more useful.

It is true that the usefulness of a calling, and thus its favour in the sight of God, is measured primarily in moral terms, and thus in terms of the importance of the goods produced in it for the community. But a further, and, above all, in practice the most important, criterion is found in private profitableness. For if that

God, whose hand the Puritan sees in all the occurrences of life, shows one of His elect a chance of profit, he must do it with a purpose. Hence the faithful Christian must follow the call by taking advantage of the opportunity.

> If God show you a way in which you may lawfully get more than in another way (without wrong to your soul or to any other), if you refuse this, and choose the less gainful way, you cross one of the ends of your calling, and you refuse to be God's steward, and to accept His gifts and use them for Him when He requireth it: You may labour to be rich for God, though not for the flesh and sin.[21]

Wealth is thus bad ethically only in so far as it is a temptation to idleness and sinful enjoyment of life; and its acquisition is bad only when it is with the purpose of later living merrily and without care. But as a performance of duty in a calling it is not only morally permissible but actually enjoined. The parable of the servant who was rejected because he did not increase the talent which was entrusted to him seemed to say so directly. To wish to be poor was, it was often argued, the same as wishing to be unhealthy; it is objectionable as a glorification of works and derogatory to the glory of God. Begging especially, on the part of one able to work, is not only the sin of slothfulness, but a violation of the duty of brotherly love according to the apostle's own word. The emphasis on the ascetic importance of a fixed calling provided an ethical justification of the modern specialized division of labour. In a similar way the providential interpretation of profit-making justified the activities of the businessman.

Here at least one thing was unquestionably new: the valuation of the fulfilment of duty in worldly affairs as the highest form which the moral activity of the individual could assume. This it was which inevitably gave everyday worldly activity a new religious significance, and which first created the conception of a calling in this sense.

Weber then tries to clarify the points in which the Puritan idea of the calling and the premium it placed upon ascetic conduct was bound directly to influence the development of a capitalistic way of life. As seen before, this asceticism turned with all its force against one thing: the spontaneous enjoyment of life and all it had to offer. For example sport was accepted by them if it served a rational purpose, that of recreation necessary for physical efficiency. But as a means for the spontaneous expression of undisciplined impulses, it was under suspicion; and in so far as it became purely a means of enjoyment, or awakened pride, raw instincts or the irrational gambling instinct, it was of course strictly condemned. Impulsive enjoyment of life, which leads away both from work in a calling and from religion, was as such the enemy of rational asceticism, whether in the form of seigneurial sports, or the enjoyment of the dance hall or the public house of the common man.

The theatre was obnoxious to the Puritans, and with the strict exclusion of the erotic and of nudity from the realm of toleration, a radical view of either literature or art could not exist. The conceptions of idle talk, of superfluities, and of vain ostentation, all designations of an irrational attitude without objective purpose, thus not ascetic, and especially not serving the glory of God, but of man, were always at hand to serve in deciding in favour of sober utility as against any artistic tendencies. This was especially true in the case of decoration of the person, for instance, with clothing. As a rule the toleration of pleasure in cultural goods, which contributed to purely aesthetic or athletic enjoyment, certainly always ran up against one characteristic limitation: they must not cost anything. Man is only a trustee of the goods which have come to him through God's grace. He must, like the servant in the parable, give an account of every penny entrusted to him, and it is at least hazardous to spend any of it for a purpose which does not serve the glory of God but only one's own enjoyment. This ethic of ascetic Protestantism, which for the first time found a consistent ethical foundation had great significance for the development of capitalism. This worldly Protestant asceticism, acted powerfully against the spontaneous enjoyment of possessions; it restricted consumption, especially luxuries. On the other hand, it had the psychological effect of freeing the acquisition of goods from the inhibition of traditionalistic ethics. It broke the bonds of the impulse of acquisition in that it not only legalized it, but (in the sense discussed) looked upon it as directly willed by God.

The irrational use of wealth in the outward form of luxury was condemned as idolatry of the flesh. On the other hand, the rational and utilitarian use of wealth which was willed by God for the needs of the individual and the community was approved. It was not wished to impose mortification on the man of wealth, but to use his means for necessary and practical things. The idea of comfort characteristically limits the extent of ethically permissible expenditures. Over against the glitter and ostentation of feudal magnificence which, resting on an unsound economic basis, prefers a sordid elegance to a sober simplicity, they set the clean and solid comfort of the middle-class home as an ideal.

On the side of the production of private wealth, asceticism condemned both dishonesty and impulsive avarice. In conformity with the Old Testament and in analogy with the ethical valuation of good works, asceticism looked upon the pursuit of wealth as an end in itself as highly reprehensible; but the attainment of wealth as a fruit of labour in a calling was a sign of God's blessing. And even more important: the religious valuation of restless, continuous, systematic work in a worldly calling, as the highest means to asceticism, and at the same time the surest and most evident proof of rebirth and genuine faith, must have been the most powerful conceivable lever for the expansion of that attitude toward life which here is called the spirit of capitalism.

When the limitation of consumption is combined with this release of acquisitive activity, the inevitable practical result is obvious: accumulation of capital through ascetic compulsion to save. Both elements, that of an unspoiled naive joy of life and that of a strictly regulated, reserved self-control and conventional ethical conduct are even today combined to form the English national character. Similarly, the early history of the North American colonies is dominated by the sharp contrast of the adventurers, who wanted to set up plantations with the labour of indentured servants and live as feudal lords, and the specifically middle-class outlook of the Puritans.

As far as the influence of the Puritans' outlook extended, under all circumstances—and this is, of course, much more important than the mere encouragement of capital accumulation—it favoured the development of a rational bourgeois economic life; it was the most important, and above all the only consistent, influence in the development of that life. It stood at the cradle of the modern economic man.

Weber further adds that as John Wesley, leader of the Methodist Church observes,

> I fear, wherever riches have increased, the essence of religion had decreased in the same proportion. Therefore I do not see how it is possible, in the nature of things, for any revival of true religion to continue long. For religion must necessarily produce both industry and frugality, and these cannot but produce riches. But as riches increase, so will pride, anger and love of the world in all its branches....So, although the form of religion remains, the spirit is swiftly vanishing away.[22]

Weber concludes by saying that one of the fundamental elements of the spirit of modern capitalism, and not only of that but of all modern culture—rational conduct on the basis od the idea of the calling—was born from the spirit of Christian asceticism. The Puritan wanted to work in a calling; we are forced to do so. For when asceticism was carried out of monastic cells into everyday life and began to dominate worldly morality, it did its part in building the tremendous cosmos of the modern economic order. This order is now bound to the technical and economic conditions of machine production which today determine the lives of all individuals.

Today the spirit of religious asceticism—whether finally, who knows?—has escaped from the cage. But victorious capitalism, since it rests on mechanical foundations, needs its support no longer. The rosy blush of its laughing heir, the Enlightenment, seems also to be irretrievably fading, and the idea of duty in one's calling prowls about in our lives like the ghost of dead religious beliefs. Where the fulfilment of the calling cannot directly be related to the highest spiritual and cultural values, or when, on the other hand, it need not be felt simply as economic compulsion, the individual generally abandons the attempt to justify it at all. In the field of its highest development, in the United States, the pursuit of wealth, stripped of its religious and ethical meaning, tends to become associated with purely mundane passions, which often actually give it the character of a sport.

No one knows who will live in this cage in the future, or whether at the end of this tremendous development entirely new prophets will arise, or whether there will be a great rebirth of old ideas and ideals; or, if neither, whether mechanized petrification, embellished with a sort of convulsive self-importance, will ensue. For the last stage of this cultural development, it might well be truly said: 'Specialists without spirit, sensualists without heart; this nullity imagines that it has attained a level of civilization never before achieved'.[23]

Here Weber also adds that he is not ignoring the fact that Protestant asceticism was in turn influenced in its development and in its character by the totality of social conditions, especially economic. This aspect he studies in his later writings, especially *Economy and Society* and *General Economic History*.

In Weber's view Asiatic religion could not supply the presuppositions of inner-worldly asceticism. It could not be established on the basis of a religiosity which also demanded of the laity life as a *bhagat*, as a holy ascetic, not simply as an ancient ideal goal but a contemporary existence as a wandering beggar during workless times of his life in general (April was the time for the assumption of a life of wandering mendicancy as a ritual duty for the members of the lower castes in India).

Other main features of Indian society

Having said so much about the religions on India and their relation to the everyday economic behaviour of the common man, let us pass on to some other main features of Indian society which Weber mentions in the last chapter of his work *The Religion of India*. These are (1) castes as a traditional system; (2) the absence of the concept of natural law and citizenship; (3) the mysterious and secretive character of Asiatic intellectuals; (4) the lack of national feeling; and (5) the passive role of intellectual strata in society, which indirectly flows from religious teachings. We may discuss these one by one.

(1) *Castes as a traditional system*

Weber observes that the single, inwardly consistent form was the caste soteriology of Vedanta brahmanism in India. Its conception of calling had to operate politically, socially, and economically in an extreme, traditionalistic manner. It is the single, logically closed form of 'organismic' holy and societal teaching which could occur. It became the peculiar objective of the priesthood, when these had the power—ritualistically—to organize the social order to their personal situation. Where the inner-worldly ethic was systematically 'specialized' with great consequences and with sufficient, workable, soteriological premises, in practice, for the corresponding relations in the Hindu inner-worldly caste ethic, it was simultaneously traditionally and ritually absolutely stereotyped. Where this was not the case, indeed, traces of 'organismic societal theories' appeared, however, without psychologically workable premises for the corresponding practical behaviour. Consequently a psychologically workable systematization was lacking.[24]

On the other hand, the Protestant stress upon the methodically rationalized fulfilment of one's vocational responsibility was diametrically opposite to Hinduism's strongly traditionalistic concept of vocations.

(2) *Absence of the concept of natural law and citizenship*

In the Occident the establishment of a rational, inner-worldly ethic was bound up with the appearance of thinkers and prophets who developed a social structure on the basis of political problems which were foreign to Asiatic culture; these were the political problems of civic status groups of the city without which neither Judaism nor Christianity, nor the development of Hellenic thought, is conceivable. The establishment of the 'city' in the occidental sense, was restricted in Asia, partly through sib power which continued unbroken, partly through caste alienation.

The interests of Asiatic intellectuality, so far as it was concerned with everyday life, lay primarily in directions other than political. The orthodox or heterodox Hinduistic and Buddhistic educated classes had the true sphere of their interests quite outside the things of this world. This was in the search for mystic, timeless salvation of the soul and the escape from the senseless mechanism of the 'wheel' of existence. Asiatic self-control found its point of gravity precisely at a point negatively evaluated in the Occident. Asiatic self-control was erected on a particular central point against distractions from the outside. The Taoistic Wu Wei, the Hinduistic 'emptying' of consciousness of worldly relations and worldly cares, and the Confucian 'distance' of the spirit from preoccupation with fruitless problems, all represent manifestations of the same type. The occidental ideal of active behaviour—be it in a religious sense concerning the beyond, be it inner-worldly—centrally fixes upon 'personality'. To all, highly developed, Asiatic, intellectual soteriology this could only appear either as hopelessly one-sided philistinism or as barbaric greed for life.

(3)   *The mysterious and secretive character of Asiatic intellectuals*

The Asiatic, the wholly- or semi-intellectual Asiatic, easily makes the impression on the Westerner of being 'mysterious' and secretive. One seeks to penetrate the presumed secret through 'psychology'. However, psycho-physical difference is not the primary way to an understanding of this character. Factors imprinted through education, and the objective elements of the respective interest situations, not 'capacity for feeling' are first palpable. What was for the Westerner pre-eminently irrational was for the Asiatic a ceremonial, ritual, and habitual condition whose meaning he did not understand. The original sense of the customs that grew up were in themselves often not clear to them. Similarly the soteriological product of Asiatic literature, which rested on the particular territories of these emergent problems, were not more ruthlessly worked through, than was done in the Occident. (It is characteristic that Chinese invention (indeed not all) is in service of art and not economically attuned, whereas the rationalization of experimentation by art and its diffusion from art to science are decisive for occidental development).

(4)   *Geographical isolation and the lack of national feeling*

The lack of economic rationalism and rational life methodology in Asia, so far as other than psychological historical causes play a part, pre-eminently was conditioned by the continental character of the social order as developed in terms of the geographic structure. Occidental culture was throughout established on the basis of the foreign or transient trade. It was different in Asia. Asiatic peoples have predominantly excluded or extremely restricted foreign trade.

Such was the case until the forceful opening of trade with China, Japan and Korea. India, the territory of least closure, still had strong ritual restrictions on travel, while with ritually impure barbarian territory, there were restrictions against active trade. Political considerations also operated towards the restriction of strangers.

However, this strong closure of local culture was not the sign of nationalistic feeling in any way. The character of the Asiatic intellectual strata had in essentials hindered the emergence of a 'national' political form of the type developed since the late times of the medieval Occident—when the full implications of the idea of the nation were developed by the modern occidental intellectual strata.

The Asiatic culture area lacked in essentials a speech community. The cultural language was a sacred one or a speech of the literary: Sanskrit in the territory of distinguished Indians; the Chinese mandarin speech in China, Korea and Japan. In Mahayanaistic cultural territory it remained in this state. In the territory of Hinayanaism (Burma, Ceylon, Siam), which basically recognized the folk idiom as a missionary language, the guru-theocracy was so absolute that there can be no talk of any sort of secular political community formation of intellectual strata outside the monks. Only in Japan did the feudal development bring about the presuppositions of a genuinely 'national' community consciousness, if also primarily on a knightly status foundation. The cultivated Asiatic strata remained quite 'confined' to its own interests.

(5) *The passive role of intellectual strata in society*

Wherever an intellectual stratum attempted to establish the meaning of the world and the character of life and—after failure of this unmediated rationalistic effort—to comprehend experience in its own terms, indirect rationalistic elements were taken into consideration. It was led in some manner in the style of the trans-worldly field of formless Indian mysticism. And where, on the other side, a status group of intellectuals rejected such world-fleeing efforts and, instead, consciously and intentionally pursued the charm and worth of the elegant gesture as the highest possible goal of inner-worldly consummation, it moved, in some manner, toward the Confucian ideal of cultivation.

Out of both these components, crossing and jostling one another, however, an essential part of all Asiatic intellectual culture was determined. The conception that through simple behaviour addressed to the 'demands of the day' one may achieve salvation which lies at the basis of all the specifically occidental significance of 'personality' is alien to Asia. This is as excluded from Asiatic thought as the pure factual rationalism of the West, which practically tries to discover the impersonal laws of the world.

The social world was divided into the strata of the wise and educated, and the uncultivated plebeian masses. The factual, inner order of the real world of nature as of art, ethics, and of economics remained concealed to the distinguished strata because it was so barren for its particular interests. Their life conduct was oriented to striving for the extraordinary, for example, in finding throughout its point of gravity in exemplary prophecy or wisdom. However, for the plebeian strata no ethic of everyday life derived from its rationally formed missionary prophecy. The appearance of such in the Occident, however—above all, in the Near East—with the extensive consequences borne with it, was conditioned by highly particular historical constellations without which, despite differences of natural conditions, developments there could easily have taken the course typical of Asia, particularly of India.

Appraisal

Most of the observations made by Weber with regard to the general characteristics of Indian religions, i.e. toleration of different faith and sects, stress on exemplary promise and mystical knowledge to get salvation, and salvation by grace are correct. But the inference drawn from the last two facts that Indian people, including the middle class and business community, had no rational practical ethic and life methodology which could lead to the development of modern capitalism, are rather too sweeping. The different occupational groups, merchants and craft guilds, had their own rules and regulations to which Weber refers in other places.[25] The importance of *grihasthasrama* in the Asrama system and emphasis on *purusharthas*, that is, the four objectives of life, viz. *dharma, artha, kama* and *moksha*, laid equal emphasis on economic progress. As stressed earlier, there were certain factors such as political subordination, lack of modern education means of communication, etc, which hindered economic development. Marx rightly laid emphasis on the social, economic and political factors which hindered economic growth. The business communities including Parsees, Jains, and vaishyas had the potentiality to start factories once they came to possess the know-how. And they did so when they got the opportunity; but the other factors, especially the political, hindered the development of industrial growth in India. Sir R. C. Dutt points out.

247

The chief sources of a nation's wealth are agriculture, commerce and manufactures, and sound financial administration. Among these the two main sources of national wealth, i.e. agriculture and industries have been crushed down by the British Government. The East India Company and the British Parliament, following the selfish commercial policy, discouraged Indian manufacturers in order to encourage the rising manufacturers of England. India was made subservient to the industries of Great Britain and was encouraged to produce raw material only in order to supply material for the looms and manufactories of Great Britain. Orders were sent out to force Indian artisans to work in the Company's factories, commercial residents were legally vested with extensive powers over villages and communities of Indian weavers; prohibitive tariffs excluded Indian silk and cotton goods from England; and English goods were admitted into India free of duty or on payment of a nominal duty.... The invention of the power-loom in Europe completed the decline of Indian industries; and when the power-loom was set up in India, England once more acted towards India with unfair jealousy. An excise duty was imposed on the production of cotton fabrics which disabled the Indian manufacturers from competing with the manufacturers of Japan and China and which stifled the new steam-mills of India.... In England and in other Western countries the state widens the income of the people, extends their markets, opens up new sources of wealth, identifies itself with the nation, grows richer with the nation. In India, the State has fostered no new industries and revived no old industries for the people. On the other hand, it intervenes at each recurring land settlement to take what it considers its share out of the produce of the soil.[27]

It is admitted that the Protestant ethics, particularly those of Calvinism, were more favourable to the accumulation of capital, less conspicuous consumption and a rational outlook on life, but the business communities of India also had similar ethics, and even some of the religious sects specifically advocated them.[28] Unfortunately Weber nowhere refers to political factors hindering economic growth, as do Marx and many Indian economists. It shows that Weber did not take into consideration the economic and political condition of India at that time. Tawney, on the other hand, rightly points out that Weber's approach to the problem seems to lay too exclusive an emphasis upon intellectual and ethical forces; his analysis of those forces themselves requires, perhaps, to be supplemented. Brentano's criticism, that the political thought of the Renaissance was as powerful a solvent of conventional restraints as the teaching of Calvin, is not without weight. He adds

> The rise of new forms of economic enterprise was the result of changes in the character of the economic environment. It was due to the influx of the precious metals from America in the sixteenth century, to the capital accumulated in extra-European commerce, to the reaction of expanding markets on industrial organisation, to the growth of population, to technological improvements made possible by the progress of natural science.

He further remarks,

> Why insist that causation can work in only one direction? Is it not a little artificial to suggest that capitalist enterprise had to wait, as Weber appears to imply, till religious changes had produced a capitalist spirit? Would it not be equally plausible, and equally one-sided, to argue that the religious changes were themselves merely the result of economic movements?
>
> Weber pursued a single line of enquiry with masterly ingenuity. His conclusions are illuminating; but they are susceptible, it may perhaps be held, of more than one interpretation. There was action and reaction, and, while Puritanism helped to mould the social order, it was, in its turn, moulded by it.[29]

Loomis and Loomis observe that the teachings of Calvinism did not make the businessmen follow the profit motive and other ascetic ethics, but the businessmen adopted the teachings because it suited them.

> The earlier teachings in Geneva had put severe restrictions on the businessman. Calvin and the church in general preached unceasingly against unjust moneylenders and avarice. The Council of Geneva, a body made up of businessmen, heard the ministers on thrift and simplicity.... They were glad to invoke the sanction of religion on traits which their secular activity found valuable—honesty, industry, sobriety, as well as the dynamic interpretation of predestination.... But Calvin in the Institutes also writes, 'With whatever kind of tribulation we may be afflicted, we should always keep this end in view, to habituate ourselves to a contempt of the present life that we may thereby be excited to meditation on that which is to come....' How far this is from a call to vigorous worldly activity to prove one's divine election! If it is claimed, as Weber does, it was not the intention of the reformers, but the unconscious and quite unexpected

effects of their teachings which were crucial in producing the capitalistic spirit.[30]

Weber's contention that caste was a dominant feature of Indian social structure, which operated politically, socially and economically in a traditionalistic manner, cannot be denied. The result was that there was difficulty in organizing the labour on rationalistic lines and in introducing the specialization of labour needed for rapid industrialization. There was also a shortage of entrepreneurial ability as compared to the expanding need of industries. The brahmins, kshatriyas and some other non-vaishya castes, including the kayastha, who had the advantage of education could not take up business because of caste restrictions. The result is that industrial development was hampered and varied from area to area according to the number of business castes available. The situation was also brought about by the British government which brought rigidity into the social structure by following certain policies. As Professor R. K. Mukherjee observes,

> Like in other parts of India, after Bengal passed into the hands of the British East India Company, the previously growing class of merchants and artisans was removed from the scene. On the other hand, in spite of rising protests from the progressive section in Indian society and also in Britain, obscurantist customs were given a new lease of life in Indian society in the name of respecting the 'traditional' customs and usages of the peoples of India. . . . While the caste system was losing its force during the earlier centuries, it regained its position in the ideological aspect under the patronage given to Brahminical religion and ethics by the British administrators like Warren Hastings and others.[31]

Weber's remarks that the Asiatic intellectuality was not concerned with the political problems of the urban citizens, and that there was no rational law developed as in the West, are partly true. As Weber himself admits, in certain cities caste and vocational groups had their own organizations and rules, and the king was governed by his court, which applied the law in an unbiased manner. He observes, 'The rules that the king is bound by the decision of the chief justice and that the lay members (viz., merchants, scribes and guild masters) must be among the members of the courts are both expressive of the rational tendencies'.[32] Even had it been otherwise, rational law would have developed with the introduction of modern education, as we find the position today. It is admitted that the special status of the town dwellers as citizens and the participation of the inhabitants in the affairs of local administration in the Western sense did not develop to the same extent owing to a different political and social structure, and in this a part was played by caste and occupational groups. But it did not in any way hinder the development of modern capitalism.

It is agreed that a good number of the Asiatic intellectuals were absorbed in mystical knowledge. But there was no dearth of intellectuals who were concerned with worldly matters. Some of the law books of the medieval period are a pointer in this direction. The main difficulty was that there was political unstability in the country, which did not allow proper development in that period. And this was the position in Europe up to the end of the fourteenth century. Once the Indian intellectual came into touch with Western civilization, his mind immediately reacted and he began to work in the profane fields, which eventuality Karl Marx had easily foreseen.

The claim that modern capitalism could not develop because of strong ritual restrictions on travel is also untrue. India had enough foreign trade with outside countries. Weber's assertion that the Asiatic culture area lacked in essentials a speech community may be correct to some extent. But this was the position in some cases in Europe too, where even a small state like Switzerland had three languages. And it in nowise stood in the way of the development of national feeling, once the mass media and communication systems like railways were developed.

Weber's emphasizing the fact that the wise and educated in India did not concern themselves with the real world of nature, of art, of ethics and of economics—their interests were extra-worldly and out of touch with the uncultivated plebeian masses—is also partly true. There were some educated persons and intellectuals who were with the masses and tried to boost their morale, otherwise the country could not have attained independence. However, their number was small. And this remains true even to this day. Similarly the number of those in the intellectual castes who took an active part in agriculture, commerce or industry was also small.

9 Emile Durkheim (1858–1917)

Durkheim, being the son of a rabbi, began to prepare for the rabbinate and studied the Old Testament, the Talmud, the Hebrew language and Hebrew history. He abandoned these interests early in his life, but in the latter part of his career as a sociologist religion became the subject of one of his most daring studies. 'He would often remind people that he was, after all, the son of a rabbi'.[1] In order to join the teaching profession Durkheim entered the Ecole Normale Supérieure at Paris in 1879 where entry is on the basis of nationwide competitive examination. Durkheim found the institution quite stimulating but uncongenial; the strong emphasis there on a rhetorical humanism conflicted with Durkheim's tough-minded concern for society's pressing problems. In his view the solution to these problems did not lie in pretty words or mystical ecstasy; the use of methods of science and practical, co-operative endeavour in empirical enterprises had to form the basis for any kind of diagnosis and treatment of society. He was appointed professor of Philosophy at the Lycée of Sens in 1882 and remained there until 1887. By 1886 he had made the first formulation of his theory of social solidarity and social evolution. By 1887 he was recognized in the field as an outstanding sociologist. At the University of Bordeaux a course in the social sciences was created for him in 1887—the first official recognition in France of the social sciences. In 1897 he organized the Année Sociologique. With the help of a group of brilliant men he made a detailed and critical analysis of much of the sociological and anthropological literature. The first volume of the Année which was the joint product of thirteen collaborators was published in 1898.

From the time of the publication of the first volume of the Année, right up to the beginning of the World War, sixteen years later, Durkheim's published sociological writings followed four main lines. To use the Année's terminology, we may call these major fields general sociology, juridical and moral sociology, religious sociology, and the sociological conditions of thought.[2]

Durkheim was intensely patriotic.

At the outset of the First World War he devoted himself to education and propaganda related to the war effort. As a lecturer and writer he engaged in what he called 'moral refreshment', both for the troops and the people at home. He accepted an official position with the government during this time and was known for his motto: 'Patience, Effort, Confidence'.[3]

His son was wounded twice in the war and died in 1915. He was seriously shocked by his death. He became ill in 1916 and made one last effort to complete a large work in the field of ethics, but died in 1917 with much of his contemplated work unfinished.

His major works

Among Durkheim's most important works which are of concern to us are (1) *Division of Labour in Society* (1893), *Suicide* (1897) and *The Elementary Forms of the Religious Life* (1912). Professor Aron observes about these works,

Durkheim wrote three great books which mark his intellectual itinerary and which represent three variations on the fundamental theme of consensus. The first 'The Division of Labour in Society' may be reduced to the following theme: modern society implies an extreme differentiation of jobs and professions. How are we to ensure that a society divided among innumerable specialists will retain the necessary intellectual and moral coherence? Durkheim's second great book, 'Suicide', is an analysis of a phenomenon regarded as pathological, intended to shed light on the evil which threatens modern or industrial societies: anomie. The third book is 'The Elementary Forms of the Religious Life', whose purpose is to seek the essential characteristics of religious order at the dawn of human history, not out of curiosity about what might have happened thousands of years ago, but in order to rediscover in the simplest societies the essential secret of all human societies—in order to understand what the reform of modern societies requires in the light of primitive experience.[4]

With these preliminaries in view we shall deal with his views on Indian society which he discusses in these three important works. His views may be discussed under the following heads:

1 Greater homogeneity in the pariah tribes and Todas of India
2 Revealed law in ancient India
3 The spirit of altruism in primitive societies as shown by widows in *Sati*
4 The rule of adoption among Hindus
5 The formation of castes
6 The disadvantages of the caste system in modern society
7 Causes of suicide in India.
   Suicides
   (a) among Brahmans and Hindu sages,
   (b) among Buddhists and Jains, and
   (c) among Hindus
   Indian religions—their characteristics:
8 Indian religions are complex
9 The negation of God in Buddhism, Jainism and Hinduism
10 Some special characteristics of Vedic religion:
   (a) Rituals as part of Vedic religion
   (b) Vedic religion—the oldest religion among civilized people
   (c) Fire—an important element in Vedic religion
11 Asceticism in Buddhism
12 Sacrifices in Hinduism

(1) *Greater homogeneity in the pariah tribes and Todas of India*

The main theme of Durkheim's thought and consequently the theme of his first book *Division of Labour in Society* (which was his doctoral thesis) is the relation between individuals and the collectivity. The problem might be stated thus: how can a multiplicity of individuals make up a society? How can individuals achieve what is the condition of social existence, namely a consensus? Durkheim's answer to this central question is to set up a distinction between two forms of solidarity, mechanical solidarity and organic solidarity. Mechanical solidarity is a solidarity of resemblances. The major characteristic of a society in which mechanical solidarity prevails is that the individuals differ from one another as little as possible. The individuals, the members of the same collectivity, resemble each other because they feel the same emotions, cherish the same values and hold the same things sacred. The solidarity is coherent because the individuals are not yet differentiated.

The social molecules which can be coherent in this way can act together only in the measure that they have no actions of their own as the molecules of inorganic bodies. That is why we propose to call this type of solidarity mechanical[5].

The more primitive the societies, the more resemblances there are among the individuals who compose them. Dr Lebon has been able to establish in an objective fashion this homogeneity growing proportionally as one goes back to origins. He has compared the crania indigenous to different races and different societies, and has found

> that the differences in cranial volume existing among individuals of the same race are as great as the race is more elevated in the scale of civilization. After grouping the cranial volumes of each race in progressive series, being careful to establish comparisons only in series numerous enough for the terms to be reliable, in gradual fashion, I have found that the difference in volume between the greatest male adult cranium and the smallest is roughly 200 cubic centimeters in the case of the gorrilla, 280 in the case of the Pariahs of India, 310 among the Australians, . . . and 700 among the Germans.[6]

There are even some people where the differences are non-existent. 'The Andamans and the Todas are all alike. We can almost say the same for the Greenlanders. Five Patagonian Crania that Broca has in his laboratory are identical'.[7]

There is no doubt that the organic likenesses correspond to psychic likenesses. Originality is not simply very rare there, but it has no place. Everybody professes and practises, without demurring, the same religion; schisms and dissents are unknown, they would not be tolerated. Religion comprises all, and extends to all. It contains in a confused mass, besides beliefs properly religious, morality, law, the principles of political organization, and even science, or at least what passes for it. Religion even regulates details of private life.

The characteristics of pariah tribes and Todas given by Durkheim are almost correct and need no further comment. However, it needs to be stated that some changes are now being brought about in such primitive communities through expansion of education, new technology, communications and other developmental activities.

(2) *Revealed law in ancient India*

According to Durkheim the collective consciousness is the body of beliefs and sentiments common to all members of the group. The collective consciousness varies in extent and force from one society to another. In societies where mechanical solidarity predominates, the collective consciousness embraces the greater part of individual consciousness. On the other hand, in societies of which differentiation of individuals is a characteristic, everyone is free to believe, to desire, and to act according to his own preference in a large number of circumstances. The force of collective consciousness coincides with its extent. In primitive societies, not only does the collective consciousness embrace the greater part of the individual existence, but the sentiments experienced in common have an extreme violence which is manifested in the severity of the punishments inflicted on those who violate the prohibitions. On the assumption that the hostile forces in man require some kind of enforced co-operation for survival, Durkheim undertakes an examination of social rules of conduct, both legal and moral, in order to discover the conditions of social solidarity. It must be possible, he thought, to find variations in a society which will serve as reliable clues to the internal structure and function of that society. He found these variations in legal and moral codes, social statistics (such as suicide rates) and religious practices. *Division of Labour* concentrates on the legal and moral codes, which are seen as expressing the social needs of a society.

Durkheim turned to a study of legal and moral codes as the place to look for the true sources of social cohesion, since, as he states, 'the characteristic of moral rules is that they enunciate the fundamental conditions of social solidarity'. He finds there is a distinction between two types of law: 'repressive' and 'restitutive'.[8]

Repressive law is simply an expression of the traditional customs, beliefs and sanctions of a society and is blindly adhered to under threats of punishment. Restitutive law on the other hand stresses restitution instead of punishment and affects only certain segments of the group at any one time. Its function is to preserve the status quo, not to inflict punishment for crimes against the community. Restitutive law is an indication of organic solidarity that is, a solidarity based on the co-operation of specialized individuals.

There are sanctions involved in both types of laws, but they are of a different nature. In one case they involve suffering, or at least a loss, inflicted on the agent. They make demands on his fortune, or on his honour, or on his life, or on his liberty, and deprive him of something which he enjoys. We call them repressive. As for the other type, it does not necessarily imply suffering for the agent, but consists only of the return of things as they were, in the re-establishment of troubled relations to their normal state, whether the incriminated act is restored by force to the type whence it deviated, or is annulled, that is, deprived of all social value.[9] It is difficult to separate moral rules from the juridical rules.

As far as the juridical rules are concerned they can be divided into two great classes, accordingly to whether they have organized repressive sanctions or only restitutive sanctions. The first comprise all penal law; the second, civil law, commercial law, procedural law, administrative and constitutional law, after abstraction of the penal rules which may be found there. Whereas the penal laws are remarkable for their neatness and precision, the purely moral rules are generally somewhat nebulous. For example, the wayward son and even the most hardened egotist are not treated as criminals. We may quite generally say that a man ought to work, that he ought to have pity on others, but we cannot determine in what fashion and in what measure.

Durkheim then considers the basis of the punishment of the offender. He says it is true that punishment has changed its character; it is no longer to avenge itself that the society punishes; it is to defend itself. It punishes, not because chastisement offers it any satisfaction for itself; but so that the fear of punishment may paralyse those who contemplate evil. But, in truth, punishment has remained, at least in part, a work of vengeance.

In the modern society it is society that punishes. What puts beyond doubt the social character of punishment is that, once pronounced, it cannot be lifted except by the government in the name of society. Among more primitive peoples punishment sometimes seems still more completely private, as the custom of the vendetta would seem to prove. But, as common as this theory of vengeance is, it is contrary to facts better established. Not a single society can be instanced where the vendetta has been the primitive form of punishment. On the contrary it is certain that the penal law was essentially religious in its nature.

It is an evident fact in India and Judea, since the law which was practised there was considered as revealed. In Judea, the judges were not priests, but every judge was the representative of God, the man of God. In India, it was the king who judged, but this function he regarded as essentially religious.[10]

In Egypt, the ten books of Hermes, which contained the criminal law with all other laws relative to the government of the state, were called sacerdotal; and Elien affirms that from earliest times, the Egyptian priests exercised judicial power. But religion is an essentially social phenomenon. Far from pursuing only personal ends, it exercises, at all times, a constraint upon the individual. It forces him into practices which subject him to small or large sacrifices which are painful to him. Religious life consists entirely in abnegation and disinterestedness. If, then, in primitive societies, criminal law is religious law, we can be sure that the interests it serves are social. It is their own offences that the gods avenge by punishment and not those of particular persons. But offences against the gods are offences against society.

Thus, in lower societies, the most numerous delicts are those which relate to public affairs; delicts against religion, against custom, against authority, etc. We need only look to the Bible, the laws of Manu, at the monuments which remain of the old Egyptian law, to see the relatively small place accorded to prescriptions for the protection of individuals, and contrariwise, the luxuriant development of repressive legislation concerning the different forms of sacrilege, the omission of certain religious duties, the demands of cermonial, etc. At the same time these crimes are the most severely punished.

As far as we can judge of the state of law in very inferior societies, it appears to be entirely repressive. Lubbock says:

> The savage is in no part free. Throughout the entire world, the daily life of the savage is regulated by a number of customs (as imperious as laws), complicated and very importunate, of prohibitions and interdictions. Numerous severe rules, although not written, encompass all the acts of his life.[11]

Even such is the case in societies where there is written law. Four books of the Pentateuch, Exodus, Leviticus, Numbers and Deuteronomy, represent the oldest monuments of this kind that we have. In these four or five thousand verses, there is a relatively small number wherein laws which can rigorously be called other than repressive are set down. Restitutive law—co-operative law in particular— holds a very minor position. Most of them bear the mark of religion. They all come, in the same degree, from the divinity; to violate them is to offend the divinity, and such offences are sins which must be expiated. When they are violated, public conscience does not content itself with a simple reparation, but demands expiation which avenges it. Since what gives penal law its peculiar character is the extraordinary authority of the rules which it sanctions, and since men have never known nor imagined any authority higher than that which the believer vests in God, law which is agreed to be the word of God himself cannot fail to be essentially repressive. As all penal law is more or less religious, in general fashion, repression dominates all law in lower societies. It is because religion completely pervades juridical life, as it does, indeed, all social life.

Indeed, this character is still very marked in the laws of Manu. We have only to look at the high rank accorded to criminal justice in the system of national institutions. 'To help the king in his duties', says Manu,

> God made him the guiding genius of punishment, the protector of all living beings, the administrator of justice, his very son, whose essence is wholly divine. It is the fear of punishment which makes all mobile and immobile creatures do their duty and accomplish their tasks. . . . Punishment rules humanity; punishment protects humanity. Punishment works while the world sleeps, punishment is justice, say the wise men. . . . All classes would be torn asunder, all barriers would be broken, there would be only confusion in the universe if punishment no longer held its sway.[12]

On the other hand, the degree of dissociation between law and religion is one of the best indications by which we can recognize whether one society is more or less developed than another. In the developed society, criminal law no longer occupies the whole field. The rules sanctioned by punishments and those which have only restitutive sanctions are now very distinct from each other. Restitutive law is separated from repressive law which formerly absorbed it; it now has its own characteristics, its peculiar structure, its own individuality. It exists as a distinct juridical species, with special organs, and a special procedure. Penal law, however, while losing its primitive preponderance, still remains great.

In simple societies where tradition is all-powerful and where nearly everything is held in common, the most puerile usages become, by force of habit, imperative duties. In China the doctor who has not correctly made out his prescription is punished. 'The State', says Fustel de Coulanges, 'exercised its tyranny over the smallest things. At Locris, the law forbade men to drink pure wine. It was the usual thing for dress to be fixed invariably by the laws of each city-state. . . . In Sparta, it forced every man to shave his moustache'. In our time, we believe, it would be difficult to find any such offences in our law.

But much the most important loss penal law suffered is that due to the total, or almost total, disappearance of religious crimes. Thus, a world of sentiments ceased to count among the strong and defined states of the common conscience. Political functions, very early separated from religious functions, subordinated them. Ultimately the religious criminality ended by completely departing, or almost completely departing from penal law.

The observations made above by Durkheim regarding the character of law in ancient India are mostly correct. The law had a religious tinge and was of a repressive nature. The restitutive law held a very insignificant place. To violate such laws was to offend the community and expiation was demanded for that purpose. However, it needs to be mentioned that recently, with the impact of Western education and ideas, there have come many changes in this field too. Besides penal law we now have in India much restitutive law in the form of contract law, constitutional law, administrative law, etc.

(3) *The spirit of altruism in primitive societies as shown by widows in* sati

Durkheim observes that it is a historical law that mechanical solidarity which first stands alone, or nearly so, progressively loses ground, and that organic solidarity becomes, little by little, preponderant. According to Spencer the place of the individual in society, of no account in its origins, becomes greater with civilization. But this incontestable fact, according to Durkheim, is presented to us under an aspect totally different from the English philosophy, so that, ultimately, our conclusions are opposed to his more than they are in agreement. First of all, according to him, this absorption of the individual into the group would be the result of force and of an artificial organization necessitated by the state of war in which lower societies chronically live. It is especially in war that union is necessary to success. It is an organized despotism which would annihilate individuals, and since this organization is essentially military, it is through militarism that Spencer defines these types of society. On the contrary what Durkheim has seen is that this effacement of the individual has as its place of origin a social type which is characterized by a complete absence of all centralization. It is a product of that state of homogeneity which distinguishes primitive societies.

Durkheim further observes that the theory is false which makes egotism the point of departure for humanity and altruism only a recent conquest. What gives this hypothesis authority in the eyes of certain persons is that it appears to be the logical consequence of the principles of Darwinism. In the name of the dogma of the struggle for existence and natural selection, they paint for us in the saddest colours this primitive humanity whose hunger and thirst, always poorly satisfied, were their only passions. Nothing is less scientific than this prejudice in the opposite direction. If the hypotheses of Darwin have a moral use, it is with more reserve and measure than in other sciences. They overlook the essential element of moral life, that is, the moderating influence that society exercises over its members, which tempers and neutralizes the brutal action of the struggle for existence and selection. Wherever there are societies, there is altruism, because there is solidarity. Thus, we find altruism from the beginning of humanity and even in a truly intemperate form.

For these privations that the savage imposes upon himself in obedience to religious tradition, the abnegation with which he sacrifices his life when society demands such sacrifice, the irresistible desire of the widow of India to follow her husband to the grave, of the Gaul not to survive the head of his clan, of the old Celt to free his companions from useless trouble by voluntary death—is not all this altruism? Shall we treat these practices as superstitions?

Scientifically, conduct is egotistical in the measure that is determined by sentiments and representations which are exclusively personal. In the lower societies the conscience of the individual is wrapped in the collective conscience, and it is a thing totally different from the individual himself, that is it is completely altruistic, as Condillac would say: this conclusion, however, would be exaggerated, for there is a sphere of psychic life which, however developed the collective type may be, varies from one man to another and remains peculiar to each. It is that which is formed by representations, by sentiments and tendencies which relate to the organism and to the state of the organism. To speak rigorously, these two sides of the conduct are found present from the beginning in all human consciences, for there cannot be things which do not reflect both of these aspects, the one relating to the individual alone and the other relating to the things which are not personal to him. Durkheim's observation that not only egotism but altruism was also the characteristic of primitive societies is correct. That a man's conduct is egotistical in a measure is true. But that the conscience of the individual is also wrapped in the collective conscience cannot be denied. He rightly points out that the desire of the widow of India to follow her husband to the grave was governed by the collective conscience and the spirit of altruism. However, this custom of *sati* is followed no more in India as it was abolished by an enactment in 1829.

(4) *The rule of adoption among Hindus*

Durkheim observes that it is true that contractual relations, which originally were rare or completely absent, multiply as social labour becomes divided. But what Spencer seems to have failed to see is that non-contractual relations develop at the same time. In this connection Durkheim examines that part of law which is improperly termed private, and which, in reality, regulates diffuse social functions. For example, domestic law, which was simple in the beginning, becomes more and more complex. Marriage and adoption are sources of domestic relations, and they are contracts. But it rightly happens that the closer we get to the most elevated social types, the more too do these two juridical operations lose their properly contractual character. In the lower societies marriage is an entirely private affair. The Christians early got into the habit of having their union consecrated by a priest. An act of the emperer Leo the Philosopher converted this usage into a law for the East. The Council of Trent sanctioned it likewise for the West. From then on, marriage ceased to be freely contracted, and was concluded through the intermediary of a public power, the Church. Later on the civil authority was substituted in this function for the religious authority.

Similarly in the case of adoption, which was practised on a large scale among the Indian tribes of North America. It could give rise to all the forms of kinship. If the adopted was of the same age as the one who adopted, they became brothers and sisters; if the adopted was already a mother, she became the mother of the one who adopted her. Among the Germans, adoption was probably quite as easy and frequent. Very simple ceremonies were enough to establish it. But in India, Greece and Rome it was already subordinated to determined conditions. The one adopting had to be of a certain age, and could not stand in such a relation to the age of the adopted that it would be impossible to be his natural father. Ultimately, this change of family became a highly complex juridical operation which necessitated the intervention of a magistrate. At the same time, the number of those who could enjoy the right of adoption became more restricted. Only the father of a family or a bachelor *sui juris* could adopt, and the first could, only if he had no legitimate children. In our current law the restrictive conditions have been even more multiplied. As Durkheim points out, the law of adoption, which was domestic in nature in the beginning became social later on. In India, the law of adoption was subordinated to certain conditions. The one adopting had to be of a certain age and could not stand in such a relation to the age of the adopted that it would be impossible to be his natural father. However, he fails to mention that adoption could only be made by the male and not the female. There have been some changes in this law in India since Independence and now even the females can adopt a son or daughter according to their wishes.

EMILE DURKHEIM (1858–1917)

(5) *The formation of castes*

Durkheim observes that in societies where organic solidarity is preponderant, there structure is constituted, not by a repetition of similar, homogeneous segments, but by a system of different organs, each of which has a special role. Individuals are here grouped, no longer according to their relations of lineage, but according to the particular nature of the social activity to which they consecrate themselves. Their natural milieu is no longer the natal milieu, but the occupational milieu. It is no longer real or fictitious consanguinity which marks the place of each one, but the function which he fills. But, when this new organization begins to appear, it tries to utilize the existing organizations and assimilate it. The segments, or at least the groups of segments united by special affinities become organs. It is thus that the clans which together formed the tribe of the Levites appropriated sacerdotal functions for themselves among the Hebrew people. In a general way, classes and castes probably have no other origin nor any other nature; they arise from the multitude of occupational organizations being born amidst the pre-existing familial organization. However, it is only a very rudimentary division of labour which can adapt itself to those rigid, defined moulds which were not made for it. As soon as it has passed a certain stage of development, the social material must enter into entirely new combinations in order to organize itself upon completely different foundations. But the old structure, so far as it persists, is opposed to this. That is why it must disappear.

In so far as labour is divided, there arises a multitude of occupational moralities and laws. But this regulation, nonetheless, does not contract the sphere of action of the individual. This is because the occupational mind can only have influence on occupational life. Beyond this sphere, the individual enjoys a greater liberty. True, the caste extends its action further, but it is not an organ, properly speaking. It is a segment transformed into an organ, it has the nature of both. At the same time, as it is charged with special functions, it constitutes a distinct society in the midst of the total aggregate.

Race (heredity) and individuality are two contradictory forces which vary inversely with each other. As long as we only continue to follow in the path of our ancestors, we tend to live as they lived, and remain adamant to all innovation. But as soon as division of labour appears in characteristic fashion, it is fixed into a form trasmitted by heredity. Thus castes grow up. India offers the most perfect model of this organization of work, but it is found elsewhere. With the Jews, the only functions which were sharply

263

separated from others, sacerdotal functions, were strictly hereditary. It was the same at Rome for all public functions, which implied religious functions, which were the privilege of the patricians alone. When castes tend to disappear, they are replaced by classes, which in order to keep their close exclusion and privileges, rely on the same principle.

Assuredly this institution is not a simple consequence of the fact of hereditary transmission. A great many causes have contributed to bring it into being. It is certain that reasons, social or politic, or even prejudices, have had to contribute to its development and its strength, but it would be absurd to believe that it was invented.

It is a well known fact that progress is slow and difficult in these societies. For centuries, work remains organized in the same manner without any thought of innovation. 'Heredity is shown to us here with its habitual characteristics: conservation, stability'.[13] Consequently, for the division of labour to be able to develop, men had to succeed in shaking off the yoke of heredity, progress had to break up castes and classes.

It is an established truth that the degree of simplicity of psychic facts gives the measure of their transmissibility. In fact, the more complex states are, the more easily do they decompose since their great complexity keeps them in a state of unstable equilibrium. Consequently, the more special faculties are, the more difficult they are to transmit. Cases have nevertheless been cited where occupational aptitudes appear to be hereditary. From tables arranged by Galton, there seem to have been veritable dynasties of scholars, poets and musicians. But these observations have no demonstrative value. In the Middle Ages, the nobleman, to fulfil his duty, had no need of a great deal of knowledge, or of very complicated practices, but did need courage, and he inherited that. The Levite and the brahman, for their work, had no need of a voluminous science—we can measure its dimensions from the books containing it—but they had to have a native superiority in intelligence which made them susceptible to ideas and sentiments closed to the vulgar. To be a good doctor in the time of Aesculapius, it was not necessary to receive a wide culture; it was enough to have a natural taste for observation and concrete things, and as this taste is general enough to be easily transmissible, it inevitably was perpetuated in certain families, and, consequently, the medical profession was hereditary. The causes leading to the formation of castes in India as mentioned by Durkheim are mostly correct. These included occupational, racial, social, political and even prejudicial ones. Durkheim does not believe that the caste system was invented. However, these were not the only factors which led to the formation of castes. The traditional theory that castes were formed because of marriages between different *varnas* cannot be ruled out.

(6) *The disadvantages of the caste system in modern society*

In these conditions, it is clear, heredity became a social institution. To be sure, these wholly psychological causes could not give rise to the organization of castes, but once the latter were born through other circumstances, it lasted because it was found to conform perfectly both to the tastes of individuals and the interests of society. However, to make the hereditary legacy valuable in the modern society, a great deal more must be added than formerly. In effect, in so far as functions are more specialized, simply general aptitudes are not longer enough. They must be submitted to active elaborations, and acquire a whole world of ideas.

Durkheim further points out that the division of social labour can be distinguished from the division of physiological labour by an essential characteristic. In the organism, each cell has its defined role, and cannot change it. In societies, tasks have never been so immutably distributed. Even where the forms of organization are most rigid, the individual can move about in the interior of the form in which he is fixed with a certain liberty. In primitive Rome, the plebeian could freely undertake all the functions not exclusively reserved to the patricians. Even in India, the careers which were allowed to each caste had sufficient in generality to permit some choice.[14]

Though normally the division of labour produces social solidarity, it sometimes happens that it has different, and even contrary results, e.g. the industrial or commercial crisis, the conflict between capital and labour, too much specialization in sciences with no proper co-ordination, etc. If the division of labour does not produce solidarity in all these cases, it is because the relations of the organs are not regulated, because they are in a state of anomie. However, the division of labour does not produce these consequences because of a necessity of its own nature, but only in exceptional and abnormal circumstances. In order for it to develop without having such a disastrous influence on the human conscience, it is not necessary to temper it with its opposite, but to correct the anomaly. For, normally, the role of each special function does not require that the individual close himself in, but that he keep himself in constant relations with neighbouring functions, take cognizance of their needs and of the changes which they undergo, etc. For that, he need not embrace vast portions of the social horizon, it is sufficient that he perceive enough of it to understand that his actions have an aim beyond themselves.

It is not sufficient that there be rules, however, for sometimes the rules themselves are the cause of evil. That is what occurs in class-wars. The institution of classes and of castes constitutes an organization of the division of labour, and it is a strictly regulated organization, although it often is a source of dissension. The lower classes, not being, or no longer being, satisfied with the role which has devolved upon them from custom or by law, aspire to functions which are closed to them and seek to disposses those who are exercising these functions. Thus civil wars arise which are due to the manner in which labour is distributed.

For the division of labour to produce solidarity, it is not sufficient, then, that each have his task; it is still necessary that this task be fitting to him. If the institution of classes and castes sometimes gives rise to anxiety and pain instead of producing solidarity, this is because the distribution of social functions on which it rests does not respond, or rather, no longer responds, to the distribution of natural talents. Through changes produced in society, some must have become apt at functions which were at first beyond them, while the others lost their original superiority. When the plebeians aimed to dispute the right to religious and administrative functions with the patricians, it was not only in imitation of the latter, but it was also because they had become more intelligent, richer, more numerous and their tastes and ambitions had in consequence been modified. In accordance with these transformations, the agreement between the aptitudes of individuals and the kind of activity assigned to them is found to be broken in every region of society; constraint alone, more or less violent and more or less direct, links them to the functions. Consequently, only an imperfect and troubled solidarity is possible.

That this perfect spontaneity is never met with anywhere is a realized fact. However, the more we advance on the social scale the more the segmental type disappears into the organized type, and the more these inequalities tend to completely level out. The progressive decline of castes, beginning from the moment the division of labour is established, is an historical law, for, as they are linked to the politico-familial organization, they necessarily regress along with this organization. The task of the most advanced societies is, then, a work of justice. Just as the ideal of lower societies was to create or maintain as intense a common life as possible, in which the individual was absorbed, so our ideal is to make social relations always more equitable, so as to assure the free development of all our socially useful forces.

Durkheim here rightly stresses that at a time when there was not much specialization of labour, the castes were not so harmful for they were found to conform perfectly both to the tastes of the individuals and to the interests of the society. But in a modern society where the functions are more specialized, general aptitudes are no longer enough and people must be submitted to active elaborations and acquire a whole world of ideas. For the division of labour to produce solidarity it is not sufficient that each has a task; it is still necessary that this task be fitting to him. The institution of classes and castes sometimes gives rise to anxiety and pain instead of producing solidarity, as the distribution of social functions on which it rests does not respond to the distribution of natural talents. He is also optimistic that castes will gradually disappear as he observes that the more we advance on the social scale the more the segmental type disappears into the organized type. In his view the progressive decline of castes, beginning from the moment the division of labour is established, is an historical law. As they are linked to the politico-familial organization, they necessarily regress along with this organization. However, he seems to have ignored the fact that castes are also related to religious institutions in India and, unless they change, the abolition of the caste system in the strict sense may not be possible there.

(7) *Causes of suicide in India*

In *Division of Labour* Durkheim had cited the increased suicide rate in the nineteenth century as an argument against the 'happiness' principle of the utilitarian. He now selects the phenomenon of suicide for intensive analysis. On the basis of statistical studies and theoretical constructs he isolates three factors operating in the suicide rate; he calls these the 'altruistic', the 'egoistic', and the 'anomic'.[15] In the egoistic factor there is progressive emphasis on the value of individuality and the individual tends to become exalted over all other objects and ideas, such as God, society, country, and all other repositories of collective sentiments. In times of dislocation, stress, and anxiety he finds himself without group support and is likely to take his own life out of desperation. At the other pole is the altruistic factor. The anomic (normless) factor operates where the social norms are upset by rapid change in the interior of a society. In times of extreme prosperity or poverty, for example, the suicide rate goes up. The altruistic factor is associated with the idea of extreme mechanical solidarity where the collective attachments and pressures are so strong that the individual life becomes relatively unimportant. With so little value placed on the individual, both by himself and others, it takes little pressure to cause a person to

267

take his own life. Also, there may actually occur a social command to commit suicide.

In this connection Durkheim takes many instances from India and other countries where altruistic factors prevail. In India generally three types of suicide are found among various classes of people. There are (a) suicides among Brahmans and Hindu sages (this category includes suicides among widows), (b) suicides among Buddhists and Jains, and (c) suicides among Hindus.

(a) *Suicides among brahmans and Hindu sages*   Durkheim points out that it has sometimes been said that suicide was unknown among lower societies. Thus expressed, the assertion is inexact. Bartholin in his book, *De causis contemptae mortis a Danis,* reports that Danish warriors considered it a disgrace to die in bed of old age or sickness, and killed themselves to escape this ignominy. Silvius Italicus says of the Spanish Celts: 'They are a nation lavish of their blood and eager to face death. As soon as the Celt has passed the age of mature strength, he endures the flight of time impatiently and scorns to await old age; the term of his existence depends upon himself'.[16] Accordingly they assigned a delightful abode to those who committed suicide and a horrible subterranean one to those who died of sickness or decrepitude. The same custom has long been maintained in India. Perhaps this favourable attitude toward suicide did not appear in the Vedas, but it was certainly very ancient. Plutarch says, concerning the suicide of the brahman Calanus: 'He sacrificed himself with his own hands as was customary with sages of this country'.[17] And Quintus Curtius:

> Among them exists a sort of wild and bestial men to whom they give the name of sages. The anticipation of the time of death is a glory in their eyes, and they have themselves burned alive as soon as age or sickness begins to trouble them. According to them, death, passively awaited, is a dishonour of life; thus no honours are rendered those bodies which old age has destroyed. Fire would be contaminated did it not receive the human sacrifice still breathing.[18]

Suicide among Hindu widows   Besides the old men, women are often required among the same people to kill themselves on their husband's death. This barbarous practice is so ingrained in Hindu customs that the efforts of the English are futile against it. In 1817, 706 widows killed themselves in the one province of Bengal and in 1821, 2366 were found in all India. Moreover, when a prince or chief dies, his followers are forced not to survive him. Such was the case in Gaul. In the above cases the suicides fall into the following three categories: (1) suicides of men on the threshold of old age or stricken with sickness, (2) suicides of women on their husbands' death and (3) suicides of followers or servants on the death of their chiefs. Now, when a person kills himself, in all these cases, it is not because he assumes the right to do so but, on the contrary, because it is his duty. If he fails in this obligation, he is dishonoured and also punished, usually, by religious sanctions. This sacrifice is imposed by society for social ends. However, as Durkheim points out, not every altruistic suicide is necessarily obligatory. Some are not so expressly imposed by society, having a more optional character. In other words, altruistic suicide is a species with several varieties.

(b) *Suicides among Buddhist, and Jains* In the same societies mentioned above, or others of their sort, suicide may often be encountered with the most futile immediate and apparent motives. Titus, Livy, Caesar and Valerius Maximus all tell us, not without astonishment mixed with admiration, of the calmness with which the Gallic and German barbarians kill themselves. The readiness of the Japanese to disembowel themselves for the slightest reason is well known. A strange sort of duel is even reported there, in which the effort is not to attack one another but to excel in dexterity in opening one's own stomach. In such cases, a man kills himself without being explicitly forced to do so. Yet these suicides are of the same nature as obligatory suicides. Though public opinion does not formally require them, it is certainly favourable to them. What is done in the one case to escape the stigma of insult is done in the other to win esteem. When people are accustomed to set no value on life from childhood on, and to despise those who value it excessively, they inevitably renounce it on the least pretext. So valueless a sacrifice is easily assumed.

In the above two cases a man kills himself only with the concurrence of circumstances. Either death had to be imposed by society as a duty, or some question of honour was involved, or at least some disagreeable occurence had to lower the value of life in the victim's eye. But it even happens that the individual kills himself purely for the joy of sacrifice, because, even with no particular reason, renunciation in itself is considered praiseworthy. India is the classic soil for this sort of suicide. The Hindu was already inclined to self-destruction under Brahmanic influence. Manu's laws, to be sure, command suicide, only with some reservations. A man must already have attained a certain age and he must at least have left one son. But if these conditions are satisfied, he has nothing more to do with life. 'The Brahman who had freed himself from his body by one of the methods employed

269

by the saints, freed from grief and fear, is honorably received in the abode of Brahma'.[19]

Though Buddhism has often been accused of having carried this principle to its most extreme consequences and elevated suicide into a religious practice, it actually condemned it. It is true that it taught that the highest bliss was self-destruction in nirvana; but this suspension of existence may and should be achieved even during this life without need of violent measures for its realization. Of course, the thought that one should seek to escape existence is so thoroughly in the spirit of the Hindu doctrine and so conformable with the aspirations of the Hindu temperament that it may be encountered in various forms in the chief sects sprung from Buddhism or formed simultaneously with it.

It is thus with Jainism. Though one of the canonical books of the Jainist religion reproves suicide, accusing it of really augmenting life, inscriptions found in many sanctuaries show that, especially among the southern Jainist religious, suicide was very often practised.[20] The believer allowed himself to die of hunger.[21]

(c) *Suicides among Hindus* In Hinduism the custom of seeking death in the waters of the Ganges or of other sacred rivers was widespread. 'Inscriptions represent to us kings and ministers preparing to end their days thus and we are assured that these superstitions had not wholly disappeared at the beginning of the century'.[22]

Among the Bhils there was a rock from the top of which men cast themselves with religious motives, to devote themselves to Shiva;[23] even as late as 1822 an officer attended one of these sacrifices. The story of the fanatics who let themselves be crushed to death in throngs under the wheels of the idol Juggernaut has become classic.[24] Charlevoix in his time had observed rites of this sort in Japan: 'Nothing is commoner', he says, 'than to see ships along the seashore filled with these fanatics who throw themselves into the water weighed with stones, or sink their ships and let themselves be gradually submerged while singing their idol's praises'.[25]

There are no suicides with a more definitely altruistic character. We actually see the individual in all these cases seek to strip himself of his personal being in order to be engulfed in something which he regards as his true essence. Impersonality is here carried to its highest pitch; altruism is acute. While the egoist is unhappy because he sees nothing real in the world but the individual, the intemperate altruist's sadness, on the contrary, springs from the individual's seeming wholly unreal to him. One is detached from life because, seeing no goal to which he may attach himself, he feels himself useless and purposeless; the other because he has a goal but one outside this life, which henceforth seems merely an obstacle to him. Thus, the difference of the causes reappears in their effects, and the melancholy of one is quite different from that of the other. That of the former consists of a feeling of incurable weakness and sad depression; it expresses a complete relaxation of activity, which, unable to find useful employment, collapses. That of the latter, on the contrary, springs from hope; for it depends on the belief in beautiful perspectives beyond this life. It even implies enthusiasm and the spur of a faith eagerly seeking satisfaction, affirming itself by acts of extreme energy.

In conclusion Durkheim adds that altruistic suicides are of three types, viz. Obligatory altruistic suicide, optional altruistic suicide, and acute altruistic suicide, the perfect pattern of which is mystical suicide.[26]

The various facts stated above with regard to the types of suicides committed in India are mostly correct. Even among some sects of Buddhism the tradition of suicide prevailed. This is confirmed by Charles Eliot when he says, 'In theory the Buddha taught a middle way, rejecting alike self-indulgence and self-mortification. But even Pali Buddhism admits such practices as the Dhutanagas and the more extravagant sects, for instance in Tibet, allow monks to entomb themselves in dark cells'.[27] Lately the practice of suicide among Hindu sages and old brahmans has gradually diminished owing to the lesser vogue of the asrama system. The custom of *sati* among widows has been totally abolished since 1829 with the passing of the Regulation Act and such cases are now very rare.

Indian religions—their characteristics

In his last major work *'The Elementary Forms of the Religious Life'* (1912), instead of a comprehensive survey of the field (in the manner of Tylor, Frazer or Smith), Durkheim selected a specific case for intensive study; namely Australian totemism. He undertook this study with the familiar assumptions that religion, like any other institution, must be regarded as a response to specific social needs and that, as a social phenomenon, it is a product of collective thought.

Durkheim defines religion as 'a unified system of beliefs and practices relative to sacred things, that is to say, things set apart and forbidden—beliefs and practices which unite into one single moral community called a Church, all those who adhere to them'.[28] He insists at the outset that religion must have its origin in

271

some concrete reality. Such a persistent and universal phenomenon cannot be based on illusion, such as is required by Tylor's animism or Morgan's naturalism.[29]

Durkheim makes two distinctions which are basic to his entire study: the distinction between beliefs and rites as categories of religious phenomena and the distinction between *sacred* and *profane*. The first distinction separates the elements of *thought* and *action* in religion, and the second separates religious attitudes from other human attitudes. There is nothing inherent in an object, such as the totem, which evokes a sacred attitude; rather it is the projection of belief upon an object that makes it sacred.

A society cannot exist unless the conditions of solidarity and co-operation are kept intact. The function of religion is to foster and perpetuate, largely on unconscious levels, the kind of human behaviour necessary for social existence: restrictions on the indulgence of individual whims, sacrifice for a social cause, a disposition toward co-operation, and the recognition of a power superior to the individual. The ideals of all great religions are the ideals of society, and although never perfectly realized by man, they keep him at least a little this side of destruction.

The general conclusions reported above result from Durkheim's analysis of the totemism of Australia. 'He has been shown to be factually mistaken on important points in totemism, and his detailed analysis has been weakened accordingly, but the insights emphasized above are still worthy of attention'.[30] With these main findings in view we shall study Durkheim's views on Indian religions and religious practices in India. These may be discussed under five main heads, viz. (a) Indian religions are complex, (b) the negation of God in Buddhism, Jainism and Hinduism, (c) some special characteristics of Vedic religion, (d) asceticism in Buddhism and (e) sacrifices in Hinduism.

(8) *Indian religions are complex*

As Durkheim wanted to study the characteristics of a simple and primitive religion, he distinguishes them from some complex religions. According to him a religious system may be said to be the most primitive which we can observe when it fulfils the two following conditions: in the first place, it is found in a society whose organization is surpassed by no others in simplicity; second, it is possible to explain it without making use of any element borrowed from a previous religion. In order to study a religion we should study some of its certain fundamental characteristics. Since all religions are species of the same class, there are necessarily many elements which are common to all. They have some external resemblances. But at the foundation of all systems of beliefs and of all cults there ought necessarily to be a certain number of fundamental representations or conceptions and of ritual attitudes, which, in spite of the diversity of forms which they have taken, have the same objective significance and fulfil the same functions everywhere. These are the permanent elements which constitute that which is permanent and human in religion.

However, these elements are not to be picked up by observing the complex religions which appear in the course of history. Every one of these is made up of such a variety of elements that it is very difficult to distinguish what is secondary from what is principal, the essential from the accessory. Suppose that the religion considered is like that of Egypt, India or the classical antiquity. It is a confused mass of many cults, varying according to the locality. The temples, the generations, the dynasties, the invasions, etc. Popular superstitions are there confused with the purest dogmas. Neither the thought nor the activity of the religion is evenly distributed among the believers; according to the men, the environment and the circumstances, the beliefs as well as the rites are thought of in different ways. Here they are priests, there they are monks, elsewhere they are laymen; there are mystics and rationalists, theologians and prophets, etc. In these conditions it is difficult to see what is common to all. Things are quite different in the lower societies. The slighter development of individuality, the small extension of the group, the homogeneity of external circumstances, all contribute to reducing the differences and variations to a minimum. The above-noted observations made by Durkheim with regard to Indian religions are correct. It is admitted that the three major religions having their origin in India, i.e. Hinduism, Buddhism and Jainism, are complex ones as there are various cults and sects in these religions.

(9) *The negation of God in Buddhism, Jainism and Hinduism*

Durkheim observes that if we are going to look for the most primitive and simple religion which we can observe, it is necessary to begin by defining what is meant by a religion. And for that we must see the characteristics of religion so far observed before we give our own definition. One idea which generally passes as characteristic of all that is religious, is that of the supernatural. By this is understood all sorts of things which surpass the limits of our knowledge; the supernatural is the world of the mysterious, of the unknowable, of the un-understandable. Thus religion would be a sort of speculation upon all that which evades science or distinct thought in general. Max Muller sees in religion 'a struggle to conceive the inconceivable, to utter the unutterable, a longing after the Infinite'.[31] However, it is certain that this idea does not appear until late in the history of religions; it is completely foreign, not only to those peoples who are called primitive, but also to all others who have not attained a considerable degree of intellectual culture.

Another idea by which the attempt to define religion is often made, is that of divinity. 'Religion', says M. Reville, 'is the determination of human life by the sentiment of a bond uniting the human mind to that mysterious mind whose domination of the world and itself it recognizes, and to whom it delights in feeling itself united'. In this sense according to Tylor, 'It seems best . . . simply to claim as a minimum definition of Religion, the belief in Spiritual Beings'.[32] But however evident this definition may appear, thanks to the mental habits which we owe to our religious education, there are many facts to which it is not applicable, but which appertain to the field of religion nevertheless.

The absence of gods and spirits in Buddhism   In the first place, there are great religions from which the idea of gods and spirits is absent, or at least, where it plays only a secondary and minor role. This is the case with Buddhism. Buddhism, says Burnouf, 'sets itself in oppostion to Brahmanism as a moral system without god and an atheism without Nature'.[33] As it does not recognize a god upon whom man depends, its doctrine is absolutely atheistic. According to Oldenberg, 'it is a faith without a god'.[34] In fact, all that is essential to Buddhism is found in the four propositions which the faithful call the four noble truths. The first states the existence of suffering as the accompaniment to the perpetual change of things; the second shows desire to be the cause of suffering; the third makes the suppression of desire the only means of suppressing sorrow; the fourth enumerates the three stages through which one must pass to attain this suppression: they are uprightness, meditation and finally wisdom, the full possession of the doctrine. These three stages once traversed, one arrives at the end of the road, at the deliverance, at salvation by the nirvana. In none of these principles is there any question of a divinity. The Buddhist is not interested in knowing whence came the world in which he lives and suffers; he takes it as a given fact, and his whole concern is to escape it. On the other hand, in this work of salvation, he can count only upon himself, he has no god to thank, as he had previously no god to invoke during his struggle. Instead of praying, in the ordinary sense of the term, instead of turning towards a superior being and imploring his assistance, he relies upon himself and meditates. This is not saying 'that he absolutely denies the existence of the beings called Indra, Agni and Varuna';[35] but he believes that he owes them nothing and that he has nothing to do with them, for their power can only extend over the goods of this world, which are without value for him. Then he is an atheist, in the sense that he does not concern himself with the question whether gods exist or not. Besides, even if they should exist, and with whatever powers they might be armed, the saint or the emancipated man regards himself superior to them; for that which causes the dignity of being is not the extent of the action they exercise over things, but merely the degree of their advancement upon the road of salvation.

It is true that Buddha, at least in some divisions of the Buddhist Church, has sometimes been considered as a sort of god. He has his temples; he is the object of a cult, which, by the way, is a very simple one, for it is reduced essentially to the offering of flowers and the adoration of consecrated relics or images. It is scarcely more than a commemorative cult. But more than that, this divinization of Buddha, granting that the term is exact, is peculiar to the form known as Northern Buddhism. 'The Buddhist of the South', says Kern, 'and the less advanced of the Northern Buddhists can be said, according to the data known today, to speak of their founder as if he were a man'.[36] Of course, they attribute extraordinary powers to Buddha, which are superior to those possessed by ordinary mortals; but it was a very ancient belief in India, and one that is also very general in a host of different religions, that a great saint is endowed with exceptional virtues; yet a saint is not a god, any more than a priest or magician is, in spite of the superhuman faculties frequently attributed to them. On the other hand, according to the most authoritative scholars, all this theism and the complicated mythology which generally accompanies it, are only derived and deviated forms of Buddhism. At first, Buddha was only regarded as 'the wisest of men'.[37]

Jainists as atheists   All that has been said in the above section on the Buddhists can be applied equally well to another great religion of India, Jainism. The two doctrines have nearly the same conception of the world and of life. 'Like the Buddhists', says Barth, 'the Jainas are atheists. They admit of no creator; the world is eternal; they explicitly deny the possibility of a perfect being from the beginning. The Jaina became perfect; he was not always so'.[38]

Just like the Buddhists in the north, the Jainists, or at least certain of them, have come back to a sort of deism; in the inscriptions of Dekhan there is mention of a Jinapati, a sort of supreme Jina, who is called the primary creator; but such language, says the same author, is 'in contradiction to the most explicit declarations extracted from their most authorized writings'.[39]

Atheism in Hinduism   If this indifference to the divine is developed to such a point in Buddhism and Jainism, it is because its germs existed already in the brahmanism from which the two were derived. In certain of its forms at least, brahmanic speculation ended in 'a frankly materialistic and atheistic interpretation of the universe'.[40] In time, the numerous divinities which the people of India had originally learned to adore came to merge themselves into a sort of principle deity, impersonal and abstract, the essence of all that exists. This supreme reality, which no longer has anything of a divine personality about it, is contained within man himself, or rather, man is but one with it, for nothing exists apart from it. To find it, and unite himself to it, one does not have to search for some external support outside himself; it is enough to concentrate upon himself and meditate. 'If in Buddhism', says Oldenberg,

> the proud attempt be made to conceive a deliverance in which man himself delivers himself, to create a faith without a God, it is Brahmanical speculation which has prepared the way for this thought. It thrusts back the idea of a god step by step; the forms of the old gods have faded away, and besides the Brahma, which is enthroned in its everlasting quietude, highly exalted above the destinies of the human world, there is left remaining, as the sole really active person in the great work of deliverance, man himself.[41]

Here, then, we find a considerable portion of religious evolution which has consisted in the progressive recoil of the idea of a spiritual being from that of a deity. Here are great religions where invocations, propitiations, sacrifices and prayers, properly so called, are far from holding a preponderating place, and they consequently do not present that distinctive sign by which some claim to recognize those manifestations which are properly called religions. But even within deistic religions there are many rites which are completely independent of all ideas of gods or spiritual beings. For example, the Bible orders that a woman live isolated during a determined period each month; a similar isolation is obligatory during the lying-in at childbirth. As much can be said for the majority of the dietetic regulations. It is true that these rites are purely negative, but they do not cease being religious for that.

The above-noted observations of Durkheim that there is a

negation of God in Buddhism, in Jainism and in some schools of Hinduism is quite correct.

(10) *Some special characteristics of Vedic religion*

While studying the common characteristics of various religions as a whole Durkheim points out three significant characteristics of Vedic religion, viz. (a) Vedic religion laid more emphasis on rituals, (b) it was the oldest religion among civilized people, and (3) fire was an important element in Vedic religion. Let us discuss these one by one.

(a) *Rituals as part of Vedic religion* Durkheim points out that besides negative rites which are independent of all ideas of gods or spiritual beings, discussed above, there are also rites which demand active and positive services of the faithful, but which are nevertheless of the same nature. They work by themselves, and their efficacy depends upon no divine power; they mechanically produce the effects which are the reason for their existence. They do not consist either in prayers or in offerings addressed to a being upon whose good will the expected result depends; this result is obtained by the automatic operation of the ritual. Such is notably the case with the sacrifice of the Vedic religion. 'The sacrifice exercises a direct influence upon the celestial phenomena', says Bergaigne, 'it is all powerful of itself and without any divine influence'.[42] In the same way there are special hymns which, by their direct action, made the waters of heaven fall upon the earth, and even in spite of the gods. The practice of certain austerities has the same power. Bergaigne speaks of many sacrifices, where divinities play no role whatsoever. Nor is this fact peculiar to the Vedic religion; it is, on the contrary, quite general. In every cult there are practices which act by themselves, by a virtue which is their own, without the intervention of any god between the individual who practises the rite and the end sought after.

Thus Durkheim concludes that there are rites without gods, and even rites from which gods are derived. All religious powers do not emanate from divine personalities, and there are relations of cult which have other objects than uniting man to a deity. Religion is more than the idea of gods or spirits, and consequently cannot be defined exclusively in relation to these latter.

On the other hand religion is a complex system of myths, dogmas, rites and ceremonies. There are various elementary phenomena which combine to form religion. Religious phenomena can be arranged in two fundamental categories: beliefs and rites. The first are states of opinion, and consist in representations; the second are determined modes of action. Further, all known religious beliefs, whether simple or complex, present one common characteristic: they presuppose a classification of all the things, real and ideal, of which men think, into two classes called *profane* and *sacred*. The religious thought in the nature of beliefs, myths, dogmas and legends express the nature of sacred things. These sacred things include not only personal beings which are called gods and spirits, but also a rock, a tree, a spring, a pebble, a piece of wood etc. A rite can also have this character; in fact, the rite does not exist which does not have it to a certain degree. There are words, expressions and formulae which can be pronounced only by the mouths of consecrated persons; they are gestures and movements which everybody cannot perform.

If the Vedic sacrifice has had such an efficacy that, according to mythology, it was the creator of the gods, and not merely a means of winning their favour, it is because it possessed a virtue comparable to that of the most sacred beings.

The circle of sacred objects cannot be determined, then, once for all. Its extent varies infinitely according to different religions. That is how Buddhism is a religion: in default of gods, it admits the existence of sacred things, namely, the four noble truths and the practices derived from them.

When a certain number of sacred things sustain relations of co-ordination or subordination with each other in such a way as to form a system having a certain unity, but which is not comprised within any other system of the same sort, the totality of these beliefs and their corresponding rites constitutes a religion. Thus religion is a whole made up of distinct and relatively individualized parts.

(b) *Vedic religion—the oldest religion among civilized people*
Durkheim, while examining the theories of the naturalistic school of religion, points out that the Vedic religion is the oldest among civilized people and this he tried to prove with the help of comparative mythology. He points out that ever since the work of the Grimm brothers, who pointed out the interest that there is in comparing the different mythologies of the Indo-European peoples, scholars have been struck by the remarkable similarities which they present. Mythical personages were identified who, though having different names, symbolized the same ideas and fulfilled the same functions; even the names were frequently related, and it has been thought possible to establish the fact that they are not unconnected with one another. Such resemblances seemed to be explicable only by a common origin.

The discovery of the Vedas aided greatly in stimulating these ambitions. In the Vedas, scholars had a written text, whose antiquity was undoubtedly exaggerated at the moment of its discovery, but which is surely one of the most ancient which we have at our disposal in an Indo-European language. Here they are enabled to study, by the ordinary methods of philology, a literature as old as or older than Homer, and a religion which was believed more primitive than that of the ancient Germans. A document of such value was evidently destined to throw a new light upon the religious beginnings of humanity and the science of religions could not fail to be revolutionized by it.

The conception which was thus born was so fully demanded by the state of the science and by the general march of ideas, that it appeared almost simultaneously in two different lands. In 1856, Max Muller exposed its principles in his Oxford Essays entitled *Comparative Mythology.* Three years later appeared the work of Adalbert Kuhn on *The origin of Fire and the Drink of the Gods* (1859), which was clearly inspired by the same spirit. Then followed the works of Schwartz *The Origin of Mythology* (1860) and many others. Durkheim examines the principles followed by all these mythologists and particularly by Max Muller. According to Max Muller religion like all other knowledge begins with sensuous experience.[43] Religion here does not appear as a sort of vague and confused dreaming (as in animism), but as a system of ideas and practices well founded in reality. The sensations which give birth to religious thought, he studies with the help of Vedic literature.

The names of the gods are generally either common words, still employed, or else words formerly common, whose original sense it is possible to discover. Now both designate the principal phenomena of nature. Thus Agni, the name of one of the principal divinities of India, originally signified only the material fact of fire, such as it is ordinarily perceived by the senses and without any mythological addition. Even in the Vedas, it is still employed with this meaning; in any case, it is well shown that this signification was primitive by the fact that it is conserved in other Indo-European languages: the Latin *ignis,* the Lithuanian *ugnis,* the old Slav *ogny* are evidently closely related to *Agni.* Similarly the relationship of the Sanskrit *Dyaus,* the Greek *Zeus,* the Latin *Jovis* and the *Zio* of High German is today uncontested. This proves that these different words designate one single and the same divinity, whom the different Indo-European peoples recognized as such before their separation. Now *Dyaus* signifies the bright sky. These and other similar facts tend to show that among these peoples the forms and forces of nature were the first objects to which the religious sentiment attached itself: they were the first things to be deified. Going one step further in his generalization, Max Muller thought that he was prepared to conclude that the religious evolution of humanity in general had the same point of departure.

(c) *Fire—an important element in Vedic religion* It is almost entirely by considerations of a psychological sort that Muller justifies these inferences. The varied spectacles which nature offers man seemed to him to fulfil all the conditions necessary for arousing religious ideas in the mind directly. In order to illustrate his idea, he applies it to a natural force, which holds a rather large place in the Vedic religion, fire. He says,

> If you can for a moment transfer yourselves to that early stage of life to which we must refer not only the origin, but likewise the early phases of Physical Religion, you can easily understand what an impression the first appearance of fire must have made on the human mind. Fire was not given as something permanent or eternal, like the sky, or the earth, or the water. In whatever way it first appeared, whether through lightning or through the friction of the branches of trees, or through the sparks of flints, it came and went, it had to be guarded, it brought destruction, but at the same time, it made life possible in winter, it served as a protection during the night, it became a weapon of defence and offence, and last, but not least, it changed man from a devourer of raw flesh into an eater of cooked meat. At a later time it became the means of working metal, of making tools and weapons, it became an indispensable factor in all mechanical and artistic progress, and has remained so ever since. What should we be without fire even now?[44]

There is no aspect of nature which is not fitted to awaken within us this overwhelming sensation of an infinity which surrounds us and dominates us. It is from this sensation that religions are derived.

However, as Durkheim points out, if the objects of nature really became sacred because of their imposing forms or the forces which they manifest, then the sun, the moon, the sky, the mountains, the sea, the winds, in a word, the great cosmic powers, should have been the first to be raised to this dignity; for there are no others more fitted to appeal to the senses and the imagination. However, the first beings to which the cult is addressed are humble vegetables and animals, in relation to which men could at least claim an equality: they are ducks, rabbits, worms, frogs, etc. Similarly, as Oldenberg points out, recent researches would tend to show that Vedic divinities did not all have the exclusively naturistic character attributed to them by Max Muller and his school.[45] Durkheim's assertion that Vedic religion had three special characteristics is true. These were (1) that rites are an important element of Vedic religion, (2) that it is the oldest religion among civilized people, and (3) that fire has a significant place in Vedic religion.

(11) *Asceticism in Buddhism*

As pointed out earlier, Durkheim defines religion as a system of beliefs and practices. He examines in detail the different types of beliefs in part II and rituals in Part III of *The Elementary Forms of the Religious Life*. These rituals, according to him are of two main types, viz. negative and positive. He observes that every cult presents a double aspect, one negative, the other positive, though they are closely associated.[46] In the negative cult they do not prescribe certain acts to the faithful, but confine themselves to forbidding certain ways of acting; so they all take the form of interdictions or, as is commonly said by ethnographers, of taboos. Although the negative cult is generally presented as a system of abstentions, in the form of inhibiting activity, yet it is found to exercise a positive action of the highest importance over the religious and moral nature of the individual.

In fact, owing to the barrier which separates the sacred from the profane, a man cannot enter into intimate relations with sacred things except after ridding himself of all that is profane to him. He cannot lead a religious life of even a slight intensity unless he commences by withdrawing more or less completely from the temporal life. So the negative cult is in one sense a means in view of an end: it is a condition of access to the positive cult. It does not confine itself to protecting sacred beings from vulgar contact; it acts upon the worshipper himself and modifies his condition positively. The man who has submitted himself to its prescribed interdictions is not the same afterwards as he was before.

For example, in certain Australian tribes a whole system of interdiction is followed at the time of the initiation. The neophyte is submitted to a great variety of negative rites. A multitude of foods are forbidden to him; he is allowed only that quantity of food which is absolutely indispensable for the maintenance of life; he is even sometimes bound to a rigorous fast, or must eat impure foods. The result of all these interdictions is to bring about a radical change of condition in the initiate. The metamorphosis is so complete that it is sometimes represented as a second birth. They imagine that the profane person, who was the young man up till then, has died, that he has been killed and carried away by the god of the initiation, Bunjil, and quite another individual has taken the place of the one that no longer is. So here we find the very heart of the positive effects of which negative rites are capable.

In the light of these facts, he enables us to understand what asceticism is, what place it occupies in the religious life and whence come the virtues which have generally been attributed to it. In fact, there is no interdict, the observance of which does not have an ascetic character to a certain degree. So in order to have real asceticism, it is sufficient for these practices to develop in such a way as to become the basis of a veritable scheme of life. Thus a systematic asceticism is born which is consequently nothing more than a hypertrophy of the negative cult. The pure ascetic is a man who raises himself above men and acquires a special sanctity by fasts and vigils, by retreat and silence, or, in a word, by privations, rather than by acts of positive piety (offerings, sacrifices, prayers, etc.). History shows what high religious prestige one may attain by this method; the Buddhist saint is essentially an ascetic, and he is equal or superior to the gods.

Asceticism is not a rare, exceptional and nearly abnormal fruit of the religious life, as some have supposed it to be, on the contrary it is one of its essential elements. Every religion contains it, at least in germ, for there are none in which a system of interdicts is not found. The existence of the negative cult in different religions in the form of interdictions, particularly in the form of asceticism as seen by Durkheim, seems to be correct. We agree with Durkheim that asceticism has a high place among Buddhist saints. He also mentions that asceticism is an essential element in other religions, but somehow he fails to stress the importance of asceticism among Hindus and Jains, Pareto, on the other hand, rightly stresses its special significance among Indian saints.

(12) *Sacrifices in Hinduism*

Durkheim observes that, whatever the importance of the negative cult may be, and though it may indirectly have positive effects, yet, people have always believed that they should uphold positive and bilateral relations with religious forces. To this system of ritual practices he gives the name of the positive cult. The system of rites found in some Australian tribes contains all the essential principles of a great religious institution, and it was destined to become one of the foundation stones of the positive cult in the superior religions; this is the institution of sacrifice. He also adds that no matter how little importance the religious ceremonies may have, they put the group into action; the groups assemble to celebrate them. So their first effect is to bring individuals together, to multiply the relations between them and to make them more intimate with one another.

These ceremonies sometimes served different purposes. According to the circumstances, one and the same ceremony serves two distinct functions. It may even lend itself to other uses. We know that as blood is a sacred thing, women must not see it flow. Yet it happens sometimes that a quarrel breaks out in their presence and ends in the shedding of blood. Thus an infraction of the ritual is committed. Among the Arunta, the man whose blood flowed first must, to atone for this fault, 'celebrate a ceremony connected with the totem either of his father or of his mother'. This ceremony has a special name, *alua uparilima,* which means the washing away of blood. But in itself, it does not differ from those celebrated at the time of the initiation or in the *Intichiuma*: it represents an event of ancestral history. So it may serve equally to initiate, to act upon the totemic species or to expiate a sacrilege.

Hubert and Mauss have already pointed out a functional ambiguity of this same sort in the case of sacrifice and more especially, in that of Hindu sacrifice.[47] They have shown how the sacrifice of communion, that of expiation, that of a vow and that of a contract are only variations of one and the same mechanism. We now see that the fact is much more primitive, and in no way limited to the institution of sacrifice. Perhaps no rite exists which does not present a similar indetermination. Inversely, just as a single rite may serve many ends, so many rites may produce the same effect and mutually replace one another. In fact rites are means by which the social group reaffirms itself periodically. From this, we may be able to reconstruct hypothetically the way in which the totemic cult should have arisen originally. Men who feel themselves united, partially by bonds of blood, but still more by a community of interest and tradition, assemble and become conscious of their moral unity.

He concludes this book by saying that

> howsoever simple the system which we must have studied may be, we have found within it all the great ideas and the principal ritual attitudes which are at the basis of even the most advanced religions: the division of things into sacred and profane, the notions of the soul, of spirits, of mythical personalities, and of a national and even international divinity, a negative cult with ascetic practices which are its exaggerated form, rites of oblation and communion, imitative rites, commemorative rites and expiatory rites, nothing essential is lacking.[48]

Durkheim rightly stresses the role of religious ceremonies (including sacrifice) which put the group into action and make them more intimate with one another. Here he specifically refers to the importance of Hindu sacrifice in the form of communion, that of expiation, that of a vow and that of contract, which are only variations of one and the same mechanism. A rite or sacrifice may serve different ends and similarly many rites may produce the same effect mutually replacing one another. However, in all these cases the object is the same: that the social group reaffirms itself periodically. People who feel themselves united by blood, by a community of interests and tradition, assemble and become conscious of their moral unity. This is one of the important functions of any religion. This function, particularly, played an important role in Hindu society where such rites and sacrifices are more in vogue than in many other religions. During political crisis these occasions helped them sometimes to feel as one and act united against any aggression.

Appraisal

Taking an overall view we may say that Durkheim did not make any special study of Indian society as did Marx and Weber. Whatever aspects of Indian society he observed they were studied as part of his larger studies in the field of 'division of labour in society', 'suicide', and 'religion'. But whatever facts he collected about Indian society whether with regard to Hindu law, the caste system, various types of suicide among Indian people and the nature of Indian religions, they were mostly correct. His knowledge about Buddhism was better even than that of Max Weber. His assertion that the castes will gradually give way to occupational groups and associations as specialization in society increases is true to a great extent, and this is happening in India too. But owing to certain peculiar circumstances prevailing in India where urbanization cannot proceed on a large scale as it has in Western countries, where the caste system is connected with religion, and where because of mass illiteracy conservatism and traditionalism prevails among rural masses, the caste system may take much longer to disappear than it did in Western countries.

10   Vilfredo Pareto
(1848–1923)

Vilfredo Pareto, a trained engineer, was an economist, political scientist and sociologist.

> The age in which he grew up was dominated by belief in social and material progress, in human perfectibility, and in scientific positivism. The paths by which thinkers and believers reached these common conclusions were various, but the outcome was much the same. In their various ways the fashionable arguments reached a consensus for democracy and rationality, for free trade and the market economy, for pacifism and humanitarianism. . . . Pareto was from ten to fifteen years older than either Freud or Durkheim or Bergson or Weber, but as his interest in social science awoke so late in life, he came to it at roughly the same time as they did—in the 1890s. At the outset he was a devout, albeit critical, believer in the dominant philosophies of reason, democracy and progress. With ten years, however, in complete independence of these contemporaries, he had run up against their common problem and came up with a similar answer. Like them he sensed the intrusion of the human personality into the framing of what had hitherto been regarded as objective laws established by naked intellect. . . . He became an antidemocrat; and this new attitude intensified with every passing year.[1]

He was astonished to see the popularity of Marxism in Italian youth and the idea suddenly came to his mind that the bulk of human activity is not due to rational processes at all, but to sentiments. Men feel an urge and act; they invent justifications afterwards. The *Treatise on General Sociology* reflects his mind in old age.

Some of his major works are: (1) *Cours d'economie politique*

(1896), (*Course of Political Economy*); (2) *Les Systèmes socialistes* (1902), (*Social Systems*); (3) *Manuale di economia politica* (1906), (*Manual of Political Economy*); (4) *Trattato di Sociologia generale* (2 vols, 1916), (*Mind and Society*); (5) *Traite de sociologie gènèrale* (2 vols, 1917), (*A Treatise on General Sociology*); (6) *Fatti e teorie* (1920); (*Facts and Theory*); (7) *Transformazione della democrazia* (1922), (*Transformation of Democracy*).[2] Among these, *A Treatise on General Sociology* (serial nos. 4 and 5), which is in four volumes and deals with some aspects of Indian society, is of major concern to us as sociologists. This is the first work of his which was translated into English, in 1935.

According to Professor Finer the three main sociological contributions of Pareto are: (1) The postulate of society as a system, together with important associated concepts; (2) the destructive critique of positivistic-rationalistic theories and the corresponding stress on the role of the irrational in social behaviour; and (3) the emphasis on the importance of social stratification and social mobility.[3] In order to explain these principles Pareto took facts from various societies, but mostly from Western countries. As he points out in the *Treatise*, 'To go farther still in our avoidance of difficulties, we shall confine our investigations to the people of Europe and of the Asian and African sections of the Mediterranean basin. That will free us of the many serious—and unsolved—questions that are connected with race.'[4] The *Treatise* in which he deals with these principles is divided into four volumes. In the first volume he deals with the fact that residues and derivations are an important element of society with which sociology deals. Here he deals with non-logical actions which take the form of beliefs, religions, rites, laws, morals, etc. In the second volume he explains the six main residues in detail. The third volume deals with derivations, while the fourth volume contains general conclusions, i.e. society as a system and social mobility in society.

Residues and derivations as important elements of a social system

Pareto observes that he had the choice of two models for his enquiry: the model of society as an organism, and the alternative model of society as a system of mutually interacting particles which move from one state of equilibrium to another (i.e. the mechanical analogy). He chose the latter deliberately because, as he says in the *Cours*,

the way in which living organisms are arranged is much more rigid and defined than is a system of material points. Now in political economy and social science our task is, precisely, to affect considerable variations in a continuous fashion in the motion of certain parts.... The organic model does not permit this operation. On the other hand, it is the better of the two, when the problem is one of forming an idea of the evolution of societies.[5]

He observes that the form of a society is determined by all the elements acting upon it and it, in turn, reacts upon them.[6] Those movements and counter-movements adjust themselves to one another to produce a state of equilibrium. So numerous are the elements which together determine the form of society that only the most important can be considered in the first instance. Those which Pareto elects to consider are, on the one side, the psychological characteristics and motivations of men and, on the other, the reflections of these in the stratification of society. Thus race, natural selection, geography and climate he takes as given. So he considers only four: residues, interests, derivations, and social heterogeneity and circulation.[7] Whereas interests are spurred by instincts and reason to acquire possession of material goods that are useful, or otherwise pleasurable, for purposes of living.[8] Residues are the manifestations of sentiments and instincts. Derivations are the manifestations of the need of logic that the human being feels. They partially correspond to sentiments, to non-logical conduct, but they clothe them with logical or pseudo-logical reasonings. In other words instincts (constant), residues, appetites, tastes, inclinations, interests, etc. are the main factors in determining the social equilibrium.

Residues and derivations

Even the actions and reactions among these four elements, (a) residues, (b) interests, (c) derivations and (d) social heterogeneity and circulation, are very complex. In one case (a) acts upon (b), (c) and (d); in the second (b) acts upon (a), (c) and (d); in the third (c) upon (a), (b) and (d); and in the fourth (d) upon (a), (b) and (c). All the combinations are important in their own way, though the second combination was considered most important by the economists. Interests are mostly economic and rational. Residues and derivations are irrational or non-logical and subjective.

Pareto further observes that the theories may in concrete cases be divided into at least two elements, one of which is much more stable than the other. Besides factual data there are two principal elements in them: (a) a substantial element (non-logical conduct, the expresssion of certain sentiments) and (b) a contingent element which is the manifestation of the need for logic that the human being feels.[9] The substantial element exists in the mind of the human being; the contingent is the explanation (or explanations) of the substantial, the inference (or inferences) that he draws from it. For example, there is a sentiment by virtue of which certain numbers are deemed worthy of veneration. But the human being, not satisfied with merely associating sentiments of veneration with numbers, wants to 'explain' how that comes about, wants to 'demonstrate' that in doing what he does he is prompted by force of logic. The contingent element (b) also has its effect upon the equilibrium. Sometimes the effect may be insignificant, but at other times it may be considerable.

The theories of 'social Darwinism', 'economic determinism' the 'theory of limits' expounded by the Spencerian school (in other words, the theory of evolution) are all of this category. In each case the limit which a writer assumes to be determined strictly by his facts turns out to be identical with the limit towards which he is sentimentally inclined.

> If he is a pacifist, as Spencer was, most obliging facts show him that the limit towards which human societies are tending is universal peace; if he is a democrat, there is no doubt that the limit will be a complete triumph of democracy; if he is a collectivist, the triumph of collectivism; and so on. Hence, a suspicion arises, and grows stronger as we proceed, that the facts are serving merely to conceal more potent motives of persuasion.[10]

If you strip from the theory its variable parts you are left with a residuum. This is the constant element and Pareto calls it the residue. (From residues we have certain derivatives.) Their number is fifty-two and again these are classed into six major groups. Class I and class II are more important. Class I is the instinct for combination or the instinct combining. Class II is the persistence of aggregates (or group persistence). Class III consists of residues impelling men to express emotions by means of outward acts. Classes IV and V relate to the individual and his personality. These are called residues of sociality and maintaining individual integrity. Class VI residues pertain to sex. Sometimes these residues are intermixed and difficult to separate. As a result they are divided into various sub-classes. These residues observe not only the mode of outer behaviour, but also the sentiments and psychic states, which they manifest. Sentiments are both innate and socially acquired. These residues have remained the same, though their form has changed. For example, in case of class I, magic and rituals, etc. have declined and their place has been taken by science.

In class II in place of religion we have nationalism, socialism, etc. Derivations have the power to make residues more or less intense.

Except in natural science, technology and economics, almost all conduct is dictated by residues, and not by reason. Rational argument is in most cases an appearance which serves to justify action or brighten the basic residues from which the action springs. Nowhere is it more apparent than in the ruler–ruled relationship. All governments are ruled by a mixture of force and persuasion and this persuasion consists of so many derivations.

Having explained that non-logical conduct plays an important role in human affairs, Pareto explains their manifestation in various forms taking examples from different societies. In volume 1 he explains that the various types of beliefs, rites, myths, allegories, religions, morals and laws, etc. are based on these sentiments. Then he discusses six types of residues in volume 2 and different types of derivations in volume 3. We shall deal with some of them where he takes examples from Indian society.

In volume 1, where he discusses logical developments in non-logical conduct, he explains the following facts about Indian society:

1 The Hindu belief in rites and magic and their effects on natural phenomena, i.e. rain, storm, etc.
2 The need for religion, and Buddhist non-belief in God.
3 The Hindu belief in the sacredness of fire and water.

In volume 2, while discussing the six main classes of residues he takes the following facts from Indian society:

Class I residues: The combination of things

4 Buddha's conception in his mother's womb as a divine act.
5 The soma drink gave ecstatic exhilaration in Vedic religion.
6 The Hindu belief that objects belonging to saints act mysteriously.

Class II residues: Group persistence (the persistence of aggregates)

7 Patriarchal family structure in India.
8 The formation of castes in India.
9 Personification and Hindu divinities.

Class III residues: Expressing sentiments by means of outward acts (activity, self-expression, etc.)

10 The worship of stones among Hindus.

Class IV residues: Residues connected with sociality and social ranking

11 Various types of ascetics among Hindus.
12 Asceticism among Buddhists.

Class V residues: The integrity of the individual and his belonings

13 Rules about the purification of sins and impurities among Hindus.
14 The importance of the son among Hindus and the system of niyoga.

Class VI residues: The sex residue and its manifestations

15 The prohibition of meat among Hindus.
16 The sex taboo and prostitution in temples.

In volume 3 while dealing with the theory of derivations as well as the properties of residues and derivations he quotes the following facts from Indian society:

17 Different arguments used by Englishmen to occupy India.
18 Englishmen's disrespect of Indian sentiments leading to the Revolt.

Logical developments in non-logical conduct

In volume 1, where Pareto deals with non-logical conduct, he points out that the human being has such a weakness for adding logical developments to non-logical behaviour that anything can serve as an excuse for him to turn to that favourite occupation. By virtue of a most interesting persistence of associations of ideas and acts, words seem to possess some mysterious power over things. In this way magic words, charms and incantations seem to possess some power. Individually, one by one, our wisest minds have no faith in such things; but in the mass, in their everyday lives, people believe in them unconsciously. In many cases there is an appeal to conscience rather than to reason. Why do we wish each other a happy new year on the first day of each year? Why do we select men with propitious names to lead the victims in public sacrifices? Why do we believe that odd numbers are more effective than others? These actions, in which words act upon things, belong to that class of operations which ordinary language more or less vaguely designates as magic. In the extreme type, certain words or acts, by some unknown virtue, have the power to produce certain effects. Next a first coating of logic explains that power as being due to the intervention of higher beings, of deities. Going on in that direction we finally get to another extreme where the action is logical throughout—the medieval belief, for instance, that by selling his soul to the devil a human being could acquire the power to harm people. When a person interested strictly in logical actions happens on pehnomena of the kind just mentioned, he looks at them contemptuously as pathological states of mind, and goes his way without thinking further of them. But anyone aware of the important part non-logical behaviour plays in human activity must examine them with great care.[11]

For countless ages people have believed in such nonsense in one form or another; and there are some who take such things seriously even in our day. Only in the past two or three hundred. years has there been an increase in the number of people who laugh at them as Lucian did. But the vogue of spiritualism, telepathy, Christian Science, and what-not, is enough to show what enormous power these sentiments and others like them still have today. There are many cases where there is a belief that by means of certain rites and practices it is possible to raise or quell a storm. In many cases, meteorological phenomena are considered dependent upon certain rites and practices, either directly, or else indirectly, through the intervention of higher powers.

(1) *The Hindu belief in rites and magic and their effects on natural phenomena*

Pareto observes that the notion that winds, rains and tempests, can be produced by art of magic is a common one in ancient writers. Seneca discusses the causes of weather at length and derides magic. He does not admit the possibility of forecasting the weather by observation, regarding observation as just a preparation for the rites commonly performed for averting storms. He says that at Cleonae there were public officials known as 'hail-observers'. As soon as they gave warning of the approach of a storm, the inhabitants rushed to the temple and sacrificed, some a ewe others a fowl. Those who had nothing to sacrifice pricked a finger and shed a little blood, and the clouds moved on in another direction.
Philostratus observes that,

coming to the place where the brahmans dwelt, Apollonius and
his companions beheld two black stone jars, one the jar of
rain and the other the jar of the winds. If India is suffering from
a frought, the one containing the rain is opened, and it sends
clouds and rains over all the land. If there is too much rain, the
jar is closed, and the storm ceases. The jar of the windworks, I

should say, something like the bag of Aeolus. If it is opened, one of the winds gets out, and it blows where it is needed and dries the land.[12]

The above observation of Pareto that Hindus believe in the art of magic and that magic can produce rain or stop a storm is correct. Even in these days such beliefs are held among the village folk.

(2) *The need for religion, and Buddhist non-belief in God*

Pareto observes that there is often rationalization of non-logical conduct. The notion that non-logical actions have been logically devised to attain certain purposes has been held by many writers. Even Polybius, an historian of great sagacity, speaks of the religion of the Romans as originating in deliberate artifice. After noting the great role of religion in Roman public life, Polybius adds,

> That will seem strange to many. As for me, I believe that religion was established with an eye to the masses. In fact, if the city were made up entirely of educated people, such an institution might never have been called for. But since the masses everywhere are fickle and untrustworthy, full of lawless passions, unreasoning angers, violent impulses, they can be controlled only by mysterious terrors and tragic fears. It seems to me, therefore, that not by chance and not without strong motive did the ancients introduce these beliefs in gods and hells to the multitude.[13]

Montesquieu gives another interpretation of Roman religion. He says,

> Neither fear nor piety established religion among the Romans, but the same necessity that compels all societies to have religion. ... I note this difference, however, between Roman legislators and the lawgivers of other peoples, that the Romans created religion for the State, the others the State for religion.[14]

Pareto adds that it is curious that Voltaire and Montesquieu followed opposite, though equally mistaken, lines, and that neither of them thought of a spontaneous development of non-logical conduct.[15]

In some religions, a belief in higher beings with whom it is possible to establish relations is called religion. In others (for example primitive religions) the principal elements in those religions are the scruples, i.e. taboos and fetishes. However, there again is a sect of Buddhism that shows no trace of relations

VILFREDO PARETO (1848–1923)

established with higher beings, as witness the conservation between Guimet and three Japanese theologians:[16]

Q. My first question bears on the origin of the heavens, the earth, and everything about us. How do you explain their formation, according to the principles of the Buddhist religion?

A. The Buddhist religion ascribes the existence of all things to what it calls In–En (Cause–Effect). Each thing is only a combination of infinitely minute atoms. These atoms combine to form mountains, rivers, plains, metals, stones, plants, and trees. Such objects come into being from the natural relationship of their *In* and their *En*, exactly as all living beings are born by virtue of their In–En.

Q. Is there no creator of the heavens, the earth, and all other things?

A. No.

Q. What is this thing which you call In–En?

A. Nothing is formed naturally and of itself. It is always the relation of a this to a that that constitutes a thing. . . .

Q. . . . I now ask you whether the conduct of human beings depends in any way of God?

A. A man is responsible for his own conduct. It in no way depends on God. [No trace so far of any relations with higher beings, which, according to Lagrange, everybody recognizes!]

Q. Do you not admit that God exerts an influence on humanity and guides us in the performance of our various acts of invention or improvement?

A. The Buddhist religion admits of no creator. It ascribes everything to the In–En. It thereby declares that every human act is performed on the individual's initiative without any interference on the part of God.

Q. It is evident that the term God is not the proper one. Nevertheless your religion does recognize a higher being, Amida, which it venerates and devoutly worships. Well, does not the power of Amida have some influence on human conduct?

A. The difference prevailing among individual human beings, as regards their personal value and the value of what they do, depend more or less on the education they have received, and 'not at all on the will of Amida . . .

293

Q. I would readily admit that knowledge may be increased by effort … but, at the same time, in the domain of ethics, in the distinction between right and wrong, between what is just and what is unjust, does it not seem that there must be a higher being who rewards and punishes us for our conduct, much as the social authority punishes us for the infractions of the rules of public order?

A. Every good and every evil act has as its consequence a blessing or a sorrow. That results from the altogether natural conception of the In–Goua (synonym of In–En).

From the above facts he concludes that there are theories which are not logico-experimental, but which are nevertheless beneficial for society. Pareto's assertion that religion was created to satisfy and control the emotions of masses is correct to some extent. His observation that Buddhists do not believe in God is also correct as seen in the foregoing pages.

(3) *The Hindu belief in the sacredness of fire and water*

Pareto observes that in the collection and verification of facts, in certain cases (particularly in the field of religion, customs, etc.) experience is given little or no place. It is authority, divine authority, known through one or more individuals, or the authority of one or more individuals, which is given more weight.[17]

In some cases the extra-experimental origin of the abstract entities that are introduced is not explicitly stated. Either they are mere abstractions arbitrarily deduced from experience, or else they have an independent existence that implicitly may be non-experimental. In such cases may be included myths, religious narratives and other legends of the kind which may be historically real or have an historical element combined with an unreal element.

In the first case, the authority is used as an instrument for logicalizing non-logical actions. Divine revelation in so far as it is not considered an historical fact, belongs to this category, as do also the divine injunction and the divine prophecy. For example, the Mohammedans accepted the authority of Mohammed just as educated people at a certain period in our history accepted the authority of Aristotle; so also the humanitarian who swoons over a passage of Rousseau; so the socialist who swears by the word of Marx or Engels as a treasure-store of all human knowledge; and so, further, the devout democrat who bows a reverent head and submits judgment and will to the oracles of suffrage, universal or limited, or what is worse, to the pronouncements of parliaments and legislators, though they are known to house not a few politicians of unsavoury reputation. Each of such believers of course considers his own beliefs rational and other beliefs absurd. Sometimes opposite conclusions can be drawn from the same principle.

For example, there is a widespread belief that water and fire are pure and sacred. From it the Hindus conclude that the bodies of the dead ought to be either burned or thrown into the Ganges. The Parsees conclude, to the precise contrary, that neither fire nor water should be defiled through contact with a corpse. Fire, say the brahmans, is a thing essentially 'pure'. The dead body therefore must go through fire and leave all its impurities there, so that the deceased may enter the eternal realm of *yama* thoroughly cleansed. Thereafter the fire that has been so contaminated can be relieved of its noxious properties by a rite of lustration. On the other hand, say the Mazdeans, fire is a thing essentially pure: Who, then, would dare violate its sanctity by thrusting upon it the abominable task of devouring the most loathsome thing in the world, a corpse in the process of putrefaction.[18]

It seems that in India cremation was not the absolute rule. It has, however, remained the principal means of disposing of the dead. The corpse is laid on a pyre that has been reared in the midst of three fires kindled from the three sacred fires of the deceased (in the event of his having kept them burning). There it is burned with certain ceremonies. 'As fire watches over the Hindu's birth, so it watches over the fundamental phases of his life'.[19] Corpses are still burnt in India in our times. Says Sonnerat,

> As soon as the pyre has burned out, milk is sprinkled over the ashes, and the bones that have been spared by the fire are gathered up, put into urns, and kept till occasion offers to throw them into some sacred stream, or into the Ganges. The Hindus are convinced that the man whose bones get into a sacred river will enjoy infinite bliss for millions of years. Those living on the river-banks often throw corpses into the water whole, after hastening death by making the sick drink all the water they can hold, since they attribute miraculous properties to it.[20]

Sonnerat also adds,

> The Brahmans who worship Vishnu believe that the fire purifies them of their sins. Devotees of Siva (Chivan) claim that since they have been consecrated to the service of the god they do not need to go through fire, the sins they may have committed not being imputable to them. It is sufficient if they be sprinkled with lustral water, of which they make lavish use.[21]

Pareto's contention that water and fire are considered as pure and sacred by the Hindus is quite correct. And it is for this reason that the bodies of the dead are either burnt or thrown into the river.

Residues and their forms of manifestation

As stated before, Pareto discusses in volume 2 the various residues and their forms of manifestation in differnt societies. Here we shall deal with their forms of manifestation in Indian society.

Class I residues: The combination of things

While studying residues of class 1 Pareto points out that this class embraces the residues corresponding to the instinct for combinations, which is intensely powerful in the human species. Figuring as a residue in vast numbers of phenomena is an inclination to combine certain things with certain other things. There may be combinations of similars or opposites, or there may be unusual things and exceptional occurrences, or objects and occurrences inspiring awe and terror, felicitous states associated with good things, infelicitous states with bad, assimilation, i.e. physical consumption of substances to get effects of associable mysterious workings of certain things, or mysterious effects of certain acts, etc.

(4) *Buddha's conception in his mother's womb as a divine act*

While explaining the manifestation of class I residues Pareto observes that constant over many centuries is the ascription of divine origins to heroes and great men. Every individual, be he real or imaginary, whose name figures at all prominently in history or legend, owes his birth to some divine act; or his birth is at least attended by prodigies. For example, the conception of Buddha was attended by so many that it would be a long and not very profitable task to recount them even briefly. Kern observes,

> The virtuous queen Maya dreamed that the four divine
> sovereigns, the Cardinal Points, gathered her up with her bed and
> transported her to the Himalayas, where they set her down in the
> shade of a wide-spreading tree. . . . The Bodhisatva assumed the
> form of a white elephant, departed from the Golden Mount on
> which he dwelt, ascended the Mount of Silver, entered the

Golden Grotto with a terrible thunder and, bearing a white water-lily in his trunk, marched thrice about the bed where Maya was resting, moving to the right as a sign of courtesy, opened the right side of the queen, and so entered her body.... At the moment of the Bodhisatva's conception in his mother's womb all nature was set in motion, and thirty-two presages were observed: an incomparable radiance encompassed the Universe.[22]

Pareto's assertion that many people subscribe to a belief in the divine origin of Buddha and of some other great men is correct to a great extent.

(5) *The soma drink gave ecstatic exhilaration in Vedic religion*

Included in class I is the residue of assimilation, where there is physical consumption of substances to get effects of associable character. Pareto observes that human beings have often believed that by eating certain substances one may come to partake of the properties of those substances. Familiar is the important part played by the 'soma' in the Vedic religion. Oldenberg observes,

The drink that gives Indra the strength to execute his mighty feats is a juice pressed from the soma plant. The notion of an intoxicating beverage belonging to the gods seems to go back to Indo-European days. A liquor that instils a mysterious vigour, an ecstatic exhilaration, in the human being must be divine by nature and an exclusive perquisite of the gods.[23]

So among the American Indians tobacco was called a 'sacred plant' as a source of supernatural inspiration, and they believed that the gods smoked it in order to taste the same ecstasy.

It is praised, (Rig-Veda, VIII, 48, V.3) for the joy it brings to men. We have drunk of the soma, and, lo, we are immortals: we have ascended to the light and found the gods! What have we now to fear, O deathless ones, from the hatred or malice of men?[24]

Pareto's observation that the soma drink gave a mysterious vigour, an escstatic exhilaration in Vedic religion is quite correct.

(6) *The Hindu belief that objects belonging to saints act mysteriously*

In the same class of residues, i.e. class I, Pareto observes that there is the belief that there are certain mysterious operations in general. There are believed to be certain virtues of relics. Numberless are the cases where an object belonging to a saint operates apparently in and of itself. In general terms, people may believe in the efficacy of certain rites of a religion without believing in the religion, a fact that emphasizes the non-logical character of the conduct. Logically, one ought first to believe in a given religion and then in the efficacy of its rites.... But generally there is first an instinctive belief in the efficacy of a rite, then an 'explanation' of the belief is desired, then it is found in religion. This is one of the many cases where the residue figures as the principal element and the derivation as the secondary. In the particular, there are numberless instances where objects connected with saints function of and by themselves upon anybody who comes into contact with them. J. B. Fraser in his *Travels and Adventures in the Persian Provinces*, tells a story of an old man who wore a copper box hanging about his neck. It contained two small figures, the one a copper Lama, the idol usual in worship of the Grand Lama, and which is presented to pilgrims visiting His temple; the other a small Chinese image, painted on porcelain or terra cotta. The two relics were wrapped in a piece of yellow silk. He said he had received them from the Grand Lama at the Hassa, whither he had gone on a pilgrimage some years before. The man was a Hindu by religion, and worshipped idols in the Hindu manner. Nevertheless, the relics came to him from the high-priest of another faith whom he had doubtless visited with a religious purpose. The man offered an interesting example of tolerance and ignorance at the same time.

Pareto's observation that there is a belief among Hindus that objects belonging to saints act mysteriously is correct. This observation was also made by Spencer.

Class II residues: Group-persistence (the persistence of aggregates)

Pareto observes that aggregate is an aggregate (combination, association, group) of sensations. The tendency to consolidate such groups of sensations and make them permanent in time Pareto regards as one of the great and fundamental forces in society.[25] There is persistence of relations between a person and other persons and places, there are relationships of family and kindred groups, relationships of social class, personifications, etc. The concept of 'group persistence' is basic in Pareto's theories of the social equilibrium and class-circulation, and, in general, in his whole conception of history. In this connection he observes three important phenomena in Indian society. These are: the patriarchal form of family structure, caste formation and the personification of divinities in India.

(7) *Patriarchal family structure in India*

Pareto observes that the relationships of family and kindred groups are present both in animals and human societies. Among human beings, probably because the young need their parents for a much longer time, interesting and sometimes very powerful residues develop. These correspond to the forms of family association prevalent in the given country, and they also serve to strengthen or modify such forms. The best known, or rather the only, literature we have comes from peoples who have had a patriarchal family system—and they, after all, are the civilized peoples; so the only residues with which we are at all familiar are residues corresponding to the patriarchal type. We find them all through Graeco-Roman antiquity, in the Bible, and in the literatures of China, India and Persia.

That fact gives grounds for the notion that the patriarchal type of family was the only one concretely existing, and that deviations from it, which had been noted even in ancient times, were of little or no account. Those good souls who dreamed of a 'natural law' did not fail to conclude that the patriarchal family was part of that law. But the day came when it was discovered, to the extreme astonishment of the learned world, that not only were other types of family extant among uncivilized or barbarous peoples, but that these may have played a part in the family organization of our own prehistoric ancestors, leaving traces that were still discernible in historic times.

The observation that the patriarchal form of family structure prevailed in India as well as in some other countries is quite correct. His contention that other types of family extant also prevailed in those countries is also correct.

(8) *The formation of castes in India*

Pareto observes that it also happened that the nucleus of such groups is constituted by individuals bound to one another by ties of kinship. Some sociologists consider the groups as natural formations growing up about a nucleus which is generally the family, with appendages of one sort or another, and the permanence of such groups in time engenders or strengthens certain sentiments that, in their turn, render the groups more compact, more stable, better able to endure. These general considerations apply in particular to the Roman *gens*, the Greek *revos* and the Hindu caste.

It is certain that in historical times the family was the nucleus of the Roman *gens*; but it is just as certain that the tie of kinship was not the only thing that figured in making up the *gens*. We must not become involved here in the intricate question as to whether the *gens* was made up of one, or of more than one, family. In the historical period girls of one *gens* were given in marriage to men of another *gens*. Further, legitimate birth was not alone enough to make a male child a member of the *gens*. He was presented to the father soon after birth, and the father might accept or repudiate him. This arrangement was common to Greece and Rome.

Then came the appendage to the family. So in India now the practice of admitting outsiders into a caste is regarded as an abuse, and an abuse it may well be today; but who can be sure that in ancient times that was not one of the ways in which a caste was formed? Senart observes,

> There has always been a rank growth of sects in India, and that sort of vegetation is far from dying out to-day. New sects turn up from year to year—only to be absorbed very soon, to be sure, in the rising tide of orthodox Hinduism, so called in spite of its composite character. As a rule such religious movements are very circumscribed, coming down to mere handfuls of ascetics who decide to consecrate themselves to penitence and celibacy and therefore reject the basic premise of caste heredity. They recruit their forces from voluntary applicants or from children borrowed from other castes. All the same a number of such brotherhoods have members from both sexes and themselves develop into castes that are more or less hereditary. The movements so arising in the castes and continually modifying their inner structure are either individual or collective. Now by favour of influential patrons, now by trickery, now by fraud, now by corruption, certain people find ways of getting into this caste or that as individuals. This is the frequent case in the frontier districts, where observances are less strict. There have been instances, where observances are less strict. There have been instances where individuals from all the different castes have been made Brahmans by caprice of some ruler. A caste, moreover, may not be very strict and may open its ranks quite readily under cetain conditions. There are clans of nomads and criminals that make a practice of admitting new members on money terms.[26]

Such things have always happened. It is the grossest of errors to imagine that reality always tallies exactly with the abstractions of law makers and men of letters.

All that being undeniable, the tie of common descent had to be supplemented with the tie of religion in order to account for family, *gens* and *revos*. And in that we do get a little closer to reality, since religion is indeed one of the forms in which the ties of fact that supplement the tie of blood find expression.

There also exist relationships of social class, observes Pareto. Living in a given group impresses the mind with certain concepts, certain ways of thinking and doing, certain prejudices, certain beliefs, which, as is the case with so many other entities of the kind, endure in time and acquire a pseudo-objective individuality. The residues corresponding to them have in the past often assumed the forms of residues of family relationships. It has been imagined that social classes and even nations were so many lineages each with some common ancestor, real or mythical, and each indeed with its own gods, who were enemies of the gods of other groups. But the latter is a mere derivation, and among modern peoples it has fallen into desuetude.

The form of the caste in India is unique but the underlying substance is very, very general. Something similar is observable in all countries, and often with greatest intensity in countries that make a show of some principle of equality. This distance between an American millionaire and a plain American is greater than the distance between a German nobleman and a German factory-hand. It is something like the distances between the castes in India, which is nothing like the distance between whites and blacks in the United States.[27]

Pareto's contention that castes were formed on a kinship basis and that the tie of descent was supplemented by a religious tie is correct. Furthermore, that some outside members were admitted in certain castes is also correct to some extent. But it must be stated that it was not a general rule. The upper castes and particularly the brahmans did not allow outsiders to enter into their group and only fraud could get one in. Thus, on the whole, the caste system was quite rigid and for an individual to change his caste was very difficult, virtually impossible. Elsewhere Pareto observes that social classes are not entirely distinct, even in countries where a caste system prevails; and that in modern civilized countries circulation among the various classes is exceedingly rapid. However, we may state that, so far as India is concerned, caste is still a barrier to a person changing his status, particularly for those belonging to lower castes.

(9) *Personification and Hindu divinities*

Pareto observes that the lowest degree of personification lies in the naming of an abstraction, a uniformity, or a sentiment, and so transforming it into an objective individuality. Thence, step by step, we mount to the highest degree, where the personification is complete and we get anthropomorphism. Bringing in the sex residue we may get male and female principles, or divinities, in every respect similar to men and women. Places and things may also be personified, without there being on that account any deification. In the case of Rome, sentiments begin by suggesting a mere image. They then develop in intensity to the point of a deification. They end by degenerating into objects of poetic or literary admiration, which state endures right down to our own day.

Lyall classifies the various styles of deification among the Hindus, and they hold, with some slight modification, for many other peoples. He observes,

1. The worship of mere stocks and stones and of local configurations, which are unusual or grotesque in size, shape or position [cf. class I residues]. 2. The worship of things inanimate, which are gifted with mysterious motion. 3. The worship of animals which are feared. 4. The worship of visible things, animate or inanimate, which are directly or indirectly useful or profitable, or which possess any incomprehensible function or property. (These, so far, have been groups of sensations of the simpler forms. The following involves a process of abstraction more remote from simple sensation.) 5. The worship of a Deo, or spirit, a thing without form and void—the vague impersonation of the uncanny sensation that comes over one at certain places. (Then come categories involving the persistence of certain sensations in time.) 6. The worship of dead relatives and other deceased persons known in their lifetime to the worshipper. 7. The worship of persons who had a great reputation during life, or who died in some strange or notorious way—at shrines. (From there we go on to abstractions of greater and greater complexity.) 8. The worship in temples of the persons belonging to the foregoing class as demigods or subordinate deities. 9. The worship of manifold local incarnations of the older deities, and of their symbols. 10. The worship of departmental deities. 11. The worship of the supreme gods of Hinduism and of their ancient incarnations and personifications, handed down by the Brahmanic scriptures.[28]

So far Lyall's description is perfect; but thereafter he succumbs to the general weakness for logical explanations, assuming that the worship of certain inanimate objects is to be attributed to the 'intelligence, which argues that a stock or stone embodies divinity only because it has a queer, unusual form'. He inadvertently refutes himself when he says:

302

Now the Brahmanic explanation of this reverence for curious looking things, expecially for things conical and concave is always at hand and producible to the earnest inquirer after divine emblems and manifestations; but these interpretations appear to belong to a later symbolism, which is habitually invented by the more ingenious to account for orthodox principles for what is really nothing but primitive fetishism rising into a higher sphere.

Lyall continues,

For the feeling which actuates the uninitiated Indian worshipper of stocks and stones, or what are called freaks of nature, is in its essence that simple awe of the unusual which belongs to no particular religion. It survives in England to this day in the habit of ascribing grotesque and striking landmarks or puzzling antiquities to the Devil, who is, or has been, the residuary legatee of all obsolete Pagan superstitions in Christian countries. In any district of India such objects or local configurations as the Devil's Quoits ... would be worshipped. Similar things are actually worshipped all over Berar, and in every case some signification, either mythical or symbolical, has been continued or sanctioned by some expert Brahman to justify and authorize the custom.
(The derivation, and admirably described.)

Examining the facts directly, Lyall was able to get at the underlying residues. If the residues are not always apparent, it is because we do not get the facts directly, but know them only under the gloss laid over them by poets, philosophers, theologians, and men of letters. Of the ancient religion of the Vedas, for instance, we know nothing but a literary–theological product passed on to us in religious hymns of a prolix vacuity that is truly remarkable, which are quite as devoid of sense as of definiteness. And we have no other documents for determining the character of parallel forms of popular belief that in all probability existed then, as they exist now, expressing themselves in the facts studied by Lyall.

Abstractions become outworn or untenable for one reason or another; they disappear or lose their appeal. But the need for them endures and new abstractions are required to take the place of those which disappear or weaken. So popular mythologies are superseded, among the educated, by scholarly, subtle, abstruse mythologies. Supernatural abstractions give ground to metaphysical abstractions. Not only does the human being need abstractions, he also needs to develop them—he wants them alive in his mind, not dead.

Pareto's observation that there is personification of living beings, places and things among people and this was particularly common among Hindus is correct. There is worship of stocks and stones, local configurations, animals, *Deo* or spirit, dead relatives or persons who had a great reputation during life or died in some strange or mysterious way. Such practices are in vogue even now among the masses, but they have lessened among educated urban people.

Class III residues: Expressing sentiments by means of outward acts (activity, self-expression, etc.)

Pareto observes that powerful sentiments are for the most part accompanied by certain acts that may have no direct relation to the sentiments but do satisfy a need for action. Something similar is observable in animals. A cat moves its jaws at the sight of a bird; the dog twists and turns and wags its tail at the sight of its master; the parrot flaps its wings. Such kinds of action are also found among the Hindus.

(10) *The worship of stones among Hindus*

Lyall observes,

> The present writer knew a Hindu officer of great shrewdness and very fair education who devoted several hours daily to the elaborate worship of five round pebbles which he had appointed to be his symbol of Omnipotence. Although his general belief was in one all-pervading Divinity, he must have something symbolic to handle and address.[29]

Notable in this is not merely the need for the symbol, but the need for 'doing something', acting, moving the limbs, fixing the attention on something concrete—escaping, in a word, from a state of passive abstraction. No doubt the type of worship mentioned by Pareto is found among Hindus. But there is nothing extraordinary in it. Such types of action are also found among peoples of other religions.

Class IV residues: residues connected with sociality and social ranking

Pareto points out that this class is made up of residues connected with life in society. People want to live in groups, and when they do they also want to have some discipline. Among these sentiments may be included: the need for uniformity which may mean voluntary conformity on the part of the individual or uniformity enforced upon others; pity and cruelty, which may mean self-pity extended to others or reasoned repugnance to useless suffering; self-sacrifice for the good of others in the form of risking one's life or sharing one's property with others; sentiments of social ranking or feeling of inferiority and superiority; and asceticism. Pareto points out that the need for uniformity is felt even by animals. If a hen is painted red and returned to its flock, the other hens at once attack it. The need for uniformity is much more strongly felt among uncivilized than among civilized people. The human being not only attempts to imitate others and become like them; he wants others to do likewise.

Further, there are any number of shadings, between the state of mind where one gives up one's life and a milder form of sentiment where there is a mere renunciation of certain enjoyments for the benefit of other individuals. At the first blush one might imagine that this residue was at work in all individuals of the ruling class who sided with the subject classes. But that is not the case. Some persons who assume leadership of the subject classes do so to attain some political, financial or other advantage. However, it cannot be denied that conceivably there may be individuals of energy, knowledge, and good sense who propound social and 'solidarian' doctrines out of a sincere desire to share their goods with others; but it is not easy to find examples of them.

Observable in human beings is a special group of sentiments that has no counterpart in animals. They are sentiments that prompt the human being to seek sufferings or abstain from pleasures without an eye to personal advantage, to go counter to the instinct that impels living creatures to seek pleasurable things and avoid painful things. Such sentiments constitute the controlling nucleus in the phenomena known as asceticism.

However, all social phenomena are complex mixtures of many elements involving many residues. In the ascetic, along with the residue of asceticism one often notes a residue of pride. He feels himself superior to the generality of mortals. Again there are various forms of asceticism. For example, four men abstain from drinking wine; the first because he has discovered that wine is injurious to his health; the second in order to save the money for the benefit of children; the third to set an example of abstinence for a drunkard who is ruining himself; the fourth to inflict a pain upon himself. Not only are the purposes different, the intensities are different too. In the last case the intensities are greater than in the other cases.

Outstanding among the residues that are alien to asceticism but appear in concrete phenomena in combination with the ascetic residue are the residues of personal integrity. They manifest themselves in the ascetic's pride, and through them asceticism becomes a kind of sport.

(11) *Various types of ascetics among Hindus*

In all time and places, the ascetic life, genuine or partly genuine, stimulated or partly stimulated, has helped many individuals to honours and money at the expense of the plain man. Heber observes,

> A few days since I saw a tall large elderly man, nearly naked, walking with three or four others, who suddenly knelt down one after the other and catching hold of his foot kissed it repeatedly. The man stood with much gravity to allow them to do so but said nothing. He has the string (*pectu*) of a Brahmin. Another man passed us on Sunday morning last hopping on one foot. He was a devotee who had made a vow never to use the other, which was now contracted and shrunk close to his hams. Lately, too, I saw a man who held his hands always above his head, and had thus lost the power of bringing them down to his sides.... The crowd on the meidan was great and very picturesque.... The devotees went about with small spears through their tongues and arms, and still more with hot irons pressed against their sides.... From time to time as they passed us, they laboured to seem to dance, but in general their step was slow, their countenance expressive of resigned and patient suffering, and there was no appearance, that I saw, of anything like frenzy or intoxication.... [The ceremony ended with a voluntary torture.] The victim was led, covered with flowers and without any apparent reluctance, to the foot of the tree: hooks were then thrust through the muscles of his sides, which he endured without shrinking, and a broad bandage was fastened round his waist, to prevent the hooks from being torn through by the weight of his body. He was then raised up and whirled round. At first the motion was slow, but by degrees was increased to considerable rapidity. In a few minutes it ceased; and the by-standers were going to let him down, when he made signs that they should proceed. This resolution was received with great applause by the crowd, and after drinking some water he was again spun round.[30]

It should not be forgotten either that not all men are to the same degree sensitive to pain, and just as in olden days there were those who could endure prolonged tortures while others immediately succumbed, so there are people who readily endure suffering as ascetics that no one else could possibly withstand. The history of tattooing, of various types of mutilation, of the cruelties practised on prisoners of war among the American Indians and other people, corroborate these inferences.

Extraordinary cases of asceticism have been and are still to be witnessed in the East. Orientals have the endurance of savages and brute animals for physical pain, and it is no great wonder therefore if individuals are to be found among them who submit to cruel tortures for the sake of attracting attention, or at times for a price. Sonnerat gives a good description of the multifarious forms of asceticism in India and it may serve as typical of the thing in general.

The Sanjassi (or Sanachi) is either a Brahman of a Chouta. He dedicates himself exclusively to the divinity. He takes a vow to be poor, chaste, and sober. Owning nothing, with no interest in anything, he wanders from place to place, his head shaven, almost naked with a single strip of yellow cloth to cover his back. He lives altogether on alms and eats only enough to keep himself alive. (Those traits are typical of many ascetic associations.) The Pandaroons are not less revered than the Sanjassis. They are worshippers of Siva. They smear their faces, chests, and arms with ashes of cow's dung, and go about the streets carrying peacock-plumes in their hands, begging alms, and singing hymns of praise to Siva.... The Kare-Patre Pandaroon is a variation on the Pandaroon proper. He takes a vow of perpetual silence (cf. the Western Trappist). He enters a house and claps his hands in begging alms, in order not to speak. His name is significant: Kare means 'hand', Patre 'plate'.... The Tadin goes begging from door to door, dancing and singing hymns of praise, and recounting the metamorphoses of Vishnu.... The Hindus, finally, have religious Penitents. The Penitents correspond among the Gentiles to the Fakirs among the Mongols. They are inspired by their fanaticism to abandon family, property, and so on, and lead lives of utter misery.... The only articles they are allowed to possess are a lingam, to which they pay continuous worship, and a tiger's skin on which they sleep. They inflict on their bodies everything that a fanatical fury can suggest. Some tear their flesh with whips (Cf. the discipline of our Catholics) or have themselves chained by the feet to trees to be released only when they die. Others take a vow to remain all their lives long in some uncomfortable position, keeping their hands always closed, for instance, so that their finger-nails, which they never cut, in the end grow through their hands. Some sit with their arms folded across their chests or raised above their heads, so that they have lost the power to bend them. Not a few bury themselves in the ground, breathing only through little openings. Others, less fanatical, bury themselves no higher than their necks. Some have taken a vow to spend their lives standing, without even lying down. They sleep with their bodies leaning against walls or trees, and to prevent themselves from slipping into comfortable postures, they wear frames of lattice-work about their necks. Others stand for hours at a time on one foot, staring open-eyed at the sun. To acquire greater merit still others stand with one foot off the ground, their weight resting on the great toe and their arms, into the bargain, raised above their heads. They stand between four cauldrons in which fires are burning and gaze at the sun with unwinking eyes. There are those who appear in public stark-naked to show that they have become insusceptible to any passion, that on abandoning their bodies to the Divinity they have returned to a state of innocence. The people are convinced of their virtue, look upon them as saints (Generally observable among many peoples.) and think they can get from God anything they ask for. In the belief that they are doing a very pious act, people assiduously provide them with food (Also very general,) put the morsels into the mouths of such as have vowed never to use their hands, and clean them. While the penitent is sunk in his contemplation, there are women who approach, kiss his private parts, and pay worship to them. ... Characteristic of the Penitents is an overweening pride; they have a very great esteem for themselves and believe in their own sanctity. They refuse to be touched by members of the lower castes and by Europeans, fearing pollution. They will not even allow their personal articles to be touched, and at once move on if anyone approaches them. They evince sovereign contempt for anyone not of their calling and look upon such as profane things. Everything about them is supposed to hide some mysterious property and to be worthy of devout worship.[31]

Monks and ascetics have been known in India from most ancient times. The student of the Vedas had to live with his master, obey him, serve him. In that, evidently, residues of rank are at work in combination with the ascetic residue, as is the case with monks in the Christian monasteries. He must, furthermore, be strictly chaste, temperate, humble, and live in poverty.

The various types of ascetics mentioned above are found among the Hindus. But some of the extraordinary cases of asceticism, for example, taking a vow to remain all their lives in some uncomfortable position (e.g. keeping their hands always closed or burying themselves in the ground, etc.) are an exception rather than the rule. As Ernest Wood rightly points out, to weaken (and ultimately to destroy) five kinds of affliction (*kleshas*), i.e. ignorance, egotism, liking and disliking, and possessiveness, the Patanjali's *raja-yoga* suggests three kinds of practices. These are called *tapas* (austerities including mortification), *swadhyaya* (study of books that concern oneself as an immortal being) and *ishwara-pranidhana* (devotion to God). But *tapas* is not self-torture; it is doing for the body what you know is good for it, not allowing laziness, selfishness, or thoughtlessness to stand in the way of one's doing what one can to make the body and mind healthy and efficient. Wood asserts,

> It is true that there has grown up a system of painful practices, such as that of holding the arm still until it withers, or sitting in the sun in the midst of a ring of fires, but these are superstitions which have grown up round a valuable thing, as they are liable to do everywhere. Those who follow these methods are few as compared with the true Yogi. All over the country there are Indian gentlemen—many of them Government servants who have a routine task with short working hours—who every day spend some time in meditation, deliberately guiding themselves by the 'Yoga sutras'.[32]

(12) *Asceticism among Buddhists*

Pareto observes that Buddhism has a complete code for the ascetic life, in some respect very like the rule devised by St Francis of Assisi—and that is another of the many cases where similar institutions have grown up spontaneously without any imitation. Kern observes,

> One of his strictest obligations is to observe absolute chastity: he must not touch a woman or look at one, if there is any danger to his purity. He must strive incessantly and earnestly to control his tongue, his appetite, and his hands. Play, menial labour, the acquisition of objects that have not been offered to him, unkindness to living creatures, unkind works, are all strictly forbidden him, and likewise the use of wines and strong drinks (at least among the Brahmans). He must abstain from salt, honey, meat, spices. He must not sleep during the daytime. He must not use perfumes or ointments, nor wear smart clothes. He must in general avoid anything tending to encourage effeminacy,

> such as dancing, singing and instrumental music.... One of the
> most characteristic duties of the student is that he should each
> day beg alms for his maintenance.[33]

Each Veda has to be studied twelve years; but only one Veda was
required, whereupon the student was free to return to life as a
layman and marry. If he chose, he could remain a student all his
life.

The mendicant monk, the *bhikshu,* differs from the student in
that he is not subject to a master:

> The rules of conduct for the Bhikshu may be summarised as
> follows: He has no home and no personal property. He leads a
> roving life, save during the rainy season, when he has to have a
> fixed residence. He begs alms once a day in the village for his
> maintenance. He must renounce all desires, master his tongue,
> his eyes, his conduct, and observe the strictest continence. He
> may have one garment to hide his nakedness, or wear cast-off
> rags, first washing them. He must keep his head shaven, save for
> one turf on the very top of the crown. (Such a person is hardly
> distinguishable from the Franciscan).... Not to be confused with
> the mendicants properly so called, the Bhikshus ... are the
> hermits, who live lives of mortification in solitude in order to
> accustom themselves to renunciation of worldly things and
> prepare themselves for the hereafter. (As Christian hermits do.)
> Though they are allowed to beg alms for their support, it is
> exceptional for them to do so.... The hermit lives in the jungle,
> getting his own living from the fruits and wild vegetables and
> practising asceticism.... The Buddhists have in the Dhutangas a
> complete set of rules for the ascetic life. The Dhutangas are
> thirteen in number among the Buddhists of the South, twelve in
> the North: I. To wear a garment made of rags gathered from a
> dunghill or a dump. (As a rule the monks are inclined to
> disregard this provision).... II. To own three such
> garments.... III. To take no food save such as is received in
> alms.... IV. While begging alms for one's living to go
> systematically from door to door, to the poor as well as to the
> rich, neglecting no one.... V. To remain seated at the same place
> during a meal.... VI. To eat only from a single ladle or alms-
> plate.... VII. To take no second repast after the morning
> meal.... VIII. To live in solitude.... IX. To live at the foot of a
> tree.... X. To sleep out of doors.... XI. To live in a
> cemetry.... XII. To spend the night at the spot one happens to
> reach without design.... XIII. To sleep in a sitting posture.... In
> the Northern rule articles IV and VI are missing. It has,
> however, another provision—prohibiting the use of felt.[34]

Just such practices, with minor variations, are to be noted among many different peoples at many different periods of history. In our day there are people who admire them. Thus this residue plays a significant role in the sentiments of certain people. Derivations draw sharp distinctions between the dirty practices of Hindu ascetics, Athenian cynics, the Franciscans and similar sects; but identical residues underlie them all.

As a rule, people laud ascetics of their own faith and censure others. Christians deride Hindu ascetics and revere their own. Humanitarians cannot endure Christian asceticism, but glorify the asceticism of teetotallers and prudes. Horror for sexual relations is an obsession seldom missing in asceticism, especially in its intenser manifestations, where it approximates insanity.

There is no doubt that the Essenes were people like the Hindu ascetics, and the 'perfects' of the Albigenses were, in turn, like them.

> To the westward of the shores (of Lake Asphaltides) and far
> enough away not to be harmed by its fumes, dwell the Essenes, a
> solitary people and marvellous beyond all others in the world.
> They live without any women, forswearing love, and without
> money, in the company of the palms. Their numbers are
> replenished day by day, because many who are weary of life and
> the fluctuations of fortune are attracted by their manner of
> living.[35]

The observations of Pareto regarding asceticism among Buddhists are mostly correct and need no comment.

Class V residues: The integrity of the individual and his belongings

Pareto points out that this class is in a sense the complement of class IV (sociality). To defend one's own things and strive to increase their quantity are two operations that frequently merge. So defence of integrity and development of personality are two operations that may differ little or even be one and the same. This residue may take the form of sentiments of resistance to alterations in the social equilibrium, sentiments of equality in inferiors, restoration of integrity by acts pertaining to the individual whose integrity has been impaired, restoration of integrity by acts pertaining to the offender (vengeance), etc.

While discussing the restoration of integrity by acts pertaining to the individuals whose integrity has been impaired, Pareto points out that this variety embraces the purifications that were so generally used in ancient societies and which are still common among uncivilized or barbarous peoples.

(13) *Rules about the purification of sins and impurities among Hindus*

Pareto points out that integrity may be altered profoundly or just slightly, so that the restoration may involve regeneration of the whole personality. So to restore integrity material instrumentalities may be used, or moral and intellectual means may do; but in general the latter have to be supplemented by material agencies. Very often an evolution seems to have taken place whereby material means have come to be supplemented by notions of a moral and intellectual character, these latter in the end coming to prevail exclusively, the material means figuring as mere symbols— something altogether secondary. Oldenberg observes,

> On the one hand ... sin is a transgression of the will of the gods, which has provoked their wrath. The expiation, therefore, is addressed to them, it aims to satisfy and appease them. The suppliant brings them his gifts, humbles himself before them. But on the other hand, sin is a sort of fluid that sticks to the sinner like the glue. In that sense the expiatory rite involves magic practices calculated to dissolve the glue, destroy it, or remove it to a distance at which it can do no harm, so that the sinner is left free and pure again, much as a man reeking with sweat is relieved of his grime by a bath, or the way a feathered bird is freed of its egg.... This second point of view is not altogether inconsistent with a divine act. The elimination of the sinful matter may be conceived of not as the direct consequence of the incantation, but as due to the power or ingenuity of the god whose succour has been invoked.[36]

That gives rise to the common error of assuming that the material element has always been incidental, that it has never served any other purpose than to give external form to the moral and spiritual concept. Water removes material stains. It is therefore taken for granted that it can also remove moral stains. Dubois observes,

> These hermits (the *vanaprasta*) made no distinction between soiling of soul and body. They were convinced that the soul communicated its stains to the body and vice versa and thought that the bath in washing the body also served to purify the soul, especially if the water came from the Ganges, or from other reputedly sacred sources. Fire completed purification, and that was why the bodies of such penitents were burned when they departed this life.[37]

312

Ordinarily, water used by human beings to remove material impurities, becomes chief among the agencies for removing moral impurities. Blood, sulphur and other things have been used in purification. An interesting extension of the idea of purification is the belief that the Flood was a purification of the Earth.

The forms of impurity were countless, but they all corresponded to a single sentiment, real or imaginary, of alteration in personal integrity; and they were remedied by appropriate ceremonies of purification. In such a plethora of dreaded impurities the superstitious soul was afraid of everything. Juvenal ridicules the purifications of a superstitious woman who in the early morning in mid-winter goes to the Tiber, breaks the ice, plunges in three times, and shivering washes her head in the eddying current.[38]

The impurity extends from the person who has incurred it to others who have been in contact with him or are otherwise related to him—from parents to children, from the individual to the group to which he belongs, to animals, material things, a whole country. To lend credence to the so-called Laws of Manu the mere fact that a close relative has died is a cause of impurity, though the corpse has neither been seen nor touched.

> Such the [ten-day] rule of impurity caused by the death of a relative when one is on the spot. But in case of absence at a distance the rule laid down for *spindas* and *samanodakas* prescribed as follows: If news of the death of a relative in a distant locality arrives within the ten days' period of impurity, the impurity holds for the remainder of the period. If the tenth day has lapsed, the impurity holds over three nights. If a year has passed, a bath is sufficient for purification. If the news of the death of a relative or the birth of a male child arrives after the expiration of the ten days, one may be purified by plunging fully dressed into water.[39]

Evidently, therefore, it is a question of a nebula extending to greater or lesser distances about a nucleus.

Biblical prescriptions, subsequently developed in the Talmud, yield a luxuriant harvest of prescriptions pertaining to impurities and purifications. Once impurities are thoroughly identified, the next thing is to get rid of them. Luckily, washing in water happened to be lavishly recommended. That tended at least towards cleanliness. However, minute prescriptions usually guided the believer in his purification. The Bible gives numbers of them and the Talmud lengthens the list.

As was the case with other peoples, Jewish purifications were performed with special waters and in special ways. A notable method among the Israelites was the sacrifice of a red heifer. It had to be undefiled and without blemish. After killing it, the priest 'shall take of her blood with his finger and sprinkle her blood directly before the tabernacle. . . . seven times'. However, the niceties of the Jews are not at all exceptional. Their counterparts are to be met with among other peoples, especially among the Hindus and the Mohammedans. Many Hindu prescriptions tally almost word for word with the Hebrew. Dubois observes,

> Menstruation and childbirth lend temporary uncleanness to women. The mother of a new-born babe lives a whole month apart from other people . . . and women are subjected to the same segregation for the periodic seasons of uncleanness. . . . When the days of expiation are over, the clothing such women have been wearing is given to the washerwoman. It is carefully kept from entering the house, and no one would dare to let his eyes rest on it. However, to purify themselves of such uncleanness, the wives of Sivaites (*lingamistes*) merely rub their foreheads with ash of cow's dung; and that simple ceremony they hold sufficient. . . . Earthen vessels are by nature susceptible of irremediable pollution, a thing not true of metal-ware. To be purified the latter need simply be washed. The others, being no longer usable, have to be destroyed. It is the same with clothing as with dishes; some are susceptible of defilement, others are not. . . . A scrupulous Brahman must be careful where he puts his feet when he walks. He would be defiled and required to take a bath if, by oversight, he chanced to set foot on a bone, a piece of hide or leather, a lock of hair—anything unclean. The place where he sits down also requires his careful inspection . . . nor is his manner of eating a matter of indifference. . . . Contact with one animal or another, the dog especially, defiles the person of the Brahman, and it is amusing to watch the capers they cut, the precautions they take, to avoid the intimate caresses of one of the most faithful comrades of man. If in spite of their efforts the dog manages to reach them, they have no recourse but to hurry away and plunge fully dressed into a bath to be free of the pollution that the touch of the unclean animal had brought upon their persons and their garments.[40]

In all such cases the nucleus is an instinctive repugnance to dead bodies or to filth of one kind or another. The repugnance is in certain cases beneficial to the human beings, just as it is beneficial to animals to abstain from poisonous foods. However, in many cases the actions are non-logical. One may insist that rules on menstruation are rules of hygiene; but in that case, why distinguish the menstruation of a Jewess from the menstruation of a Gentile, and the corpse of a Jew from the corpse of a Gentile?

The observations of Pareto regarding the rules followed for the purification of sins and impurities by Hindus are mostly correct. However, with the spread of education some of the rules are now neglected by educated people.

(14) *The importance of the son among Hindus and the system of* niyoga

Pareto observes that among Hindus, if a man has neither sons nor daughters, the family integrity is altered and something has to be done about it. Hence the various arrangements for permitting a man married to a barren woman to take another wife, either divorcing or keeping the first. As Loiseleur observes,

> He alone is the perfect man who is made up of three persons combined—to wit, his wife, himself, and his son; and the Brahmans have propounded this maxim: 'The husband makes but one same person with his wife'.... The owner of the male that has sired with cows, mares, sheep, female camels, buffaloes, and goats, and slave-girls has no property-right over the offspring. The same it is with the wives of other men.... An elder brother who cohabits with the wife of a younger brother, and a younger brother with the wife of an elder brother, are degraded even if they have been invited to do so by the husband or by the relatives, unless the marriage be barren.... When one has no children the desired progeniture may be obtained through the union of one's wife, on suitable authorization, with a brother or another relative (*sapinda*).... Rubbed with liquid butter and observing silence, let the relative assigned that office approach at night a widow or a childless woman and beget a single son, but never a second.... A man without a male child may bid his daughter rear a son for him.[41]

His observation that Hindus gave more importance to a male child is correct. For an ideal family it was necessary to have at least one male issue so that he could give water to his parents after their death. He could hold property, cultivate land during his father's old age and carry his lineage after death. It is for these reasons that importance was given to the male issue in a family. Such an idea also existed to some extent in other societies as was seen in chapter 2.

Class VI residues: The sex residue and its manifestations

Pareto observes that mere sexual appetite, though powerfully active in the human race, is no concern of ours here. We are interested in it only in so far as it influences theories, modes of thinking—as a residue. In general terms, the sex residue and the sentiments in which it originates figure in huge numbers of phenomena.

Graeco-Roman antiquity thought of the sexual act as satisfying a bodily need, on a par with eating, drinking, adorning one's person, and the like; and all such things the ancients regarded with indifference, generally condemning abuses and, less frequently, excessive refinements in pleasures. In the Western races three abstinence taboos come down across the ages, in order of increasing virulence: abstinence from meat, abstinence from wine, abstinence from everything pertaining to sex. The early Christians advised a moderate use of wine, or indeed abstinence from it as well as from meat, first as a means of doing penance, but also and more especially as a means of attenuating impulses to carnal sin. There are plenty of prescriptions in such regards by the Church Fathers. However, the Catholic Church has always aimed at a golden mean. Requiring abstinence from meat on certain days, it permitted the use of wine, so showing itself more liberal than many a modern pseudo-scientist.

Residues in these phenomena are compounds. The element most important for the first two taboos (meat and wine), and of considerable importance for the third as well (sex), is a residue of asceticism. It manifests its presence in the fact that such taboos are accompanied by abstentions and mortifications that certainly belong to asceticism. The prohibitionists of our day pretend to be interested strictly in public welfare. But it is by no mere chance that they are also as a rule humanitarians, religious zealots, moralists, and champions of sexual purity.

(15) *The prohibition of meat among Hindus*

Religious exaltation sometimes figures in the three taboos. The meat taboo assumes a religious form in India, but not in the Western countries. Scattered examples in connection with the wine taboo are observable here and there among our contemporaries. With the sex taboo the fact is general all the way from antiquity down to our own time.

There are actually localities where the meat and wine taboos are more or less scrupulously observed, where, that is, groups of people actually abstain from meat and fermented drinks. For that matter, in such communities or countries the abstinence is at times merely apparent, as is the case in present-day Turkey.

It is true that in India in certain communities the eating of meat is prohibited on religious grounds. The basis is *ahimsa* or non-injury to living creatures. This was particularly prevalent during the Buddhist period, but even among Hindus meat is considered to be taboo on the above-mentioned grounds.

(16) *The sex taboo and prostitution in temples*

But as regards the sex taboo, differences in substance are negligible, there being notable differences only in forms. Prostitution is prohibited in Mohammedan countries, but it has substitutes in concubinage and in even worse practices. It was also prohibited in Western countries in days when morals were far from being better than they are at present.

In the religion of sex, as in many other religions, inflexibility in forms gives rise to perversion and hypocrisy; the fable of forbidden fruit belongs to all periods of history. Dubois found widespread and offensive incontinence among the brahmans in India. He observes,

> And yet—who could imagine such a thing after what I have just been saying?—there is no country in the world where the outer semblances of decency, properly so called, are more generally observed. What we call *galanterie* is altogether unknown to them. That free, *risqué* chatter, those insipid allusions, that endless flattery, that boundless solicitude and attentiveness that is the stock in trade of our parlour 'dandy' would seem insulting to a Hindu lady, even to one not very strict in her morals, if she were offered them in public. If a husband ventured on any familiarities with his legitimate wife he would be set down as a ridiculous person of no very good taste.[42]

This may be repeated to the letter for many centuries in Europe and America where words are hypocritically chaste and conduct unpleasantly indecent.

Dubois further observes,

> Though adultery in a woman entails disgrace and is condemned by the rule of the Brahmans, it is nevertheless not punished in their caste as severely as in most others. If it is kept secret, little importance is attached to it. Publicity is the only thing that worries them, and in case of gossip, husbands are the first to contradict aspersions on the honour of their wives, in order to avoid the consequences of a public scandal.[43]

In one respect, however, India is free of the hypocrisy observable in Western countries.

317

Relations with a prostitute or an unmarried person are not regarded as crimes by the Brahmans. Those men, who have associated notions of sin with violations of the most inconsequential rules, see no sin whatever in the extremest gratifications of sense. It was largely for their benefit originally that bayaderes and prostitutes were attached to service in the temples. They may often be heard reciting a scandalous line to the effect that 'commerce with a prostitute is a virtue that erases all sin'.[44]

Some of the observations made above by Pareto in connection with sexual immorality among Hindus are correct. However, it needs pointing out that the system of attaching prostitutes to temples has now been given up under legal obligations.

Derivations and their properties

In volume 3 Pareto deals with the theory of derivations as well as the properties of residues and derivations. As pointed out in the beginning, derivations account for the production and acceptance of certain theories, the ways in which people try to dissemble, change, explain, the real character of this or that mode of conduct. The proof of a derivation is very often different from the reason for its acceptance. Sometimes again the proof and the reason may coincide. A precept may be demonstrated by appeal to authority and accepted in deference to the same authority, but then again the two things may be altogether at odds. The derivation may be based (1) on assertion, (2) on authority, (3) on accord with sentiments or principles, or (4) on verbal proofs, i.e. indefinite terms designating real things, terms with numbers of meanings, metaphors, allegories, analogies or vague and indefinite terms corresponding to nothing concrete.

Having explained the different types of derivations used by people, Pareto explains with concrete examples their use at different times and in different societies. Here we shall refer to examples cited in connection with Indian society.

(17) *Different arguments used by Englishmen to occupy India*

The residues (or sentiments) are among the elements which determine the social equilibrium. The term 'sentiments', 'residues' and so on, are convenient makeshifts in sociology, just as the term 'force' has proved convenient in mechanics. The derivations proper are the need of logical developments that human beings feel. However, derivations have no objective existence; in other words they change according to the sentiments and interests of person. Take, for instance, the 'natural law', or the 'law of nations'. In chemistry I draw the logical inference that a certain weight of sodium chloride contains a definite weight of chlorine. I perform an analysis and verify my inference. Not so when the logical inference is to be drawn from entities of that vague and indefinite variety known as the 'law of nations', 'natural law' and the like.

> Still keeping to Montenegro, the British Foreign Secretary declared that Montenegro could not be permitted to occupy Scutari because the population was not of the same race, did not speak the same language, did not have the same religion. It would seem, therefore, that a country does not have the 'right' to occupy another country when the latter presents those differences. Now let someone ask whether the Hindus are of the same race, language, and religion as the English; and if the answer is no, it must remain a mystery why Montenegro does not have the 'right' to occupy Scutari while the English have the 'right' to occupy India.[45]

Pareto's assertion that people use different types of argument at different times to justify their actions is correct. Many examples can be cited where Englishmen used different arguments to justify their actions. We have already seen in chapter 1 such arguments, quoted by Marx, which Englishmen used to bring the princely states under their subjugation one after another.

(18) *Englishmen's disrespect of Indian sentiments leading to the Revolt*

Pareto observes that 'When one group of residues is weakened, the other residues are intensified, by way of compensation'. A truly imposing mass of fact shows the scant efficacy of trying to influence residues by attacking their manifestations or, what is worse, derivations inspired by them. Did the severities visited upon expressions of thought in the press serve to prevent the French Revolution? On the other hand Rome enjoyed the favour and goodwill of the peoples she conquered precisely because she respected their sentiments. English rule in India continues to endure on the same ground; and for identical reasons. Tunis is of all the French colonies the one where French rule is most popular and most willingly accepted, for there the sentiments, usages, and customs of the natives have been best respected. People more readily submit to heavy burdens than to offences after their manners and customs, however slight and insignificant these may seem to be. The Revolt of the Sepoys in India was provoked, it is said, by a rumour that the English were tying their cartridges with strings greased in pork-fat. Minor acts of arbitrary disregard in matters of language, religious usage, and, in Oriental countries, behaviour toward women, are tolerated grudgingly. The art of government, therefore, lies in finding ways to take advantage of such sentiments, not in wasting one's energies in futile efforts to destroy them, the sole effect of the latter course very frequently being only to strengthen them. Facts connected with the sex religion furnish another excellent example of the futility of attempts to destroy residues by suppressing the manifestations that they provoke. It is doubtful whether over the course of the centuries the hosts of laws and measures against sexual immorality have had the slightest effect upon it.

Pareto's assertion that the Revolt of the Sepoys in India was provoked by attack on their sentiment is correct. The rumour that the English were tying their cartridges with strings greased in pork-fat was one of the reasons for the Mutiny.

Appraisal

Reviewing the views of Pareto on Indian society as a whole we may say that most of his observations are correct. Although Pareto studies various aspects of Indian society yet his attention is specially drawn to three peculiar features which he studies in some detail. These were: personification of Hindu divinities, various types of asceticism among Hindus, and rules of purification among Hindus. Such phenomena have generally attracted the attention of Western writers because these are the special features connected with Indian religion rarely found in Christian communities. However, he does not go deeply into the asceticism of various types practised in India. This we shall take up in the last chapter. He also refers to the caste system in India, which many other Western writers also discuss. However, his analysis of the caste system as compared to that of other writers is very shallow. He does not realize at all the peculiarity and the complexity of the caste system in India as do the other writers. Of course, he refers to certain other features of Indian society such as the Buddhists' non-belief in God, the special sacredness of fire and water among Hindus, the importance of a son for the family and prostitution in the temples, but these features have been studied by other writers too and in a more methodical way.

11   A retrospect

In the foregoing pages we have discussed the views which five great sociologists expressed on different aspects of Indian society. Among these Karl Marx and Max Weber were the two sociologists who made a special study of the Indian society, while the others, i.e. Herbert Spencer, Emile Durkheim and Vilfredo Pareto, studied some aspects of Indian society in a comparative perspective while studying a particular social phenomenon, to arrive at certain conclusions, taking instances from different societies of the world. However, Spencer also studied to some extent the effects of British rule in India which Durkheim and Pareto did not. Here we would like to discuss some of the main features of Indian society as noted by the above-mentioned sociologists, and will also see how far they stand valid in the present context and the future progress of this country. These aspects can be discussed under the following heads:

1   The tribes of India
2   Indian civilization—an ancient one
3   Indian religion
4   Marriage and family structure
5   The caste system as an important aspect of the Hindu social system
6   Village communities and communal regulations
7   Cities in India
8   Ancient Hindu law and its effect
9   Development of the sciences and philosophy in ancient India
10 The military system
11 Bureaucracy in India
12 Political organization and colonial rule
13 Economic conditions and development
14 The educational system
15 Hindu beliefs and customs

1 The tribes of India

Certain features of tribes in India have been studied by Spencer, Weber and Durkheim. According to Spencer the tribal population of India is accepted to be the oldest population of the land. These communities have lived for centuries in the forest and hilly regions. Besides these, there were certain other tribes including criminal ones, living in the plains. They are made up of a few pastoral communities which could not adjust themselves to the economy of settled life. Some of them developed a peculiar concept of property and practised antisocial activities like thieving, begging etc. Out of a total population of 361 millions in 1951, the tribal population made 19 millions (5.3%) and the criminal tribes 4 millions (1.1%). The tribes whose details are given by Spencer in his work *Descriptive Sociology* include Todas, Khonds, Gonds, Bhils, Santals, Karens, Kukis, Bodo, Dhimals, etc. Some of these tribes such as Todas, Khonds, Santals, Bodo and Dhimals possess some good characteristics which are not found in many of the tribes in other countries. Therefore Spencer praises these tribes for their good characteristics, i.e. their high moral character, their voluntary co-operation in industrial and other activities, their better treatment of women and children etc. However, he also mentions some of their weak features which are often antisocial or lead to their ruin. For example in one tribe (Todas) with the death of the head of the family his entire herd of oxen was sacrificed with the result that his widow and children had to suffer. Among some tribes robbery as well as murder has had a religious sanctification. Weber also mentions some of the tribes who carried out antisocial activities such as begging and robbery, and to this we shall refer later. Durkheim notes that the Todas and the other Pariah tribes of India have a psychic likeness and behave in the same way.

At present the majority of the Scheduled Tribes are dependent upon agriculture (91%) and the rest on other forms of labour.[1] A large number of tribes dwell in hills and forests and have shifting cultivation. After Independence special schemes have been drawn under the five-year plans to settle them permanently on agricultural lands or in cottage industries, and improve their living conditions. However, so far as their religious and social life is concerned, no changes are brought about unless the initiative comes from the tribal people themselves.

2 Indian civilization—an ancient one

All the sociologists agree that Indian civilization is one of the oldest. The Indian civilization is generally taken from the Vedic period of which some written records are available. However, it needs to be mentioned that Indian civilization is older than that. 'The excavations at Harappa and Mohenjodaro and those in Saurāshtra have disclosed the existence of a highly evolved culture long before the Aryan immigration, perhaps dating back to 3000 B.C. or earlier.'[2]

The Indian civilization is generally dealt with by these writers under three main periods, i.e. ancient, medieval and modern. There is no unanimity among the writers about the period of each epoch, but generally the ancient period is taken from 3000 B.C. to A.D. 1200. From 1200 to the end of the eighteenth century is taken as the medieval period, corresponding with the Muslim rule. From then on starts the modern period which begins with the British rule. The British rule ended in 1947 when a new era of post-independence starts. For the sake of discussion the Hindu period may generally be divided into five phases, i.e. the pre-Vedic period (3000 B.C. to 2000 B.C.), the Vedic period (2000 B.C. to 1000 B.C.), the Brahman period (1000 B.C. to 500 B.C.), the Buddhist period (500 B.C. to 200 B.C.) and the Hindu period from 200 B.C. to A.D. 1200. Reference to these five phases is made by these sociologists.

3 Indian religion

One of the most important social institutions of India, to which reference is made by all the sociologists under study, is Indian religion. And they have rightly done so, for as Dr Arnold A. Toynbee in his book *A Study of History* observes,

the principal civilizations of the world lay different degrees of emphasis on specific lines of activity. Hellenic civilization, for instance, displays a manifest tendency towards a prominently aesthetic outlook of life as a whole. Indic civilization, on the other hand, shows an equally manifest tendency towards a predominantly religious outlook.

Dr Toynbee's remark sums up what has been observed by many other scholars. Indeed the study of Hinduism has to be, in a large measure, 'a study of the general Hindu outlook on life'.[1]

Of the sociologists referred to above, the most exhaustive study is made by Max Weber, though the other sociologists also discuss one or other aspect of Indian religion. All the sociologists agree that the Indian religion is a complex one and is one of the oldest religions.

According to Spencer, Hindu religion is a polytheistic one where, besides ancestor worship, people believe in various types of gods and goddesses. Not only is there a hierarchy of certain gods, but there are special gods that are worshipped on particular occasions. There is a fetish worship and people worship stones, plants and animals because of their usefulness or unusualness or some extraordinary power in them. The belief in demons, i.e., *Bhutas* and *pisachas* is also found among rural folk.

However, it is much more than that.

Receptivity and all-comprehensiveness, it has been aptly stated, are the main characteristics of Hinduism. Since it has had no difficulty in bringing diverse faiths within its ever-widening fold, it has something to offer to almost all minds. Monier William in his notable book *Brahmanism and Hinduism* dwelt on this aspect about a hundred years ago. The strength of Hinduism, he emphasized, lies in its finite adaptability to the infinite diversity of human character and human tendencies. It has its highly spiritual and abstract side suited to the philosopher; its practical and concrete side congenial to the man of the world; its aesthetic and ceremonial side attuned to the man of the poetic feeling and imagination; and its quiescent, contemplative aspect that has its appeal for the man of peace and the lover of seclusion. The Hindus, according to him, were Spinozists more than 2,000 years before the advent of Spinoza, Darwinians many centuries before Darwin, and Evolutionists many centuries before the doctrine of Evolution was accepted by the scientists of the present age.

No civilization anywhere in the world, with the probable exception of China, has been as continuous as that of India. While the civilizations of Egypt, Babylonia and Assyria have disappeared, in India the ideas emanating from the Vedic times continue to be a living force.[4]

As seen in the foregoing pages, Weber discusses in some detail the chief characteristics of Hinduism, Jainism and Buddhism. But sometimes he misses some links and these we have tried to provide at relevant places in Chapters 5 to 8. However, some important lacunae are still left in his treatment, and these we need to fill up here to have a complete picture. First, he fails to discuss the various yoga systems of Hinduism in detail, and particularly the Patanjali's Yoga Sutras, the most important among them. This we need to discuss because Patanjali's yoga Sutras is rather scientific and has captured the mind of Western intellectuals more than any other aspect. In addition it is considered to be a very useful system in modern society. Secondly, he does not clearly bring out the basic similarities between these three religions.

Raja Yoga

The term yoga is used in Hindu literature in different senses.

> But in a general sense 'Yoga' means a unification of two or more
> diverse elements, a whole which includes or unites several parts.
> In Patanjali's specific sense, it is the establishment of perfect
> harmony between the every-day self and its spiritual source. It is
> what we in the western hemisphere often called mysticism.[5]

Yoga, in this sense, does not belong to any particular revealed
religion, and is to be found in the records of all revealed religions. The
true mystic may be a Christian, a Hindu or a Mohammedan.

Patanjali did not originate yoga. It is known to have existed long
before his time. Yajnavalkya, who lived at least a thousand years
before him, enjoined in his writings the duty of retirement into the
forests at a certain age, for the practice of religious devotion and
mystic contemplation. Yoga was also touched upon in other earlier
books, such as the Maitriayana Upanishad. What Patanjali did
was to collect the experiences, the knowledge and the opinions of
some other yogis and aligned them with his own. He then
formulated definite principles and summarized them in a short text
known as 'Yoga Sutras'. It needs also to be mentioned that his
system known as Raja Yoga is one of the many prevalent in the
Hindu religion. According to Paul Brunton, there are today at least
eleven other known schools, while in his researches and travels he
discovered quite a few little-known secret schools.[6] Ernest Wood
discusses ten principal ancient schools of yoga, of which there are
seven well-known surviving schools in India among Hindus.
Among the other three schools of oriental occultism he includes the
Persian Sufis, the Buddhist 'Noble Way', and the Chinese and
Japanese Zen. Among the seven well-known varieties of yoga
practice he lists the *Raja Yoga* of Patanjali, the *Karma* and *Buddhi
Yoga* of Sri Krishna, the *Gnyana Yoga* of Shri Shankaracharya,
Hatha Yoga, Laya Yoga, Bhakti Yoga and *Mantra Yoga*.[7]
However, here we shall deal only with the Patanjali's Yoga Sutras
as this is more popular and scientific. He also remarks,

> There is great interest in the Western world at the present time
> on the subject or Oriental occultism, and very rightly so, for the
> time has come for it to be blended in with the practical material
> civilization which has been so wonderfully developed in the
> modern world. There will be two benefits in this blending—more
> success in the outer world and more peace in the inner life. The
> time has gone for any of us—East or West—to think of
> Occultism as an escape from material reality and responsibility
> into some vague inner condition in which one retreats from all

that material life stands for. Rather it is to make of this world a place where consciousness can enjoy to the full all the powers of its own mind and at the same time discover that there is more to the mind than is commonly known—that is practical Occultism.[8]

As stated before, foremost of the yoga teachings among Hindus, comes that of Patanjali, dating back, according to popular tradition, at least to 300 B.C.[9] He begins with a description of Yoga as *chitta vritti nirodha*. Here *chitta* means the mind, *vritti* means literally a whirlpool, and *nirodha* signifies restraint or control. Thus yoga is controlling the activities of the mind.[10] Before proceeding with the systematic description of the practice of Yoga, Patanjali mentions two things which are necessary for success in controlling the *vrittis* or thoughts, namely *abhyasa* and *vairagya*. *Abyhyasa* means constant practice in the effort to secure steadiness of mind. *Vairagya* means detachment which is the deliberate renunciation of desire for objects seen or heard.[11]

Patanjali's systematic instruction for practical training is given in two portions. The first called Kriya Yoga, is often translated as preliminary yoga because a person who has not first practised it is not likely to succeed in the main portion, the *ashtanga* or 'eight limbs' of yoga practice. But it is much more than preliminary. It is the yoga of action, the yoga which must be practised all the time in daily life. Without it, meditation would be useless, for yoga involves not retirement or retreat but a change in attitude towards the world. . . . The object of the preliminary yoga or yoga of action is to weaken what are called the five *kleshas* (or afflictions).[12]

These five afflictions are *avidya, asmita, raga, dwesha* and *abhinivesha*.[13] They may be translated, ignorance, egoism, desire, aversion and fear. To weaken these five afflictions (and later on to completely destroy them), three kinds of practices are prescribed. These are called *tapas, swadhyaya* and *ishwar-pranidhana*. *Tapa* means austerity, which can be of body, mind, speech, etc. (continence, control of the desire for food, control of tongue by speaking the truth or observing silence, indifference to heat and cold and service of the master); *swadhyaya* means the study of books that really concern oneself as an immortal being; and *ishwara-pranidhana* means devotion to God.

When the candidate has weakened the afflictions to some extent, he is ready for Patanjali's regular course, the eight 'limbs' of yoga. These may be divided into three sets: two moral, three external and three internal as shown in the following list:[14]

	(i) *Yama,* five abstentions	Thou shalt not injure, lie, steal, be sensual or be greedy.
Ethical	(ii) *Niyama,* five observances	Thou shalt be clean (pure), content, self-controlled, studious (to repeat sacred words) and devoted. These are ten commandments. The last three are *tapa, swadhyaya* and *ishwara-pranidhana.*
External	(iii) *Asana,* balanced posture (iv) *Pranayama,* regularity of breath (v) *Pratyahara,* withdrawal of senses	
Internal	(vi) *Dharana,* concentration (vii) *Dhyana,* meditation (viii) *Samadhi,* contemplation.	

These are also known as eight steps of yoga.[15]

If we compare the above-mentioned elements of yoga in Hinduism with those of Jainism and Buddhism discussed in Chapter 6, we shall find many common points. Of the ten commandments, four or five great ones are common to all the three. Similarly out of the ten vows of the brahmanic ascetics (*sannyasin*) mentioned in Baudhayana (the five great ones are *ahimsa,* truthfulness, abstention from appropriating the property of others, continence and liberty; the five minor ones are abstention from anger, obedience towards the guru, avoidance of rashness, cleanliness and purity in eating) many are followed by *gainas* and Buddhist *bhikshus.*[16] Jacobi also refers to some fifteen other rules to be observed by a brahmanic ascetic, as mentioned in Gautama's and Baudhayana's law books, which are also followed by *gainas* and Buddhist monks.[17] Jacobi further states that there are certain other common tenets among these three. These are the belief in the regeneration of souls, the theory of the *karma,* or merit and demerit resulting from former actions which must take effect in this or another birth and the beliefs that by perfect knowledge, and good conduct, man can avoid the necessity of being born again and again, etc.[18] Common too is the theory that from time immemorial prophets (buddhas or *tirthankaras* or avatars) have come to the world to liberate the souls. All the three lay emphasis on concentration, meditation and contemplation to attain liberation.

The basic differences between these three religions have already been discussed in chapter 8.

Religion and asceticism

As pointed out by Durkheim and Pareto, asceticism is part of every religion. However, there are special ascetic practices found in Indian ascetics and it is for this reason that these practices have been discussed by Durkheim, Pareto and Weber. Among Hindu ascetics there are two schools which differ on the question of *asanas* and *pranayama* practices to be followed to attain illumination or *mukti*. One is known as the *Raja Yoga* school, expounded by patanjali, and the other is known as *Hatha Yoga*. 'The practice of *Hatha Yoga* is composed chiefly of *pranayama,* which is regulation of breath, *asana*, the practice of various postures and a set of six *bandhas* or body-purifications'.[19] In some cases this *Hatha Yoga* takes some treacherous forms. This aspect we discuss later on under the heading 'Beliefs and customs'.[20]

Religion and economic development

The question whether Indian religion is a hindrance in the economic development of the country has been discussed by Weber and Marx. Weber, as stated in chapter 8, is of the view that all the three Indian religions, Hinduism, Buddhism and Jainism, are other-worldly and do not lay emphasis on a rational outlook on life. However, as pointed out there, Weber's generalization is too sweeping, and does not fit in with the historical facts. Marx observes that Indian religion lays more emphasis on fate than on a rational outlook. But in spite of that Indian people are capable of making material progress once they are politically free. Here Marx is more correct than Weber.

Relation between priesthood and nobility

According to Weber, everywhere state and society have been greatly influenced by the struggle between military and temple nobility, between royal and priestly following. However, this struggle did not always lead to an open conflict, but it produced

328

distinctive features and differences. As a rule priestly charisma compromised with the secular power, most of the time tacitly but sometimes also through a concordat. Thus their spheres of control were mutually guaranteed and each power was permitted to exert certain influences in the other's realm in order to minimize collisions of interest. As observed by Spencer, in India the Hindu kings were often guided by an advisory council of brahmans, and they also served as judges. All these facts are mostly true of Indian society.

4 Marriage and family structure

Spencer observes that although monogamy has been the rule in most societies, yet polygamy also exists in Indian society in the form of polyandry as well as polygyny. Polyandry was found among Nairs and certain other groups. Among Hindus the chief reason for allowing polygamy was that a son must necessarily be born to the father. If the legitimate wife was barren, the defect could be remedied by a second wife. Weber refers to endogamous, exogamous, hypergamous and *kulin* marriages among the Hindus. In the *kulin* marriage a man may be married to a number of women and be supported by their parents, travelling from one household to another. However, such types of marriages have now been stopped and monogamy is the only form of marriage in vogue at present.

Spencer argues that the patriarchal system was most prevalent in advanced societies where the authority in family affairs rested in the male head. In Hindus, a joint family system was the rule where all the members mess together, live in the same house and have a common purse. He also agrees with Sir Henry Maine that disintegration of the joint family accompanies industrialization and urban growth. Some of the reasons for the dissolution of the joint family were dissatisfaction with the family head, opportunities for employment outside the village and a desire to retain what one had earned. Similar views were expressed by Weber.

Preference for the male child

As pointed out by Spencer, the urgent need to augment the number of warriors, the sacred duty of blood revenge and the development of ancestor worship were some of the reasons for the preference for the male child. However, he also notes that the status of children, in common with that of women, rises in proportion as the militant activities are replaced by the voluntary co-operation characterizing industrial activities. These facts are almost true of Indian society.

5 The caste system as an important aspect of the Hindu social system

Next to religion the most important feature of Indian society is the caste system. In fact it is a part of Hindu religion. All the five sociologists under the study have dealt with this aspect, although the most exhaustive treatment of this subject has been given by Max Weber who devoted about one third of his book *The Religion of India* to the caste system, and also refers to it in his other two works. We have already dealt with Weber's views on the caste system in chapter 4 on the Hindu social system. There Weber pointed out the various important aspects of the Hindu social system, viz. India was a land of villages and of the most inviolable organization by birth, i.e. caste but at the same time the land of trade including foreign trade, particularly with the Occident and with the settlement of some Jews in the south and of Zoroastrians in the north-west; a land that was politically united into one unit at certain periods both under the Mogul rule and before, but for long periods was divided into numerous constantly warring political dominions; a land that had urban development on the western pattern for a long time and also had state creditors, tax farming, state contracting, trade and communication monopolies, etc. on occidental lines. In the field of the sciences, there was the development of the contemporary rational number system, of rational science (including mathematics and grammar); there were numerous philosophical schools and religious sects (tolerant towards each other), numerous forms of justice, handicraft and occupational specialization, and also the development of the caste system. The last phenomenon became one great hindrance in the development of modern capitalism. He then discusses certain main features of the caste system and how it was a hindrance in the industrialization of the country.

He observes that in Hinduism there was a definite type of priest, the brahman, who was a leader of the religion. The brahmans constituted a caste and the institution of caste was rigid and hereditary. Caste played and continues to play a role in the social life of India. In the laws of Manu four main castes are mentioned, brahmans, kshatriyas, vaishyas and shudras. Apart from the exclusiveness of the upper castes, there are important processes of recruitment in some lower castes. In some cases lower castes admit excommunicated members of other castes, while people from tribes or pariah groups were taken into the fold in a special way. A ruling stratum of an 'animistic' tribal territory begins to imitate some specific Hindu customs, tribal priests are eliminated and their place is taken by brahmans who provide testimony to the fact that they—the rulers of the tribes—were of ancient, only temporarily forgotten, knightly (kshatriya) blood. He further observes that the persons belonging to a caste may be followers of different religious sects. Thus one may observe the general rites of a caste and at the same time the special rites of a sect. The everyday *dharma* of the caste derives its content in large measure from the distant past with its taboos, magical norms and witchcrafts. All Hindus consider the Vedas a sacred book, but it is not absolutely indispensable for religious purposes. On the other hand the sacredness of the cow and the prohibition against killing cows is a part of universal Hindu *dharma*. A beef-eater is either barbarian or low caste.

Caste, that is the ritual rights and duties it gives and imposes, and the position of the brahmans, is the fundamental institution of Hinduism. Before everything else, without caste there is no Hindu. There is an extraordinary complexity of the rank relations of the caste system (rules of hypergamy, dietary rules, etc). The caste order is oriented religiously and ritually to a degree not even partially attained elsewhere.

Weber also observes that today the Hindu caste order is profoundly shaken, by the railway system, the taverns, the changing occupational stratification, the concentration of labour through imported industry, Western education, colleges, etc. However, for the time being the caste structure stands quite firmly.

According to Weber the truly strict caste order was originally based on the professional castes, but sometimes ethnic differences also led to the formation of castes. The stability of the caste order blocked technological change and occupational mobility, which from the point of view of caste were objectionable and ritually dangerous. The ritual law, in which every change of occupation, every change in work technique, may result in ritual degradation is certainly not capable of giving birth to economic and technological revolutions from within itself or even of facilitating the first germination of capitalism in its midst. The religious promise of the caste system in the form of two basic principles, the *samsara* belief in the transmigration of souls and the related *karma* doctrine of compensation, did not allow much change in the social structure. The Indian views the individual as born into the caste merited by conduct in a prior life. It meant that in this life there is no escape from the caste, at least no way to move up in the caste order. He can gain heaven or become a god, not in this life but in the life of the future after rebirth and that by doing his (caste) duty faithfully, even without reward. It is difficult to imagine more traditionalistic ideas of professional virtues than those of Hinduism. So long as the *karma* doctrine was unshaken, revolutionary ideas or progressivism were inconceivable.

The anyalysis of the caste system and the Hindu social system given by Weber is mostly correct. However, his interpretation that the caste system was one great hindrance to technological change and industrial development was too narrow, as he totally ignored the political situation of that time. On the other hand, Karl Marx was too optimistic when he foresaw that, once India was politically free, the caste system would not stand in the way of economic and technological revolution. Spencer agreed with Weber, while Durkheim and Pareto stood with Marx. The three latter sociologists did not understand correctly the relation between the caste system and Hinduism. Actually the situation was a complex one and could not be interpreted correctly by any of these sociologists. So far as the trader castes are concerned, as soon as they got Western education and opportunity to invest money in a more profitable way they left their traditional trades and took to new industries. On the other hand the brahmans, kshatriyas and other high castes who had the opportunity of modern education preferred to enter into administrative or professional services but did not enter into business or other services where manual labour was required, e.g. farming with personal labour, with the result that the development of both industries and agriculture was less than desired. This can be seen from the regional imbalance in the economic development of various states. Thus the states of Punjab, Haryana, Gujerat, Maharashtra and Madras were more advanced that the other states, whereas the states like Uttar Pradesh, Orissa, Bihar and West Bengal were the most backward, where the non-trading upper castes still followed the traditional occupations. Of course, there were certain factors in the social system responsible for this phenomenon, e.g. the zemindari system introduced by the British in the region, the broader outlook of people in some regions, particularly of the Punjabis who went abroad during the First and Second World Wars as army recruits, and later on as migrants. But the abolition of the caste system and with it the new religious teaching in these regions were also responsible. The teachings of Sikhism, which preached against the caste system, praised the dignity of manual labour and honesty in professional dealings, were also responsible for this development. How the British Rule affected the economic development of the country is discussed later.

6 Village communities and communal regulations

The subject of village communities in India has been of great interest to Western scholars. Besides Marx, Spencer and Weber, whose studies are included here, the subject has been studied by many writers, both Westerners and Indians.[21] According to Sir Henry Maine, whose studies have been quoted by many social scientists, including Spencer, the existing structure of the village communities was as follows:

> There was first, a certain number of families, who are traditionally said to be descended from the founder of the village. . . . Belôw these families, descended from the originators of the colony, there were others distributed into well ascertained groups. The brotherhood, in fact, forms a sort of hierarchy, the degrees of which are determined by the order in which the various sets of families are amalgamated with the community.[22]

At another place in the same book he observes,

> That in certain villages of Central and South India, there is a hereditary class of 'outsiders' who are looked upon as 'essentially impure', and who, though not included in the village . . . are an appendage solidly connected with it; they have definite village duties, one of which is the settlement of boundaries. . . . They evidently represent a population of alien blood whose lands have been occupied by the colonists or invaders forming the community.[23]

He further adds,

> The Indian cultivating group includes a nearly complete establishment of occupations and trades for enabling them to continue their collective life without assistance from any person or body external to them. . . . They include several families of hereditary trades, the blacksmith, the harness maker, the shoemaker. . . . There is invariably a village accountant. . . . But the person practising any one of these hereditary employments is really a servant to the community as well as one of its component members. He is sometimes paid by an allowance in grain, more generally by the allotment to his family of a piece of cultivated land in hereditary possession.[24]

Spencer further observes,

> The village communities have a local self-government. The village life of these small communities comprises an agricultural and a government element and the village community has to decide all manner of questions; judicial, criminal, social, fiscal or any other which may arise.

So far as the structure and working of village communities of that time is concerned, the observations made by Spencer are mostly correct. Similar views have been expressed by Marx and Weber. However, Spencer does not go into detail about the system of land ownership and tax collection in Indian villages which are discussed by Weber and Marx in more detail.

Land Tenure system

Weber observes that in India two different forms of village organization are met with. Common to the two is the common pasture and a garden area corresponding to the tract of arable on which in the German system wage labourers and cottagers lived. Here are settled craftsmen, temple priests, barbers, laundrymen, and all kinds of labourers belonging to the village— the village 'establishment'. They hold on a 'demiurgic' basis; that is, they are not paid for their work in detail, but stand at the service of the community in return for a share in the land or in the harvest.

The villages differ in regard to land ownership. In the ryotwari village the land ownership is individual and the tax burden likewise. At the head of the village is a reeve. The peasants have no share in the common mark, which belongs to the king (rajah). One who wishes to clear land must pay for the privilege. Another type is represented by the village placed under a 'joint body' a community of a number of a privileged nobles, a village aristocracy of full freeholders or hidemen without an individual head. These farmers grant out the land and to them belongs the common mark; thus they stand between the true cultivators and the rajah. Within this category two classes of villages may be further distinguished; one is the pattidari village, where the land is definitely divided out and appropriated. On the death of the occupant his share goes to his descendants by blood and is redivided when it again passes by inheritance. The other is the bhayacharya village. Here the land is distributed in accordance with the labour force, or the rank of the individual holder. Finally, there are also villages in which an individual is in complete control as tax farmer and overlord. These are zemindari villages, and the pattidari villages also developed through the partition of feudal holdings. The special feature of Indian conditions is that a large number of rent collectors have intervened between the sovereign and the peasantry through the farming out and refarming of the taxes.

The complex system of land ownership in villages as described by Weber is almost correct. The three forms of village organization so far as land ownership is concerned, vis., the ryotwari system, the pattidari system and the bhayacharya system mentioned

334

by Max Weber, were found in different parts of country before the British came. The British government introduced the zemindari system under which 'tax farmers' were made the landowners of many villages. Later on many intermediaries came in between the zeemindars and the actual tiller of the soil.

A similar description of land ownership in villages is given by Marx. However, the ideas of Weber are more clear than Marx in this respect. Marx became rather confused in this matter as he himself admits,

> In some of these communities the lands of the village are cultivated in common, in most cases each occupant tills his own land. The waste lands are for common pasture. . . . As to the question of property, this is a very controversial one among the English writers on India.[25]

However, Marx went further and criticized both the tenure systems introduced by the British, i.e. the zeemindari system and the modified ryotwari system. In the first case the people were dispossessed at once of their hereditary rights to the soil in favour of the native tax gatherers called zeemindars, who increased the rent from time to time. In the ryotwari system also the ryot was not given a permanent title to the land, and the taxation changed every year in proportion to the soil.

After Independence many changes were brought out in the land ownership system in India. The zeemindars and the other intermediaries were eliminated and the tiller of the soil was made the owner of the land as far as possible. Not only that, but further reforms were introduced in the land tenure system. Ceilings have been fixed on the individual holdings and the surplus land distributed among the smaller cultivators or landless labourers. However, the system still suffers from many defects.[26]

7 Cities in India

A study of the structure of Indian cities *vis-a-vis* the occidental pattern in the ancient as well as medieval period is made by Max Weber. He makes an exhaustive study of different types of cities in the West as well as in the East. In his opinion the city-commune in the full meaning of the word, where the patrician 'families', owning urban land and participating either in peaceful commerce or in the bellicose pursuits of piracy, governed the city autonomously, appeared as a mass phenomenon only in the Occident. To develop into a city-commune a settlement had to be of the non-agricultural-commercial type, at least to a relative extent, and to be equipped with the following features: (1) a fortification; (2) a market; (3) its

335

own court of law and at least in part, autonomous law; (4) an associational structure and, connected therewith, (5) at least partial autonomy and autocephaly, which includes administration by authorities in whose appointment the burghers could in some form participate. But the cities of Asia could not fit into this classification. It is true that they all had markets and that they also were fortresses. Separate court districts for the larger trade and craft towns of these countries were also quite frequent. The seat of the administrative authorities of the larger political associations was always in these towns. However, these cities did not know a special substantive or trial law applicable to the 'burghers' by virtue of their membership in the city-commune, or a court autonomously appointed by them. They experienced an approximation only in the case of guilds or (in India) castes, which, if they primarily or exclusively inhabited a single city, might then develop a special law and their own courts. But, from the point of view of the law, the urban seat of these organizations was purely accidental and of no significance. Autonomous administration of the city was unknown or merely vestigial. Thus the special status of the town dweller as a citizen, in the ancient or medieval sense, did not exist and a corporate character of the city was unknown. On the other hand, in the Orient, the confederation of the elders was particularly all-powerful in the villages. In the Asian city this could never occur because it was usually the seat of high officials or the prince himself and thus under his military bodyguards. The city was administered by officials and military officers of the prince, who held judicial powers. However, in certain cases guilds or other occupational associations had certain competencies or claimed them in such a way that officials had to reckon with them.

In India the cities were royal seats or official centres of the royal administration as well as fortresses and market centres. We also find merchant guilds and the castes, to a large extent coterminous with the occupational associations, both of which enjoyed considerable autonomy, above all in the fields of legislation and administration of justice. But the hereditary caste structure of Indian society with its ritual segregation of the occupations, precludes the emergence of a 'bourgeoisie' as well as of a 'city commune', as the caste barriers prevented all intercaste fraternization. However, in the period of the great religions of salvation we find in India the guilds, combined into an association in many cities, which was led by a common urban *shreshtha* corresponding to a Western Lord Mayor. But all this later disappeared with the triumph of ritual caste barriers. as the royal bureacracy in alliance with the brahmans swept away all such budding developments. In the absence of a concept of 'citizenship' and

cent capitalism. It is agreed that, as pointed out by Weber, the
concept of citizenship could not develop in India, owing to the
prevalence of caste inequality, but as the system of modern
education was introduced into India the concept of self-
government in urban towns also developed.

8 Ancient Hindu law and its effect

The ancient Hindu law has been studied by three of the
sociologists, i.e. Spencer, Weber and Durkheim. Among these the
most exhaustive study is made by Weber who, being a jurist, wrote
a detailed essay on the sociology of law in *Economy and Society*.
These sociologists were of the view that the Hindu law was mostly
a sacred law and not a rational one. In the beginning little
distinction is made between sacred and secular law, and the code of
Manu was a kindred mixture of sacred and secular regulations of
moral dictates and rules for carrying out ordinary affairs. Sir Henry
Maine observes that, in common with other Indian codes, the code
of Manu, according to Hindu mythology, is an emanation from the
supreme God. Possessing a supposed supernatural sanction, its
rules have a rigidity enabling them to restrain men's actions in a
greater degree than could any rules having an origin recognized as
natural. Spencer observes that while the unchangeableness of law,
which is due to its supposed sacred origin, is greatly conducive to
social order during those early stages, there, of course, results a
lack of adaptability which impedes progress, where there arise new
conditions to be met.

According to Weber the Dharma books, and specially one of the
latest, viz. that of Manu, were important for a long time in the
courts, as 'books of authority', i.e. private works of legal scholars,
until they were displaced in legal practice by the systematic
compilations and commentaries of the schools. This displacement
was so complete that by the time of the British conquest legal
practice was dominated by one such tertiary source, the Mitakshara dating from the eleventh century. In his view legal erudition
was to a great extent purely scholastic, theoretical, and systematizing, having little contact with legal practice. As the law was to
serve holy ends, these law books were a summary not just of law,
but also of rituals, ethics and, occasionally, of social conventions
and etiquette. The consequence was a moralistic (conscience)
treatment of the legal data that lacked definiteness and concreteness, remaining juridically informal. A dominant priesthood was
able to regulate the whole range of life ritualistically and thus to a

337

considerable extent to control the entire legal system. According to prevailing Hindu theory, all law was contained in the Dharma Sutras. The purely secular development of law was confined to the establishment of particular systems of law for the various vocational groups of the merchants, artisans and so forth. No one doubted the rights of the vocational groups and castes to establish their own laws. However, this type of secular law which covered almost the entire field of matters of daily life was disregarded in priestly doctrines and in the philosophical schools.

Appeals from the organized tribunals of the consociations to the public courts were permitted as a general rule. Ordeals were reserved for cases in which the results of the rational means of evidence were not sufficiently clear. Thus practically complete parallelism of sacred and secular law existed in criminal procedure.

In the villages, the village communities had their own autonomy as mentioned earlier. The Hindu law recognized liturgical collective liability and the corresponding collective rights of the compulsory organizations, especially of village communities, but also of craftsmen. Besides, the oldest procedures approximating a trial are compulsory arbitration of conflict within the household or the kin group, either by the household head or the kin elder who best knows the customs and mutually agreed arbitration between several households and kin groups.

The law of adoption and inheritance

Besides the laws in general, Spencer and Durkheim discuss the law of adoption in India. In Spencer's view the primitive and long-surviving belief in a second life prompted the practice of adoption which supplies the childless with heirs. Among the eastern Aryans there was the great desire to have vacant inheritances filled up, in order that there might be some one to perform the sacred rites, which were specially called for at the time of death. Durkheim observes that in India, Greece and Rome, the law of adoption was subordinated to certain conditions. The one adopting had to be of a certain age and could not stand in such a relation to the age of the adopted that it would be impossible to have been his natural father. Only the father of a family could adopt and only if he had no legitimate child.

Similar was the position with regard to the law of inheritance. Sir Henry Maine, speaking of the elaborate liturgy and ritual for ancestor-worship among the Hindus says, 'In the eyes of the ancient Hindu sacerdotal, the whole law of inheritance is dependent on its accurate observance'. Hunter, however, remarked that the earliest notions of succession to deceased persons were connected with duties rather than rights, with sacrifices rather than with property.

The above observations of most of these writers with regard to ancient Hindu law are correct. It was only during British rule that rational law was gradually developed and introduced and this was equally applicable to all strata of society except in certain spheres where personal law was still applicable such as the law of inheritance, marriage, adoption, etc., though in a modified form. There have since been certain changes in the law of adoption and inheritance where equal rights have been given to females.

9 Development of the sciences and philosophy in ancient India

There was development of various sciences and philosophy in ancient India. This fact is mentioned in some detail by Weber and Spencer and is also referred to by Marx. Weber observes that it is typical of Hinduism, in contrast to the anti-professionalism of Confucianism, to do justice in their own terms to the informing spirit of most varied spheres of life and knowledge, promoting and developing special sciences. Thus it was that alongside important mathematical and grammatical contributions they developed especially a formal logic as the technology of rational proof. A special philosophical school, Nyaya (founded by Gotama) occupied itself with the technology of the syllogism and the Vaisesika school (recognized as orthodox), by applying these formal aids to cosmology, arrived at the theory of atomism.

Indian natural sciences in many areas arrived at a level which Western science had attained about the fourteenth century. There are noteworthy contributions to anatomy, medicine (excepting surgery but including veterinary science) and music (*tosolfa*). In all disciplines, including astronomy, developed for ritual purposes and in mathematics (outside of algebra), Indian science, measured by the standards of occidental science, has essential achievements to its credit. It had the advantage of not having to contend with certain prejudices of Western religious ideas, i.e. the belief in resurrection which blocked the dissecting of corpses.

In India all science of social life remained in the form of a policing and cameralistic technology. This can well compare with the contributions of seventeenth and early eighteenth century cameralism. Whereas Weber holds the view that the science of surgery was not much developed in India, Spencer views it otherwise. He points out that, along with differentiation of medicine and surgery, there has gone on, within each division, minor differentiations. A special branch of surgery was devoted to rhinoplasty, or operations for improving deformed ears and noses and forming new ones. The specialization thus illustrated was otherwise marked; is implied by the statement that no less than 127 surgical instruments were described in the works of the ancient surgeons, and by the statement that in the Sanskrit period the number of medical works and authors is extraordinarily large. The former are either systems embracing the whole domain of the science, or highly special investigations of single topics. Spencer also adds that Indian architecture as a sacred science was well developed in ancient India.

However, Weber also gives a peculiar reason for the deteriorating conditions later on. He observes, 'Considering natural science and technical philosophy, however, one has the impression that noteworthy developmental beginnings were somehow hindered. Unlike Hellenic science it did not even come near the beginning of rational experimentation'. The reason attributed is that the socially anchored unshakability of certain metaphysical presuppositions pushed all philosophy in the direction of individual salvation-striving. For example the Vedanta school conceived the empirical world as a cosmic illusion (*maya*). And the philosophic position taken on all problems was dominated by salvation interests. This served as a barrier to the development of special sciences as well as to a framing of the problem of thought in general. However, this argument of Weber does not seem to be convincing. He always wants to emphasize one factor, ignoring the others. On the other hand, Sri R. C. Dutt rightly observes that factors of deterioration were partly religious and more political and social. He adds,

Indeed, in many respects the tenth and eleventh centuries in India resembled the Middle Ages in Europe. A noble religion had become the monopoly of priests, and had been all but smothered with childish legends and image worship. War and sovereignty were the monopoly of another caste, the Rajput Kshatriyas of India, and the feudal barons of Europe, who had both come to the forefront from the struggles of the preceding Dark Ages. The people were ignorant, dispirited, enslaved, in one country as in the other. . . . Everything bore the appearance of disintegration and decay; and national life seemed extinct.

But here the parallel ends. The sturdy feudal barons of Europe soon mixed with the people, fought the people's battle in the field, the council board or the counting-house, and thus infused a new and vigorous life in modern nations. In India the caste system prevented such a fusion and the Rajput Kshatriyas, isolated from the people, soon fell a prey to foreign invaders, and were involved in a common ruin.

Great is the penalty which Hindus have paid for their caste

disunion and their political weakness. For six centuries after 1200 A.D. the history of the Hindus is a blank. They were the only Aryan nation in the earth who were civilised four thousand years ago; they are the only Aryan nation in the earth who are socially lifeless and politically prostrate in the present day. After six centuries of national lifelessness, there are indications of reviving life. There is a struggle in the land to go beyond the dead forms of religion, and to recover what is pure, nourishing, life-giving. There is an effort to create a social union which is the basis of national union. There are beginnings of national consciousness among the people.[27]

10 The military system

The military system in India has been discussed by three sociologists, viz. Spencer, Weber and Marx. As pointed out by Spencer, in the beginning all adults were warriors and their primary military gathering is also the primary political gathering. In the normal course of social evolution, the military head grows into the political head. Later on when political subordination is established the army usually coincides with the body of freemen, who are also the landowners. So natural is this incidence of military obligation, that in ancient Japan and medieval India there were systems of military tenure like that of medieval Europe. Weber points out that in India the jagirdar provided and equipped a military unit from the proceeds of his tax benefice. The use of land in return for military service is found throughout the Orient since early antiquity. In India, particularly it became an independent and highly developed practice. The usual arrangement was the granting of rights to these sources of income in return for the provision of military contingents and the payment of administrative costs. The king expressing his power in the form of a military monopoly is the basis of the distinction between the military organization of Asia and that of the West. The military or royal officer is the central figure of the process, while in the West both were absent.

As pointed out by Spencer, a dissociation of military duty from land ownership begins when land ceases to be the only source of wealth. The growth of a class of free workers, accumulating property by trade, is followed by imposing on them too the obligation to fight or to provide fighters. Thus a new military system with the full-time job of soldier comes into vogue. This system existed in ancient India as well as during the British rule. Here Marx adds, 'The native army, organized and trained by the British drill-sergeant, was the *sine qua non* of Indian self-emancipation, and of India ceasing to be the prey of the first foreign intruder'. Most of the observations made above by these sociologists are correct.

11 Bureaucracy in India

About the structure of bureaucracy in India study is made by Marx and Weber. Weber observes that in the cultural evolution of Egypt, western Asia, India and China the question of irrigation was crucial. The water question conditioned the existence of the bureaucracy, the compulsory service of the dependent classes, and the dependence of the subject classes upon the functioning of the bureaucracy of the king. In Asia the royal official and army officer is from the beginning the central figure of the process, while in the West both were originally absent. According to Marx there have been in Asia, generally, from time immemorial, but three departments of government; that of finance, or the plunder of the interior, that of war, or the plunder of the exterior; and finally the department of public works. Climate and territorial conditions, especially the vast tracts of desert, extending from the Sahara, through Arabia, Persia, India and Tartary, to the most elevated Asiatic highlands, dictated artificial irrigation by canal and waterworks, the basis of Oriental agriculture. This artificial fertilization of the soil, dependent on a central government and immediately decaying with the neglect of irrigation and drainage, explains the otherwise strange fact that we now find whole territories barren and deserted that were once brilliantly cultivated.

It is true that there were departments of public works to build and maintain canals in certain parts of the country. But in many places the work of construction and maintenance of small irrigation works like tanks was entrusted to local self-government. There was regular machinery for the collection of revenue by government, whether this was entrusted to special officers appointed by the government, or to jagirdars who also had some military functions to perform. During the British rule a new trained civil service was created by the British government which was responsible for the maintenance of law and order, revenue collection and other welfare work. As Marx observes, 'From the Indian natives, reluctantly and sparingly educated at Calcutta, under English superintendence, a fresh class is springing up, endowed with the requirements for government and imbued with European science'. The bureaucratic machinery has much increased since Independence with the expansion of government functions.

12 Political organization and colonial rule

The political structure in India is discussed by Spencer, Weber and Marx. Spencer points out that political organization is essential for every nation to maintain law and order within the territory and save it from foreign aggression. The political organization as it extends itself throughout masses of increasing size, directly furthers welfare by removing that impediment to co-operation which the antagonisms of individuals and of tribes cause, while indirectly with the increase in population within the territory there is more specialization and complex division of labour leading to economical modes of production. However, this political organization is not without disadvantages if it becomes oppressive, as was the position in India in the nineteenth century. Spencer adds

> notwithstanding the boasted beneficence of our rule in India the extra burdens and restraints it involves, have the effect that the people find adjacent countries preferable: the ryots in some parts have been leaving their homes and settling in the territory of the Nizam and Gwalior where the local rulers reigned.

We shall discuss his further views on colonial rule later on. Let us first turn to Weber who discusses the political situation during the ancient period.

Weber observes that as the patron of the *rayat* (client), the kshatriya had the ascribed *dharma* of 'protection' essentially in the sense of defence against the outside. The kshatriya was also responsible for the administration of justice and integrity of trade and related matters. Such ethical commandments were his *dharma*. For the rest it was the primary duty of the prince, to support and further the brahmans, especially by sustaining their authoritarian regulation of the social order according to holy right, not to tolerate attacks upon the brahman's station. The struggle against anti-brahman heterodoxy is clearly required and it did occur. But this in no way altered the place of the prince and politics retained their autonomy in a peculiarity significant manner.

The problem of 'political ethics' had never preoccupied Indian theory and in the absence of ethical universalism and natural right, it could hardly be otherwise. The *dharma* of the prince was to conduct war for the sake of pure power. He had to destroy his neighbour by cunning and fraud and by no matter what crafty, unknightly and ruseful means, by surprise attack, when in distress through instigation of conspiracies among his subjects and bribing his trusted friends. However, elsewhere Weber also mentions that in the Mahabharata emphasis was laid on the ethic of the just war.

Marx, while stating the political conditions in India, points out that, just like Italy, there was dismemberment in the political configuration of the country.

Just as Italy has from time to time been compressed by the conqueror's sword into different national masses, so do we find Hindustan, when not under pressure of the Mohammedan, or the Mogul, or the British dissolved into as many independent and conflicting states as it numbered towns or even villages.

He further observes that from time immemorial there have been misery and political unstability in India as he says,

he shares not the opinion of those who believe in a Golden Age of Hindustan. Take for example the times of Aurangzebe, or the epoch, when the Mogul appeared in the North, and the Portuguese in the South, or the age of Mohammedan invasion and of the Heptarchy in Southern India; or if you will go still further back to antiquity, take the mythological chronology of the Brahmin himself, who places the commencement of Indian misery in an epoch even more remote than the Christian creation of the world.

Regarding the colonial rule of the British in India, Spencer points out that for political integration certain conditions are essential. These include the homogeneity of nature among the population within a territory, which is ensured by greater or less kinship in blood, community of religion, community of their traditions, ideas, sentiments; as well as a community of speech. In the absence of considerable likeness, the political aggregates formed are unstable, and can be maintained only by a coercion which, some time or another, is sure to fail. So from this point of view the governing of India and other territories by the British was unjustified. He further adds that a government cannot undertake to administer the affairs of the colony, and to support for it a judicial staff, a constabulary, a garrison, and so forth, without trespassing against the parent society. Also there is no profit in trade as that trade only is advantageous to a country which brings in return what is directly and indirectly given, a greater worth of commodities than could otherwise be obtained. Further, the interests of those people cannot be properly looked after by a foreign government, and they can manage their affairs better than the British official sitting in London. There is the grevous salt monopoly, and the pitiless taxation that wrings from the poor ryots nearly half the produce of the soil.

Marx goes further than this. He points out that all the civil wars, invasions, revolutions, conquests, famines, strangely complex, rapid and destructive as the successive action in Hindustan may appear, did not go deeper than its surface. England has broken down the entire framework of Indian society without any symptoms of reconstruction yet appearing. There was neglect of irrigation facilities leading to various famines, an abominable system of taxation and an abominable state of justice and law. The different interests, i.e. the manufacturers, the commercial class and oligarchy have been exploiting Indian people in different ways. The cottage industries of India, particularly textiles, were destroyed and the cities were depopulated (as we shall see later on). However, Marx also pointed out one great advantage of British rule, that it united the country into one political unit, which will be beneficial for its future progress, once the country became free. He remarks,

> The political unity of India, more consolidated and extending further than it ever did under Great Moguls, was the first condition of its regeneration. That unity, imposed by the British sword, will now be strengthened and perpetuated by the railways and electric telegraph. The native army, organized and trained by the British drill-sergeant, was the *sine qua non* of Indian self-emancipation, and of India ceasing to be the prey of the first foreign intruder.

The above observations of Marx, Weber and Spencer regarding political organization and political conditions in India before Independence are mostly correct. However, Marx was incorrect when he said that there was always political instability and misery in India. On the other hand Spencer and Weber are more correct when they say that in India at certain times the political conditions were much better than at other places. For example, during the time of Alexander people in the villages were quite prosperous and extra produce was burnt in order that they might renew their labour and not remain inactive. As observed by Weber, King Ashoka was one of the most benevolent kings in the world, as there was the development toward a patriarchal ethical and charitable ideal of a welfare state. The king who has to care for the country and people must work for the public welfare in order that the subjects be happy and attain heaven. Such good periods in the history of India were reported by many foreigners who visited the country at various times.

13 Economic conditions and development

All the five sociologists say something about the economic progress of the country in the past, as seen under the heading, 'The caste system as an important aspect of the Hindu social system'. Spencer observes that in the early periods there was no restriction of occupation on the basis of caste and there was all-round progress in the field of science as well as in industry. During the social evolution among the civilized there were, in the beginning, specializations of function caused by natural aptitude. The Hindus in the ancient period had no caste barriers. The Aryan vaisyas followed different trades and professions in ancient India without forming separate castes; they were scribes and physicians, goldsmiths and blacksmiths, etc., all these occupations of relatively skilled kinds having fallen into the hands of the most intelligent. It was during the intermediate stages that men's occupations became regulated by castes and guilds and individuals were restrained from following their natural bent.

The proper industrial growth of India is evinced by the fact that it had good foreign trade, particularly with the West, as observed by Weber and Marx. In the villages the auxiliary industrial work was performed for a village. The hand workers were small farmers who were not able to live from the produce of their allotments alone. They were attached to the village subject to the disposal of anyone who had need of industrial service. They were essentially serfs, receiving a share in the products or money products. In other words those persons in villages who have very small farms or have no land may work as village artisans or menials. Such a description is given by Spencer, Weber and Marx. In the urban areas craft work is carried out by skilled labour if it is to any extent specialized, either through differentiation of occupations or technical specialization. In India, the caste system, where members of a group do not eat together or intermarry, has had tremendous consequences for the whole social organization. It has stereotyped all craft work and thus made impossible the utilization of inventions or the introduction of any industry based on capital. Every Indian caste had its production process traditionally fixed and one who abandoned the traditional process not only lost caste, but also lost his chance in the future world. Hence the system became the most conservative of possible social orders. The caste stood in the way of the complete subjugation of the craftsman to the merchant. The latter could not take possession of the means of production to the extent found necessary where these were hereditary in the caste. The workshop system could not develop into the factory, the exclusiveness of the caste being partly responsible. The different rest pauses and the demands for different holidays also stood in their way. Similarly in case of trade and banking there were exclusive castes for certain types of trade and banking business as a result of which further developments were hindered in this field. Under British influence it has gradually broken down and even now in India capitalism is slowly making its way.

As seen before, whereas Weber was very pessimistic about

India's future economic development, Spencer was sceptical, while Marx was very much the optimist. Spencer says that the natural rulers, if given the freedom, would have facilitated improvements, and we should not have seen, as now, rivers unnavigable, roads not bridged or metalled and the proved capabilities of the soil neglected. Private enterprise would long ago have opened up these sources of wealth, as in fact it is at length doing, in spite of the discouragements thrown in its way by conquest-loving authorities. England would have been better supplied with raw material, and the markets for her goods would have been enlarged. Here it may be seen that Spencer although he believed that the Indians could develop certain resources, yet thought that they were not capable of setting up industries and could only produce raw material.

Marx like Spencer was critical of British economic policy but was optimistic about India's industrial development. He said that the British Parliament, following the prejudicial policy because of pressure from the industrial class, discouraged Indian manufacturers in order to encourage the rising manufacture of England. The policy was to make India subservient to the industries of Great Britain, and to make the Indian people grow raw produce only. The handloom and the spinning wheel, producing their regular myriads of spinners and weavers, were the pivot of the structure of that society. From time immemorial, Europe had received the admirable textiles produced by Indian labour, sending in return for them her precious metal. It was the British intruders who broke up the Indian handloom and destroyed the spinning wheel. Till 1813 India had been chiefly an exporting country, while it has now become an importing one. The decline of Indian towns, celebrated for their fabrics, was by no means the worst consequence. British science and steam uprooted, over the whole surface of Hindustan, the union between agriculture and manufacturing industry.

Marx further stated that Indians were capable of making material progress once they were politically free, as he remarked, 'we may safely expect to see, at a more or less remote period, the regeneration of that great and interesting country'. None of these sociologists could make a correct analysis, though they were right to a great extent. We have already expressed our own views in this connection under the heading 'The caste system as an important aspect of the Hindu social system'.

Indian revenue and taxation

Marx observed that during the British rule both the utilization of public revenue and the taxation system were defective. While the bulk of the public revenue goes out of the country in the form of home charges, very little is spent on developmental activities. On the other hand, nearly three-fifths of the whole net revenue is derived from the land, about one-seventh from opium and upward of one-ninth from salt. Therefore the revenue system was defective. Spencer also held the same view that Englishmen maintained a salt monopoly, charged excessive land revenue from the poor cultivators, and made no efforts to develop resources, i.e. construct roads, provide irrigation facilities, etc. The observations of both these sociologists in this respect are correct.

14 The educational system

The educational system has been studied by Spencer, Marx and Weber. As noted by Spencer, in ancient India education consisted of learning the Vedas and in the latter, as in the earlier, periods it was done under the priests.

> There were Parishads or Brahmanic settlements for the cultivation of learning . . . and young men went to these Parishads to acquire learning. Besides, learned Brahmins who had retired to forests in their old age often collected some students round them, and much of the boldest speculations in the Epic Period proceeded from these sylvan and retired seats of sanctity and learning.

Thus teaching in the beginning was exclusively concerned with religious doctrines and rites and gradually gave rise to teaching in subjects other than the religion. Weber observes that the *bramacharin* (novice) was personally subordinate to the strict authority and household discipline of the teacher. He was enjoined to chastity and mendicancy and his life was ascetically ordered throughout. As observed by Marx, the modern system of Western education was introduced by the British and he could foresee that this would bring many changes in Indian society. It would produce many scientists, bureaucrats and other personnel for business management, professions and political leadership. Most of the observations made by these sociologists regarding the educational system in India are correct.

The Indian intellectual

According to Weber, whereas in China the mandarins form a stratum of officials and candidates for office, in India the brahmans represent a status group of literati comprising partly princely chaplains, partly counsellors, theological teachers and jurists, priests and pastors. The Hindu intellectuals (including kshatriyas and others during the Buddhist period) largely constituted a stratum of men educated in literature and philosophy and dedicated to speculation and discussion of ritualistic, philosophical and scientific questions. The character of the Asiatic intellectual strata had in essentials hindered the emergence of a 'national' political form of the type developed since the late times of the medieval Occident. At the same time they attempted to establish the meaning of the world and the character of life in the style of the trans-worldly field of formless mysticism. The conception that through simple behaviour addressed to the 'demands of the day' one may achieve salvation was alien to Asia. This excluded from Asiatic thought the pure factual rationalism of the West, which practically tries to discover the impersonal laws of the world. However, here Weber seems to be too one-sided, as he did not take into consideration the political conditions of the country, which compelled the intellectuals to follow irrational pursuits.

15 Hindu beliefs and customs

Some Hindu beliefs and customs were studied by all these sociologists. It may be stated here that most of the Hindu beliefs and customs are connected with religion or a particular caste or sect and we might have referred to them in the foregoing pages. However, in order to have a clearer picture of some of these beliefs and customs which have often caught the eye of Western writers, it may be appropriate to discuss them in brief separately. They include (a) the Hindu preference for a male child and ancestor worship, (b) prostitution in temples, (c) the custom of *sati* and other types of suicide in India, (d) the sacredness of fire and water among Hindus, (e) the Hindu belief in magic, (f) the rules of pollution and purification, (g) sacrifices and practices of asceticism, (h) vegetarianism among Indians, (j) the Hindu love of gold and silver, (k) the robber and begging castes in India.

(a) *The Hindu preference for a male child and ancestor worship*

The subject of the Hindu preference for a male child has been discussed by four sociologists. Pareto observes that there are the residues of the integrity of the individual and to so defend the integrity and for the development of personality certain acts are to be performed. If a man has neither sons nor daughters the family integrity is altered (daughters are not considered when the family is perpetuated through the male line) and something has to be done about it. Hence the various arrangements for permitting a man married to a barren woman to take another wife, divorcing, or keeping, the first. Among Hindus the belief is that a married person must have a son to offer libations and hence various arrangements to get a son, including the system of *niyoga*, where a brother or a relative of the husband can cohabit with a childless woman or widow to beget one son but never a second. We have already referred to the views of Spencer, Durkheim and Weber under the headings 'Marriage and family structure' and 'Ancient Hindu law and its effect'. Here it may also be mentioned that preference for a male child is also connected with ancestor worship. As Spencer observes, among Hindus the daily offerings to ancestors is made by the head of the family, who must be a male member. He further adds that there are specific passages in the laws of Manu in this regard. There we have the statement that the manes eat of the funeral meal and we have the direction to the head of the family to make a daily offering to get the goodwill of the manes, and also a monthly offering. However, Manu also says that the offerings to the gods are to be made at the beginning and end of the Sraddha, with an oblation to the Pitris in between. It shows that higher rank is given to gods than to ancestors. Such practices continue even now among orthodox Hindus.

(b) *Prostitution in temples*

The custom of prostitution in temples has been observed by Spencer, Weber and Pareto. Weber points out that prostitution is not a product of monogamy and private property, but is of immemorial age. Prostitution, however, not only appears in the form of an unregulated sexual submission but is also met within the sacramentally regulated form of ritualistic prostitution, as for example, the hieroduli in India and the ancient East. These were female slaves who had to function in the temple in connection with the religious services, of which a part consists in their sex orgies. The hieroduli are also found submitting themselves to the public for pay. The institution of the hieroduli goes back to sacerdotal sources, to animistic magic of a sexual character which has a way of running into sexual promiscuity in view of the progressive self-excitement of an ecstatic situation.

According to Pareto sex taboos are found in almost all societies, the differences being in forms. Prostitution is prohibited in Mohammedan countries, but it has substitutes in concubinage and in even worse practices. It was also prohibited in Western countries at certain periods, without success. In the religion of sex, as in many other religions, inflexibility of form gives rise to perversion and hypocrisy; the fable of the forbidden fruit applies to all periods of history. Dubois found widespread and offensive incontinence among the brahmans in India. It was largely for their benefit that bayaderes and prostitutes were originally attached to service in the temple. According to Spencer, prostitution in temples was a religious observance among Hindus.

Temple prostitution continued to exist in India even during the British period. It was only after 1933 that certain steps were taken to abolish this system. The Bombay Devadasi Protection Act, 1934, and Madras Devadasi (Prevention of Dedication) Act 1947 were passed to check this system. However, sterner measures were taken in this regard after Independence and such practices were totally banned by legislation.

(c) *The custom of* sati *and other types of suicide in India*

The custom of *sati* among Hindus has been noted by Durkheim and Spencer. The other types of suicide have also been studied by these writers. Durkheim, who makes a special study of suicide in different societies, refers to various types of suicide among Hindus. He says that there are three factors which operate in suicide: (i) altruistic, (ii) egoistic and (iii) anomic. Under the altruistic factor, he mentions certain types of suicides committed in India. These included (i) suicides among brahmans and Hindu sages, (ii) suicides by widows, (iii) suicides by Hindus in general and (iv) suicides by Buddhists and Jains. The old brahmans and other sages anticipating their time of death during old age tried to burn themselves in fire. Even widows tried to kill themselves on their husbands' death. Similarly the custom of seeking death in the waters of the Ganges or other sacred rivers was widespread. There were also fanatics who let themselves be crushed to death in throngs under the wheels of the idol Juggernaut. These types of suicide still continue, though on a lesser scale, except for the custom of *sati* which has been abolished since 1829.

In Buddhism the suicide is reproved in principle yet in certain sects suicide is committed by the followers of Buddhism. In Jainism, too, one of the canonical books of the Jainist religion reproves suicide, accusing it of really augmenting life, yet in many cases religious suicides are often practised among Jains particularly among southern Jains. The believer allows himself to die of hunger. Such types of practice were also noted by Weber and Marx, as seen in the foregoing chapters.

(d) *The sacredness of fire and water among Hindus*

There were three sociologists, i.e. Durkheim, Pareto and Spencer who observed that fire and water were treated as sacred by Hindus.

351

Durkheim points out that fire held a rather large place in Vedic religion. The reason for this was that the first appearance of fire must have made a deep impression upon the human mind. Fire was not given as something permanent or eternal, like the sky or the earth or water. In whatever way it first appeared, whether through lightning or through friction of the branches of trees, or through the sparks of flints, it came and went, it had to be guarded. It made life possible in winter, it served as a protection during the night and it changed man from a devourer of raw flesh into an eater of cooked meat. Later on it became an indispensable factor in mechanical and artistic progress, and has remained so ever since. The reasons given for the sacredness of fire by Durkheim seem to be convincing, However, Pareto holds a different view and argues that in the field of religion or custom experience is given little place. It is authority divine or of certain individuals, which is given more weight. He points out that there is a belief among Hindus that water and fire are pure and sacred and therefore they conclude that the bodies of the dead ought to be either burned or thrown into the Ganges. The Parsees conclude to the precise contrary, that neither fire or water should be defiled through contact with a corpse. We have already mentioned the sacredness of Ganges water in which some old people drowned themselves rather than wait for death.

Spencer mentions that there is reference in the Vedas to Agni as the god who is called the ruler of the universe, and Indra is celebrated as the strongest god.

Here Pareto also mentions the ceremonies which are performed at the time of death. As soon as the pyre has burnt out, milk is sprinkled over the ashes, and the bones that have been spared by the fire are gathered up, put into urns and later thrown into some sacred stream or into the Ganges. Hindus believe that the man whose bones get into a sacred river will enjoy infinite bliss for millions of years.

(e) *The Hindu belief in magic*

Pareto, Weber, and Spencer hold the view that Hindus believe in magic. Pareto observes that just like some other societies, Hindus believe in magic. For example as Apollonius and his companions saw in India, where brahmans dwelt, two jars of black stone, one jar of rain and the other the jar of the winds. If they wanted rain one jar was opened, and it sent clouds and rain all over the land. If the rain was too much it was closed and the storm ceased. If the jar of the winds was opened, one of the winds got out, and it blew where it was needed and dried the land.

Weber makes similar observations about tantric magic. There always existed that massive popular orgiasticism against which the intellectuals had closed the doors. Alcoholic, sexual, and meat orgies, magical compulsion of the spirit, personal deities, living and apotheosized saviours, ardent cultist love of personalized helpers-in-need conceived as incarnations of great merciful goods all these were familiar elements of popular religiosity.

Tantric magic was originally a form of orgiastic ecstasy called forth through common indulgence of the five *nukara,* the five things beginning with the letter 'M': alcohol, meat, fish, sexual intercourse and holy finger gestures. The goal of the orgy was doubtless ecstatic self-deification for magical purposes. He who had obtained possessions of the god, Bhairava or Vira, has magical power. Magic was also observable in the caste craft. As Weber points out, magic involves a stereotyping of technology and economic relations. Every new technological process which an Indian employs signifies for him first of all that he leaves his caste and falls into another, necessarily lower. Similarly accepting food or water from others involved pollution. Obviously capitalism cannot develop in a society where people are bound hand and foot by magic beliefs. Most of these observations about belief in magic are correct.

(f) *The rules of pollution and purification*

Pareto observes that there are residues connected with the integrity of individual. To restore the integrity of the individual which has been impaired for some reason, certain ceremonies are performed in many societies. To restore integrity there may be used material instrumentalities or moral or intellectual means. Sometimes gifts are offered to appease the deities, while in certain cases expiatory rites may involve magical practices to destroy the sin. Among Hindus, water and fire are used to remove not only material stains but moral stains too. Water removes material stains. It is, therefore, taken for granted that it can also remove moral stains. There is a belief among the Hindus, as observed by Dubois, that there is a close conncection between body and soul. They were convinced that the soul communicates its stains to the body and vice versa and therefore a bath, in washing the body, also served to purify the soul, especially if the water comes from the Ganges. Fire completed purification so the body was burned after the death of a person.

Hindus believe that impurities extend from the person who has incurred it to others who have been in contact with him or otherwise related to him. The laws of Manu say that the mere fact that a close relative has died is a cause of impurity, though the corpse has neither been seen nor touched by the relative. The impurity holds for a particular number of days and is removed by taking a bath and performing some other ceremonies. Menstruation and childbirth lend temporary uncleanness to women. The mother of a new-born baby lives a whole month apart from other people. Women are also subjected to the same segregation for their monthly periods. When the days of expiation are over, the clothing such women have been wearing is given to the washerman. Similarly a scrupulous brahman must be careful where he puts his feet when he walks. He would be defiled and required to take a bath, if by oversight he chanced to set foot on a bone, a piece of hide or leather, a lock of hair—anything unclean. Contact with one animal or another, the dog especially, defiles the person of a brahman. If in spite of his efforts the dog manages to touch him, he has to plunge fully dressed into a bath to be free of the pollution that the touch of the unclean animal may have brought about.[28] In all such cases the nucleus is an instinctive repugnance for dead bodies or to filth of one kind or another. Such repugnance is in certain cases beneficial to the human beings, but in many cases the actions are non-logical.

The observations of Pareto are mostly correct. Such types of beliefs are found among the Hindus. Connected with these rites and ceremonies are some other practices discussed by Durkheim under the heading 'Sacrifices and practices of asceticism'.

(g) Sacrifices and practices of asceticism

Durkheim observes that there are two types of cults observed in different religions. These may be positive as well as negative. The existence of negative cults is in the form of interdictions particularly in the form of asceticism. The positive cult takes the form of certain ceremonies and sacrifices. These sacrifices are made to uphold positive and bilateral relations with religious forces. He adds, however little importance the religious ceremonies may have, they put the group into action and multiply their relations. In such cases men feel themselves united, partially by bonds of blood, but still more by a community of interest and tradition; they assemble and become conscious of their moral unity. Hubert and Mauss have shown that the sacrifice of communion, that of expiation, that of a vow and that of a contract are found among the Hindus.

Spencer observes that in India a woman adores the basket which serves to bring or to hold her necessaries; and she offers sacrifices to it, as well as to the rice-mill, and other implements that assist her in her household labours. A carpenter pays like homage to his hatchet, his adze, and other tools; and likewise he offers sacrifices to them. A brahman does so to the style with which he is going to write; a soldier to the arms he is to use in the field; a mason to his trowel. Besides this individual fetish worship there is common worship too as observed by Weber and Marx.

Practices of asceticism Durkheim points out that while in the positive cult they prescribe certain acts for the faithful, in the negative cult they confine to forbidding certain ways of acting, and they take the form of interdictions commonly called taboos. Although the negative cult is generally presented as a system of abstentions, in the form of inhibiting activity, yet it is found to exercise a positive action of the highest importance over the religious and moral nature of the individual. A pure ascetic is a man who raises himself above men and acquires a special sanctity by feasts and vigils, by retreat and silence, or, in a word, by privations rather than by acts of positive piety (offerings, sacrifices, prayers, etc.). The Buddhist saint is essentially an ascetic, and he is equal or superior to the gods.

Pareto also mentions such practices among Hindu saints and Buddhists. He observes that in some Hindu sects the saints inflict on their bodies everything that a fanatical fury can suggest. Some tear their flesh with whips, or have themselves chained by the feet to trees to be released only when they die. Others take a vow to remain all their lives in some uncomfortable position, keeping their hands always closed, for instance, so that their fingernails which they never cut, in the end grow through their hands. Not a few bury themselves in the ground, breathing only through little openings.

The above observations of the sociologists are mostly correct. However, as mentioned earlier, some of the extraordinary ascetic practices are exceptions rather than the rule.[29]

(h) *Vegetarianism among Indians*

While explaining the sex residues, Pareto points out that in the Western races three abstinence taboos come down across the ages, in order of increasing virulence: abstinence from meat, abstinence from wine, abstinence from everything pertaining to sex. The early Christians advised a moderate use of wine, or indeed abstinence from it as well as from meat, first as a means of doing penance, but also and more especially as a means of attenuating impulses to carnal sin.

Residues in these phenomena are compound. The elements most

important for two taboos, i.e. meat and wine, and of considerable importance for the third as well (sex), is a residue of asceticism. But they also as a rule are humanitarian. Religious exaltation sometimes figures in the three taboos. The meat taboo assumes a religious form in India, but does not in the Western countries.

According to Weber, the intensification of vegetarianism and abstinence from alcohol among Hindus clearly developed out of opposition to meat orgies; the very strong tabooing of adultery and the admonition to control the sexual impulse in general has similar anti-orgiastic roots. Among Jains the practice of *ahimsa*, the absolute prohibition on the killing of living beings, originated in the rejection of the meat sacrifice which the brahmans had illogically preserved out of the ancient Vedic sacrificial ritual. Such was the position in Buddhism too.

(j) *The Hindu love of gold and silver*

Weber and Marx observe that Hindus had a fancy for precious metals like gold and silver. Marx observes that the Europeans received the admirable fabrics of Indian labour, sending in return for them her precious metals and furnishing thereby his material to the goldsmith, that indispensable member of Indian society. Weber observes that in the period of Roman power India imported an enormous mass of precious metal.

The observations made by Marx and Weber are correct. The main reason for preserving gold among Indians was that it served as a security during famines or political upheaval. Owing to the uncertainty of rain in India, famines occurred and this metal could be used as money at that time. Similarly during political upheavals gold could easily be carried during migration to some other place.

(k) *The robbers and begging castes in India*

Weber observes that in India we find secular castes of beggars and elsewhere particularly in China, organized groups of beggars are formed. In India there have existed ritually separate castes of 'thieves' and 'robbers' and in China sects and secret societies with a similar method of economic provision. Spencer mentions that robbery as well as murder has had and has still in some places a religious sanction. The robber-tribe among the Chibchas regard as the most acceptable sacrifice that which they offer up out of their spoils to certain idols of gold, clay and wood, whom they worship. Among the freebooters like the Domras a successful theft is always celebrated by a sacrifice to their chief god Gandak.

These facts about certain tribes (later on converted into castes) are correct. However, it may be mentioned that the government has recently taken measures to crush their antisocial activities and rehabilitate them to a normal existence.

The future of Indian society

All the five sociologists under study have said something about the future progress of society in general and that of Indian society in particular. However, there are two sociologists, viz. Weber and Marx, who made a special study of Indian society and said something definite about its future progress. Spencer made some observations about Indian society in a general way, while Durkheim and Pareto did not see Indian society in any special context.

Spencer observed that two main obstacles in the way of India's progress were political subordination and the caste system. If India was politically set free, the Indians would be able to develop their resources by providing irrigation facilities, roads and other means of communication etc. However, they would not be able to develop complex industries on account of the caste system which prevents innovations in technology.

Both Durkheim and Pareto looked into the caste system of India in a general way and were of the view that with specialization and more division of labour the caste system would disappear as had been the case in the West, and then Indian society would progress like any other society. However, they did not go into detail in this matter and could not see the link between the caste system and Hindu religion. Karl Marx saw that political subordination was one of the important factors which hindered India's future progress. He observed that the British government has introduced certain new elements into Indian society which have laid the material foundations of Western society in Asia. These were the political unity of India, the introduction of railways, the post and telegraph service, the training of the army on modern lines, the free press, the new system of modern education, regular and rapid communication with Europe through steam vessels, new irrigation facilities, the introduction of certain industrial processes to meet the needs of railway locomotion, etc. Some of these elements would remove caste barriers and would help in introducing modern techniques in other fields. Once the country was politically free, it was capable of making material progress just like other countries of the world. Most of the observations made by Marx are proving true, except that the caste barriers still stand in the way of rapid material progress, as discussed earlier.

On the other hand, Weber held the view that two factors, i.e. the caste system which was a part of Hindu religion and the Indian

357

religions whose philosophy was other-worldly, stood in the way of industrial development. Therefore he did not see rapid progress of Indian society. Weber made a more detailed study of the caste system as well as of Indian religion than did any other sociologist. But somehow he totally ignored the political subordination of India, which stood in the way of its progress, as discussed in chapter 8. He positively stated that colonialism could not be a factor in the development of capitalism, which was far from the truth. On the other hand, his contention that the caste system stood in the way of industrial development is true to some extent, as seen in the foregoing pages. His contention that Indian religion was other-worldly and did not lay emphasis on a rational outlook of life was again wrong to a great extent. There is no doubt that his knowledge of Hinduism was very incisive yet the conclusions which he drew from its philosophy were too wide of the mark. His contention that the Protestant ethic, particularly that of Calvinism, was more favourable to the accumulation of capital, to less conspicuous consumption and to a rational outlook on life, and therefore responsible for the rapid industrial growth of Europe, is true to a great extent. However, to assume that other religions had no such ethic was rather an erroneous conclusion. But if such an ethic was not rightly interpreted to the masses, another problem arises.

From our point of view, what was more important was the organizational aspect of the Church. In the Western countries new religious instructions were given in a more methodical way and on a regular basis. On the other hand, in India, in spite of there being some good basic ethics present in Indian religion, they were not rightly interpreted to the laity. Thus the organizational aspect of religion was quite defective. People hardly attended the religious institutions where good sermons were imparted on a regular basis. Religious instruction was imparted by the traditional priests in a traditional way occasionally. Moreover the political and social environment were also not conducive to frugal living.

The way of imparting religious teaching was ineffective and also the priests were not well trained. In some sects where the tenets were reinterpreted to suit the new needs, and sermons given on a regular basis, such teaching was helpful in changing their attitudes so they could change their occupation to suit their capacity, to work honestly and diligently. Here it may be sufficient to add some examples from Sikhism, a new sect in Hindu religion. Nanak the founder of the Sikh religion preached hard work, honesty in business and the love for manual labour, which were conducive to prosperity. This is clear from his precepts and teachings.

Once Guru Nanak, while passing through the streets of Sialkot (a town now in Pakistan), stopped at the shop of a grain dealer and began to examine his weights. The shopkeeper became terrified and requested the guru to grace his house with a visit. The guru said, 'Not now, but I will come when your gains are no more contaminated with wrong dealings. A dealer in grain is the sustainer of life and must be honest and true in his dealings. When you become a true dealer and giver of food I will come to your house'.[30]

Nanak did not favour the renunciation of the world to realize God and disliked living on the alms of others. Once a baker followed Guru Nanak for a number of days and wanted to become a fakir. But then Nanak asked him to return home and said, 'It is not by shirking our duty that we become saints, but by daily performance of that which is ordained'.[31]

Nanak much praised the dignity of manual labour and started a small farm at Kartarpur which he cultivated by following the plough himself. He held that the right way to live was by the produce of one's own labour. He produced not only enough for himself and his family but gave the surplus to the free kitchen.

He denunciated the caste system and preached for the equality of human beings. Once the guru halted at Saidpur (a town now in Pakistan) and lodged at the house of a carpenter named Lalu, who lived by sweat of his labour. It happened that Malik Bhago, the Dewan of the Pathan Governor, was giving a sacrificial feast on that day and expected all religious and holy men to join and partake of his repast to enable him to acquire merit. The news that a saint was staying at the house of Lalu reached Malik Bhago. He immediately sent a servant to invite the guru along with his followers. The guru, however, refused to accept the invitation. Bhago said, 'You are a strange man. You can eat the food cooked by a Shudra'. Nanak said, 'I have no caste. Nor do I sit in a *chauka* to eat, for me the whole earth is pure'.[32] When Bhago insisted on his joining the feast, the guru asked him to bring some food from his house. Lalu also brought a piece of bread made of barley flour. The guru took a piece from each in his right and left hand respectively and squeezed the two. From the Lalu's food oozed out drops of milk and from that of Bhago's drops of blood. Then guru told Bhago, 'You see that your food is bloodstained and drawn from others. Lalu enjoys what he earns by hard labour and shares his earnings with others. No sanctified *chauka* can make your food pure'. This made the people realize the value of hard and honest labour.

Later on the Arya Samaj movement in the Punjab, Brahmo Samaj in West Bengal and the Prarthana Samaj movement in Bombay and other areas had similar effects.[33] But still their teachings were confined to few educated persons in the urban areas. The majority of the people were still untouched. Rigidity of occupation, aversion for manual work and trading occupations among some upper castes, and shabby dealings in business among all were still prevalent in Indian society.

Notes

1 Karl Marx (1818–83)

1 Aron, R., *Main Currents in Sociological Thought,* vol. I (London, Weidenfeld & Nicolson, 1965), p. 109

2 Hobsbawm, E. J. (ed.), *Karl Marx, Pre-capitalist Economic Formations* (London, Lawrence & Wishart, 1964), p. 20.

3 Hobsbawm, E. J., *Karl Marx,* p. 21.

4 Ibid., p. 51.

5 Among his various articles in *New York Daily Tribune* the two most important are 'The British Rule in India' and 'The Future Results of British Rule in India', published on 25 June and 8 August 1853 respectively. These were despatched from London on 10 June and 22 July 1853.

6 It may be pointed out here that all the rulers (except one) who earlier came to India settled here permanently and did not take away the riches of the country as did the British. Once they had conquered the country they looked to the welfare of the people as far as possible.

7 *New York Daily Tribune,* 12 July 1853.

8 *Ibid.,* 20 July 1853.

9 *Ibid.,* 25 July 1853.

10 Marx, Karl, 'The British Rule in India', *New York Daily Tribune,* 25 June 1853.

11 Mukerjee, R. K., *The Economic History of India: 1600–1800* (Calcutta, Longmans, 1946), p. 1.

12 From another report in his letter dated 14 June 1853 to Engels, Marx mentions that besides the Joshee, or astrologer who announces the seed time and harvests, and the lucky or unlucky days or hours for all the operations of farming, the smith and the carpenter frame the rude instruments of husbandry, and the ruder dwelling of the farmer. The potter fabricates the only utensils of the village. The washerman keeps clean the few garments.... The barber and the silversmith who often at the same time is also a poet and schoolmaster of the village—all in one person.

13 Marx, Karl, 'The British Rule in India'.
14 Letter Marx to Engels dated 14 June 1853. See Karl Marx and Frederick Engels, *Selected Correspondence* (Moscow: Foreign Languages Publishing House, 1953), p. 103.
15 Marx, Karl, 'The Future Results of British Rule in India'.
16 Letter Marx to Engels dated 2 June 1853.
17 Letter Marx to Engels dated 14 June 1853.
18 Ibid.
19 Altekar, A. S., *A History of Village Communities in Western India* (Bombay Oxford University Press, 1927), pp. 80–5. For Baden-Powell's views see his book, *The Origin and Growth of Village Communities in India* (London, Swan Sonnenschein, 1899).
20 Maine, Sir Henry, *Village Communities in the East and West* (London, John Murray, 1871), pp. 41, 107, 109, 112.
21 *New York Daily Tribune,* 25 July 1853.
22 Marx, Karl, *Notes on Indian History (664–1858)* (Moscow: Foreign Languages Publishing House, 1947), pp. 98–9.
23 *New York Daily Tribune,* 25 July 1853.
24 Marx, Karl, 'The Future Results of British Rule in India'.
25 Marx, Karl, *Capital,* vol. III (Moscow: Foreign Languages Publishing House, 1960), p. 328.
26 Dutt, R. C., *The Economic History of India Under Early British Rule* (London, Kegan Paul, Trench, Trubner, 1901), p. ix.
27 *New York Daily Tribune,* 25 July 1853.
28 For details see R. C. Dutt's two books, *The Economic History of India Under Early British Rule,* pp. 398–420, and *The Economic History of India in the Victorian Age* (London, Kegan Paul, Trench, Trubner, 1906), pp. vii–xix.
29 This means: more delicate and clever than Italians. It is quoted from Soltykov's book *Lettres sur l'Inde* (*Letters about India*) (Paris, Garnier, 1848).
30 Marx, Karl, 'The Future Results of British Rule in India'.
31 Of course, China attacked India in November 1962 and captured a part of the territory on the eastern side. But it was an unexpected attack as rarely in the history of India had there been any attack from this side.
32 Hobsbawm, E. J., *Karl Marx,* p. 34.
33 'Manifesto of the Communist Party', in Karl Marx and Frederick Engels, *Selected Works,* vol. I (Moscow: Foreign Languages Publishing House, 1962), pp. 34–5.
34 Ibid., p. 363.

2 Herbert Spencer (1820–1903)

1 Fletcher, R., in Andreski, S. L. (ed.) *Herbert Spencer: Structure, Function and Evolution* (London, Michael Joseph, 1971), p. 1.
2 Andreski, S. L. (ed.), 'Editor's Introduction' in *Herbert Spencer: Principles of Sociology* (London, Macmillan, 1969), p. x.
3 Abraham, J. H., *Sociology* (London, English Universities Press,

1966), p. 25. Also see Spencer, *First Principles* (London, Williams of Norgate, 1887), chapters XIV and XV.

4 Duncan, David, *The Life and Letters of Herbert Spencer* (London, Methuen, 1908), p. 246.

5 Spencer, Herbert, *Principles of Sociology,* vol. II (London, Williams & Norgate, 1902), p. 234. Also see Hunter, W. W., *Annals of Rural Bengal* (London, Smith, Elder, 1868), p. 248.

6 Harkness, H., *The Neilghery Hills,* (London, Smith Elder, 1832), p. 18.

7 Macpherson, S. C., *Report upon the Khonds of Ganjam and Cuttack* (Calcutta, Huttmann, 1842), p. 196.

8 Shortt, J., *Hill Ranges of Southern India* (Madras, Higginbotham, 1870–83), p. 9.

9 Hunter, W. W., *Statistical Account of Bengal* (London, Trubner, 1875–7), p. 330.

10 Hodgson, B. H., 'On the Origin, Location, etc., of the Kocch, Bodo and Dhimal People', in *Journal of the Asiatic Society of Bengal,* vol. 18 (Calcutta, 1849).

11 Shortt, J., *Ethnological Society Transactions* (London: 1859–69), vol. VII, p. 240.

12 Ibid, p. 245.

13 Spencer, Herbert, *Principles of Sociology,* vol. I (London, Williams & Norgate, 1904), p. 785. Also see vol. III (London, Williams & Norgate, 1897), p. 141.

14 Nesfield, J. C., 'An Account of the Kanjars of Upper India', *Calcutta Review,* Oct. 1883, p. 12.

15 Fergusson, J., *Tree and Serpent Worship in India* (London, 1873; Delhi, Oriental Publishers, 1971), p. 80.

16 Cunningham, A., *The Bhilsa Topes* (London, Smith Elder, 1854), p. 11.

17 Lyall, A. C., *The Fortnightly Review* (Feb. 1872), p. 133.

18 Jones, W., *Works,* 9 vols (London, Stockdale, 1799–1804), vol. III, p. 147.

19 Spencer, Herbert, *Principles of Sociology,* vol. I, p. 787.

20 Lyall, Sir Alfred C., *Asiatic Studies Religious and Social* (London, John Murray, 1882), p. 20.

21 Spencer, Herbert, *Principles of Sociology,* vol. I, p. 317.

22 Lubbock, J., *Origin of Civilization* (London, Longmans, 1882), p. 286.

23 Lyall, A. C., *The Fortnightly Review* (Feb. 1872), p. 131.

24 Spencer, Herbert, *Principles of Sociology,* vol. I, p. 327.

25 Muir, J., *Original Sanskrit Texts,* vol. II (London, Trubner, 1868–70), p. 471.

26 *Journal of the Anthropological Institute,* vol. V, pp. 408–22.

27 Spencer, Herbert, *Principles of Sociology,* vol. I, p. 422.

28 Muller, Max, *A History of Ancient Sanskrit Literature* (London, Williams & Norgate, 1889), p. 533. See also 2nd edn (Allahabad, Panini, 1912), p. 275.

29 Weber, Max, *The Religion of India* (New York, Free Press, 1962), pp. 318–28.

30 Maine, H. S., *Dissertations on Early Law and Customs* (London, John Murray, 1883), p. 85.
31 Duncker, Max, *History of Antiquity,* vol. IV (London, Richard Bentley, 1880), p. 252.
32 Sangermano, F., *A Description of the Burmese Empire* (Rangoon, Government Press, 1885), p. 53.
33 Mitra, Rajendralala, *Indo-Aryans* (Calcutta, Newman, 1881), p. 423.
34 Sherring, M. A., 'The Natural History of Hindu Caste', in *Calcutta Review,* vol. LXXI (1880), p. 33.
35 Spencer, Herbert, *Principles of Sociology,* vol. III, p. 153.
36 McLennan, J. F., *Primitive Marriage* (Edinburgh, A. & C. Black, 1865), pp. 184–5.
37 Duncker, Max, *History of Antiquity,* vol. iv, pp. 264–5.
38 Spencer, Herbert, *Principles of Sociology,* vol. I, p. 701.
39 Maine, H. S., *Early Institution* (London, John Murray, 1875), pp. 99–100.
40 Ghosh, J. C., 'Caste in India', in *Calcutta Review,* vol. LXXI (1880).
41 *The Laws of Manu,* trans. G. Buhle, vol VIII (Oxford, Clarendon Press, 1886), p. 416.
42 Nelson, H. H., *A View of the Hindu Law* (Madras, Higginbotham, 1877), pp. 56–7.
43 Mommsen, T., *History of Rome,* vol. I (London, Macmillan, 1868), p. 71.
44 Maine, H. S., *Dissertations on Early Law and Customs,* p. 264.
45 Ghosh, J. C., 'The Village Community of Bengal and Upper India', in *Calcutta Review,* vol. LXXIV (1882).
46 See Kapadia, K. M., *Marriage and Family in India* (Bombay: Oxford University Press, 1966), pp. 52–86.
47 Dutt, R. C., *History of Civilization in Ancient India,* vol. III (London, Thacker, Spink, 1889), p. 75.
48 Spencer, Herbert, *Principles of Sociology,* vol. II, p. 467.
49 Ghosh, J. C., 'Caste in India', in *Calcutta Review,* vol. LXXI (1880).
50 Strabo, *Geography* (London, Bohn's Series, 1848), p. xv.
51 Ghosh, J. C., 'The Village Community of Bengal and Upper India', p. 15.
52 Elphinstone, M., *History of India* (London, John Murray, 1874), pp. 71–2.
53 Maine, H. S., *Village Communities in East and West* (London, John Murray, 1871), pp. 176–7.
54 Ibid., pp. 127–8.
55 Ibid., pp. 20, 41.
56 Ibid., pp. 125–6.
57 Spencer, Herbert, *Principles of Sociology,* vol. III, p. 436.
58 For details see Mookerji, R. K., *Local Government in Ancient India* (London, Oxford University Press, 1920).
59 Metz, F., *Tribes Inhabiting the Neilgherry Hills,* (Mangalore, 1864), pp. 17–18.
60 Maine, H. S., *Ancient Law* (London, John Murray, 1861), p. 18.
61 Maine, H. S., *Dissertations on Early Law and Customs,* p. 55.

62 Hunter, W. A., *Introduction to Roman Law* (London, Sweet & Maxwell, 1880), p. 149.

63 Dutt, R. C., *History of Civilization in Ancient India,* vol. III, p. 388.

64 Wise, T. A., *Review of the History of Medicine,* 2 vols (London, Churchill, 1867), vol. I, p. 25.

65 Hunter, W. W., *The Indian Empire* (London, Smith Elder, 1893), p. 149.

66 Dutt, R. C., *History of Civilization in Ancient India,* vol. III, p. 393.

67 Weber, Albrecht, *The History of Indian Literature* (London, Trubner, 1878), p. 269.

68 Ibid., p. 29.

69 Thibaut, G., 'On the S'ulvasutras', in *Journal of the Asiatic Society,* Bengal (1875), vol. XLIV, p. 227.

70 Dutt, R. C., *History of Civilization in Ancient India* vol. II, (1893), p. 127. 127.

71 Ibid., vol. I (1891), pp. 264–5.

72 Hunter, W. W., *The Indian Empire,* p. 142.

73 Dutt, R. C., *History of Civilization in Ancient India,* vol. II, p. 163.

74 Ibid., vol. II, p. 96.

75 Ibid., vol. I, pp. 248–9.

76 Manning, (Mrs) Speir, *Ancient and Medieval India* (London, W. H. Allen, 1869), vol. I, p. 416.

77 Hunter, W. W., *The Indian Empire,* p. 154.

78 Tennent, J. E., *Ceylon—an account of the Island,* vol. I (London, Longmans, 1859), p. 476.

79 Dutt, R. C., *History of Civilization in Ancient India,* vol. II, p. 333.

80 Spencer, Herbert, *Principles of Sociology,* vol. II, p. 252.

81 Ibid., p. 252.

82 Ibid., p. 278.

83 Spencer, Herbert, *Social Statics* (London, Williams & Norgate, 1850), p. 390.

84 Spencer, Herbert, *Principles of Sociology,* vol. III, p. 572.

85 Ibid., vol. III, p. 575.

86 For a lucid analysis of their comparative views see Professor S. L. Andreski's 'Introduction', in *Herbert Spencer: Principles of Sociology,* pp. ix–xxxvi.

3 Max Weber (1864–1920) on general characteristics of Indian society

1 Parsons, Talcott (ed.), *Max Weber: Theory of Social and Economic Organization* (trans. Henderson, A. M. and Parsons, Talcott) (Chicago, Free Press, 1947), p. 1.

2 Roth, G., 'Introduction' in Roth, G. and Whittich C., (eds.), *Max Weber's Economy and Society* (New York, Bedminster Press, 1968), p. xxxiv. The exact titles of the theses were 'The History of Trading Companies During the Middle Ages' and 'Roman Agrarian History in Its Bearing on Public and Private Law'.

3 *Verhandlungen der ersten Deustchen Soziologentages,* p. 101. Also see Roth, G., 'Introduction', p. lxiv.

4 Roth, G., 'Introduction', p. lviii.

5   Weber, Max, *The Sociology of Religion* (trans. E. Fischoff) (London, Methuen, 1965), p. 282.

6   Roth, G., and Wittich, C., *Max Weber's Economy and Society*, p. 340.

7   Ibid., p. 333.

8   Ibid., p. 316.

9   Roth, G., 'Introduction', p. lxxxii.

10 Ibid., p. xxix.

11 It may be mentioned here that this work has been prepared from his lectures which he delivered in 1919–20 on the request of his students and which were reconstructed from students' notes. These lectures were delivered under the title 'Outlines of Universal Social and Economic History'. No manuscripts or even coherent outlines by Weber himself were available. There was found in his papers only a bundle of sheets with notes, little more than catch words, as at that time his interest was entirely centred on the great sociological labours which he had taken up. See Roth, G., and Wittich, C., *Max Weber's Economy and Society* (1968), p. lviii, and Weber, Max, *General Economic History* (London, Allen & Unwin, 1927), p. xviii.

12 Roth, G., and Wittich, C., *Max Weber's Economy and Society*, pp. lxxi–lxxiv.

13 The exact title of this introductory essay was 'The Economic Ethic of the World Religions, Comparative Essays in the Sociology of Religion, Introduction'.

14 Weber, Max, *Protestant Ethic and the Spirit of Capitalism* (trans. Talcott Parsons) (London, Allen & Unwin, 1930), 'Introduction', pp. 24–5.

15 Ibid., p. 26.

16 Tawney, R. H., in Max Weber's *Protestant Ethic and the Spirit of Capitalism*, Foreword, pp. 1–3.

17 Parsons, Talcott, *Max Weber*, p. 27.

18 In addition he had done work on Islam, early Christianity and Talmudic Judaism, but they were not yet in a condition fit for publication in any form.

19 Roth, G., and Wittich, C., *Max Weber's Economy and Society*, p. 357.

20 Weber, Max, *General Economic History*, p. 3.

21 Ibid., p. 34. Here Weber points out that it is not these arrangements which explain the stability of Indian conditions as Marx affirms but rather the caste system.

22 Roth, G., and Wittich, C., *Max Weber's Economy and Society*, p. 261.

23 Weber, Max, *General Economic History*, p. 84.

24 Roth, G., and Wittich, C., *Max Weber's Economy and Society*, p. 195.

25 For details see Madan, G. R., *Indian Social Problems*, vol. II (Calcutta, Allied Publishers, 1973, 2nd edn), pp. 269–71.

26 It may be mentioned here that Weber makes no reference to bureaucracy in India in the chapter on bureaucracy or the city in *Economy and Society*. He makes reference to bureaucracy in India only in *General Economic History* as referred above.

27 Weber, Max, *General Economic History*, p. 40.

28 Madan, G. R., *Indian Social Problems*, vol. I (Calcutta, Allied Publishers, 1969, 2nd edn), p. 212.

29   Weber, Max, *General Economic History,* p. 123. Also see Baden-Powell, B.H., *The Land Systems of British India* (3 vols) (London: Oxford University Press, 1892).
30   Weber, Max, *General Economic History,* p. 175.
31   Ibid., p. 207.
32   Ibid., pp. 275–80 and 354–6.
33   Roth, G., and Wittich, C., *Max Weber's Economy and Society,* p. 792.
34   Ibid., p. 816.
35   In Hindu law, the house priest of the king is a member of his law court. All important cases have to come before the king's court. The unity of the secular and religious administration of justice is thus guaranteed and there is, therefore, no place for any licensed class of responding legal *honoratiores.*
36   See Weber, Max, *Economy and Society,* vol. III, p. 1221.
37   On the guild-*shreshth* (or *sheth*) of Ahmedabad in Gujrat, India, see Hopkins, E. Washburn, 'Ancient and Modern Hindu Guilds' in his *India Old and New* (New York, Scribner's, 1901), pp. 169ff, esp. 178f. See also Weber, Max, *The Religion of India—The Sociology of Hinduism and Buddhism* (trans. and ed. H. H. Gerth and D. Martindale (Chicago, Free Press, 1958), pp. 51, 87, 90, 107. On the council of the elephant-supplying notables in Vaicali, see *The Religion of India,* p. 89.
38   Weber, Max, *Economy and Society,* pp. 1252–3.
39   Weber, Max, *General Economic History,* p. 354.
40   Weber, Max, *Gesammelte Aufsatze zur Religioussoziologie,* 3 vols (Tubingen, Mohr, 1920–1), vol. I, pp. 63ff, 163ff, 207ff. Also see chapter 8.
41   Ibid., vol. I, pp. 181ff, note 2.
42   See chapter 8, p. 248.

4   The Hindu social system

1   Weber, Max, *The Religion of India—The Sociology of Hinduism and Buddhism* (trans, and ed. H. H. Gerth and Don Martindale) (Chicago, Free Press, 1958), p. 1.
2   Ibid., p. 4. Some of the other factors have already been discussed in the last chapter and to these he refers in this book too.
3   Weber, Max, *The Religion of India,* p. 10.
4   Ibid., p. 16.
5   Ibid., p. 25.
6   Dasgupta, Surma, *Development of Moral Philosophy in India* (Calcutta, Orient Longmans, 1961), pp. 14–15. However, Weber considers these universal ethic principles as colourless as he discusses these later on, and not positive ones conducive to better worldly life as were Protestant ethics. For the first point see chapter 5, p. 143 and for the second chapter 8.
7   There are castes among the Mohammedans of India, taken over from the Hindus. And castes are also found among the Buddhists. Even the Indian Christians have not quite been able to withhold themselves from practical recognition of the castes. These non-Hindu castes have

lacked the tremendous emphasis that the Hindu doctrine of salvation placed upon the caste, as we shall see later, and they have lacked a further characteristic, namely, the determination of the social rank of the castes by the social distance from other Hindu castes, and therewith, ultimately, from the brahman. This is decisive for the connection between Hindu castes and the brahman, a rank position is determined by the nature of its positive or negative relation to the brahman.

8   Weber, Max, *The Religion of India*, p. 55.
9   According to legend the old kshatriyas were wiped off the face of the earth, in vengeance for their enmity towards the brahmans. There is certainly a grain of truth in this as there is in the legend of the struggle of Vicvamithra's against Vaishtha. Ibid., p. 65.
10   Ibid., p. 103.
11   Ibid., p. 118.
12   Ibid., p. 122.
13   Ibid., p. 131.
14   Madan, G. R., *Economic Thinking in India* (New Delhi, Chand, 1966), p. 268.

5   The main characteristics of Hinduism in early times

1   Schroder, V., *Mysterium und Mimus in Regveda* (1908). See also Weber, Max, *The Religion of India* (Chicago, Free Press, 1958), p. 137.
2   See p. 148.
3   For instance B. K. Sarkar in *The Sacred Books of the Hindus* (ed. B. D. Basu) (Allahabad, the Panini Office, Bhuvaneswari Asrama, 1914), vols XIII and XVI, translated under the title *The Positive Background of Hindu Sociology*, commentaries with an appendix by Brajendra Nath Seal, points out that Sukraniti was quite characteristically conceived as 'organic social science' somewhat in the way Comte comprehended the steps of social science knowledge. However, this was completely unscientific 'organismic' systematics of the so-called positivism. Similarly, in mechanics all remained on a pre-Galilean level. In minerology Indian science remained essentially at the seven metal doctrine which was also known in the occident. (For further details see Max Weber *The Religion of India*, pp. 357–8.)
4   It may be mentioned here that though he deals with asceticism and mysticism, yet it merges into gnosis and yoga techniques, which he discusses later on. All these aspects cannot be separated from each other.
5   At this time there was also the flowering of Hellenic and Chinese philosophy and some borrowing was possible.
6   The Quakers are a sect of Christians known for their quiet manner.
7   In this case, it is the Samkhya philosophy.
8   *Brihadaranyaka Upanishad*, trans. E. Roer, under title *Bibliotheca Indica* (Calcutta, Asiatic Society of Bengal, 1856), vol. 2.
9   Ibid., p. 179.
10   See Hopkins, E. W., *Religion of India* (London, Ginn, 1895).

11 *Bhagavadgita* (Leipzig, 1901 edn), chapter XVIII, 4. See also edition
   translated by J. D. Goyandka (Gorakhpur, Gita Press, 1943).
12 Ibid., (Leipzig edn), ch. XVII, 5.
13 Ibid., ch. VI, 46.
14 Ibid., ch. V, 27.
15 Ibid., ch. XVI, 21.
16 Ibid., ch. XVI, 22.
17 Ibid., ch. XVIII, 66.
18 Ibid., ch. XIII, 13.
19 Ibid., ch. III, 26.
20 Professor Barth designates this religion as Brahmanism, the religion
   of the brahmans. He points out that Buddhism and Jainism, very
   different from it, broke off first. The others, the different forms of
   Vishnuism and Shivaism, were adopted by them and flourished under
   their guidance, but never belonged to them to such an extent that they
   could not dispense with their services. Many of them adopted,
   alongside their own doctrines, religious beliefs of different origins,
   and we shall notice later on some of the religious forms due to these
   compromises. In their theoretical studies, however, they were conformable to their traditional customs and their ancient literature. This is
   not only among the Mimamsists who were tradition incarnate, but
   even among the Vedantists who had very many more points of affinity
   with all the innovations. When Patanjali, the reputed author of the
   Yoga-Sutras, pleads in the introduction to his *Mahabhashya* (in 200
   B.C.) the claims of grammatical studies, he takes up the same ground
   as the ancient Yaska, that of the Vedic exegesis. Cankara in the eighth
   century and Sayana in the fourteenth were Vaishnavas, though of this
   there is not much evidence when they comment, the one on the
   Vedanta-Sutras and the Upanishads and the other on the whole of the
   great Vedic collections. In the philosophical treatises, a conspicuous
   element is polemic against the different doctrines of the sects, but it is
   one which is strictly scholastic. With the art of writing becoming
   general, attempts were made by some sects to reproduce some
   literature of general interest (e.g. some Upanishads adapted to
   common intelligence, old epic and legendary collections, the ancient
   Itihas and the ancient Puranas etc.). The cultus of the new religions was
   never more than a, special devotion, a rendering of a system of acts of
   homage, a *puja* which was radically different from the *yajna*, the
   sacrifice of tradition. The *dana,* i.e. making of presents to brahmans,
   became more meritorious than sacrifice. The observances, such as
   pilgrimages, ablutions in the Ganges, etc., were now held in high
   esteem (see Barth, A., *The religions of India,* (London, Kegan Paul,
   Trench, Trubner, 1891), pp. 87–97).
21 The Sutras are divided into three categories, Sruata-Sutras, Grhya-
   Sutras and Dharma-Sutras (known as Dharma-Castras). The first
   comes under Sruti and the other two under Smriti. According to some
   scholars the whole body of Vedic works composed in the Sutra style
   can be divided into six categories called Vedangas. These are *siksa,* or
   phonetics; *chandas,* or metre; *vyakarna,* or grammar; *nirukta,* or

etymology; *kalpa*, or religious practice; and *jyotisa*, or astronomy. The first four were meant as aids to the correct reciting and understanding of the sacred texts; the last two deal with religious rites and duties, and their proper seasons. See Macdonell, Arthur A., *A History of Sanskrit Literature* (Delhi, Munshi Ram, Maaohar Lal, 1899, 1971), chapters II and IX.

22　The *purusha* seated in the heart occurs in *Rig-Veda-Samhita*, ed. Max Muller, 6 vols (London, Oxford University Press, 1849–74), X, 90, 1. See also *Die Hymnen des Rigveda*, ed. Theodor Aufrecht (Bonn, Marcus, 1877). Compare *Athar-Veda Samhita*, ed. R. Roth and W. D. Whitney (1855–6), X, 8, 43.

23　Barth, A., *The Religions of India*, pp. 71–3.

24　Ibid., p. 83.

25　Barth points out that almost all ancient religious literature was esoteric, or became so at length. No profane person would have been able to read a Sutra, though gradually some of the Upanishads, particularly the smaller ones, were adapted to the common intelligence. At a later stage the Dharma-Castras, or codes of laws, such as those of Manu, of Yajnavalkya, and others, were drawn up, without any sectarian admixture. They laid emphasis on the role of Brahma, the creator, the father of gods and men, a figure majestic indeed, unknown to the ancient cult. Through this eclectic and monotheistic tendency the recognition of a personal God and a divine providence became by degrees a settled dogma.

26　*Rig-Veda*, ed. Muller, I, 104, 6; 108, 6; II, 26, 3; X, 151.

27　See Barth, A., *The Religions of India*, p. 32.

28　*Rig-Veda*, ed. Muller, II, 12, 5; VIII, 100, 3, 4.

29　Taittir Samh., vi, 1, 1, 1 (this is part of Vajur Veda which is divided into two main parts: the White Yajus and the Black Yajus. Taittiriya Samhita is part of Black Yajus. See *Die Taittiriya-Samhita herausgegeben von A. Weber* (1871–72) forming vols. xi and xii of the *Indische Studien*); Katha Up., i, 1, 20 (see several Upanishads published under the title *Bibliotheca Indica*, Collection of Oriental Works (ed.) Dr E. Roer, Calcutta: Asiatic Society of Bengal, 1856–60).

30　Nirukta, i, 15, 16 (see *Yaska's Nirukta*, (ed.) K. K. Rajavade, Poona: Bhandarkar Oriental Research Institute, 1940).

31　Expecially those who deny a future life. Compare the eloquent passage directed against them—Bhagavad-Gita, XVI, 6. (*Miscellaneous Essays* by H. T. Colebrooke, new edn with notes by E. B. Cowell, 2 vols (London: Trubner & Co., 1873), vol. I, p. 456).

32　Barth, A., *The Religions of India*, p. 85. Sayana has devoted to the Carvakas the first chapter of his Sarvadarcanasangraha; the greatest part of this chapter will be found, as translated by Cowell, in his edition of *Colebrooke's Miscellaneous Essays* vol. I, p. 456. The false Science of Brihaspati is denounced. Maitrayana Up. (*Bibliotheca Indica*, Calcutta: Asiatic Society of Bengal, 1856–60), vii, 9.

6　Jainism and Buddhism in India

1　See Kalp-Sutra in *Sacred Books of the East*, trans. H. Jacobi

(London, Oxford University Press, 1884), vol. 22, 138ff. It may be mentioned here that according to Jainism there are five degrees of knowledge that lead to omniscience. These were the Mati-Jnana, Sruta-Jnana, Avadhi-Jnana, Manah-paryaya-Jnana (by which one can know the thoughts of all sentient beings of five senses) and Kevala-Jnana (or omniscience) (see Stevenson, S., *The Heart of Jainism* (London, Oxford University Press, 1915), pp. 32–3).

2 Weber, Max, *The Religion of India* (Chicago, Free Press, 1958), p. 195.

3 Balfour, E. (ed.), *Cyclopaedia of India,* vol. II, s.v. 'Jain' (Madras, Higginbotham, 1857–8), p. 403. This is no longer the case.

. 4 See p. 160.

5 See Smith, V. A., *Ashoka* (London, Oxford University Press, 1901).

6 Rock Edict, no. VI. See also Smith, V. A., *Ashoka,* ch. 1 and p. 164.

7 Rock Edict, no. IX. See also Smith, V. A., *Ashoka,* ch. 1 and p. 167.

8 St Julien, *Sung Yun,* p. 197.

9 Ibid., p. 111.

10 See Jacobi, H., 'Introduction', in *Sacred Books of the East* (ed. Max Muller), vol. 22 (London, Oxford University Press, 1884), p. xxiii.

11 See Stevenson, S., *The Heart of Jainism*. Also see Barth, A., *The Religions of India* (London, Kegan Paul, Trench, Trubner, 1891), p. 142.

12 Ibid., p. 144.

13 Ibid., p. 151.

14 There are twelve vows for the Jain laity which are divided into three categories. The first five, i.e. *ahimsa, asatya tyaga* (truthfulness), *asteya, brahmacarya* and *aparigraha* are known as *anuvrata*. (They are for both the ascetics and the laity), followed by three *gunavrata* which help the keeping of the first five vows. These include self-restriction on one's travels, a limit on the number of things one may use and not harming anyone (not to think evil of anyone). The remaining four are known as *siksavrata* and are related to meditation (increasing the time of meditation gradually), control of body and mind, taking to fasts and limiting the use of clothes to two or three on one's body like an ascetic and, finally, to give to *sramana* in charity any of the fourteen things, i.e. food, drink, fruit, etc., which he may need.

Besides these twelve vows which help the laity in climbing the fourteen steps to attain *moksha* there are eleven *pratimas*, which lead the laity gently on towards the point when they will be able to take the five great vows of the ascetic. By the first, a layman undertakes to worship the true *deva* (i.e. a *tirthankara*), to reverence a true guru and to believe in the true *dharma* (i.e. Jainism). By the second *pratima* he promises to keep each of the twelve vows, and when death comes to receive it in absolute peace (*samadhi marana*). By the third *pratima* he vows that he will engage in meditation (*samayika*) at least three times a day (forty-eight minutes each time). By the fourth *pratima* he vows that he will observe *posadha* (fast) at least six times a month. By the fifth he promises to avoid all uncooked vegetables (to avoid taking vegetable life). By the sixth *pratima* he promises never to eat between sunset and sunrise lest in the darkness he might unwillingly devour some insects. By the seventh he promises to observe *brahmacarya* and to keep away from the society of his own wife. By the eighth *pratima* he promises not to begin anything that might entangle him in worldly pursuits or involve the destruction of life. So he undertakes not to build a house or take a trade (like a blacksmith's) which entails the taking of life. By the ninth *pratima* he hands over all his property to his children or gives it to charity. By the tenth *pratima* he promises to keep the *sadhu* rule of never allowing any special cooking to be done for him. By the eleventh and last *pratima* he becomes practically a monk, for he has promised to wear a *sadhu*'s dress, to live apart in some religious building, or in the jungle and to act according to the rules laid down in the scriptures for the *sadhus*.

15 Stevenson, S., *The Heart of Jainism*, p. 234.
16 *Kasaya* means anger, pride, deceit and greed.
17 Stevenson, S., *The Heart of Jainism*, p. 239.
18 See Gard, R. A. (ed.), *Buddhism* (London, Prentice-Hall International, 1961), p. 128.
19 Barth, A., *The Religions of India*, pp. 117–18.
20 Ibid., pp. 118–19.
21 Gard, R. A., *Buddhism*, p. 67.
22 Ibid., pp. 152–3. *Digha-Nikaya* (London, Pali Text Society, 1890–1911), 3 vols (vol. III, p. 220).
23 Barth, A., *The Religions of India*, pp. 138–9.
24 Gard, R. A., *Buddhism*, p. 132.
25 Ibid., p. 135. Also see Rhys Davids, T. W. and C.A.F. (trans.), *Dialogues of the Buddha* (London, Pali Text Society, 1952), pp. 343–5.
26 Gard, R. A., *Buddhism*, p. 141. There are a number of schools in Buddhism in the two main traditions i.e. Mahayana and Hinayana. In the latter alone there are eighteen schools including the Theraveda (Ceylon), where as Mahasaṅghika, Sarvastivada Sautrantika and Vajrayana (Tibet) come under Mahayana traditions. For details see pp. 22–30 of the same book.
27 Ibid., pp. 143–4.
28 Ibid., p. 148.
29 See p. 192.
30 Gard, R. A., *Buddhism*, p. 242.

7 Hinduism in the Middle Ages and after

1 Weber, Max, *The Religion of India* (Chicago, Free Press, 1958), p. 293.
2 Even in the epics the types of officially accepted conjuring and animist practice greatly developed. Sympathetic and symbolic conjuring which approaches fetishism, spirits of holy rivers, ponds and mountains, word formulae and finger-pointing magic and writing magic, all these appear.
3 See Grierson, G. A., 'The Modern Hindu Doctrine of Works', *Journal of the Royal Asiatic Society* (London, 1908), vol. 40, p. 337.

4   So according to the Indologist G. A. Grierson. See also Blunt, E. A.
    H., *Census of India 1911*, vol. XV *United Provinces of Agra and Oudh*
    (Allahabad, Government Press, 1915), Introduction.
5   See Liebich, *Sanskrit-Lehrbuch* (Leipzig, 1905), p. 265, nos 41, 42.
    Also see Max Weber, *The Religion of India,* p. 387.
6   Barth, A., *The Religions of India* (London, Kegan Paul, Trench,
    Trubner, 1891, 1969), pp. 90–6.
7   Varadachari, V., *A History of Samskrta Literature* (Allahabad, Ram
    Narain Lal, 1952), p. 242.
8   Ibid., p. 243.
9   Ibid., p. 257.

8   General characteristics of Indian religion and other conclusions

1   Weber, Max, *Economy and Society* (New York, Bedminster Press,
    1968), p. 466.
2   Oldenberg, H., *Die Religion der Veda* (Berlin, Von Wilhelm Hertz,
    1894), 4th edn (1923).
3   Weber, *Economy and Society,* p. 525.
4   Ibid., pp. 526–7.
5   Ibid., p. 528.
6   Ibid., p. 551.
7   Ibid., p. 542.
8   Ibid., p. 544.
9   Ibid., p. 547.
10 Weber, Max, *The Religion of India* (Chicago, Free Press, 1958), p.
    334.
11 Ibid., p. 334.
12 Weber, Max, *Economy and Society,* p. 557.
13 Ibid., p. 559.
14 Ibid., p. 571.
15 Weber, Max, *The Religion of India,* p. 335.
16 Ibid., p. 399.
17 Ibid., p. 336. Also see chapter 4, p. 120.
18 Weber, Max, *Economy and Society,* p. 627.
19 Ibid., p. 629.
20 See Weber, Max, *The Protestant Ethic and the Spirit of Capitalism*
    (trans. Talcott Parsons), (London, Allen & Unwin, 1930), p. 157.
21 Baxter, R., *Saints' Everlasting Rest* (Liverpool, Nuttall, Fisher &
    Piron, 1809), chapter X, 1, 9 (par. 24). Also see Max Weber,
    Protestant Ethic, p. 162.
22 Weber, Max, *Protestant Ethic,* p. 175.
23 Ibid., p. 182.
24 Weber, Max, *Religion of India,* p. 337.
25 See pp. 83 and 90.
26 See Prabhu, P. N., *Hindu Social Organization* (Bombay, Popular
    Prakashan, 1963), pp. 73–100.
27 Dutt, R. C., *Economic History of India under Early British Rule*
    (London, Kegan Paul, Trench, Trubner, 1961), vol. I, pp. viii to xi.

Also see Madan, G. R., *Economic Thinking in India* (New Delhi, Chand, 1966), pp. 67–8.

28 See chapter 11.
29 Tawney, R. H., 'Foreword' in Weber, Max, *The Protestant Ethic,* pp. 8–10.
30 Loomis, C. P., and Loomis, Z. K. (eds), *Socio-Economic Change and the Religious Factor in India—An Indian Symposium of Views on Max Weber* (New Delhi, Affiliated East-West Press, 1969), pp. 16–18.
31 Mukherjee, R. K., *The Dynamics of a Rural Society* (Berlin, Akademie-Verlag, 1957), p. 82.
32 See chapter 3, p. 91.

9 Emile Durkheim (1858–1917)

1 Kardiner, A. and Preble, E., *They Studied Man* (London, Secker & Warburg, 1962), p. 109.
2 Alpert, H., *Emile Durkheim and His Sociology* (New York, Columbia University Press, 1939), pp. 52–3.
3 Kardiner, A. and Preble, E., *They Studied Man,* p. 111.
4 Aron, Raymond, *The Main Currents in Sociological Thought* (London, Weidenfeld & Nicolson, 1965), p. 16.
5 Durkheim, E., *The Division of Labor in Society* (Chicago, Free Press, 1939), p. 130.
6 Lebon, G., *Les Sociétés* (Paris, Société, 1881), p. 193. Also see Durkheim, E., *The Division of Labor,* p. 134.
7 Topinard, P., *Anthropologie* (Paris, Reinwald, 1884), p. 343. Also see Durkheim, E., *The Division of Labor,* p. 134.
8 Kardiner, A. and Preble, E., *They Studied Man,* p. 120.
9 The restitutive sanction is not expiatory (i.e. paying the penalty of, making amend for sin), but consists of a simple return in state. Suffering proportionate to the misdeed is not inflicted on the one who has violated the law or who disregards it; he is simply sentenced to comply with it. If certain things were done, the judge reinstates them as they would have been. He speaks of law; he says nothing of punishment. Damage-interests have no penal character. However, sometimes there is a sort of civil penalty in the payment of costs by the defeated party.
10 Loiseleur- Deslongchamps, *Lois de Manou* (Paris, 1840), vol. VIII, v. 303–11. Also see Durkheim, E., *The Division of Labor,* pp. 91–2.
11 Lubbock, J., *Les Origines de la civilisation* (Paris, Ballière, 1872), p. 440. Also see Durkheim, E., *The Division of Labor,* p. 138.
12 Durkheim, E., *The Division of Labor,* p. 141. Also see Loiseleur-Deslongchamps, *Lois de Manou,* VII, v. 14–24.
13 Durkheim, E., *The Division of Labor,* p. 308. Also see Ribot, L., *Herédité* (Paris, Balliere, 1882), 2nd edn, p. 360.
14 Loiseleur- Deslongchamps, *Lois de Manou,* I, 87–91.
15 Kardiner, A. and Preble, E., *They Studied Man,* p. 123.
16 Siloius Halicus, *Punica,* 1, 225 and ff. Also see Durkheim, E.,

Suicide—A study in Sociology (London, Routledge & Kegan Paul, 1952), p. 218.

17 Plutarch, *Life of Alexander,* trans. J. Dryden (New York, The Modern Library), CXIII, pp. 849–50. Also see Durkheim, E., *Suicide,* p. 218.

18 Durkheim, E., *Suicide,* p. 218.

19 Loiseleur-Deslongchamps, *Louis de Manou,* VI, 32. Also see Durkheim, E., *Suicide,* p. 223.

20 Barth, A., *The Religions of India* (London, Kegan Paul, Trench, Trubner, 1891), p. 146.

21 Bühler, Johann Georg, *Über die Indische Sects der Jaina* (Vienna, Imperial Academy of Sciences, 1887), pp. 10, 19 and 37.

22 Heber, *Narrative of a Journey through the Upper Provinces of India* (London, John Murray, 1828), vol. I, ch. XII.

23 Forsyth, J., *The Highlands of Central India* (London, Chapman & Hall, 1871), pp. 172–5. Also see Durkheim, E., *Suicide,* p. 224.

24 Stirling, *Asiatic Studies,* vol. XV, p. 324. Also see Durkheim, E., *Suicide,* p. 224.

25 Charlevoix, P. F., *Histoire du Japan* (Paris, Gandouin, 1736), vol. II. Durkheim, E., *Suicide,* p. 225.

26 Durkheim, E., *Suicide,* p. 227.

27 Eliot, C. *Hinduism and Buddhism,* vol. I (London, Ed. Arnold, 1921), p. 72.

28 Durkheim, E., *The Elementary Forms of the Religious Life* (trans. Swain, J. S.), (London, Allen & Unwin, 1905), p. 47.

29 Kardiner, A. and Preble, E., *They Studied Man,* p. 127.

30 Ibid., p. 129.

31 Muller, Max, *Introduction to the Science of Religion* (London, Longmans, 1897), p. 18.

32 Tylor, Edward B., *Primitive Culture* (London, John Murray, 4th edn, 1903), p. 424.

33 Burnouf, Par E., *Introduction a l'histoire du Bouddhisme indien* (Paris, Maisonneuve, 2nd edn 1876, p. 264.

34 Oldenberg, Hermann, *Buddha* (trans. Howey) (London, Humphreys, 1904), p. 53.

35 Barth, A., *The Religions of India,* p. 109.

36 Kern, H., *Histoire du bouddhisme dans l'inde,* vol. I (Haarlem, 1882–4), p. 289.

37 Burnouf, *Introduction,* p. 120.

38 Barth, A., *The Religions of India,* p. 146.

39 Ibid., p. 146.

40 Barth, A., in *Encyclopédie des sciences religieuses* (Paris, 1879), vol. VI, p. 548.

41 Oldenberg, *Buddha,* p. 53.

42 Bergaigne, A. H. J., *La religion Védique* (Paris, Vieweg, 1878), vol. 1, p. 122. Also see Durkheim, E., *The Elementary Forms,* p. 34.

43 Muller, Max, *Natural Religion* (London, Longmans, 1898), p. 114. Also see Durkheim, E., *The Elementary Forms,* p. 73.

44 Muller, Max, *Physical Religion* (London, Longmans, 1891), p. 120.

45 Oldenberg, H., *Die Religion des Vedas* (Berlin, Von Willhelm Hertz, 1894), pp. 59ff. Also see Durkheim, E., *Elementary Forms*, p. 79.
46 Durkheim, E., *Elementary Forms,* p. 299.
47 See 'Essai sur le Sacrifice', in *Mélanges d'histoire des Religions,* p. 83. Also see Durkheim, E., *Elementary Forms,* p. 385.
48 Durkheim, E., *Elementary Forms,* p. 415.

10 Vilfredo Pareto (1848–1923)

1 *Vilfredo Pareto, Sociological Writings,* selected and introduced by S. E. Finer (trans. D. Mirfin), (London, Pall Mall Press, 1966), 'Introduction', pp. 3–11.
2 See Pareto, V., *Mind and Society (Trattato di sociologia generale)*, volume I (London, Cape, 1935), p. xviii.
3 Ibid., p. 86.
4 Pareto, V., *The Mind and Society—a Treatise on General Sociology* (ed. and trans. A. Livingstone), (New York, Dover, 1963), art. 2065, p. 1434.
5 Finer, S. E., *Vilfredo Pareto, Sociological Writings,* p. 33.
6 Pareto, V., *A Treatise on General Sociology,* vol. IV, art. 2060, p. 1433.
7 Ibid., art. 2205, p. 1541.
8 Ibid., art. 2009, p. 1406.
9 Ibid., art. 798
10 Ibid., art. 832, p. 494.
11 Ibid., art. 183.
12 Philostratus, *Vita Apollonii,* III, 14 (New York, Loeb, 1912). Also Pareto, V., *Treatise,* vol. I, art. 194.
13 Polybius, *Historiae,* VI, 56, 8–12 (New York, Loeb, 1922–7), vol. III, p. 395. See also Pareto, V., *Treatise,* vol. I, art. 313.
14 Montesquieu, Charles de, *Dissertation sur la politique des Romains dans la religion* in *Oeuvres* (Paris, 1822), vol. V, p. 303. Pareto, V., *Treatise,* vol. I, art. 314.
15 Pareto, V., *Treatise,* art. 315.
16 *Annales du Musée Guimet,* vol. I, pp. 307–44. Also see Pareto, V., *Treatise,* vol. I, art. 394.
17 Pareto, V., *Treatise,* vol. I, art. 575.
18 Henry, *Le Parsisme* (Paris, 1908), p. 16. Also see Pareto, V., *Treatise,* vol. I, art. 587.
19 Oldenberg, *Die Religion des Veda* (Berlin, 1894), p. 338. See also Pareto, V., *Treatise,* art. 587
20 Sonnerat, *Voyage aux Indes Orientales* (Paris, L'auteur, 1872), vol. I, p. 92.
21 Ibid., p. 85. Also see Pareto, V., *Treatise,* art. 587.
22 Kern, Histoire du bouddhisme (Haarlem, 1882–4), vol. I, pp. 23–4.
23 Oldenberg, *Die Religion,* pp. 175–6, 181.
24 Griffith, T. H., *The hymns of the Rigveda* (Benares, Lazario, 1889–92), vol. III, p. 265. See also Pareto, V., *Treatiqe,* vol. II, art. 938.
25 Pareto, V., *Treatise,* art. 991.
26 Senart, E., *Les Castes dans l'Inde* (Paris, Leroux, 1896), pp. 94f. Also see Pareto, V., *Treatise,* art. 1025.

27 Pareto, V., *Treatise,* art. 1044.
28 Lyall, A. C., *Asiatic Studies, Religious and Social* (London, John Murray, 1882), pp. 7–9.
29 Ibid., p. 10.
30 Heber, R., *Narrative of a Journey through the Upper Provinces of India* (London, John Murray, 1882), vol. I, pp. 99–100, 110–11.
31 Sonnert, *Voyage,* vol. I, pp. 256–62.
32 Wood, Ernest, *Great Systems of Yoga* (New York, Philosophical Library, 1954), p. 24.
33 Kern, *Histoire du bouddhisme,* vol. II, pp. 3–5, 14–16.
34 Ibid., vol. II, pp. 3–5, 14–16.
35 Pliny, *Historia naturalis,* v. 17 (Bostock-Riley), vol. I, pp. 430–1. See also Pareto, V., *Treatise,* art. 1186.
36 Oldenberg, *Die Religion,* pp. 317–18.
37 Dubois, J. A., *Moeurs institutions et cĕrĕmonies des peuples de l'Inde* (Paris, Impremere Royale, 1825), vol. II, p. 257. Also see Pareto, V., *Treatise,* art. 1246.
38 Pareto, V., *Treatise,* art. 1260.
39 Loiseleur-Deslongchamps, *Lois de Manou,* in G. Panthier, *Les Livres sacrés de l'orient* (Paris, 1840), vol. V, 74–7 (p. 382).
40 Dubois, *Moeurs,* vol. II, pp. 245–52. Also see Pareto, V., *Treatise,* art. 1272.
41 Loiseleur-Deslongchamps, *Lois de Manou,* IX, 45f., pp. 422–56.
42 Dubois, *Moeurs,* vol. I, pp. 440–1. Also see Pareto, V., *Treatise,* art. 1330.
43 Dubois, *Moeurs, pp. 437–8.* Also see Pareto, V., *Treatise,* art. 1330.
44 Dubois, *Moeurs,* p. 438. Also see Pareto, V., *Treatise,* art. 1330.
45 Pareto, V., *Treatise,* art. 1680.

11 A retrospect

 1 Government of India *The Gazetteer of India* (New Delhu, Ministry of Information, 1965), vol. 1, p. 314.
 2 Ibid., ch. VIII, 'Religion', p. 414. Also see MacKay, E., *The Indus Civilization* (London, Lovat, Dickson & Thompson, 1935).
 3 *Gazetteer of India* (1965), p. 413.
 4 Ibid., p. 413.
 5 Brunton, Paul, 'Introduction' in Wood, E. E., *Practical Yoga Ancient and Modern* (New York, Philosophical Library, 1957), p. 10.
 6 Ibid., p. 9.
 7 Wood, E. E., *Great Systems of Yoga* (New York, Philosophical Library, 1953), p. 8.
 8 Ibid., p. 3.
 9 Ibid., p. 15.
10 Bhagwan Shree Patanjali, *Aphorisms of Yoga* (trans. Shree Purohat Swami), (London, Faber, 1938), book I, sutra 2.
11 Ibid., book I, sutra 12–16.
12 Wood, E. E., *Great Systems of Yoga,* p. 19.
13 Patanjali, *Aphorisms of Yoga,* book II, sutra 1.
14 Wood, E. E., *Great Systems of Yoga,* p. 27.

15 Patanjali, *Aphorisms of Yoga,* book II, sutra 29.
16 Jacobi, Hermann, *Jaina Sutras, The Sacred Books of the East* (London, Oxford University Press, 1884), vol. XXII, p. xxiv. Also see chapters 5 and 7 and chapter 10 where Weber and Pareto mention the rules of ascetics and yogis.
17 Ibid., p. xxx.
17 Ibid., p. xxx.
18 Ibid., p. xxx.
19 Wood, E. E., *Great Systems of Yoga,* p. 87. The Sanskrit works relating to Hatha-Yoga are Hatha-Yoga Pradipika, Shiva Sanhita, Gheranda Sanhita, Shandilya Upanishad, Yoga Kundali Upanishad, etc.
20 See p. 355.
21 For example, see Maine, Sir Henry, *Village Communities in the East and West* (London, John Murray, 1872); Baden-Powell, *Origin and Growth of Village Communities* (London, Swan Sonnenschein, 1899); Altekar, A. S., *A History of Village Communities in Western India* (Bombay, Oxford University Press, 1927); Mukerjee, R. K., *Democracies of the East* (London, King, 1923); Mukerjee, R. K., *Local Self Government in Ancient India* (London, Oxford University Press, 1920).
22 Maine, H. S., *Village Communities in the East and West,* pp. 171–7.
23 Ibid., pp. 127–8.
24 Ibid., pp. 125–6.
25 Letter Marx to Engels dated 14 June 1853. See Karl Marx and Frederick Engels, *Selected Correspondence* (Moscow, Foreign Languages Publishing House. 1953), p. 103.
26 See Madan, G. R., *Changing Pattern of Indian Villages* (New Delhi, Chand, 1964), pp. 451–2 and 478–9.
27 Dutt, R. C., *A History of Civilization in Ancient India Based on Sanskrit Literature,* vol. II (Delhi, Vishal, 1972), pp. 333–4.
28 For details about such impurities and ceremonies for purification see Dubois, Abbé J. A., *Hindu Manners, Customs and Ceremonies* (London, Oxford University Press, 1897).
29 See ch. 10, p. 309. Also see p. 328 of this chapter.
30 Singh, Daljit, *Guru Nanak* (Lahore, Lion Press, 1943), p. 29.
31 Ibid., p. 30.
32 Ibid., p. 28.
33 For details see Madan, G. R., *Indian Social Problems,* vol. II (Calcutta, Allied Publishers, 1973), pp. 71–3.

Index

Index

communistic household, 72
  husbandry, 75
Communities, 29
  ascetic, 76
  European, 17
  family, 13
  idyllic village, 13
  pastoral, 29
  primitive, 75
  tribal, 33, 40, 84
compassionate acosmic love, 172
Company, East India, 5, 6, 7
Company's Court of Directors, 7
Cornwallis, Lord, 17, 18
cosmos, 121
cosmic illusion (maya), 131, 144, 145
  semblance, 146
Coulanges, Fustel De, 259
Council of Geneva, 249
cow, killing of, 109, 331
  sacredness of, 109, 331
  worship of, 109
Craddha, 156
craft guilds, 46
Cravakas laity, 180
craya (daily rites), 222
Cruti, 144
cult:
  Bhakti, 207
  see also seets
Cunningham, A., 34
Curtius, Quintus, 268

Dacca, 11, 21
Daau Panthi, 211
Dahra, caves of, 58
Dakshina, 216
Dakshinacharas, 216
Dandi, 204, 209
Darwin, 260, 324
Darwinians, 324
Darwinism, 260, 288
dasa-sikkhapadani, 194, 195
dasa-sila, 195
Das Gupta, S., 108
Dayabhaga, 45
Deacons, sub-deacons, 40
deceptive magic of God (maya), 155
deities, 219
  functional, 140
  greater, 34
  local, 140
  provincial, 35
defilement, ritualistic, 84
Dekhan, 275

demiurgic, 74, 334
demon-worship, 37
derivations, 286, 287
despotism, Asiatic, 4
  European, 4
  machinery of, 4
  oriental, 13
destruction of hand industries, 10
De Tocqueville, 28
Devadasi, 82
development of,
  capitalist civilization 69
  economic rationalism, 68
  market capitalism, 78
  philosophy, 53, 130, 321, 339
  sciences, 52, 130, 131, 321, 339
  soteriology, 148
Devi, 201
Devis, 36
dhamapatakas, 136
Dharma, 129, 143, 148, 174, 204, 236,
    247, 327, 331
  books, 90, 327
  caste, 108
  castras (social order), 136, 220
  everyday, 331
  kaya, 182
  Kshtriya, 343
  of Buddha, 175
  of Hinduism, 109
  of protection, 130
  Sadharan, 109
  sangrah, 196
Dharma-Shastras, 90
  Sutras, 90, 127, 338
  universal, 331
  vashisha, 127
Dhimals, 29, 30, 332
Dhyana, 327; yoga, 156
difficulties in the growth of modern
    capitalism:
  absence of communes, 97; rational
    law, 89; rational spirit, 99;
    rationalistic economic ethics, 99
  caste exclusiveness, 97
  lack of military strength, in bourgeo-
    isie, 98
  lack of specific type cities, 92
  lack of specific type citizens, 92
Digambara, 160, 161, 186
directeurs de l'âme, 209
District boards, 5
Division of labour, 253, 256, 265–6, 285
Doctrine (mata), 108, 120
  of karma, 120

Routledge Social Science Series

Routledge & Kegan Paul   London, Henley and Boston

39 Store Street, London WC1E 7DD
Broadway House, Newtown Road,
Henley-on-Thames, Oxon RG9 1EN
9 Park Street, Boston, Mass. 02108

Contents

*Authors wishing to submit manuscripts for any series in
this catalogue should send them to the Social Science Editor,
Routledge & Kegan Paul Ltd, 39 Store Street,
London WC1E 7DD*

●*Books so marked are available in paperback
All books are in Metric Demy 8vo format (216 × 138mm approx.)*

International Library of Sociology

General Editor   John Rex

GENERAL SOCIOLOGY

Barnsley, J. H. The Social Reality of Ethics. *464 pp.*
Brown, Robert. Explanation in Social Science. *208 pp.*
● Rules and Laws in Sociology. *192 pp.*
Bruford, W. H. Chekhov and His Russia. *A Sociological Study. 244 pp.*
Burton, F. and **Carlen, P.** Official Discourse. *On Discourse Analysis, Government Publications, Ideology. About 140 pp.*
Cain, Maureen E. Society and the Policeman's Role. *326 pp.*
●**Fletcher, Colin.** Beneath the Surface. *An Account of Three Styles of Sociological Research. 221 pp.*
Gibson, Quentin. The Logic of Social Enquiry. *240 pp.*
Glucksmann, M. Structuralist Analysis in Contemporary Social Thought. *212 pp.*
Gurvitch, Georges. Sociology of Law. *Foreword by Roscoe Pound. 264 pp.*
Hinkle, R. Founding Theory of American Sociology 1883-1915. *About 350 pp.*
Homans, George C. Sentiments and Activities. *336 pp.*
Johnson, Harry M. Sociology: *a Systematic Introduction. Foreword by Robert K. Merton. 710 pp.*
●**Keat, Russell** and **Urry, John.** Social Theory as Science. *278 pp.*
Mannheim, Karl. Essays on Sociology and Social Psychology. *Edited by Paul Keckskemeti. With Editorial Note by Adolph Lowe. 344 pp.*
Martindale, Don. The Nature and Types of Sociological Theory. *292 pp.*
●**Maus, Heinz.** A Short History of Sociology. *234 pp.*
Myrdal, Gunnar. Value in Social Theory: *A Collection of Essays on Methodology. Edited by Paul Streeten. 332 pp.*
Ogburn, William F. and **Nimkoff, Meyer F.** A Handbook of Sociology. *Preface by Karl Mannheim. 656 pp. 46 figures. 35 tables.*
Parsons, Talcott, and **Smelser, Neil J.** Economy and Society: *A Study in the Integration of Economic and Social Theory. 362 pp.*
Podgórecki, Adam. Practical Social Sciences. *About 200 pp.*
Raffel, S. Matters of Fact. *A Sociological Inquiry. 152 pp.*
●**Rex, John.** (Ed.) Approaches to Sociology. *Contributions by Peter Abell,* Sociology and the Demystification of the Modern World. *282 pp.*
●**Rex, John** (Ed.) Approaches to Sociology. *Contributions by Peter Abell, Frank Bechhofer, Basil Bernstein, Ronald Fletcher, David Frisby, Miriam Glucksmann, Peter Lassman, Herminio Martins, John Rex, Roland Robertson, John Westergaard and Jock Young. 302 pp.*
Rigby, A. Alternative Realities. *352 pp.*
Roche, M. Phenomenology, Language and the Social Sciences. *374 pp.*
Sahay, A. Sociological Analysis. *220 pp.*

Strasser, Hermann. The Normative Structure of Sociology. *Conservative and Emancipatory Themes in Social Thought. About 340 pp.*

Strong, P. Ceremonial Order of the Clinic. *About 250 pp.*

Urry, John. Reference Groups and the Theory of Revolution. *244 pp.*

Weinberg, E. Development of Sociology in the Soviet Union. *173 pp.*

FOREIGN CLASSICS OF SOCIOLOGY

● **Gerth, H. H.** and **Mills, C. Wright.** From Max Weber: *Essays in Sociology. 502 pp.*

● **Tönnies, Ferdinand.** Community and Association. *(Gemeinschaft and Gesellschaft.) Translated and Supplemented by Charles P. Loomis. Foreword by Pitirim A. Sorokin. 334 pp.*

SOCIAL STRUCTURE

Andreski, Stanislav. Military Organization and Society. *Foreword by Professor A. R. Radcliffe-Brown. 226 pp. 1 folder.*

Carlton, Eric. Ideology and Social Order. *Foreword by Professor Philip Abrahams. About 320 pp.*

Coontz, Sydney H. Population Theories and the Economic Interpretation. *202 pp.*

Coser, Lewis. The Functions of Social Conflict. *204 pp.*

Dickie-Clark, H. F. Marginal Situation: *A Sociological Study of a Coloured Group. 240 pp. 11 tables.*

Giner, S. and **Archer, M. S.** (Eds.). Contemporary Europe. *Social Structures and Cultural Patterns. 336 pp.*

● **Glaser, Barney** and **Strauss, Anselm L.** Status Passage. *A Formal Theory. 212 pp.*

Glass, D. V. (Ed.) Social Mobility in Britain. *Contributions by J. Berent, T. Bottomore, R. C. Chambers, J. Floud, D. V. Glass, J. R. Hall, H. T. Himmelweit, R. K. Kelsall, F. M. Martin, C. A. Moser, R. Mukherjee, and W. Ziegel. 420 pp.*

Kelsall, R. K. Higher Civil Servants in Britain: *From 1870 to the Present Day. 268 pp. 31 tables.*

● **Lawton, Denis.** Social Class, Language and Education. *192 pp.*

McLeish, John. The Theory of Social Change: *Four Views Considered. 128 pp.*

● **Marsh, David C.** The Changing Social Structure of England and Wales, 1871-1961. *Revised edition. 288 pp.*

Menzies, Ken. Talcott Parsons and the Social Image of Man. *About 208 pp.*

● **Mouzelis, Nicos.** Organization and Bureaucracy. *An Analysis of Modern Theories. 240 pp.*

Ossowski, Stanislaw. Class Structure in the Social Consciousness. *210 pp.*

● **Podgórecki, Adam.** Law and Society. *302 pp.*

Renner, Karl. Institutions of Private Law and Their Social Functions. *Edited, with an Introduction and Notes, by O. Kahn-Freud. Translated by Agnes Schwarzschild. 316 pp.*

Rex, J. and **Tomlinson, S.** Colonial Immigrants in a British City. *A Class Analysis. 368 pp.*

Smooha, S. Israel: Pluralism and Conflict. *472 pp.*

Wesolowski, W. Class, Strata and Power. *Trans. and with Introduction by G. Kolankiewicz. 160 pp.*

Zureik, E. Palestinians in Israel. *A Study in Internal Colonialism. 264 pp.*

SOCIOLOGY AND POLITICS

Acton, T. A. Gypsy Politics and Social Change. *316 pp.*

Burton, F. Politics of Legitimacy. *Struggles in a Belfast Community. 250 pp.*

Etzioni-Halevy, E. Political Manipulation and Administrative Power. *A Comparative Study. About 200 pp.*

●**Hechter, Michael.** Internal Colonialism. *The Celtic Fringe in British National Development, 1536–1966. 380 pp.*

Kornhauser, William. The Politics of Mass Society. *272 pp. 20 tables.*

Korpi, W. The Working Class in Welfare Capitalism. *Work, Unions and Politics in Sweden. 472 pp.*

Kroes, R. Soldiers and Students. *A Study of Right- and Left-wing Students. 174 pp.*

Martin, Roderick. Sociology of Power. *About 272 pp.*

Myrdal, Gunnar. The Political Element in the Development of Economic Theory. *Translated from the German by Paul Streeten. 282 pp.*

Wong, S.-L. Sociology and Socialism in Contemporary China. *160 pp.*

Wootton, Graham. Workers, Unions and the State. *188 pp.*

CRIMINOLOGY

Ancel, Marc. Social Defence: *A Modern Approach to Criminal Problems. Foreword by Leon Radzinowicz. 240 pp.*

Athens, L. Violent Criminal Acts and Actors. *About 150 pp.*

Cain, Maureen E. Society and the Policeman's Role. *326 pp.*

Cloward, Richard A. and **Ohlin, Lloyd E.** Delinquency and Opportunity: *A Theory of Delinquent Gangs. 248 pp.*

Downes, David M. The Delinquent Solution. *A Study in Subcultural Theory. 296 pp.*

Friedlander, Kate. The Psycho-Analytical Approach to Juvenile Delinquency: *Theory, Case Studies, Treatment. 320 pp.*

Gleuck, Sheldon and **Eleanor.** Family Environment and Delinquency. *With the statistical assistance of Rose W. Kneznek. 340 pp.*

Lopez-Rey, Manuel. Crime. *An Analytical Appraisal. 288 pp.*

Mannheim, Hermann. Comparative Criminology: *a Text Book. Two volumes. 442 pp. and 380 pp.*

Morris, Terence. The Criminal Area: *A Study in Social Ecology. Foreword by Hermann Mannheim. 232 pp. 25 tables. 4 maps.*

Podgorecki, A. and **Łos, M.** *Multidimensional Sociology. About 380 pp.*

Rock, Paul. Making People Pay. *338 pp.*

● **Taylor, Ian, Walton, Paul,** and **Young, Jock.** The New Criminology. *For a Social Theory of Deviance. 325 pp.*

● **Taylor, Ian, Walton, Paul** and **Young, Jock.** (Eds) Critical Criminology. *268 pp.*

SOCIAL PSYCHOLOGY

Bagley, Christopher. The Social Psychology of the Epileptic Child. *320 pp.*

Brittan, Arthur. Meanings and Situations. *224 pp.*

Carroll, J. Break-Out from the Crystal Palace. *200 pp.*

● **Fleming, C. M.** Adolescence: Its Social Psychology. *With an Introduction to recent findings from the fields of Anthropology, Physiology, Medicine, Psychometrics and Sociometry. 288 pp.*

● The Social Psychology of Education: *An Introduction and Guide to Its Study. 136 pp.*

Linton, Ralph. The Cultural Background of Personality. *132 pp.*

● **Mayo, Elton.** The Social Problems of an Industrial Civilization. *With an Appendix on the Political Problem. 180 pp.*

Ottaway, A. K. C. Learning Through Group Experience. *176 pp.*

Plummer, Ken. Sexual Stigma. *An Interactionist Account. 254 pp.*

● **Rose, Arnold M.** (Ed.) Human Behaviour and Social Processes: *an Interactionist Approach. Contributions by Arnold M. Rose, Ralph H. Turner, Anselm Strauss, Everett C. Hughes, E. Franklin Frazier, Howard S. Becker et al. 696 pp.*

Smelser, Neil J. Theory of Collective Behaviour. *448 pp.*

Stephenson, Geoffrey M. The Development of Conscience. *128 pp.*

Young, Kimball. Handbook of Social Psychology. *658 pp. 16 figures. 10 tables.*

SOCIOLOGY OF THE FAMILY

Bell, Colin R. Middle Class Families: *Social and Geographical Mobility. 224 pp.*

Burton, Lindy. Vulnerable Children. *272 pp.*

Gavron, Hannah. The Captive Wife: *Conflicts of Household Mothers. 190 pp.*

George, Victor and **Wilding, Paul.** Motherless Families. *248 pp.*

Klein, Josephine. Samples from English Cultures.
  1. Three Preliminary Studies and Aspects of Adult Life in England. *447 pp.*
  2. Child-Rearing Practices and Index. *247 pp.*

Klein, Viola. The Feminine Character. *History of an Ideology. 244 pp.*

McWhinnie, Alexina M. Adopted Children. *How They Grow Up. 304 pp.*

● **Morgan, D. H. J.** Social Theory and the Family. *About 320 pp.*

● **Myrdal, Alva** and **Klein, Viola.** Women's Two Roles: *Home and Work. 238 pp. 27 tables.*

Parsons, Talcott and **Bales, Robert F.** Family: Socialization and Inter-action Process. *In collaboration with James Olds, Morris Zelditch and Philip E. Slater. 456 pp. 50 figures and tables.*

SOCIAL SERVICES

Bastide, Roger. The Sociology of Mental Disorder. *Translated from the French by Jean McNeil. 260 pp.*

Carlebach, Julius. Caring For Children in Trouble. *266 pp.*

George, Victor. Foster Care. *Theory and Practice. 234 pp.*
   Social Security: *Beveridge and After. 258 pp.*

George, V. and **Wilding, P.** Motherless Families. *248 pp.*

● **Goetschius, George W.** Working with Community Groups. *256 pp.*

Goetschius, George W. and **Tash, Joan.** Working with Unattached Youth. *416 pp.*

Heywood, Jean S. Children in Care. *The Development of the Service for the Deprived Child. Third revised edition. 284 pp.*

King, Roy D., Ranes, Norma V. and **Tizard, Jack.** Patterns of Residen-tial Care. *356 pp.*

Leigh, John. Young People and Leisure. *256 pp.*

● **Mays, John.** (Ed.) Penelope Hall's Social Services of England and Wales. *About 324 pp.*

Morris, Mary. Voluntary Work and the Welfare State. *300 pp.*

Nokes, P. L. The Professional Task in Welfare Practice. *152 pp.*

Timms, Noel. Psychiatric Social Work in Great Britain (1939-1962). *280 pp.*

●   Social Casework: *Principles and Practice. 256 pp.*

SOCIOLOGY OF EDUCATION

Banks, Olive. Parity and Prestige in English Secondary Education: a Study in Educational Sociology. *272 pp.*

● **Blyth, W. A. L.** English Primary Education. *A Sociological Description.* 2. Background. *168 pp.*

Collier, K. G. The Social Purposes of Education: *Personal and Social Values in Education. 268 pp.*

Evans, K. M. Sociometry and Education. *158 pp.*

● **Ford, Julienne.** Social Class and the Comprehensive School. *192 pp.*

Foster, P. J. Education and Social Change in Ghana. *336 pp. 3 maps.*

Fraser, W. R. Education and Society in Modern France. *150 pp.*

Grace, Gerald R. Role Conflict and the Teacher. *150 pp.*

Hans, Nicholas. New Trends in Education in the Eighteenth Century. *278 pp. 19 tables.*

●   Comparative Education: *A Study of Educational Factors and Tra-ditions. 360 pp.*

● **Hargreaves, David.** Interpersonal Relations and Education. *432 pp.*

●   Social Relations in a Secondary School. *240 pp.*

   School Organization and Pupil Involvement. *A Study of Secondary Schools.*

● **Mannheim, Karl** and **Stewart, W.A.C.** An Introduction to the Sociology of Education. *206 pp.*
● **Musgrove, F.** Youth and the Social Order. *176 pp.*
● **Ottaway, A. K. C.** Education and Society: An Introduction to the Sociology of Education. *With an Introduction by W. O. Lester Smith. 212 pp.*
　Peers, Robert. Adult Education: *A Comparative Study. Revised edition. 398 pp.*
　Stratta, Erica. The Education of Borstal Boys. *A Study of their Educational Experiences prior to, and during, Borstal Training. 256 pp.*
● **Taylor, P. H., Reid, W. A.** and **Holley, B. J.** The English Sixth Form. *A Case Study in Curriculum Research. 198 pp.*

SOCIOLOGY OF CULTURE

　Eppel, E. M. and **M.** Adolescents and Morality: *A Study of some Moral Values and Dilemmas of Working Adolescents in the Context of a changing Climate of Opinion. Foreword by W. J. H. Sprott. 268 pp. 39 tables.*
● **Fromm, Erich.** The Fear of Freedom. *286 pp.*
● 　The Sane Society. *400 pp.*
　Johnson, L. The Cultural Critics. *From Matthew Arnold to Raymond Williams. 233 pp.*
　Mannheim, Karl. Essays on the Sociology of Culture. *Edited by Ernst Mannheim in co-operation with Paul Kecskemeti. Editorial Note by Adolph Lowe. 280 pp.*
　Zijderfeld, A. C. On Clichés. *The Supersedure of Meaning by Function in Modernity. About 132 pp.*

SOCIOLOGY OF RELIGION

　Argyle, Michael and **Beit-Hallahmi, Benjamin.** The Social Psychology of Religion. *About 256 pp.*
　Glasner, Peter E. The Sociology of Secularisation. *A Critique of a Concept. About 180 pp.*
　Hall, J. R. The Ways Out. *Utopian Communal Groups in an Age of Babylon. 280 pp.*
　Ranson, S., Hinings, B. and **Bryman, A.** Clergy, Ministers and Priests. *216 pp.*
　Stark, Werner. The Sociology of Religion. *A Study of Christendom.*
　　Volume II. *Sectarian Religion. 368 pp.*
　　Volume III. *The Universal Church. 464 pp.*
　　Volume IV. *Types of Religious Man. 352 pp.*
　　Volume V. *Types of Religious Culture. 464 pp.*
　Turner, B. S. Weber and Islam. *216 pp.*
　Watt, W. Montgomery. Islam and the Integration of Society. *320 pp.*

SOCIOLOGY OF ART AND LITERATURE

Jarvie, Ian C. Towards a Sociology of the Cinema. *A Comparative Essay on the Structure and Functioning of a Major Entertainment Industry. 405 pp.*

Rust, Frances S. Dance in Society. *An Analysis of the Relationships between the Social Dance and Society in England from the Middle Ages to the Present Day. 256 pp. 8 pp. of plates.*

Schücking, L. L. The Sociology of Literary Taste. *112 pp.*

Wolff, Janet. Hermeneutic Philosophy and the Sociology of Art. *150 pp.*

SOCIOLOGY OF KNOWLEDGE

Diesing, P. Patterns of Discovery in the Social Sciences. *262 pp.*

● **Douglas, J. D.** (Ed.) Understanding Everyday Life. *370 pp.*

Glasner, B. Essential Interactionism. *About 220 pp.*

● **Hamilton, P.** Knowledge and Social Structure. *174 pp.*

Jarvie, I. C. Concepts and Society. *232 pp.*

Mannheim, Karl. Essays on the Sociology of Knowledge. *Edited by Paul Kecskemeti. Editorial Note by Adolph Lowe. 353 pp.*

Remmling, Gunter W. The Sociology of Karl Mannheim. *With a Bibliographical Guide to the Sociology of Knowledge, Ideological Analysis, and Social Planning. 255 pp.*

Remmling, Gunter W. (Ed.) Towards the Sociology of Knowledge. *Origin and Development of a Sociological Thought Style. 463 pp.*

URBAN SOCIOLOGY

Aldridge, M. The British New Towns. *A Programme Without a Policy. About 250 pp.*

Ashworth, William. The Genesis of Modern British Town Planning: *A Study in Economic and Social History of the Nineteenth and Twentieth Centuries. 288 pp.*

Brittan, A. The Privatised World. *196 pp.*

Cullingworth, J. B. Housing Needs and Planning Policy: *A Restatement of the Problems of Housing Need and 'Overspill' in England and Wales. 232 pp. 44 tables. 8 maps.*

Dickinson, Robert E. City and Region: *A Geographical Interpretation. 608 pp. 125 figures.*

The West European City: *A Geographical Interpretation. 600 pp. 129 maps. 29 plates.*

Humphreys, Alexander J. New Dubliners: *Urbanization and the Irish Family. Foreword by George C. Homans. 304 pp.*

Jackson, Brian. Working Class Community: *Some General Notions raised by a Series of Studies in Northern England. 192 pp.*

● **Mann, P. H.** An Approach to Urban Sociology. *240 pp.*

Mellor, J. R. Urban Sociology in an Urbanized Society. *326 pp.*

Morris, R. N. and **Mogey, J.** The Sociology of Housing. *Studies at Berinsfield. 232 pp. 4 pp. plates.*

Rosser, C. and **Harris, C.** The Family and Social Change. *A Study of Family and Kinship in a South Wales Town. 352 pp. 8 maps.*

● **Stacey, Margaret, Batsone, Eric, Bell, Colin** and **Thurcott, Anne.** Power, Persistence and Change. *A Second Study of Banbury. 196 pp.*

RURAL SOCIOLOGY

Mayer, Adrian C. Peasants in the Pacific. *A Study of Fiji Indian Rural Society. 248 pp. 20 plates.*

Williams, W. M. The Sociology of an English Village: *Gosforth. 272 pp. 12 figures. 13 tables.*

SOCIOLOGY OF INDUSTRY AND DISTRIBUTION

Dunkerley, David. The Foreman. *Aspects of Task and Structure. 192 pp.*

Eldridge, J. E. T. Industrial Disputes. *Essays in the Sociology of Industrial Relations. 288 pp.*

Hollowell, Peter G. The Lorry Driver. *272 pp.*

● **Oxaal, I., Barnett, T.** and **Booth, D.** (Eds) Beyond the Sociology of Development. *Economy and Society in Latin America and Africa. 295 pp.*

Smelser, Neil J. Social Change in the Industrial Revolution: *An Application of Theory to the Lancashire Cotton Industry, 1770–1840. 468 pp. 12 figures. 14 tables.*

Watson, T. J. The Personnel Managers. *A Study in the Sociology of Work and Employment. 262 pp.*

ANTHROPOLOGY

Brandel-Syrier, Mia. Reeftown Elite. *A Study of Social Mobility in a Modern African Community on the Reef. 376 pp.*

Dickie-Clark, H. F. The Marginal Situation. *A Sociological Study of a Coloured Group. 236 pp.*

Dube, S. C. Indian Village. *Foreword by Morris Edward Opler. 276 pp. 4 plates.*

India's Changing Villages: *Human Factors in Community Development. 260 pp. 8 plates. 1 map.*

Firth, Raymond. Malay Fishermen. *Their Peasant Economy. 420 pp. 17 pp. plates.*

Gulliver, P. H. Social Control in an African Society: a Study of the Arusha, Agricultural Masai of Northern Tanganyika. *320 pp. 8 plates. 10 figures.*

Family Herds. *288 pp.*

Jarvie, Ian C. The Revolution in Anthropology. *268 pp.*

Little, Kenneth L. Mende of Sierra Leone. *308 pp. and folder.*

Negroes in Britain. *With a New Introduction and Contemporary Study by Leonard Bloom. 320 pp.*

Madan, G. R. Western Sociologists on Indian Society. *Marx, Spencer, Weber, Durkheim, Pareto. 384 pp.*

Mayer, A. C. Peasants in the Pacific. *A Study of Fiji Indian Rural Society. 248 pp.*

Meer, Fatima. Race and Suicide in South Africa. *325 pp.*

Smith, Raymond T. The Negro Family in British Guiana: *Family Structure and Social Status in the Villages. With a Foreword by Meyer Fortes. 314 pp. 8 plates. 1 figure. 4 maps.*

SOCIOLOGY AND PHILOSOPHY

Barnsley, John H. The Social Reality of Ethics. *A Comparative Analysis of Moral Codes. 448 pp.*

Diesing, Paul. Patterns of Discovery in the Social Sciences. *362 pp.*

● **Douglas, Jack D.** (Ed.) Understanding Everyday Life. *Toward the Reconstruction of Sociological Knowledge. Contributions by Alan F. Blum, Aaron W. Cicourel, Norman K. Denzin, Jack D. Douglas, John Heeren, Peter McHugh, Peter K. Manning, Melvin Power, Matthew Speier, Roy Turner, D. Lawrence Wieder, Thomas P. Wilson and Don H. Zimmerman. 370 pp.*

Gorman, Robert A. The Dual Vision. *Alfred Schutz and the Myth of Phenomenological Social Science. About 300 pp.*

Jarvie, Ian C. Concepts and Society. *216 pp.*

Kilminster, R. Praxis and Method. *A Sociological Dialogue with Lukács, Gramsci and the early Frankfurt School. About 304 pp.*

● **Pelz, Werner.** The Scope of Understanding in Sociology. *Towards a More Radical Reorientation in the Social Humanistic Sciences. 283 pp.*

Roche, Maurice. Phenomenology, Language and the Social Sciences. *371 pp.*

Sahay, Arun. Sociological Analysis. *212 pp.*

Slater, P. Origin and Significance of the Frankfurt School. *A Marxist Perspective. About 192 pp.*

Spurling, L. Phenomenology and the Social World. *The Philosophy of Merleau-Ponty and its Relation to the Social Sciences. 222 pp.*

Wilson, H. T. The American Ideology. *Science, Technology and Organization as Modes of Rationality. 368 pp.*

International Library of Anthropology

General Editor Adam Kuper

Ahmed, A. S. Millenium and Charisma Among Pathans. *A Critical Essay in Social Anthropology. 192 pp.*
Pukhtun Economy and Society. *About 360 pp.*

Brown, Paula. The Chimbu. *A Study of Change in the New Guinea Highlands. 151 pp.*

Foner, N. Jamaica Farewell. *200 pp.*

Gudeman, Stephen. Relationships, Residence and the Individual. *A Rural Panamanian Community. 288 pp. 11 plates, 5 figures, 2 maps, 10 tables.*

The Demise of a Rural Economy. *From Subsistence to Capitalism in a Latin American Village. 160 pp.*

Hamnett, Ian. Chieftainship and Legitimacy. *An Anthropological Study of Executive Law in Lesotho. 163 pp.*

Hanson, F. Allan. Meaning in Culture. *127 pp.*

Humphreys, S. C. Anthropology and the Greeks. *288 pp.*

Karp, I. Fields of Change Among the Iteso of Kenya. *140 pp.*

Lloyd, P. C. Power and Independence. *Urban Africans' Perception of Social Inequality. 264 pp.*

Parry, J. P. Caste and Kinship in Kangra. *352 pp. Illustrated.*

Pettigrew, Joyce. Robber Noblemen. *A Study of the Political System of the Sikh Jats. 284 pp.*

Street, Brian V. The Savage in Literature. *Representations of 'Primitive' Society in English Fiction, 1858–1920. 207 pp.*

Van Den Berghe, Pierre L. Power and Privilege at an African University. *278 pp.*

International Library of Social Policy

General Editor Kathleen Jones

Bayley, M. Mental Handicap and Community Care. *426 pp.*

Bottoms, A. E. and **McClean, J. D.** Defendants in the Criminal Process. *284 pp.*

Butler, J. R. Family Doctors and Public Policy. *208 pp.*

Davies, Martin. Prisoners of Society. *Attitudes and Aftercare. 204 pp.*

Gittus, Elizabeth. Flats, Families and the Under-Fives. *285 pp.*

Holman, Robert. Trading in Children. *A Study of Private Fostering. 355 pp.*

Jeffs, A. Young People and the Youth Service. *About 180 pp.*

Jones, Howard, and **Cornes, Paul.** Open Prisons. *288 pp.*

Jones, Kathleen. History of the Mental Health Service. *428 pp.*

Jones, Kathleen, with **Brown, John, Cunningham, W. J., Roberts, Julian** and **Williams, Peter.** Opening the Door. *A Study of New Policies for the Mentally Handicapped. 278 pp.*

Karn, Valerie. Retiring to the Seaside. *About 280 pp. 2 maps. Numerous tables.*

King, R. D. and **Elliot, K. W.** Albany: Birth of a Prison—End of an Era. *394 pp.*

Thomas, J. E. The English Prison Officer since 1850: *A Study in Conflict.*
258 pp.
Walton, R. G. Women in Social Work. *303 pp.*
● **Woodward, J.** To Do the Sick No Harm. *A Study of the British Voluntary
Hospital System to 1875. 234 pp.*

International Library of Welfare and Philosophy

General Editors Noel Timms and David Watson

● **McDermott, F. E.** (Ed.) Self-Determination in Social Work. *A Collection
of Essays on Self-determination and Related Concepts by Philosophers
and Social Work Theorists. Contributors: F. B. Biestek, S. Bernstein,
A. Keith-Lucas, D. Sayer, H. H. Perelman, C. Whittington, R. F.
Stalley, F. E. McDermott, I. Berlin, H. J. McCloskey, H. L. A. Hart,
J. Wilson, A. I. Melden, S. I. Benn. 254 pp.*
● **Plant, Raymond.** Community and Ideology. *104 pp.*
Ragg, Nicholas M. People Not Cases. *A Philosophical Approach to Social
Work. About 250 pp.*
● **Timms, Noel** and **Watson, David.** (Eds) Talking About Welfare.
*Readings in Philosophy and Social Policy. Contributors: T. H.
Marshall, R. B. Brandt, G. H. von Wright, K. Nielsen, M. Cranston,
R. M. Titmuss, R. S. Downie, E. Telfer, D. Donnison, J. Benson, P.
Leonard, A. Keith-Lucas, D. Walsh, I. T. Ramsey. 320 pp.*
●   (Eds). Philosophy in Social Work. *250 pp.*
● **Weale, A.** Equality and Social Policy. *164 pp.*

Primary Socialization, Language and Education

General Editor Basil Bernstein

Adlam, Diana S., *with the assistance of Geoffrey Turner and Lesley
Lineker.* Code in Context. *About 272 pp.*
Bernstein, Basil. Class, Codes and Control. *3 volumes.*
●   1. *Theoretical Studies Towards a Sociology of Language. 254 pp.*
    2. *Applied Studies Towards a Sociology of Language. 377 pp.*
●   3. *Towards a Theory of Educational Transmission. 167 pp.*
Brandis, W. and **Bernstein, B.** Selection and Control. *176 pp.*

Brandis, Walter and **Henderson, Dorothy.** Social Class, Language and Communication. *288 pp.*

Cook-Gumperz, Jenny. Social Control and Socialization. *A Study of Class Differences in the Language of Maternal Control. 290 pp.*

● **Gahagan, D. M** and **G. A.** Talk Reform. *Exploration in Language for Infant School Children. 160 pp.*

Hawkins, P. R. Social Class, the Nominal Group and Verbal Strategies. *About 220 pp.*

Robinson, W. P. and **Rackstraw, Susan D. A.** A Question of Answers. *2 volumes. 192 pp. and 180 pp.*

Turner, Geoffrey J. and **Mohan, Bernard A.** A Linguistic Description and Computer Programme for Children's Speech. *208 pp.*

Reports of the Institute of Community Studies

Baker, J. The Neighbourhood Advice Centre. A Community Project in Camden. *320 pp.*

● **Cartwright, Ann.** Patients and their Doctors. *A Study of General Practice. 304 pp.*

Dench, Geoff. Maltese in London. *A Case-study in the Erosion of Ethnic Consciousness. 302 pp.*

Jackson, Brian and **Marsden, Dennis.** Education and the Working Class: *Some General Themes raised by a Study of 88 Working-class Children in a Northern Industrial City. 268 pp. 2 folders.*

Marris, Peter. The Experience of Higher Education. *232 pp. 27 tables.*

● Loss and Change. *192 pp.*

Marris, Peter and **Rein, Martin.** Dilemmas of Social Reform. *Poverty and Community Action in the United States. 256 pp.*

Marris, Peter and **Somerset, Anthony.** African Businessmen. *A Study of Entrepreneurship and Development in Keyna. 256 pp.*

Mills, Richard. Young Outsiders: *a Study in Alternative Communities. 216 pp.*

Runciman, W. G. Relative Deprivation and Social Justice. *A Study of Attitudes to Social Inequality in Twentieth-Century England. 352 pp.*

Willmott, Peter. Adolescent Boys in East London. *230 pp.*

Willmott, Peter and **Young, Michael.** Family and Class in a London Suburb. *202 pp. 47 tables.*

Young, Michael and **McGeeney, Patrick.** Learning Begins at Home. *A Study of a Junior School and its Parents. 128 pp.*

Young, Michael and **Willmott, Peter.** Family and Kinship in East London. *Foreword by Richard M. Titmuss. 252 pp. 39 tables.*

The Symmetrical Family. *410 pp.*

Community Work. *Edited by David Jones and Marjorie Mayo. 1973. Published annually.*

Economy and Society. *Vol. 1, No. 1. February 1972 and Quarterly. Metric Roy. 8vo. A journal for all social scientists covering sociology, philosophy, anthropology, economics and history. All back numbers available.*

Ethnic and Racial Studies. *Editor – John Stone. Vol. 1 – 1978. Published quarterly.*

Religion. Journal of Religion and Religions. *Chairman of Editorial Board, Ninian Smart. Vol. 1, No. 1, Spring 1971. A journal with an inter-disciplinary approach to the study of the phenomena of religion. All back numbers available.*

Sociology of Health and Illness. *A Journal of Medical Sociology. Editor – Alan Davies; Associate Editor – Ray Jobling. Vol. 1, Spring 1979. Published 3 times per annum.*

Year Book of Social Policy in Britain, The. *Edited by Kathleen Jones. 1971. Published annually.*

Social and Psychological Aspects of Medical Practice

Editor Trevor Silverstone

Lader, Malcolm. Psychophysiology of Mental Illness. *280 pp.*
● **Silverstone, Trevor** and **Turner, Paul.** Drug Treatment in Psychiatry. *Revised edition. 256 pp.*
Whiteley, J. S. and **Gordon, J.** Group Approaches in Psychiatry. *256 pp.*

Printed in Great Britain by
Lowe & Brydone Printers Limited, Thetford, Norfolk

Reports of the Institute for Social Studies in Medical Care

Cartwright, Ann, Hockey, Lisbeth and **Anderson, John J.** Life Before Death. *310 pp.*

Dunnell, Karen and **Cartwright, Ann.** Medicine Takers, Prescribers and Hoarders. *190 pp.*

Farrell, C. My Mother Said. . . . *A Study of the Way Young People Learned About Sex and Birth Control. 200 pp.*

Medicine, Illness and Society

General Editor W. M. Williams

Hall, David J. Social Relations & Innovation. *Changing the State of Play in Hospitals. 232 pp.*

Hall, David J., and **Stacey, M.** (Eds) Beyond Separation. *234 pp.*

Robinson, David. The Process of Becoming Ill. *142 pp.*

Stacey, Margaret *et al.* Hospitals, Children and Their Families. *The Report of a Pilot Study. 202 pp.*

Stimson G. V. and **Webb, B.** Going to See the Doctor. *The Consultation Process in General Practice. 155 pp.*

Monographs in Social Theory

General Editor Arthur Brittan

● **Barnes, B.** Scientific Knowledge and Sociological Theory. *192 pp.*

Bauman, Zygmunt. Culture as Praxis. *204 pp.*

● **Dixon, Keith.** Sociological Theory. *Pretence and Possibility. 142 pp.*

Meltzer, B. N., Petras, J. W. and **Reynolds, L. T.** Symbolic Interactionism. *Genesis, Varieties and Criticisms. 144 pp.*

● **Smith, Anthony D.** The Concept of Social Change. *A Critique of the Functionalist Theory of Social Change. 208 pp.*

Routledge Social Science Journals

The British Journal of Sociology. *Editor – Angus Stewart; Associate Editor – Leslie Sklair. Vol. 1, No. 1 – March 1950 and Quarterly. Roy. 8vo. All back issues available. An international journal publishing original papers in the field of sociology and related areas.*